OCR
PE
for AS

Official Publisher Partnership

OCR PE

for AS

Graham Thompson
Nesta Wiggins-James
Rob James

DYNAMIC LEARNING
Innovate · Motivate · Personalise
CD-ROM INSIDE

PART OF HACHETTE LIVRE UK

Orders: please contact Bookpoint Ltd, 130 Milton Park, Abingdon, Oxon OX14 4SB.
Telephone: (44) 01235 827720. Fax: (44) 01235 400454. Lines are open from 9.00am – 5.00pm,
Monday to Saturday, with a 24-hour message-answering service. You can also order
through our website www.hoddereducation.co.uk

If you have any comments to make about this, or any of our other titles, please send them
to educationenquiries@hodder.co.uk

British Library Cataloguing in Publication Data
A catalogue record for this title is available from the British Library

ISBN: 978 0 340 95868 1

First Edition Published 2008
Impression number   10 9 8 7 6 5 4 3 2 1
Year   2013 2012 2011 2010 2009 2008

Cover photo from Getty Images: male gymnast doing floor routine (photographer: Ryan McVay).
Typeset by Pantek Arts Ltd, Maidstone, Kent
Printed in Italy for Hodder Education, part of Hachette Livre UK, 338 Euston Road,
London NW1 3BH.

Contents

The Olympic Games
Background of the modern Olympic Games
Role of the International Olympic Committee and the British Olympic Association
The impact of commercialisation on the Games
Implications of the 2012 London Games on the host country
Role of the 2012 London Games and the host country
Impact of funding, government control and politics on the Olympics Games

What are the coursework requirements?
What activities can I be assessed in?
How will I be assessed?
What are the assessment criteria?
How can I improve my level of performance, coaching and officiating?
Evaluating and planning for improvement
What questions can I expect in the evaluating and planning for improvement section?
How should I structure my oral response?

Glossary
Further reading
Index

Acknowledgements

The authors would like to thank their families for all their support during the writing of this book. Nesta Wiggins would also like to thank Gwyneth Goodchild, Librarian of the Sixth Form College Colchester, for her assistance in compiling references for this book.

The publishers would like to thank the following for permission to reproduce their images:

George Tiedman/NewSport/Corbis	1.10
Glyn Kirk/actionplus	1.13; 1.27(a) & (b); 1.34; 1.36; 1.39; 2.11; 2.20(d); 2.29; 3.8; 3.13; 4.13; 4.3; 4.7; 4.17; 5.2; 5.4; 7.8(d); 8.8; 8.10; 8.13; 9.3; 10.5; 10.18
Roberto Tedeschi/epa/Corbis	1.14
Adam Pretty/Getty Images	1.17
Nigel Reed/QEDimages/Alamy	1.21
JUPITERIMAGES/Polka Dot/Alamy	1.22
Bradley Kanaris/Getty Images	1.23
Neil Tingle/actionplus	1.9; 1.24(a) & (b); 1.26(a) & (b); 1.38; 1.41; 2.12(a) & (b); 4.5; 4.10; 4.4; 4.14; 6.8(a) & (c); 6.12; 7.8(b) & (c); 8.3; 8.14; 9.12; 11.7; 12.3
David J. Phillip/AP Photo/PA Photos	1.25
Nucleus Medical Art, Inc./Alamy	1.29
John Giles/PA Photos	1.30
John Giles/EMPICS/PA	1.31
Robert Michael/Corbis	1.36
Ivo Lorenc/Sygma/CORBIS	1.40
Richard Saker/Allsport/Getty Images	2.9
Tim de Waele/Corbis	2.14
Photodisc	2.19
Mark Nolan/Getty Images	2.20(c)
AHMAD YUSN/AFP/Getty Images	2.21
Steve Bardens/Actionplus	2.25; 4.6
Picturebank/Alamy	2.26
Actionplus	2.27; 4.4(a)
PHOTOTAKE Inc./Alamy	2.28
Bob Sacha/Corbis	3.11
James Leynse/CORBIS	3.12
Photo News/DPPI/Actionplus	3.3
Stefan Matzke/NewSport/Corbis	3.4
Sipa Press/Rex Features	3.6
Manan Vatsyayana/AFP/Getty Images	4.1
Paul Williams/Actionplus	4.11
Mike Hewitt/Actionplus	4.12
JUPITERIMAGES/BananaStock/Alamy	4.15; 5.13
LLUIS GENE/AFP/Getty Images	4.16

Darren Hauck/epa/Corbis	4.2
Icon/Actionplus	4.4(b)
Mark Thompson/Allsport/Getty Images	4.8
Franck Faugere/DPPI/Actionplus	4.9
Reuters/CORBIS	5.11
Pete Saloutos/CORBIS	5.12
China Photos/Getty Images	5.14; 8.16(b)
Matthew Impey/actionplus	5.3
Darren Staples/Reuters/CORBIS	6.13
Matthew Clarke/actionplus	6.4
Image Source/Corbis	6.8(b)
Robert Laberge/Getty Images	7.7
Laurie Strachan/Alamy	7.8(a)
MAKKU ULANDER/Rex Features	8.16(a)
Clifford White/Corbis	8.9(a)
Chris Brown/Actionplus	8.9(b); 11.2
Ron C Angle/BEI/Rex Features	9.14
Richard Francis/actionplus	9.9
Will he do it?, Hicks, George Elgar (1824-1914)/Private Collection/The Bridgeman Art Library	10.11
Steve Grayson/actionplus	10.15
Fox Photos/Getty Images	10.2
Laurence Griffiths/Getty Images	10.3
South West News Service/Rex Features	10.4
Sipa Press/Rex Features	12.4
AKG-Images	12.6
Charles Platiau/Reuters/Corbis	13.1
Jamie Squire/Getty Images	13.2
Corbis Super RF/Alamy	13.3
Nick Potts/PA Archive/PA Photos	13.4

HODDER
EDUCATION
The Expert Choice

What does 'the expert choice' mean for you?

We work with more examiners and experts than any other publisher

- Because we work with more experts and examiners than any other publisher, the very latest curriculum requirements are built into this course and there is a perfect match between your course and the resources that you need to succeed. We make it easier for you to gain the skills and knowledge that you need for the best results.

- We have chosen the best team of experts – including the people who mark the exams – to give you the very best chance of success. Look out for their advice throughout this book – this is content that you can trust.

Innovate • Motivate • Personalise

Welcome to Dynamic Learning

Dynamic Learning is a simple and powerful way of integrating this text with digital resources to help you succeed, by bringing learning to life. Whatever your learning style, Dynamic Learning will help boost your understanding. And our Dynamic Learning content is updated online so your book will never be out of date.

- Easy access to the book's key photographs, charts and diagrams so that you can use them in your studies

- Boost your understanding through interactive activities, quizzes and from support in additional Word and PowerPoint files

- Easy-to-use PowerPoint presentations show you what each chapter is going to deliver for you, and help you to check your understanding once you have worked through the section

More direct contact with teachers and students than any other publisher

- We talk with more than 100 000 students every year through our student conferences, run by Philip Allan Updates. We hear at first hand what you need to make a success of your A-level studies and build what we learn into every new course. Learn more about our conferences at **www.philipallan.co.uk**

- Our new materials are trialled in classrooms as we develop them, and the feedback built into every new book or resource that we publish. You can be part of that. If you have comments that you would like to make about this book, please email us at: **feedback@hodder.co.uk**

More collaboration with Subject Associations than any other publisher

- Subject Associations sit at the heart of education. We work closely with more Associations than any other publisher. This means that our resources support the most creative teaching and learning, using the skills of the best teachers in their field to create resources for you.

More opportunities for your teachers to stay ahead than with any other publisher

- Through our Philip Allan Updates Conferences, we offer teachers access to Continuing Professional Development. Our focused and practical conferences ensure that your teachers have access to the best presenters, teaching materials and training resources. Our presenters include experienced teachers, Chief and Principal Examiners, leading educationalists, authors and consultants. This course is built on all of this expertise.

To start up Dynamic Learning now, make sure that your computer has an active broadband connection to the internet and insert the disk into your CD ROM drive. Dynamic Learning should run automatically if you have 'Auto Run' enabled. Full installation instructions are printed on the disk label.

Basic system requirements for your Student Edition: **PC** Windows 2000 (SP4), XP SP2 (Home & Pro), Vista; **PC (Server)** Windows 2000 and 2003; **Mac** Mac OS X 10.3 or 10.4; G4, G5 or Intel processor. Dynamic Learning is not currently Leopard-compatible: see the website for latest details. Up to 1.4Gb hard disc space per title. Minimum screen resolution 1024 x 768. Sound card. A fast processor (PC, 1GHz; Mac, 1.25 GHz) and good graphics card.
Copyright restrictions mean that some materials may not be accessible from within the Dynamic Learning edition. Full details of your single-user licence can be found on the disk under 'Contents'.

You can find out more at www.dynamic-learning.co.uk

Introduction

Welcome to the new edition of *OCR PE for AS*.

This book has been written specifically to support those students following the OCR AS specification in physical education (H154). It has been designed to follow the exact requirements of the specification and, in doing so, to prepare you for both the written and coursework units of the qualification.

The book is divided into two parts – one for each area of study:

- Part 1: An introduction to physical education (G451);
- Part 2: Acquiring, developing and evaluating practical skills in physical education (G452).

How will each part be assessed?

Unit G451: An introduction to physical education	Unit G452: Acquiring, developing and evaluating practical skills in physical education
• Externally assessed written paper • 90 marks available • Two hours • Three compulsory questions, each worth 30 marks, on the following: 1 anatomy and physiology; 2 acquiring movement skills; 3 sociocultural studies. • Each question will contain a more demanding part, assessed by levels • 60% of overall AS mark	• Internally assessed but externally moderated • 80 marks available • Assessed in two activities, each worth 30 marks (assessed as a performer and/or coach/official) • Oral assessment on evaluating and planning for improvement of performance, worth 20 marks • 40% of overall AS mark

Features and symbols

Look out for the feature boxes and symbols which appear throughout the text. There are a number of different features, which are designed to give you all the information you need to be successful and to help reinforce your learning. A brief overview of each feature is given below:

- Key terms: definitions of significant words or phrases that are required knowledge.

- In context: real-life case studies which demonstrate the application of theoretical knowledge to sporting situations.
- Activities: opportunities to apply and reinforce your knowledge through a range of student-centred tasks.
- Examiner's tips: helpful hints on examination technique and revision tips from real examiners.
- What you need to know: a summary of key points at the end of each chapter which can be

used as a quick progress check and a useful revision tool.

- Exam-style questions: apply your knowledge to the sorts of questions you can expect in your written examination.
- Review questions: check your progress with questions that address the important aspects of each chapter.
- Dynamic learning: an icon which directs you to further activities or videos on the accompanying dynamic learning CD-ROM.

Themes

There are several main themes that underpin this course and it is really important that you reflect on these when completing assessment activities.

Throughout the course you must relate and apply knowledge to lifelong involvement in an active and healthy lifestyle. You will already be aware that physical education is a multifaceted discipline which encompasses a number of theoretical areas. In part 1, for example, you will study three main theory topics:

1 anatomy and physiology;
2 acquiring movement skills;
3 sociocultural studies.

It is imperative that you reflect on the impact of each area on lifelong participation and the contribution of each to the promotion of a healthy lifestyle.

You will be required to engage in higher-order thinking, and this text will help you to develop the necessary skills of critical evaluation and analysis.

Topics marked IN DEPTH will stretch you and help you prepare for A2, but contain information beyond what is required for the AS specification.

Higher-order thinking

Higher-order thinking skills require you to do more than simply show your knowledge and understanding. To be successful on this course, you must show your abilities of application, analysis, synthesis and evaluation.

	What is involved?	What could I do?	Question cues
Application	Making use of your knowledge in a particular situation	Use your knowledge in a sporting context Problem solving (e.g. illustrate the pattern of heart rate during a game of netball)	Apply, demonstrate, illustrate, examine
Analysis	Taking something apart or breaking it down	Look at the effect that individual components have on the 'whole' (e.g. break a skill down into its component parts and identify strengths and weaknesses of each part)	Explain, classify, compare
Synthesis	Pulling ideas together, rebuilding and solving problems	Formulate an action plan or development plan for improvement (e.g. suggest how a coach can improve the skills of a performer)	Create, design, compose, formulate
Evaluation	Judging the value of material or methods as they might be applied in a particular situation	Reflect on the impact of methods or an action plan Give recommendations (e.g. judge the relative benefits of exercise compared to any negative aspects)	Assess, measure, recommend, convince, judge

An introduction to physical education (G451)

The underlying theme for this unit considers the impact of physical activity on the balanced, active and healthy lifestyle of the young participant.

There are three sections to this unit. Section A – Anatomy and Physiology – focuses on the impact of physical activity on the body's systems. This section will help you to develop your knowledge and understanding of anatomical and physiological factors, which will lead to an improvement in the effectiveness and efficiency of your performance. Section B – Acquiring Movement Skills – will help you to develop your knowledge and understanding of the factors that contribute to the development of skills. You will see how an appreciation of practice conditions, information processing and the development of motor control can help in your effective and efficient performance. The final section of this unit – Section C – addresses the socio-cultural issues relating to participation in physical activity. You will learn about the socio-cultural factors that have an impact on regular participation and the achievement of excellence in physical activity and help you appreciate the opportunities and pathways available for involvement in physical activity.

Introduction

When examining the performer in action, an understanding of anatomical and physiological concepts within a sporting context is required. For example, running a certain distance involves the interaction and coordination of many of the body's systems to enable successful performance:

- The cardiovascular and respiratory systems work together as a delivery service, distributing oxygen and nutrients to fuel the working muscles, while simultaneously ridding the body of any undesired waste products of metabolism, such as carbon dioxide.
- The skeletal and muscular systems interact, with the bones acting as levers to provide movement, and the muscles (the engines of movement) providing the power to drive the levers.
- The nervous and hormonal systems direct and control the body's actions to enhance performance.

The body is therefore a complex machine, with the components or systems working together to enable effective participation in sport.

What is exercise physiology?

Exercise or sports physiology (to ease confusion, these terms have been used interchangeably in this book) is a branch of the much broader area of anatomy and physiology:

- Anatomy is the study of the body's structure.
- Physiology seeks to discover how the body works and functions.

Sports physiology then puts these findings into a sporting context and specifically examines how the body adapts and develops in response to exercise.

Training has a significant part to play in the body's development, and as such it is vital to the study of sports physiology.

CHAPTER 1

An analysis of human movement

Learning outcomes

By the end of this chapter you should be able to:

- name the major bones and muscles of the body;
- describe the structure of a synovial joint and explain the function of its features;
- describe the movement patterns that can occur at synovial joints, using examples from a range of sporting activities;
- describe the different types of muscle contraction, using examples from a range of sporting activities;
- distinguish between the structure and function of the three types of skeletal muscle fibre in the body;
- show how an individual's mix of muscle fibre type might impact on their reasons for choosing to take part in a particular type of physical activity;
- explain the effect of a warm-up and a cool-down on skeletal muscle tissue, in relation to the quality of performance of physical activity;
- identify and explain the three types of motion, giving examples of each from sporting activity;
- apply all three of Newton's laws of motion to a range of sporting examples;
- explain the effect that the size of force, direction of force and the point of application of force has on a body in a sporting environment;
- define the term 'centre of mass' (COM) and show how changes in the position of the centre of mass can affect the stability of a body, using examples from sport;
- critically evaluate the impact of different types of physical activity on the skeletal and muscular systems.

CHAPTER INTRODUCTION

In order for humans to move and perform sporting activity, the interaction of the skeletal and muscular systems is necessary.

Muscles contract, moving bones, which pivot and rotate about the joints of the body. In doing so, a series of lever systems operate that enable a force to be transferred through the body, causing the body, or an object, to move in a desired direction. There now follows a brief discussion of each of the following components:

- bones;
- joints;
- muscles.

First, we will consider each of the components individually. Towards the end of the chapter we will look at them collectively and will see how they interact to enable the body to perform such a wide range of movements.

The skeleton

The skeletal system

The 206 bones that make up the human skeleton are specifically designed to provide several basic functions which are essential for participation in physical activity. In conjunction with other components of the skeletal system (including the ligaments and joints), the skeleton can perform certain functions, as explored below.

Functions

Support

The skeleton provides a rigid framework to the body, giving it shape and providing suitable sites for the attachment of skeletal muscle.

Protection

The skeleton provides protection for the internal organs. For example, the vertebral column

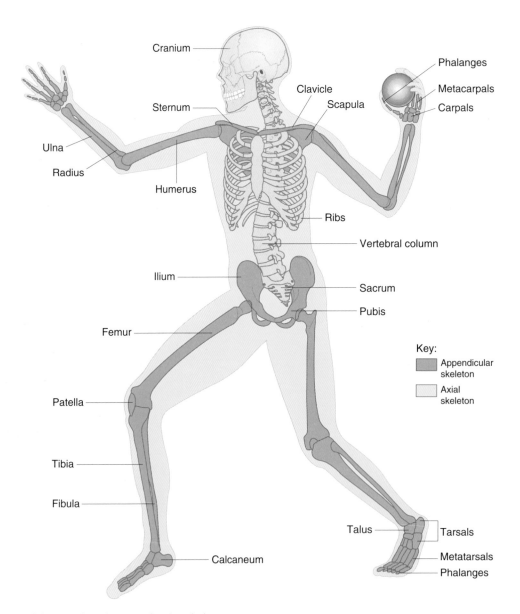

Figure 1.1 Bones of the axial and appendicular skeleton

Source: Davis, Kimmet and Auty (1986) *Physical Education, Theory and Practice,* Macmillan

protects the spinal cord; the cranium protects the brain; and the ribcage principally protects the heart and lungs.

Movement

The bones of the skeleton provide a large surface area for the attachment of muscles – the engines of movement. The long bones, in particular, provide a system of levers against which the muscles can pull.

Blood production

Within the bones, bone marrow produces both red and white blood cells. Red blood cells are generally produced at the end of long bones such as the humerus (arm) and the femur (thigh), and in some flat bones such as the pelvis and the sternum (breastbone). White blood cells are usually produced in the shafts of long bones.

Mineral storage

The bones of the skeleton have storage capabilities for vital minerals such as calcium and phosphorus, which can be distributed to other parts of the body when required.

The structure of the skeleton

The bones of the skeleton can be divided into two distinct categories: the axial and the appendicular skeleton:

- The axial skeleton provides the main area of support for the body, and includes the cranium (skull), the vertebral column (spine) and the ribcage.
- The appendicular skeleton consists of the appendages, or the bones of the limbs, together with the girdles that join on to the axial skeleton.

Take a moment to study the bones of the axial and appendicular skeleton in Figure 1.1.

Key terms

Axial skeleton: The main supporting frame of the skeleton, consisting of the skull, vertebral column and ribcage.

Appendicular skeleton: Bones of the skeleton that make up the limbs and their associated girdles (hip and shoulder).

Activity 1

Using sticky labels, label the bones on a partner's body.

Activity 2

List the bones in the axial and appendicular skeletons in Figure 1.1.

Skeletal tissues

The tissues making up the skeletal system consist of cartilage and bone.

Cartilage

Cartilage is a soft, slightly elastic tissue. It is avascular, meaning that it does not possess a blood supply and receives nutrition via diffusion from the capillary network outside the tissue.

All bones start out as cartilage in the developing foetus, and this cartilage is gradually replaced by bone.

There are three basic types of cartilage found in the body:

1   Hyaline or articular cartilage is a fairly resilient tissue and is found on the articulating surfaces of bones that form joints. It is bluish in colour and is composed of a fine network of collagen fibres. The cartilage protects the bone tissue from wear and reduces friction between articulating bones. Joint movement improves the nutrition supplied to this tissue and can encourage growth. Hyaline cartilage therefore often thickens as a result of exercise, which further protects the joints. During the exercise period, articular cartilage will soak up synovial fluid released from the synovial membrane, thus improving mobility at the joint.

2   White fibrocartilage is a much denser tissue. It is tough, and its shock absorption properties mean that it is often found in areas of the body where high amounts of stress are imposed. For example, the semilunar cartilages of the knee joint (also known as menisci) resist the huge amount of stress often incurred as a result of performing activities such as the triple jump. Other examples are the intervertebral discs and the socket of the hip joint.

Long bones

Long bones are cylindrical in shape and are found in the limbs of the body. Examples of long bones include:

• femur
• tibia
• humerus
• phalanges (although not great in length, these possess the cylindrical shape and so also fall into this category).

The primary function of long bones is to act as levers, and they are therefore essential in movement. When running for example, the psoas, iliacus, and rectus femoris muscles pull on the femur to cause flexion of the hip, effectively lifting the leg off the ground. The rest of the quadricep group (the vasti muscles as well as the rectus femoris) then pull on the tibia causing extension to take place at the knee joint, enabling the lower leg to 'snap' through. This is the first stage of a running action. Their other vital function is the production of blood cells which occurs deep inside the bone.

Flat bones

Flat bones offer protection to the internal organs of the body. Examples include:

• the sternum
• the bones of the cranium
• the bones of the pelvis
• upon close inspection, it can be seen that the ribs are also flat.

Flat bones also provide suitable sites for muscle attachment, with the origins of muscles often attaching to them. In this way the muscle contracting has a firm, immovable base against which to pull, and can therefore carry out its function effectively. For example, a major function of the quadricep muscle group is to pull on the tibia, causing extension at the knee. In order to raise the tibia, the muscle must have a stable base against which it can pull, in this case, the ilium. The bone can now act as a lever and cause movement to occur as outlined earlier. The pelvis, sternum and cranium also produce blood cells.

Irregular bones

Irregular bones are so named due to their complex, individual shapes and the difficulty in classifying them. They have a variety of functions which include protection. Examples include:

• the vertebrae (protect the spinal cord and help to absorb shock when running and jumping)
• the bones of the face.

Sesamoid bones

Sesamoid bones have a specialised function: they ease joint movement and resist friction and compression. They are usually developed in tendons and are covered with a layer of articular cartilage as they exist where bones articulate. Although generally small in appearance, sesamoid bones do vary in size, the largest and most obvious being the patella which is situated in the quadriceps femoris tendon and aids the smooth articulation and movement between the femur and the tibia. The patella also prevents the knee from hyperextending.

Short bones

Short bones are small and compact in nature, often equal in length and width. They are designed for strength and weight bearing, for example when performing a handstand, and include:

• the bones of the wrist (carpals)
• the ankle (tarsals) and calcaneum.

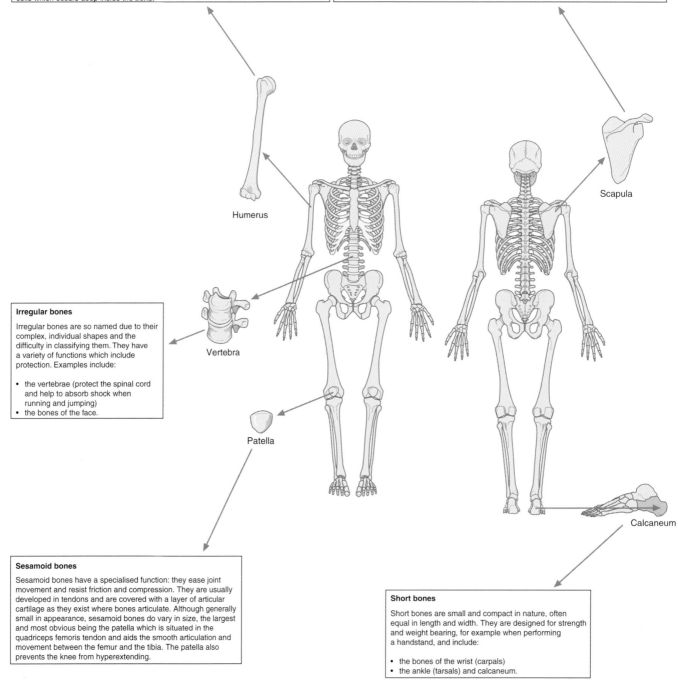

Humerus

Scapula

Vertebra

Patella

Calcaneum

Figure 1.2 Bones are designed to carry out a variety of specific functions and fall into one of five categories, largely according to their shape

3 Yellow elastic cartilage is a much more pliant and flexible tissue, giving support and also flexibility. The external ear and the epiglottis are examples.

Key term

Articular cartilage: A smooth tissue that covers the ends of bones which helps to prevent friction.

Bone

Bone differs from cartilage in that it is a rigid, non-elastic tissue and is composed of approximately 65 per cent mineral components (including calcium phosphate and magnesium salts) and 35 per cent organic tissue, such as collagen, a protein which gives the bones some resilience and prevents them from breaking on the slightest of impacts.

Bone tissue can be categorised into either compact or cancellous, and is best illustrated by viewing a longitudinal cross section of a long bone.

Compact bone, or hard bone, forms the surface layers of all bones and the whole of the cylindrical shaft of long bones. It goes some way towards protecting bones from external forces or impacts and has great weight-bearing properties. Cancellous or spongy bone lies beneath and alongside compact bone, and has a honeycomb appearance. This criss-cross matrix of bony plates is developed along lines of stress on the bones and is constantly reorganised in response to the altering orientation of stress. For example, the stress alters when an infant starts to walk as opposed to crawling.

Ligaments

Ligaments are a tough, fibrous, connective tissue that is composed almost entirely of thick bundles of collagen fibres. Their main role is to attach one bone to another; therefore, they typically occur at joints and are responsible for stabilising them to enable effective movement to take place. Take the knee joint, for instance. This joint needs to be very stable in order for us to move effectively, and consequently it is surrounded by an intricate network of ligaments, each responsible for limiting the movement in a given direction. The lateral and medial ligaments prevent any sideways movement, while the cruciate ligaments prevent

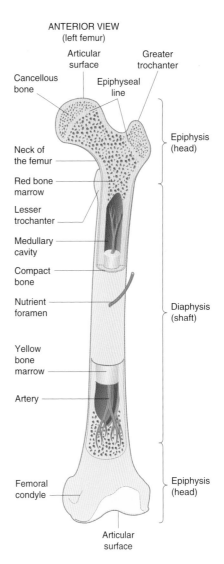

Figure 1.3 Structure of a long bone viewed in cross section
Source: Kapit and Elson (1993) *The Anatomy Coloring Book*, HarperCollins

anteroposterior (backwards and forwards) movement of the tibia.

IN CONTEXT

Ligaments are plastic rather than elastic. This means that once they have been stretched, they remain the same length and do not return to their original length. Consequently, if damage occurs to them, such as a dislocation at the shoulder, it can lead to joint instability.

Key term

Ligaments: A band of strong fibrous tissue that attaches one bone to another.

Joints and articulations

So far we have seen that some bones of the skeleton act as levers, which move when muscles contract and pull on them. Where two or more bones meet, an articulation or joint exists. However, movement does not always occur at these sites, and joints are typically classified according to the degree of movement permitted.

Classification of joints

Fixed or fibrous joints

These are very stable and allow no observable movement. Bones are often joined by strong fibres called sutures, such as the sutures of the cranium (skull).

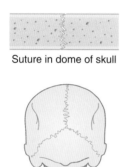

Suture in dome of skull

Figure 1.4 A fixed joint

Cartilaginous or slightly movable joints

These are joined by a tough, fibrous cartilage which provides stability and possesses shock-absorption properties. However, a small amount of movement usually exists. For example, between the lumbar bones, intervertebral discs of cartilage occur, allowing some movement, as shown in Figure 1.5.

Synovial or freely movable joints

These are the most common type of joint in the body, and the most important in terms of physical activity, since they allow a wide range of movement.

The joint is enclosed in a fibrous joint capsule, which is lined with a synovial membrane. Lubrication is provided by synovial fluid, which is secreted into the joint by the synovial membrane.

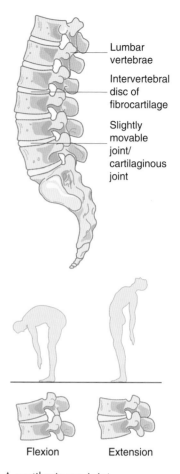

Lumbar vertebrae

Intervertebral disc of fibrocartilage

Slightly movable joint/ cartilaginous joint

Flexion   Extension

Figure 1.5 A cartilaginous joint

In addition, where the bones come into contact with each other, they are lined with smooth yet hard-wearing hyaline or articular cartilage.

Synovial joint stability is provided by the strength of the muscles crossing the joint, which are supported by ligaments that may be inside or outside the capsule. Ligaments are very elastic and lose effectiveness to some degree when torn or stretched.

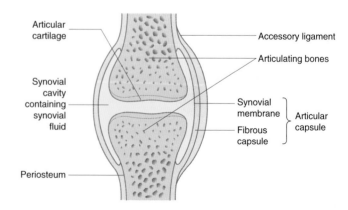

Articular cartilage

Synovial cavity containing synovial fluid

Periosteum

Accessory ligament

Articulating bones

Synovial membrane

Fibrous capsule

Articular capsule

Figure 1.6 A typical synovial joint

Some synovial joints possess sacs of synovial fluid known as bursae, which are sited in areas of increased pressure or stress and help to reduce friction as tissues and structures move past each other. Pads of fat help to absorb shock and improve the 'fit' of the articulating bones. This is particularly true in the knee joint, to help the articulation of the femur and tibia.

Key term

Synovial fluid: A protein-enriched fluid which lubricates and nourishes the articular cartilage. It helps to reduce friction between the articulating bones.

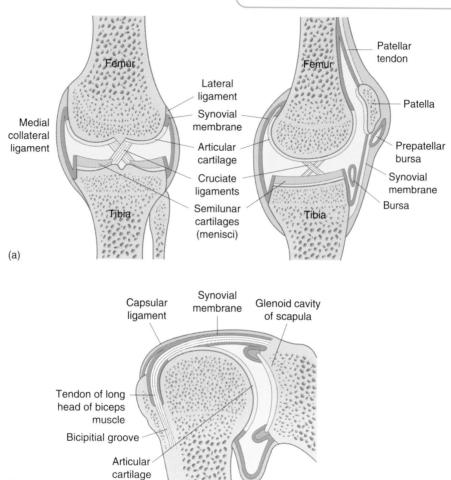

(a)

(b)

Figure 1.7 a) The knee joint b) The shoulder joint

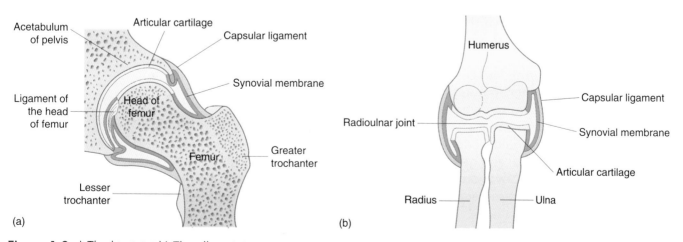

(a)

(b)

Figure 1.8 a) The hip joint b) The elbow joint

Activity 3

Copy and complete the table below.

Joint feature	Definition	Function
Joint capsule		
	Glassy smooth tissue that covers the ends of bones in a joint	
		Reduce friction between the articulating bones Nourish articular cartilage
	Small sacs of synovial fluid located in the joint at sites of friction	
Synovial membrane		
		Attaches one bone to another

Activity 4

Explain how the knee joint is structured and how this suits its function in relation to sporting activity.

Types of synovial joint

Synovial joints can be further subdivided:

1 A hinge joint is a uniaxial joint, which only allows movement in one plane. For example, the knee joint only allows movement back and forth. Strong ligaments exist in order to prevent any sideways movement.
2 A pivot joint, which is also uniaxial, only allows rotation. For example, in the cervical vertebrae, the axis rotates on the atlas.
3 An ellipsoid joint is biaxial, allowing movement in two planes. For example, the radiocarpal joint of the wrist allows movement back and forth as well as side to side.
4 A gliding joint is formed where flat surfaces glide past one another. Although mainly biaxial, they may permit movement in all directions. For example, in the wrist, the small carpal bones move against each other.
5 A saddle joint is biaxial and generally occurs where concave and convex surfaces meet. For example, the carpo-metacarpal joint of the thumb.
6 The ball-and-socket joint allows the widest range of movement; occurs where a rounded head of a bone fits into a cup-shaped cavity. For example, in the hip and shoulder.

Activity 5

Try to explain, where possible, how each type of synovial joint shown in Figure 1.9 has a role to play in sporting activity.

EXAMINER'S TIP

Synovial joints are classified according to the range and type of movement they allow. You must be able to relate the type of synovial joint to its structure. For example, hinge joints only allow movement in one plane due to the large number of ligaments crossing the joint and restricting movement. The ball-and-socket joint of the shoulder, however, enjoys a wide range of movement, due to its shallow socket and relatively few ligaments.

Movement patterns occurring at synovial joints

The movements that occur at joints can be classified according to the action occurring between the articulating bones. These are called movement patterns. A movement of a limb or body part will always have a starting point (point A) and a finishing point (point B). By analysing the position of the finishing point relative to the

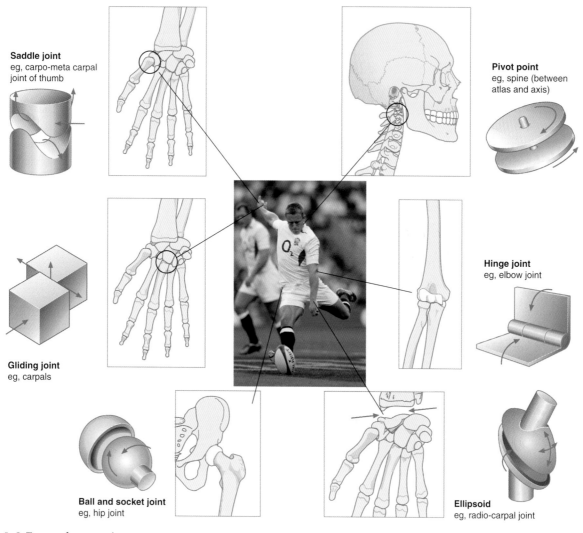

Figure 1.9 Types of synovial joint

starting point, we can form a classification of movement. A knowledge of body planes can also aid our understanding and classification of joint actions.

Major movement patterns that play a significant role in sporting activity are outlined in Table 1.1.

- Hip joint
- Shoulder joint
- Skull and cervical vertebrae
- Ribs and thoracic vertebrae
- Lumbar region

Activity 6

Using an articulated skeleton, or a partner, examine the joints listed below. Describe the type of joint and the movements possible:

- Radio-ulnar joint
- Knee joint
- Elbow joint

Activity 7

What movement patterns occur at:

- the shoulder and elbow during the performance of a tennis serve?
- the hip and knee during a squat thrust?
- the hip, knee and ankle during the recovery and kick phase in breaststroke?

Table 1.1 Movement patterns

Joint action	Diagram
Flexion: Flexion occurs when the angle between the articulating bones is decreased. For example, by raising the lower part of the arm to touch the shoulder, the angle between the radius and the humerus at the elbow has decreased. Flexion of the elbow has thus occurred. A muscle that causes flexion is known as a **flexor**. In the example at the elbow, the **biceps brachii** is the flexor muscle.	*Flexion / Extension*
Extension: Extension of a joint occurs when the angle of the articulating bones is increased. For example, when standing up from a seated position, the angle between the femur and the tibia increases, thus causing extension at the knee joint. Extreme extension, usually at an angle of greater than 180°, is known as **hyperextension**. A muscle that causes extension is known as an **extensor**. In the example of the knee joint, the **quadriceps femoris group** is the extensor.	*Extension / Flexion*
Abduction: This is movement of a body part away from the midline of the body or other body part. For example: • If arms are placed by the sides of the body and then raised laterally, abduction has occurred at the shoulder joint. • If fingers are spread out, movement has occurred away from the midline of the hand, and abduction has taken place.	*Abduction*
Adduction: Adduction is the opposite of abduction and concerns movement towards the midline of the body or body part. For example, by lowering the arm to the side of the body, movement towards the midline has occurred and this is termed adduction.	*Adduction*
Circumduction: Circumduction occurs when a circle can be described by the body part and is simply a combination of flexion, extension, abduction and adduction. True circumduction can only really occur at ball-and-socket joints of the shoulder and hip.	*Circumduction of shoulder*
Pronation: Pronation occurs at the radio-ulnar joint. It typically occurs where the palm of the hand is moved from facing upwards to facing downwards. It is a form of rotation.	*Pronation / Supination of forearm*

Joint action	Diagram
Supination: Supination is the opposite of pronation and, again, takes place at the radio-ulnar joint. It generally occurs when the palm of the hand is turned to face upwards.	
Horizontal abduction/adduction: Horizontal abduction involves movement of the arm across the body. A discus thrower will perform both horizontal abduction and horizontal adduction when preparing and executing a throw. A right-handed thrower with perform horizontal abduction when swinging their arm out to the right, and horizontal adduction when moving the arm towards the midline of the body. Sometimes horizontal abduction is known as horizontal extension and horizontal adduction as horizontal flexion.	
Rotation: Rotation of a joint occurs where the bone turns about its longitundinal axis within the joint. Rotation towards the body is termed **internal** or **medial** rotation, while rotation away from the body is called **external** or **lateral** rotation. Lateral rotation will occur at the shoulder joint of a tennis player preparing to strike a ball on their forehand with topspin whilst medial rotation will occur during the execution of the shot.	
Plantar flexion: Plantar flexion occurs at the ankle joint and is typified by the pointing of the toes. When taking off in high jump, plantar flexion of the ankle occurs. **Dorsiflexion:** This also occurs at the ankle and takes place when the foot is raised upwards, towards the tibia. When the preparing to perform a jump shot in basketball, dorsiflexion occurs at the ankle joint.	
Lateral flexion: sideways movement of the trunk.	

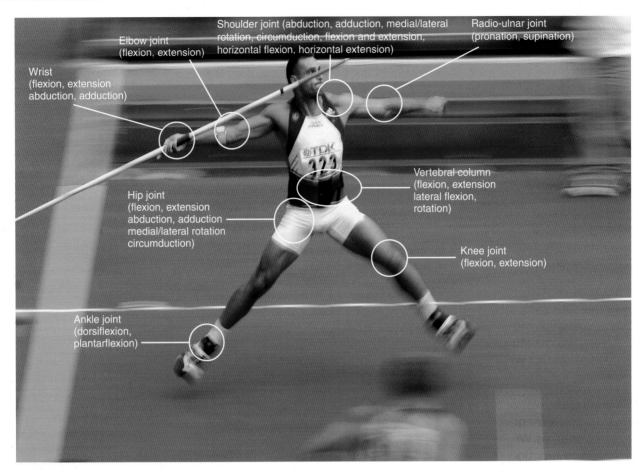

Figure 1.10 Joints and their associated movement patterns

Key term

Movement patterns: Terms used to describe the actions taking place at joints. They include flexion, extension, abduction, adduction, rotation and circumduction.

IN CONTEXT

Look at the javelin thrower in **Figure 1.10**. The humerus articulates with the scapula at the shoulder joint and moves from the preparation phase shown (starting point), through to the release point (finishing point). In doing so, the action of horizontal flexion/adduction occurs.

EXAMINER'S TIP

Candidates often get confused between rotation and circumduction. To distinguish between the two, try the following:
● Grip a ruler at the bottom with your right hand.
● Now raise your arm in front of your body and move the ruler anticlockwise. Medial rotation has just occurred at your shoulder.

● Now move the ruler clockwise so that it ends up pointing to the side. This is lateral rotation.
Circumduction occurs when you describe a circle with your hand, using your whole arm.

EXAMINER'S TIP

When answering a question on movement patterns, make sure you state the following:
● the name of the joint;
● the type of joint;
● the articulating bones;
● the movement produced.
It is often a good idea in your exam to draw up a table to show this information.

Activity 8

Participate in the circuit training session outlined in Figure 1.11. For each activity, state what movement patterns are occurring at the stated joints.

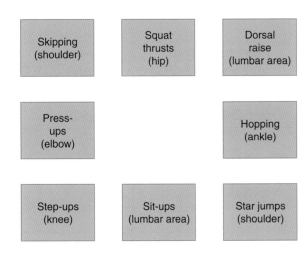

Skipping (shoulder)	Squat thrusts (hip)	Dorsal raise (lumbar area)
Press-ups (elbow)		Hopping (ankle)
Step-ups (knee)	Sit-ups (lumbar area)	Star jumps (shoulder)

Figure 1.11 A circuit of exercises

The muscular system

No study of human movement or exercise is complete without a study of the muscular system. The muscles interact with the skeleton to provide movement.

Skeletal muscle is responsible for the body's mechanical movement, and is central to our study of movement analysis. We are now going to examine its properties and functions.

Properties of skeletal muscle

Skeletal muscle possesses three essential properties:

1 Extensibility: this is the ability of muscle tissue to lengthen when contracting and provide the effort required to move the lever system (bones), producing coordinated movement.
2 Elasticity: this is the ability of muscle tissue to return to its normal resting length once it has been stretched. This can be compared to an elastic band that will always resume its resting shape, even after stretching. This enables the muscle to prepare for a series of repeated contractions, which is normally required during the performance of exercise.
3 Contractility: this refers to the capacity of a muscle to contract or shorten forcibly when stimulated by nerves and hormones (excitability).

All these properties are essential for all body actions, including locomotion, posture and facial expressions.

Functions of skeletal muscle

Skeletal muscle has several important functions within the body:

1 Movement: skeletal muscles attach to bones, against which they pull to enable movement. For example, when running, the hip flexor muscles pull on the femur to lift the leg off the ground, while the quadriceps muscles contract to pull on the tibia to straighten the leg at the knee joint.
2 Support and posture: the muscles are seldom fully relaxed and are often in a constant state of slight contraction. In order to adopt an upright position, many muscles within the legs and torso are contracting statically to ensure that the body is balanced. This is also known as muscle tone.
3 Heat production: the contraction of skeletal muscle involves the production of energy. In breaking down glycogen to provide this energy, heat is released. This accounts for why the body becomes hot when exercising. When the body is cold, the muscle often goes through a series of involuntary contractions (commonly known as shivering) in order to release heat and keep the body warm.

Muscle fibres

Muscles are composed of thousands and thousands of individual muscles fibres, which are held together by connective tissue. However, muscle fibres may differ in physiological make-up and it is the type of fibre that exists which explains, for example, the difference in performance between a sprinter and a marathon runner.

Skeletal muscle has two main fibre types: slow-twitch and fast-twitch. (See Tables 1.2 and 1.3 for their characteristics.)

Fast-twitch and slow-twitch fibres vary in different muscles and in different individuals; these proportions tend to be inherited. Essentially, a marathon runner may have almost 80 per cent

Table 1.2 Basic characteristics of fast-twitch and slow-twitch muscle fibres

Slow-twitch (Type 1)	Fast-twitch (Type 2)
red	white
contract slowly	contract rapidly
aerobic	anaerobic
endurance-based	speed/strength-based
can contract repeatedly	easily exhausted
exert less force	exert great force

Table 1.3 Structural characteristics of muscle fibres

Characteristics	Slow-twitch (Type 1)	Fast oxidative glycolytic (FOG) (Type 2a)	Fast-twitch glycolytic (FTG) (Type 2b)
speed of contraction (ms)	slow (110)	fast (50)	fast (50)
force of contraction	low	high	high
size	smaller	large	large
mitochondrial density	high	lower	low
myoglobin content	high	lower	low
fatiguability	fatigue-resistant	less resistant	easily fatigued
aerobic capacity	high	medium	low
capillary density	high	high	low
anaerobic capacity	low	medium	high
motor neuron size	small	large	large
fibres/motor neuron	10–180	300–800	300–800
sarcoplasmic reticulum development	low	high	high

Source: Adapted from Sharkey, *Physiology of Fitness*, Human Kinetics, 1990

slow-twitch fibres, which are designed for long periods of low-intensity work; while sprinters will have approximately the same percentage of fast-twitch fibres, which can generate extremely high force, but fatigue easily.

Fast-twitch muscle fibres have recently been subdivided into type 2a and type 2b:

- Type 2a, also referred to as fast oxidative glycolytic fibres (FOG), pick up certain type 1 characteristics through endurance training. They therefore tend to have a greater resistance to fatigue. Activities which are fairly high in intensity and of relatively short duration, such as a 200m swim or an 800m run, may well rely on type 2a fibres.
- Type 2b, pure fast-twitch fibres called fast-twitch glycolytic (FTG), are used for activities of very high intensity and have a much stronger force of contraction. This is because the motor neuron that carries the impulse is much larger; there are generally more fibres within a fast-twitch motor unit; and the muscle fibres themselves are larger and thicker. We would expect a powerlifter or a sprinter to possess a large proportion of type 2b fibres.

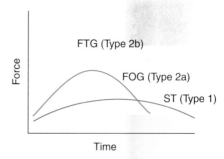

Figure 1.12 Muscle fibre twitch response: fast-twitch muscle fibres generate higher forces for a shorter space of time when compared to slow-twitch

Key terms

Slow-twitch muscle fibres: Muscle fibres designed to produce energy aerobically. They can produce a relatively small amount of force over a long period of time. Found in large quantities in the leg muscles of marathon runners or cyclists.

Fast-twitch muscle fibres: Muscle fibres designed to produce energy anaerobically. They can produce large amounts of force, but only over a short period of time, as they fatigue easily. Found in large quantities in the leg muscles of 100m sprinters and triple jumpers.

IN CONTEXT

A marathon runner such as Paula Radcliffe will have a very high percentage (80–90 per cent) of slow-twitch oxidative fibres (type 1), while a 100m sprinter such as Asafa Powell will have a very high proportion (60–70 per cent) of fast-twitch glycolytic muscle fibres (type 2b).

EXAMINER'S TIP

Make sure you can distinguish between a structural characteristic and a functional characteristic of different fibre types. A structural characteristic considers the actual make-up of the muscle fibre, while a functional characteristic considers what effect that composition has on performance. For example, a structural characteristic of a slow-twitch fibre is that it has a greater capillary density. The functional characteristic, therefore, is that slow-twitch fibres have a greater aerobic and endurance capacity, due to the enhanced blood supply.

Activity 9

Under the headings of slow-twitch, fast oxidative glycolytic and fast-twitch glycolytic, list as many sporting activities as you can which predominantly use that fibre type.

Activity 10

Construct a continuum with type 1 at one end and type 2b at the other. Collect pictures from as many different sports and activities as possible and stick them along the continuum, relating the position to the fibre type that the activity predominantly requires.

Figure 1.13 A marathon runner possesses a high percentage of type 1 slow-twitch muscle fibres

Figure 1.14 A 100m sprinter possesses a high percentage of type 2b fast-twitch muscle fibres

Table 1.4 Slow-twitch muscle fibre composition of various athletes

Athletic group	Shoulder (deltoid)	Calf (gastrocnemius)	Thigh (vastus lateralis)
Long-distance runners		79% (m) 69% (f)	
Canoeists	71% (m)		
Triathletes	60% (m)	59% (m)	63% (m)
Swimmers	67% (m) 69% (f)		
Sprint runners		24% (m) 27% (f)	
Cyclists			57% (m) 51% (f)
Weightlifters	53% (m)	44% (m)	
Shot-putters		38% (m)	
Non-athletes			47% (m) 46% (f)

Activity 11

Using Table 1.4, account for the differences in fibre content between the different classes of athletes. Explain your answers.

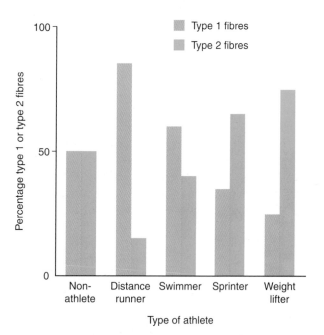

Figure 1.15 Relative percentages of fast- and slow-twitch fibres in a range of athletes

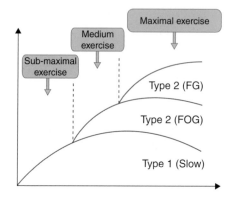

Figure 1.16 Motor unit recruitment related to intensity of exercise

Activity 12

Undertake some research to discover if there is a link between genetics and muscle fibre type. Discuss your findings in class. What evidence is there of a genetic link and how much do you think this determines a performer's choice of activity?

Connective tissue

Connective tissue is responsible for holding all the individual muscle fibres together. It surrounds individual muscle fibres and encases the whole muscle, forming tendons, which attach the muscles to bones and transmit the 'pull' of the muscle to the bones, to cause movement and harness the power of muscle contractions. Tendons vary in length and are composed of parallel fibres of collagen.

The points of attachment for each muscle are termed the origin and the insertion.

- The origin is the end of the muscle attached to a stable bone against which the muscle can pull. *This is usually the nearest flat bone.*
- The insertion is the muscle attachment on the bone that the muscle puts into action.

For example, the biceps has its origin on the scapula. This gives a firm base against which the biceps can pull in order to raise the lower arm. (The biceps is a flexor muscle, and its job is to allow flexion at the elbow.) Since the biceps raises the lower arm, it must be attached to that body part via the insertion. In fact, the biceps has its insertion on the radius.

The muscle belly is the thick portion of muscle tissue sited between the origin and the insertion. It is not unusual for a muscle to have two or more origins, while maintaining a common insertion: the term 'biceps' can be broken down to mean two ('bi') heads ('ceps'). The biceps has two origins, or heads, which pull on one insertion in the radius and put the lower arm into action.

Key terms

Tendon: A connective tissue that attaches skeletal muscle to a bone. Tendons have a great capacity to withstand stress as they must transmit large muscular forces to put a bone into action.
Origin: The tendon or point of attachment of a muscle onto a stationary bone against which the muscle can pull. Usually on the nearest flat bone to the working muscle.
Insertion: The tendon or point of attachment of a muscle onto the bone that the muscle puts into action.

EXAMINER'S TIP

The origin of a muscle is usually attached to the nearest flat bone, while the insertion is on the bone that the muscle puts into action.

Exam-style questions

1 The long jumper would use fast-twitch glycolytic fibre type (type 2b) during the take-off phase. Identify two reasons why this fibre type would be used.

2 During submaximal (aerobic) exercise, the predominant muscle fibre type would be slow-twitch (type 1). Give one structural and one functional characteristic of this fibre type.

Antagonistic muscle action

Muscles never work alone. In order for a coordinated movement to be produced, the muscles must work as a group or team, with several muscles working at any one time. Taking the simple movement of flexion of the arm at the elbow, the muscle responsible for flexion (bending of the arm) is the biceps brachii, and the muscle which produces the desired joint movement is called the agonist, or prime mover. However, in order for the biceps muscle to shorten when contracting, the triceps muscle must lengthen. The triceps, in this instance, is known as the antagonist, since its action is opposite to that of the agonist. The two muscles must work together, however, to produce the required movement.

Fixator muscles, or stabilisers, also work in this movement. Their role is to stabilise the origin so that the agonist can achieve maximum and effective contraction. In this case, the trapezius contracts to stabilise the scapula, to create a rigid platform. Neutralisers or synergist muscles in this movement prevent any undesired movements which may occur, particularly at the shoulder, where the biceps works over two joints.

It can thus be seen that for this apparently simple movement of elbow flexion, integrated and synergistic (harmonious) muscle actions are required to enable the necessary smooth movement.

Furthermore, the roles of each muscle are constantly changed for changing actions. For example, in the action of elbow extension, the roles of the biceps and triceps are reversed, so that the triceps becomes the prime mover or agonist (since the triceps is an extensor and thus produces this movement pattern), while the biceps becomes the antagonist, to enable the smooth and effective contraction of the triceps.

Below is a list of commonly used antagonistic pairings:

- pectorals/latissimus dorsi;
- anterior deltoids/posterior deltoids;
- trapezius/deltoids;
- rectus abdominis/erector spinalis;
- quadriceps group/hamstring group;
- tibialis anterior/gastrocnemius and soleus;
- biceps brachii/triceps brachii;
- wrist flexors/wrist extensors.

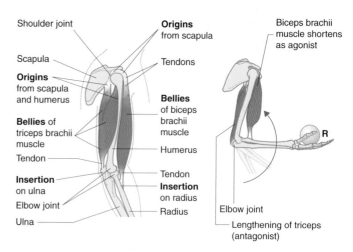

Figure 1.18 Antagonistic muscle action at the elbow joint

IN CONTEXT

When a gymnast such as Beth Tweddle takes off when performing a somersault, her quadriceps muscles are the agonists and will undergo concentric contraction as they shorten. On landing, her quadriceps undergo eccentric contraction as they lengthen while contracting and cushion the landing – they remain the agonists. To maintain the tucked position throughout the somersault, her hip flexors (iliopsoas) work isometrically – they do not change length but they are still contracting.

Key terms

Agonist/prime mover: A muscle that contracts and is directly responsible for the movement that results at a joint.
Antagonist: A muscle that has an action opposite to that of an agonist and helps in the production of a coordinated movement.
Fixator: A muscle that stabilises the origin of the agonist so that an effective contraction can take place.

Activity 13

Explain the antagonistic muscle action occurring in the leg during a kicking action in swimming front crawl.

Figure 1.17 The muscles of a gymnast will work antagonistically to produce effective and coordinated movements

Exam-style questions

1   Diagram A shows a back raise exercise. Use the diagram to help you identify the agonist and antagonist

2   Diagram B shows an athlete during the take-off phase of the long jump.

A

Complete the joint analysis below.

(a) Knee joint during extension:

- type of joint?
- articulating bones?

(b) Ankle joint during plantar flexion:

- type of joint?
- agonist?

B

C

(c) Diagram C shows a gymnast performing a tuck jump.

Apply your knowledge to complete the following movement analysis table.

Joint	Joint type	Articulating bones	Movement occurring	Agonist	Antagonist
Hip			Flexion	Iliopsoas	

3   Identify two structures of the hip joint and describe the role of each structure during physical performance.

Types of muscle contraction

In order to produce the vast range of movements of which it is capable, the body's muscles either shorten, lengthen or remain the same length while contracting. Indeed, muscle contractions are classified depending on the muscle action which predominates.

Isotonic contractions refer to those instances when the muscle is moving while contracting. This can be divided further, into concentric and eccentric muscle actions:

- Concentric contractions involve the muscle shortening while contracting, as happens in the biceps brachii during the upward phase of a biceps curl, or in the triceps during the upward phase of a push-up.

- Eccentric contractions, on the other hand, involve the muscle lengthening while contracting (remember that a muscle is not always relaxing while lengthening!). This can be seen in the biceps during the downward phase of the biceps curl, or in the triceps during the downward phase of the press-up. The eccentric contraction of the biceps during the downward phase is used to counteract the force of gravity. This is because gravity acts on the mass of the weight and forearm, causing extension at the elbow. If the biceps does not contract to control the rate of motion caused by gravity, the movement will be very quick, resulting in injury.

Plyometrics is a type of strength training based on a muscle contracting eccentrically.

Sometimes, however, a muscle can contract without actively lengthening or shortening. In this instance, the muscle is going through isometric contraction – the muscle remains the same length while contracting. In fact, the majority of muscles will contract isometrically in order for us to maintain posture. These static contractions also occur while holding a weight in a stationary position, or when performing a handstand.

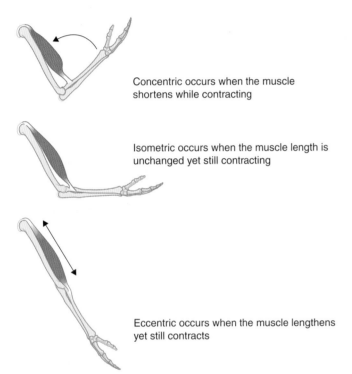

Concentric occurs when the muscle shortens while contracting

Isometric occurs when the muscle length is unchanged yet still contracting

Eccentric occurs when the muscle lengthens yet still contracts

Figure 1.19 Types of muscle contraction at the biceps brachii

IN CONTEXT

When a muscle contracts eccentrically it is often acting as a brake to counteract the effect of gravity. So a triple jumper's quadriceps muscles must contract eccentrically on landing during the hop-and-step phase to stop the leg from buckling and the jumper collapsing to the floor.

Normally, when a muscle contracts, the angular velocity of the muscle shortening or lengthening varies throughout the contraction. However, specialist hydraulic machines have been devised so that it is possible to maintain constant the speed at which the muscle lengthens or shortens, but not necessarily maintain the resistance applied. The speed of the movement cannot be increased. Any attempt to increase the velocity results in equal reaction force from the machine. In this way, isokinetic exercise, as it is called, is excellent for strength training.

Key terms

Isotonic concentric contraction: The shortening of a muscle while contracting. For example, during the upward phase of a biceps curl, the biceps contracts concentrically.
Isotonic eccentric contraction: The lengthening of a muscle while contracting. For example, during the downward phase of a biceps curl, the biceps contracts eccentrically.

Table 1.5 Types of muscle contraction

	Isotonic Concentric	Eccentric	Isometric Static
Muscle action	Muscle shortens	Muscle lengthens while contracting	Muscle remains the same length while contracting
Example	Biceps: when raising a weight	Biceps: when lowering a weight	Biceps: holding a weight in a static position

Isometric contraction: Where a muscle contracts, yet there is no visible shortening or lengthening. Also known as a static contraction. For example, when holding a barbell with the elbows flexed at 90°, the biceps contracts isometrically.

Plyometrics: A type of training designed to improve power, elastic strength and speed. It involves pre-loading the muscle with an eccentric contraction before performing a powerful concentric contraction. Activities commonly include bounding, hopping and a variety of medicine ball exercises.

EXAMINER'S TIP

Make sure you can name the four muscles of the quadriceps group and the three muscles of the hamstring group.

Figure 1.20 shows the location of the major muscles in the body, while Table 1.6 shows the movements each muscle produces and gives an idea of some simple strengthening exercises. Take a moment to study both of these.

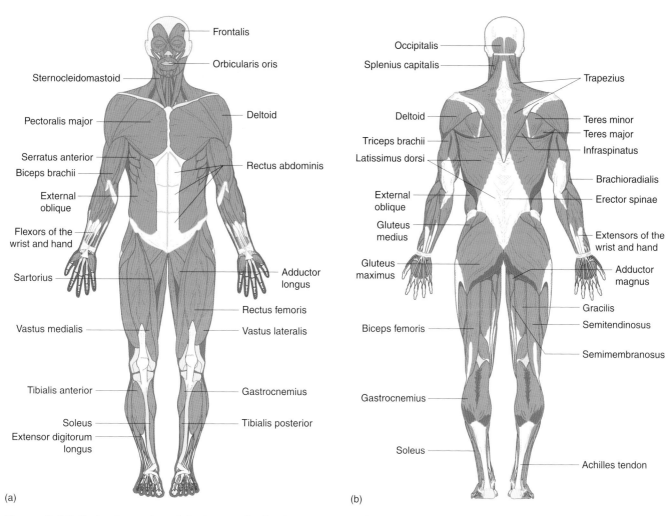

(a)

(b)

Figure 1.20 Skeletal muscles of the human body a) Anterior view b) Posterior view

Table 1.6 Major muscles, their origins and insertions, and actions performed

Major muscle/group	Origin	Insertion	Actions performed during a weights session
Trapezius Acromion process **Action** **Upper:** adducts and rotates scapula, laterally flexes neck and head. **Middle:** adducts and elevates scapula. **Lower:** rotates scapula. Spine of scapula	Base of the skull Thoracic vertebrae	Acromion process Clavicle Scapula	Shoulder shrugs
Pectoralis major Anterior view **Action** Medial rotation of the humerus. Flexes the shoulder and horizontally adducts humerus.	Sternum Clavicle Rib cartilage	Humerus	Barbell chest press

Continued

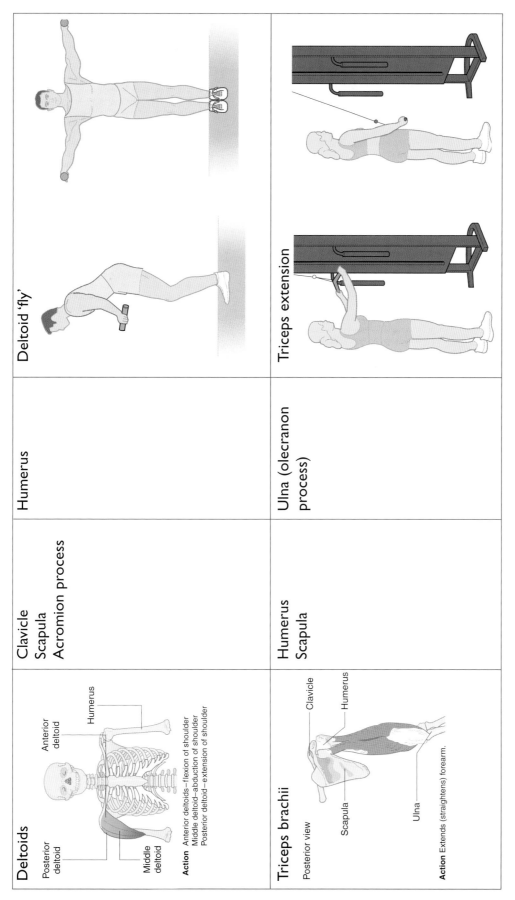

Deltoids

Posterior deltoid

Anterior deltoid

Humerus

Middle deltoid

Action Anterior deltoids—flexion of shoulder
Middle deltoid—abduction of shoulder
Posterior deltoid—extension of shoulder

Clavicle
Scapula
Acromion process

Humerus

Deltoid 'fly'

Triceps brachii

Posterior view

Clavicle

Humerus

Scapula

Ulna

Action Extends (straightens) forearm.

Humerus
Scapula

Ulna (olecranon process)

Triceps extension

Table 1.6 Continued

Major muscle/group	Origin	Insertion	Strengthening exercise
Latissimus dorsi **Action** Adduction of humerus.	Thoracic vertebrae Lumbar vertebrae Iliac crest	Humerus	'Lat' pull-down
Rectus abdominis/obliques **Action** **Transverse**: constricts abdominal contents, assists in forcing air out of lungs **Rectus**: gives anterior support to lumbar spine, holds rib cage and pubis together. **Internal/external obliques**: flex, rotate and side-bend trunk. Internal oblique Rectus abdominals External oblique	Ribs	Ilium pubis	Swiss ball abdominal crunches

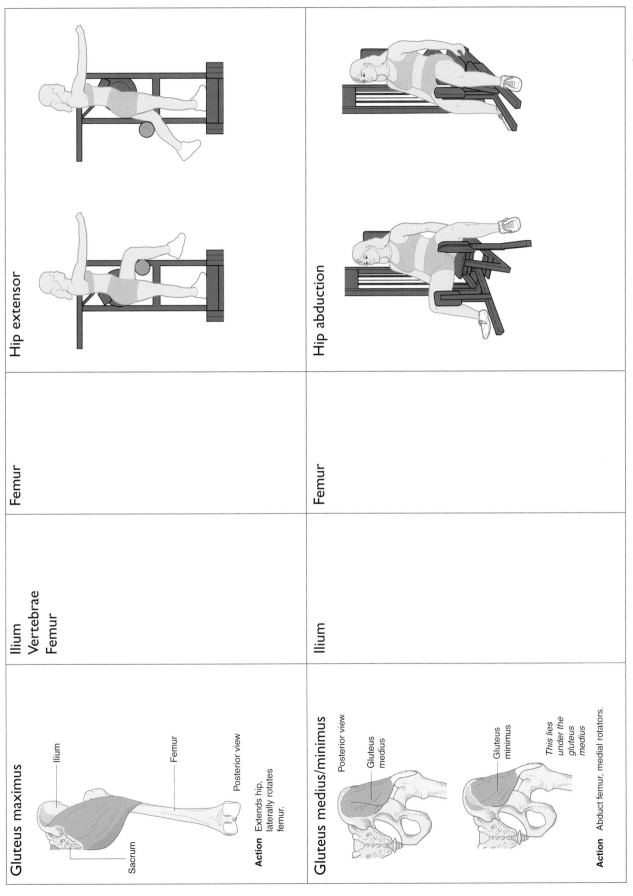

Hip extensor

Femur

Ilium
Vertebrae
Femur

Gluteus maximus

Ilium

Femur

Posterior view

Sacrum

Action Extends hip, laterally rotates femur.

Hip abduction

Femur

Ilium

Gluteus medius/minimus

Posterior view

Gluteus medius

Gluteus minimus

This lies under the gluteus medius

Action Abduct femur, medial rotators.

Continued

Table 1.6 *Continued*

Major muscle/group	Origin	Insertion	Strengthening exercise
Adductors Adductor brevis / Adductor longus / Adductor magnus **Action** Adduction of hip flexion and lateral rotation of the femur. **Origin** Front part of pubic bone and lower part of hip bone (ischial tuberosity).	Pubic bone (ischial tuberosity)	Femur	Hip adduction
Biceps brachii Anterior view — Clavicle, Scapula, Long head, Short head **Action** Flexes and supinates (turns palm upwards) the forearm.	Scapula	Radius	Barbell biceps curl

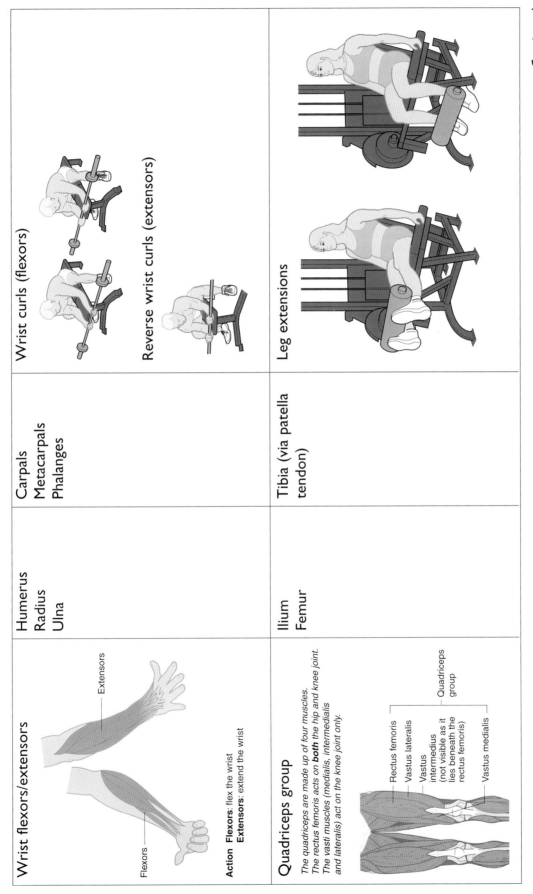

Wrist flexors/extensors

Extensors

Flexors

Action Flexors: flex the wrist
Extensors: extend the wrist

Humerus
Radius
Ulna

Carpals
Metacarpals
Phalanges

Wrist curls (flexors)

Reverse wrist curls (extensors)

Quadriceps group

*The quadriceps are made up of four muscles.
The rectus femoris acts on **both** the hip and knee joint.
The vasti muscles (medialis, intermedialis
and lateralis) act on the knee joint only.*

Rectus femoris
Vastus lateralis
Vastus intermedius (not visible as it lies beneath the rectus femoris)
Vastus medialis

Quadriceps group

Ilium
Femur

Tibia (via patella tendon)

Leg extensions

Continued

Table 1.6 Continued

Major muscle/group	Origin	Insertion	Strengthening exercise
Hamstring group Posterior view Semitendinosus Semimembranosus Biceps femoris *The hamstrings consist of three muscles.* **Action** Flexes the knee, extends the femur of the hip.	Pubic bone (ischial tuberosity)	Tibia Fibula	Hamstring curls
Gastrocnemius/soleus **Action** Plantar flexion of the ankle (pointing the toes at the feet) Femur Tibia Achilles tendon a) Gastrocnemius b) Soleus	Femur (gastrocnemius) Tibi Fibula (soleus)	Calcaneus	Calf raises

Tibialis anterior

Femur

Patella

Tibia

Fibula

Action
Dorsiflexes (lifts up) and inverts the foot towards the tibia

Tibia

Tarsals/metatarsals

Dorsiflexion

Activity 14

1   Using sticky labels, label the muscles on a partner's body. Try to label as many as you can without looking at your textbook.
2   Collect as many pictures of bodybuilders as you can and label/identify the defined muscles.

No strength-training programme is complete without due consideration of core stability. Core stability is the combined strength of all the muscles from your hips to your armpits, and it is responsible for many things, including posture. An increase in core strength can lead to increases in virtually all other types of strength and dramatically reduces the chance of injury during strength training. The best method of improving core stability is with the use of a Swiss ball. Simply performing abdominal crunches or leg raises on the Swiss ball will strengthen the abdominal and lower back muscles, the 'core' of the body's strength. The core muscles stabilise the upper body and pelvis during dynamic movement. The multifidus muscle, for example, lies deep in the back and helps to stabilise the cartilaginous joints of the spine. The transversus abdominis lies under the internal obliques and helps to stabilise the lower spine and pelvis during lifting movements. It is the body's natural corset or weightlifting belt!

Key term

Core stability: The muscles of the core that help to stabilise the trunk and create a firm foundation for coordinated movement of the legs and arms. Sports that require you to have great balance, such as snowboarding, require high levels of core stability.

EXAMINER'S TIP

You must make sure that you know the names of the muscles and the function each muscle performs (i.e. what movement patterns or joint actions they cause).

EXAMINER'S TIP

Make sure you are aware of the role of the transversus abdominis and multifidus muscles in relation to core stability.

Figure 1.21 Improving core stability with a Swiss ball (1)

Figure 1.22 Improving core stability with a Swiss ball (2)

Table 1.7 Variety of joint movements

Sport	Action	Movement pattern	Muscles working	Type of contraction
Basketball	Jump shot	Extension at knee	Quadriceps group: rectus femoris vasti muscles	Concentric

Putting it all together

Kinesiology is the study of body movement, and thus includes muscle action. When studying this unit it is helpful to consider the following:

- the function of the muscles contracting;
- how the muscle is contracting (e.g. concentric or eccentric);
- the movement patterns occurring at joints as a result of the movement.

Figure 1.23 Netball shooting – knees, ankles, elbows

Activity 15

Table 1.7 shows one joint movement used in basketball. Think of other 5 sporting situations, then copy and complete the table accordingly. You will find it useful to study the various tables throughout the chapter.

Activity 16

For each of the following joints, state which muscles are used for the movement patterns shown in brackets:

- knee (flexion and extension);
- hip (flexion, extension, abduction, adduction);
- shoulder (flexion, extension, abduction, adduction);
- ankle (plantar flexion, dorsiflexion, inversion, eversion).

Activity 17

For your course you need to be able to complete a full movement analysis for a range of skills. On the following pages there are some skills from a variety of activities. In each case, study the movement that has occurred from phase 1 to phase 2 and complete a full movement analysis on the joints specified. Use the format of Table 1.7, and don't forget to cover all aspects of the movement.

(a)
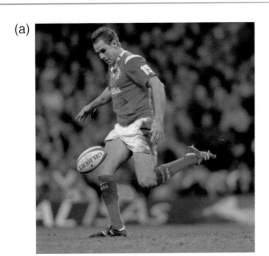

(b)
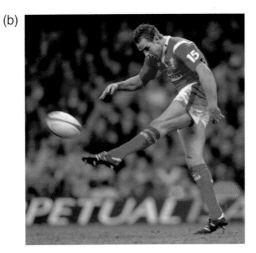

Figure 1.24 Kicking – hip, knee, ankle

(a)

(b)

Figure 1.25 Throwing the javelin – shoulder, radio-ulnar, wrist

(a)
(b)

Figure 1.27 The tennis serve – shoulder, elbow, wrist

(a)
(b)

Figure 1.26 The sprint start – hip, knee, ankle

Table 1.8 summarises the key movement patterns and muscle actions. With this information you should be able to apply your knowledge to a wide range of sporting activities.

Table 1.8 The musculoskeletal system: movement analysis

Joint	Action	Muscles used	Diagram	Example
Hip	Flexion	Psoas Iliacus Rectus femoris		Performing a tuck jump in trampolining
	Extension	Gluteus maximus Biceps femoris Semimembranosus Semitendinosus Gluteus medius (posterior)		Preparation to kick a football
	Abduction	Gluteus medius Gluteus minimus Tensor fasciae latae		Performing a cartwheel
	Adduction	Adductor magnus Adductor brevis Adductor longus Pectineus Gracilis		Kick action in breaststroke
	Medial rotation	Gluteus medius Gluteus minimus Tensor fasciae latae		Rotational movement when throwing the discus
	Lateral rotation	Gluteus maximus Adductors		Side foot pass in football
Knee	Flexion	Semitendinosus Semimembranosus Biceps femoris Popliteus Gastrocnemius		Preparing to kick a conversion in rugby
	Extension	Rectus femoris Vastus medialis Vastus lateralis Tensor fasciae latae		Rebounding in basketball
Knee	Medial rotation (when flexed)	Sartorius Semitendinosus		Breaststroke kick phase
	Lateral rotation (when flexed)	Tensor fasciae latae Biceps femoris		Breaststroke recovery

Continued

Table 1.8 Continued

Joint	Action	Muscles used	Diagram	Example
Ankle	Dorsiflexion	Tibialis anterior Extensor digitorum longus Peroneus tertius		Landing from a lay-up in basketball
	Plantar flexion	Gastrocnemius Peroneus longus Peroneus brevis Tibialis posterior Flexor digitorum longus		Pointing toes when performing a handstand
Shoulder	Flexion	Anterior deltoid Pectoralis major Coracobrachialis		Blocking of the net in volleyball
	Extension	Posterior deltoid Latissimus dorsi Teres major		Butterfly arm pull
	Adduction	Latissimus dorsi Pectoralis major Teres major Teres minor		Landing phase of a straddle jump in trampolining
	Abduction	Medial deltoid Supraspinatus		Straddle jump in trampolining
Elbow	Extension	Brachioradialis Triceps		Execution of a set shot in basketball
Radio-ulnar	Pronation	Pronator teres Pronator quadratus Brachioradialis		Putting top spin on a tennis ball
	Supination	Biceps brachii Supinator		Recovery phase of the arms in breaststroke
Wrist	Flexion	Wrist flexors		Wrist snap in basketball shot
	Extension	Wrist extensors		Initial grip of a shot against neck

Joint	Action	Muscles used	Diagram	Example
Movement of the trunk	Flexion	Rectus abdominis Internal obliques External obliques	Extension / Flexion	Crouching at start of a swimming dive
	Extension	Erector spinae Iliocostalis spinalis		Backflip in gymnastics
	Lateral flexion	Internal obliques Rectus abdominis Erector spinae Quadratus laborum	Lateral flexion	A cartwheel
	Rotation	External oblique Rectus abdominis Erector spinae		Follow-through on a tennis serve
Movement of the scapulae	Elevation	Levator scapulae Trapezius Rhomboids		Recovery phase of butterfly arm pull
	Depression	Trapezius (lower) Pectoralis minor Serratus anterior (lower)		Thrusting off a horse when performing a handspring
	Protraction	Serratus anterior		Recovery phase in breaststroke
	Retraction	Rhomboids Trapezius		Pull phase in breaststroke
	Upward rotation	Trapezius (upper) Serratus anterior		Recovery phase in front crawl
	Downward rotation	Rhomboids Levator scapulae		Front crawl arm pull

The effects of a warm-up and a cool-down on skeletal muscle tissue

Warm-ups and cool-downs should be undertaken prior to and following every training session and competitive performance, as they will improve the effectiveness and quality of performance.

The warm-up

Not only does the warm-up prepare the body for exercise, but it is fundamental to safe practice and injury prevention. To ensure the athlete gains as much as possible from the warm-up, the activities included should be specific to the sport that follows and should include exercises which prepare the muscles used.

It is a good idea to follow the three stages outlined below:

1 The first phase of a warm-up has the purpose of raising the heart rate, increasing the speed of oxygen delivery to the muscles and, of course, raising the body temperature. This can be achieved by performing some kind of cardiovascular exercise, such as jogging.

2 Now that muscle temperature has increased, the athlete can perform some mobility or stretching exercises. It is essential that both static stretches and some callisthenic-type activities are performed where the muscle is working over its full range. Press-ups, squat thrusts and lunges are good for this.

3 The final stage of a warm-up should involve a sport-specific or skill-related component, where the neuromuscular mechanisms related to the activity to follow are worked. For example, practising serving in tennis, tumble turns in swimming or shooting baskets in basketball.

Other physiological effects of a warm-up on skeletal muscle include:

● increased muscle temperature;
● improved extensibility and elasticity of muscle fibres due to decreased muscle viscosity;
● increased speed and force of contraction due to faster conduction of nerve impulses;
● it can help reduce DOMS (delayed onset of muscle soreness) (see below, under The cool-down).

Figure 1.28 shows the relationship between performance and muscle temperature.

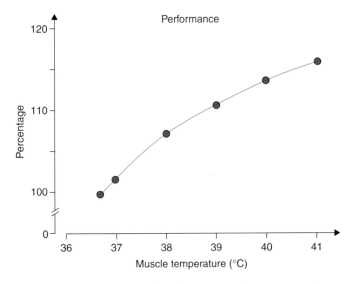

Figure 1.28 The relationship between performance and muscle temperature

The cool-down

Following exercise, a similar process to the warm-up must be followed in order to prevent unnecessary discomfort; this is a cool-down. It involves performing some kind of light, continuous exercise where the heart rate remains elevated. The purpose is to keep metabolic activity high and capillaries dilated, so that oxygen can be flushed through the muscle tissue, removing and oxidising any lactic acid that exists.

A cool-down may also result in limiting the effects of DOMS, which is characterised by tender and painful muscles, often experienced in the days following heavy and unaccustomed exercise. The explanation of this soreness is quite simple, resulting from the damage to muscle fibres and connective tissue surrounding the fibres. The soreness is usually temporary and goes within a couple of days, as the muscle fibres repair themselves. DOMS is most likely to occur following eccentric contraction, and can result from weight training, plyometrics or even walking down steep hills. The final part of the cool-down should involve a period of stretching activity, which should hopefully facilitate and improve flexibility, as the muscles are very warm at this stage.

The impact of different types of physical activity on the skeletal and muscular systems

The benefits of exercise are well documented. Table 1.9 highlights some of the benefits of regular physical activity on the skeletal and muscular systems.

Many studies have shown that children who are active throughout their teenage years have a greater chance of being healthy adults. Exercise has proven beneficial in the avoidance and prevention of certain skeletal disorders, such as osteoporosis and osteoarthritis.

- Osteoporosis is a bone condition that leads to weak or porous bones that can break easily. Bones are living tissue and are constantly being rebuilt. In osteoporosis, the rate of bone loss is greater than the rate of bone growth, leading to a reduction in overall bone mass. The risk of osteoporosis is lower for people who are active, particularly those who undertake weight-bearing activities, such as jogging, three times per week, since these activities promote bone growth, thus leading to denser and stronger bones.

Table 1.9 Benefits of regular physical activity on the skeletal and muscular systems

Skeletal system	Muscular system
- **Increased bone density.** Skeletal tissues become stronger since exercise imposes stress on the bones, which encourages the laying down of bony plates and the deposition of calcium salts along the lines of stress. This reinforces the criss-cross matrix of cancellous bone and improves the tensile stress of the bone. Strength training will be particularly beneficial in developing the strength of skeletal tissues. - **Articular cartilage thickens**, which aids the cushioning of the joint, and therefore protects the bones from wear and tear. - Flexibility and mobility training may enable ligaments to stretch slightly to enable a **greater range of movement at the joint**.	- **Increased muscle mass due to hypertrophy (enlargement) of muscle fibres.** Slow-twitch fibres respond well to activities such as jogging and cycling, while fast-twitch fibres respond well to strength-training activities, such as weight training. - **Tendons thicken** and can withstand greater muscular forces. - **Improved flexibility** due to increased extensibility of muscle fibres. - **Increased force of contraction** due to hyperplasia (splitting) of muscle fibres and increased elasticity.

- Osteoarthritis is a disease characterised by pain and impaired function at the joints, largely due to the deterioration of the joint cartilage. Regular aerobic exercise that is non- or partial weight bearing, such as swimming or cycling, should be encouraged to help control the pain associated with osteoarthritis. General mobility training will also help promote effective joint functioning. It is thought that increased activity can help promote the growth of new cartilage and nourish existing cartilage.

If done incorrectly, however, an exercise programme can cause long-term injury and damage to the body.

- Growth plate disorders: From birth, bone starts out as a shaft with cartilage at each end. The cartilage at the heads of bone gradually transforms into bone. However, a thin section of cartilage always remains to allow new growth to take place and thus make bones longer, until full maturity is reached. This is the growth plate and is the weakest part of the bone, and hence is more susceptible to injury. When a growth plate is injured, it causes it to close over prematurely, which stops the bone growing. Avoidance of explosive repetitive actions, impact activities and weight training should ensure that bones reach full maturation.
- Joint stability injuries: Extreme flexibility occurs where ligaments are lengthened excessively and, due to their inelasticity, remain lengthened, leading to joint instability and possible dislocation. Impact injuries arising from contact sports such as rugby may also lead to joint instability. Cruciate ligament damage at the knee, for example, can arise from the external force of a tackle. Similarly, the impact of performing a rugby tackle on the shoulder can lead to dislocation of this joint, as the head of the humerus sits in the relatively shallow depression (glenoid fossa) of the scapula.
- Overuse injuries: Repetitive actions, such as jogging, may lead to some wear and attrition of articular cartilage, causing excessive pronation of the foot, or inflammation of the bursa (bursitis), at the point of tendon attachment to the bone (tendonitis) in cases of tennis and golfer's elbow and stress fractures.

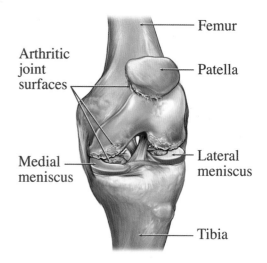

Figure 1.29 Osteoarthritis from overuse

Source: www.painreliefcushions.co.uk/images/osteoarthritis.jpg

IN CONTEXT

At the Atlanta Olympics in 1996, Kelly Holmes finished just outside the medals, in fourth place, running the 800m with a stress fracture. She spent the next seven weeks in recovery, in plaster!

Figure 1.30 Pushing the body or training too hard can lead to injury

Activity 20

'Participation in sport is dangerous and damaging to the musculoskeletal system.' Write an extended answer (minimum 500 words), showing how far you agree with this statement.

Exam-style questions

Exam-style questions

Taking part in physical activity is considered essential to maintaining a healthy lifestyle. However, taking part in some activities can result in injury and a reduction in activity levels. Discuss both the positive and the negative impacts on the joints and muscles of the body of participating in different types of physical activity.

EXAMINER'S TIP

You must be able to critically evaluate the impact of different types of physical activity on the skeletal and muscular systems.

Basic mechanics of sport and exercise

No study of human movement would be complete without the study of some basic mechanical principles. This section will investigate the following:

- force;
- an explanation and application of Newton's laws of motion to a variety of sports and activities – these are quite simply the 'rules' of motion;
- the centre of mass and how knowledge of it can be used to the advantage of a performer;
- the range of movement and types of motion that we see in sport.

Familiarity with these principles of mechanics will go some way in allowing the coach and performer to understand performance and its improvement.

The application of force in sport

Force is the 'push' or 'pull' exerted on an object or body, without which movement would not be possible. Forces can be generated internally by muscular contractions, or externally through the action of weight and frictional forces, including those of air and water.

In fact, sport and force are so inextricably linked that without force, sport could not exist. Forces applied in sport can:

Figure 1.31 Roger Federer is the master of using and manipulating force in tennis

- cause a body at rest to move (e.g. when someone tees off in golf, a force is applied to the golf ball via the club, causing the ball to accelerate away from the tee);
- cause a moving body to accelerate (e.g. when driving out of the blocks at the start of a race);
- cause a moving body to decelerate (e.g. when brakes are applied to a Formula 1 car when cornering);
- cause a moving body to change direction (e.g. when dodging in netball or sidestepping in rugby);
- cause a body to change shape (e.g. when landing in high jump, our body weight causes an impression in the crash mat).

Activity 21

'There can be no sport without force.' Write an extended answer (minimum 500 words), showing how far you agree with this statement. Make sure you include a number of sporting examples which support your answer.

When analysing force in sport it is important to consider three key aspects:

1. The size of the force
2. The point of application of the force
3. The direction in which the force acts.

It is best to explain these components of force by applying it to a sporting example.

When driving out of the blocks, a sprinter will apply a large force through the contraction of the muscles (pt1). The larger the force produced by the muscles, the greater the acceleration. The force generated by the muscles will be translated into a frictional force that occurs at the point where the spikes are in contact with the starting blocks (pt2). Because friction opposes motion, as the spikes push backwards onto the blocks the frictional force causes the sprinter to move forward out of them (pt 3).

Key term

Force: A push or pull that tends to alter the state of motion of a body.

Newton's laws of motion

Newton's laws of motion explain the principles of acceleration and movement, and are explained below, using the example of a 100m sprinter.

Newton's first law – the law of inertia

At the beginning of the race, an athlete remains stationary in the blocks. According to Newton's first law of motion: *Every body at rest, or moving with constant velocity in a straight line, will continue in that state unless compelled to change by an external force exerted upon it.*

This suggests that a body or an object has a tendency to resist any change in its state of motion – if a body is travelling in a straight line, at constant speed, it will continue to do so unless acted on by a force.

The same is true for the sprinter in the set position in the blocks. S/he will remain stationary unless a force is exerted on the blocks. The force exerted must be great enough to overcome this inertia, and in doing so the sprinter will move forward, out of the blocks. However, the inertia of an object is directly proportional to its mass, so a body with a greater mass will need a larger force to overcome its inertia than a body with less mass. Once out of the blocks, the athlete will quickly accelerate as there has been a change in velocity (which is zero when the sprinter is in the blocks).

Newton's second law – the law of acceleration

In order to generate greater acceleration, the athlete must generate greater force. This is Newton's second law of motion, which states that: *The acceleration of a body is **proportional** to the force causing it, and the acceleration takes place in the **direction** in which that force acts.*

So the 100m sprinter will seek to apply the greatest force possible to the blocks at the start of the race, in order to achieve maximal acceleration; this acceleration enables them to drive out and away from the blocks, as this is the direction in which the (reaction) force acts.

After about five seconds of a 100m sprint, we would expect the sprinter to have reached maximum velocity, and (according to Newton's first law) to remain at this constant velocity. So why does the athlete start to slow down? The explanation is relatively simple:

- physiological effect of the sprint – this is the main cause; the muscle stores of adenosine triphosphate (ATP) and phosphocreatine (PC),

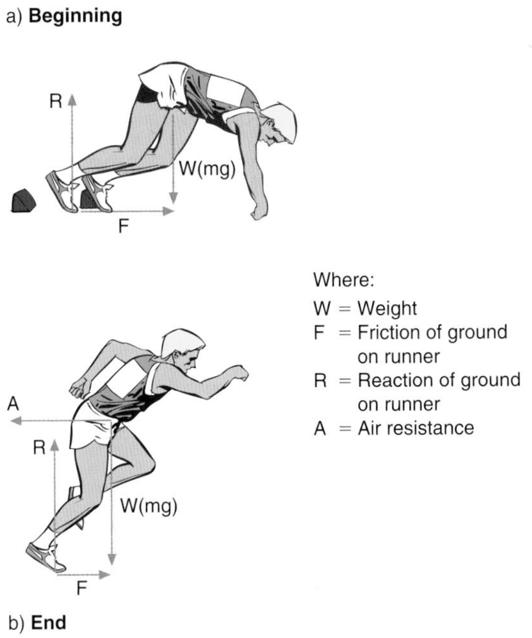

a) **Beginning**

R
W(mg)
F

Where:

W = Weight
F = Friction of ground on runner
R = Reaction of ground on runner
A = Air resistance

A
R
W(mg)
F

b) **End**

Figure 1.32 A free body diagram showing the forces acting upon a sprinter at the beginning and end of a race

which provide the energy for muscular contraction, are depleted;
- the effects of air resistance (although negligible).

This slowing down of the athlete represents a change in velocity and therefore is known as deceleration. In fact, most sprinters will start to slow down after 80–90m, and the winner will often be the person who takes longer to slow down!

Newton's third law – the action/reaction law

Newton's third law of motion states that: *When one object exerts a force on a second object, there is a force **equal** in magnitude but **opposite** in direction exerted by the second object on the first.*

More simply, to every action there is an equal and opposite reaction. The sprinter on the blocks experienced a force propelling him/her forward. From Newton's third law, we can deduce that as the athlete pushed backwards and downwards on the blocks, the blocks pushed the athlete upwards and forwards out of the blocks, with a force of equal magnitude.

Reaction forces can be seen easily in the field of sport:

- A footballer kicking a ball exerts a force on it in order to set it in motion (N1); according to Newton's third law (N3), the ball will exert an equal and opposite force on the kicking foot.
- The high jumper exerts a force on the ground in order to gain height and upward acceleration. The reaction force must be greater than the weight force of the athlete:

Reaction force = Weight force + Internal muscular force

EXAMINER'S TIP

You must be able to apply all three of Newton's laws to the same sporting performance.

Exam-style question

Apply Newton's laws of motion to a strength-training exercise for a muscle group of your choice.

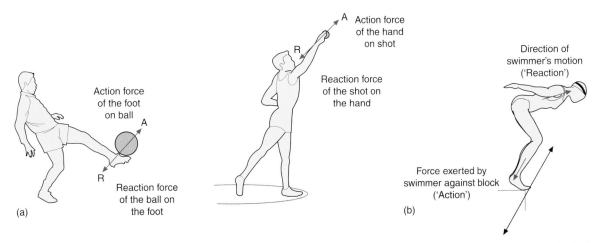

Action force of the foot on ball
A
R
Reaction force of the ball on the foot
(a)

A Action force of the hand on shot
R
Reaction force of the shot on the hand

Direction of swimmer's motion ('Reaction')
Force exerted by swimmer against block ('Action')
(b)

Figure 1.33 Action and reaction forces a) When an athlete applies force to the football or puts the shot, the ball/shot applies an equal force on the athlete's foot/hand b) Action and reaction forces in swimming

Activity 22

Copy out the table below. For each of Newton's three laws, give at least five examples from different practical activities where these laws can be applied.

	Newton's first law	Newton's second law	Newton's third law
1			
2			
3			
4			
5			

Centre of mass (COM)

The centre of mass is *where the weight of a body tends to be concentrated*. This signifies that point about which the object or body is balanced in all directions. For spherical objects, such as a shot, the mass is distributed symmetrically around its centre, which therefore indicates its centre of mass. Due to irregular body shapes, however, the centre of mass is not so obvious for humans. For a person standing erect with their hands by their sides, the point of centre of mass is approximately at navel height, but this point is constantly changing during movement. For example:

- If a person raises one arm above their head, the centre of mass will move further up the body.
- If the person adducts their arm to the right of their body, the centre of mass will move slightly to the right.

Thus, depending on the shape of the body, the centre of mass will vary.

Figure 1.34 The Fosbury flop can enable the high jumper's centre of mass to actually travel underneath the bar!

The centre of mass of an object or human body does not have to lie within its actual physical matter. Consider a quoit or rubber ring, for example; the centre of mass of these objects will actually fall at the centre, right in the middle of the hole. Similarly, by altering body shape, the human performer can manipulate their centre of mass so that it actually lies outside the body.

Athletes and coaches can use their knowledge of this concept in order to improve performance. A perfect example is the high jump. The Fosbury flop was developed so that greater heights could be achieved with similar outlay of effort. By arching the back, the centre of mass will move outside the body, and may pass underneath the bar while the jumper actually travels over it! The jumper using the Fosbury technique will therefore not need to raise their centre of mass as high as someone performing a western roll technique when clearing the same height.

Activity 23

Take part in a gymnastics lesson. Investigate your ability to balance in a number of different positions (e.g. a tucked headstand, an extended headstand, a handstand with support, a handstand without support, an arabesque with a bent supporting leg, an arabesque with a straight supporting leg). Discuss your findings with others in your class. Be sure to consider the following:
- the number of points of contact;
- the size of the base of support;
- the position (height) of the centre of mass;
- the position of the centre of mass in relation to the base of support.

Centre of mass (COM): The point where the mass of a body tends to be concentrated and is balanced in all directions.

Stability and balance

Stability is the ability of an object to resist motion and remain at rest. The more stable a body is, the greater its ability to resist motion. In sporting activity, stable positions occur when balancing or when defensive positions need to be adopted. More often, however, performers need to become unstable, as unstable positions allow performers to change their state of motion and actually move – a central part of most sporting activity!

Factors that affect stability therefore include:

- the mass of the body or object – the greater the mass, the more stable the body;
- the size of the base of support – the larger the base of support, the more stable the body;
- the height of the centre of mass – the lower the centre of mass, the more stable the body;
- the number of points of contact with the surface – the greater the number of points of contact, the more stable the body;

- the proximity of the line of gravity to the centre of the base of support – the closer the line of gravity to the centre of the base of support, the more stable the body.

Figure 1.36 A gymnast maintains balance in an arabesque by ensuring her centre of mass is over her base of support

The position of the centre of mass is also important for maintaining balance. An object or person will remain in balance as long as the centre of mass remains directly over its base of support (because the force of mass will always act directly downwards). As soon as the centre of mass moves away from the base of support, the object will become more unstable. Taking the example of a gymnast on a balance beam, as soon as the centre of mass moves outside the beam, the gymnast will become unstable and fall.

If the centre of mass is lowered or the base of support is increased, the object or body will become more stable. For example:

Figure 1.35 A judo player maximises stability by lowering their centre of mass

- Rugby players forming a platform for a ruck take a large step and lower their hips. This ensures a stable platform and enables them to stay on their feet.
- A judo player has a wide stance, in order to resist attacks from their opponent.

Activity 24

Look at Figure 1.37. Graphs a) and b) show the change in centre of mass for a 100m sprinter and a high jumper. Draw a line graph for c), d) and e), to show the change in the centre of mass for each athlete stated.

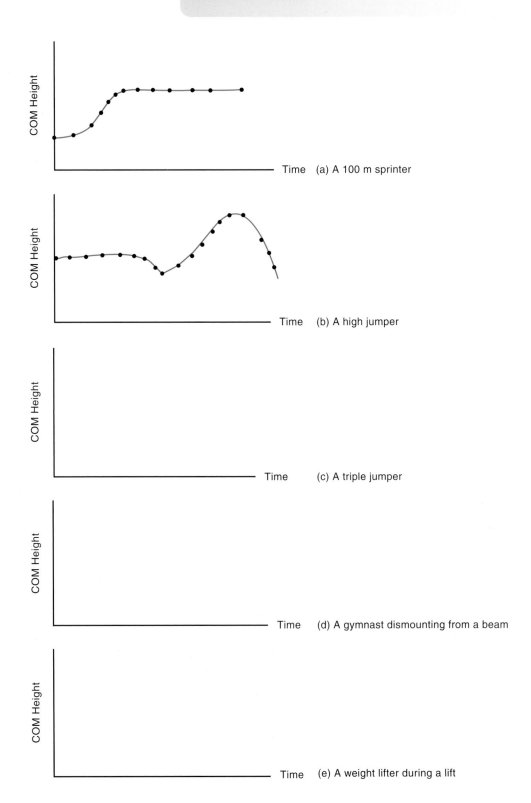

Figure 1.37
a) A 100m sprinter
b) A high jumper
c) A triple jumper
d) A gymnast dismounting from a beam
e) A weightlifter during a lift

Stability: Stability is the ability of an object to resist motion and remain at rest.
Line of gravity: An imaginary line which extends from the centre of mass directly down to the ground.

Exam-style question

The diagram below shows the position of the centre of mass while holding a balance. Describe how the position of the centre of mass can affect a balance.

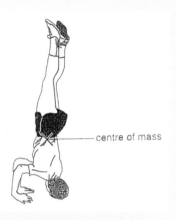

centre of mass

Types of motion

There are three recognised types of motion:

1 linear motion;
2 angular motion;
3 general motion.

Classifying motion into linear, angular or general makes the mechanical analysis of movement easier.

Linear motion

Linear motion is movement of a body or object that takes place in a straight line. It occurs when all parts of an object or body move the same distance, in the same direction, at the same time. A good example of a performer undergoing linear motion is a waterskier, where all body parts and the skis are moving the same direction, in a straight line, covering the same distance at the same speed. Sometimes linear motion can take place along a curved line, such as a projectile in flight. This is known as curvilinear motion, and an example of this would be a shuttlecock in flight.

Figure 1.38 A waterskier demonstrates linear motion

OCR PE for AS

Linear motion occurs when a force is applied through the centre of mass of the body. A force that passes through the centre of mass of a body causing linear motion is called a direct force.

Angular motion

Angular motion, or rotation, occurs when all parts of a body or object move in a circle, or part circle, about a fixed axis of rotation. A spinning ice skater, for example, rotates about the longitudinal axis which runs through the body from top to bottom. Movements of our arms and legs at the joints when running or swimming, for example, are also categorised as angular motion, as they move about an axis of rotation, in this case the joints. We only have to consider the circular path taken by the hand of a bowler in cricket to understand how movement of our limbs at the joints can be classed as angular or rotational motion. Angular motion occurs when a force is applied outside the centre of mass of the body. A force that passes outside the centre of mass of a body causing angular motion is called an eccentric force.

Figure 1.40 A twisting ice skater demonstrates angular motion

General motion

General motion is a combination of linear and angular motions and is in fact the most common type of motion we see in sport today. Running and swimming are great examples of general motion, as the trunk will often move linearly due to the angular movements of our arm and legs.

Exam-style questions

1   Use a practical example to describe how angular motion is produced.

2   When hitting a ball in tennis, an understanding of force is important. Explain how force can cause the ball to:
    ● move straight;
    ● spin.

Figure 1.39 A somersaulting diver demonstrates angular motion

Figure 1.41 A swimmer demonstrates general motion as although the body moves in a linear fashion, the arms and legs perform angular motion about the joints

Activity 25

Think of as many movements or activities in sport as you can, and consider how you would classify the movement taking place.

Key terms

Linear motion: Linear motion is movement of a body or object that takes place in a straight line, when all parts move the same distance, in the same direction, at the same time.
Angular motion: Angular motion, or rotation, occurs when all parts of a body or object move in a circle, or part circle, about a fixed axis of rotation.
General motion: A combination of linear and angular motion. Most movements in the sporting arena are general motion.
Direct force: A force applied through the centre of mass of a body, resulting in linear motion.
Eccentric force: A force applied outside the centre of mass of a body, resulting in angular motion.

What you need to know

* The skeleton has five basic functions: support, protection, movement, blood production and mineral storage.
* The axial skeleton consists of those bones that provide the greatest support, including the skull, the vertebral column and the ribcage.

* The appendicular skeleton consists of the bones of the limbs and their respective girdles.
* Bones can be categorised as either long, short, flat, irregular or sesamoid.
* There are three types of cartilage in the body: hyaline or articular cartilage, white fibrocartilage, and yellow elastic cartilage.
* Bone is a rigid, non-elastic tissue, composed of mineral and organic tissue. There are two types of bone: compact or hard bone, and cancellous or spongy bone.
* Joints are classified according to the degree of movement allowed. There are three basic types of joint: fixed or fibrous joints, cartilaginous joints and synovial joints.
* Movement at synovial joints can be classified as flexion, extension, abduction, adduction, horizontal flexion, horizontal extension, rotation, pronation, supination, circumduction, plantar flexion, dorsiflexion, inversion and eversion.
* The whole of the skeletal system can be strengthened through performing exercise.
* Skeletal muscle properties include extensibility, elasticity and contractility.
* Functions include movement, support and posture, and heat production.
* There are two basic types of muscle fibre: Slow-twitch (type 1) and fast-twitch (type 2) fibres.
* Fast-twitch fibres can be further subdivided into fast oxidative glycolytic (type 2a) and fast-twitch glycolytic (type 2b).
* Muscles are attached to bones via tendons. The origin of a muscle is the attachment to a stable bone, usually the nearest flat bone. The insertion is the muscle attachment to the bone that the muscle puts into action.
* Muscles often work together in order to produce coordinated movements: antagonistic muscle action. A muscle directly responsible for joint movement is the agonist. An antagonist often lengthens in order for the agonist to shorten.
* Muscles can contract in several ways: isotonic (shortening or lengthening), concentric (the muscle shortens), eccentric (the muscle lengthens). A muscle can also contract without any visible movement (isometric).
* The analysis of muscle contraction and joint action is called kinesiology.
* The benefits of exercise to the skeletal system include increased bone density, thickening of articular cartilage and a greater range of movement at joints.
* The benefits of exercise on the muscular system include increased muscle mass and force of contraction, increased strength of tendons and improved flexibility.
* Exercise can help prevent and improve skeletal conditions such as osteoporosis and osteoarthritis.
* Some high-impact activities can lead to growth plate disorders.

* Some contact sports can lead to joint instability.
* Some activities involving repetitive actions can lead to overuse injuries, such as bursitis, tendonitis or even stress fractures.
* All sport relies on the application of force.
* Force can move a resting body, and cause a body to accelerate, decelerate or change direction and/or shape.
* Newton's three laws of motion help us to describe and understand movement in sporting activity.
* The centre of mass (COM) is a point on a body where all the mass is said to be concentrated.
* The position of the COM influences the stability of a body and the type of motion produced.
* A stable body has a low COM, which is directly over the base of support.
* A stable body is one that has a large mass and a wide base of support.
* There are three types of motion: linear, angular and general.
* Linear motion is where all parts of a body move in a straight line, in the same direction, at the same time.
* Linear motion occurs when the line of force travels directly through the COM of a body.
* Angular motion is where a body or part of a body travels about a fixed point in a circle or part circle.
* Angular motion occurs when the line of force travels outside the COM of a body.
* General motion is the most common type of motion seen in sport. It is a combination of linear and angular motion.

Review Questions

1 Name the bones that articulate at the following joints:
  * knee;
  * hip;
  * shoulder;
  * elbow.

2 How is the knee joint structured for stability?

3 Explain how it is possible for us to bend down and touch our toes. What movement patterns are brought about during this action?

4 What is the function of articular cartilage?

5 How is the shoulder structured to enable the different types of movement patterns of which it is capable?

6 State the functions of the following:
  * bursae;
  * cruciate ligaments;
  * patella;
  * carpals.

7 Outline the benefits that training has on the skeletal tissues.

8 Analyse the action of a tennis serve. State the movement patterns and joint actions that occur at the shoulder and elbow.

9 Explain how the properties of skeletal muscle enable it to perform its function when sprinting. Use the correct names of muscles, where appropriate.

10 Skeletal muscle is composed of different types of fibre. What are they? Explain how the structure of these fibres is suited to the requirements of performers in a variety of sports.

11 When performing a jump shot in basketball, many different muscles work in the lower body. Identify the muscles working on the hip, knee and ankle joints, and state the specific roles that each of these muscles have (i.e. are they agonists, fixators, etc.?).

12 What are the essential ingredients to successful analysis of movement? Use these to analyse an overhead clear in badminton, with particular reference to the shoulder, elbow and wrist actions.

13 Identify one stroke in swimming. State the muscles that are contracting in each phase of the stroke (e.g. either the kick or recovery phase in the leg action), and state the type of contraction taking place in each muscle.

14 Outline the benefits of exercise on the muscular system.

15 Discuss the role of exercise in the prevention of musculoskeletal conditions.

16 'Exercise can cause as much harm as good.' Discuss this statement with reference to the musculoskeletal system.

17 Relate Newton's three laws of motion to a gymnast performing a vault.

18 'Without force there can be no sport.' Discuss this statement with reference to sporting activities.

19 A knowledge of centre of mass can be of great benefit to the sportsperson. Using examples from sport, show how the centre of mass and its adjustment can enhance performance.

20 Using examples from sports of your choice, explain occasions when a performer needs to be stable and when they need to be unstable.

CHAPTER 2

The cardiovascular system – the maintenance of blood supply

Learning outcomes

By the end of this chapter you should be able to:

- explain how the structure of the heart suits its function as a dual-action pump;
- explain the relationship between stroke volume, heart rate and cardiac output when resting, and the changes that occur during different intensities of exercise;
- describe the pattern of heart rate during maximal and submaximal exercise;
- relate the conduction system of the heart to the cardiac cycle;
- explain the regulation and control of the heart rate through neural, hormonal and intrinsic mechanisms;
- explain the transport of oxygen and carbon dioxide in the body, and the impact of smoking on oxygen transport in particular;
- name and describe the structure of each of the different types of blood vessel, identifying their main features in relation to their respective functions;
- explain the five facets of the venous return mechanism;
- define and explain how blood pressure is regulated and its role in the redistribution of blood;
- describe the effects of training on cardiovascular functioning;
- identify the changes that occur to the cardiovascular system in response to a warm-up and a cool-down.
- evaluate the role of exercise in maintaining a healthy and active lifestyle and in the prevention of cardiovascular diseases.

CHAPTER INTRODUCTION

This chapter will examine the structure and function of the cardiovascular system, which includes the heart, blood and blood vessels. We will investigate the response of the cardiovascular system to exercise, looking in particular at the changes in heart rate, stroke volume, cardiac output and blood pressure.

We will learn how the heart, blood vessels and blood adapt in response to the demands of exercise, and you will see how the maintenance

and control of the blood supply is the major determining factor in the effective and successful performance of aerobic or endurance-based exercise. The final section of this chapter will enable you to make a critical evaluation of the impact of different types of physical activity on the cardiovascular system in the prevention of health-related illness and disease, such as coronary heart disease, arteriosclerosis, atherosclerosis, angina and heart attack.

The structure and function of the heart

The human body is an amazing machine, and at the centre of its operation is the heart. The heart is a muscular pump that beats continuously, over 100,000 times per day. Together with the blood vessels and the blood, the heart provides the tissues and cells with the essentials for life itself – oxygen and nutrients.

The heart lies behind the sternum (breastbone) and ribs, which offer protection. In adults, it is about the size of a clenched fist – although trained athletes often experience cardiac hypertrophy, which is an enlargement of the heart.

In terms of structure, the heart is composed of four chambers:

- The two chambers at the top or superior part of the heart are called the atria.
- The two lower or inferior chambers are termed ventricles.

The ventricles are much more muscular than the atria, since it is here that the pumping action of the heart occurs which circulates the blood all round the body.

As well as being divided into upper and lower portions, the heart can also be divided into left and right halves, due to a muscular partition called the septum. Study Figures 2.1 and 2.2 and get to know the structure of the heart.

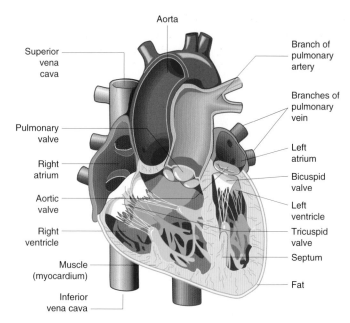

Figure 2.2 The structure of the heart

EXAMINER'S TIP

Don't forget that the left side of the heart is on the right as we look at it, and the right side of the heart is on the left.

The heart as a dual-action pump

This separation into left and right is essential for the heart to carry out its function effectively, since each side has a slightly different role:

- The left side of the heart is responsible for circulating blood rich in oxygen throughout the entire body. This is known as systemic circulation.
- The right side is responsible for ensuring that oxygen-poor blood is pumped to the lungs, where it can be reoxygenated. This is known as pulmonary circulation.

Key terms

Systemic circulation: The component of the circulatory system which conducts oxygenated blood from the left ventricle to all the major muscles and organs of the body (excluding the lungs) and returns it to the right atrium via the venae cavae.

Pulmonary circulation: The component of the circulatory system which conducts blood between the heart and the lungs.

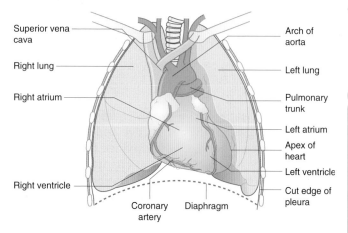

Figure 2.1 Position of the heart in the thoracic cavity

The major vessels act as entry and exit points for the blood to enter or leave the heart, and are all situated towards the top of the heart. To ensure a smooth passage of blood through the heart, a number of valves exist. These valves make sure that the blood only flows in one direction and prevent backflow of blood.

The thick muscular wall of the heart is called the myocardium and is composed of cardiac muscle fibres. It is this muscle that is responsible for the contraction of the heart and the subsequent ejection of blood from the heart.

Covering the exterior of the heart are coronary arteries, which feed the heart muscle with blood; being a muscle, it still requires fuel to keep the pump working continually. Blockages of these arteries are responsible for many problems of the heart, in particular cardiovascular diseases such as hypertension, angina pectoris and myocardial infarctions (heart attacks).

> **Key term**
>
> **Myocardium:** The muscular tissue of the heart. It is the contraction of the myocardium that is responsible for pumping blood round the body.

Blood flow through the heart

To help you understand the anatomy of the heart, you will now be taken on a journey through it. Make a note of the key structures and their functions as you go.

- Blood low in oxygen returns from the body to the right atrium via the superior (upper body) and inferior (lower body) venae cavae.
- At the same time, oxygen-rich blood returns to the left atrium from the lungs via the pulmonary veins.
- The atria are the top two chambers of the heart. You will see from Figure 2.2 that they are separated by a thick muscular wall that runs through the middle of the heart, known as the septum. This enables the two pumps to function separately – thus enabling the heart to be dual-purpose.
- Blood will eventually start to enter the larger lower chambers of the heart, called the right and left ventricles.

- In doing so, it passes the atrioventricular (AV) valves. The right AV valve is the tricuspid valve, and the left AV valve is the bicuspid valve. The purpose of these valves is not merely to separate the atria from the ventricles, but also to ensure that the blood can only flow in one direction through the heart.
- When the ventricles contract, blood on the right side of the heart is forced through the semilunar pulmonary valve into the pulmonary artery, from where it travels towards the lungs.
- Meanwhile, blood from the left ventricle enters the aorta via the semilunar aortic valve.
- The aorta branches into many different arteries, which then transport the blood around the whole body.
- Once again, the semilunar valves ensure the unidirectional flow of blood, preventing backflow of blood into the heart.

As the left side of the heart is responsible for pumping blood round the whole body, the wall of cardiac tissue (myocardium) surrounding the left ventricle is much thicker than that on the right side of the heart.

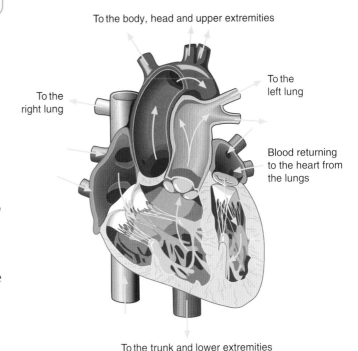

To the body, head and upper extremities

To the right lung

To the left lung

Blood returning to the heart from the lungs

To the trunk and lower extremities

Figure 2.3 The path of blood through the heart

Activity 1

1 Place the following terms in the correct sequential order to explain the flow of blood returning to the heart from the body, and its path through the heart:
   ● Aorta
   ● Pulmonary vein
   ● Lungs
   ● Pulmonary artery
   ● Tricuspid valve
   ● Left atrium
   ● Aortic valve
   ● Pulmonary valve
   ● Left ventricle
   ● Right atrium
   ● Right ventricle
   ● Bicuspid valve
   ● Venae cavae

2 Describe the location of the heart.

3 Draw a simple model to illustrate the dual role of the heart. Use red lines to highlight oxygen-rich blood and blue lines to show oxygen-poor blood.

The conduction system – how the heart works

The heart produces impulses that spread and innervate specialised muscle fibres. Unlike skeletal muscle, the heart produces its own impulses (i.e. it is myogenic), and it is the conduction system of the heart that spreads the impulses throughout the heart and enables the heart to contract.

Key term

Myogenic: The capacity of the heart to generate its own impulses which cause the heart to contract.

From Figure 2.4 it can be seen that the electrical impulse begins at the pacemaker – a mass of cardiac muscle cells known as the sinoatrial node (SA node) located in the right atrial wall. It is the rate at which the SA node emits impulses that determines the heart rate. As an impulse is emitted, it spreads to the adjacent interconnecting fibres of the atrium, which spread the excitation extremely rapidly, causing the atria to contract. It

then passes to another specialised mass of cells called the atrioventricular node (AV node). The AV node acts as a distributor and passes the action potential to the bundle of His, which, together with the branching Purkinje fibres, spreads the excitation throughout the ventricles.

There is a delay of about 0.1 seconds from the time when the AV node receives stimulation to when it distributes the action potential throughout the ventricles. This is crucial to allow completion of atrial contraction before ventricular systole begins, so that as much blood as possible is passed from the atria to the ventricles.

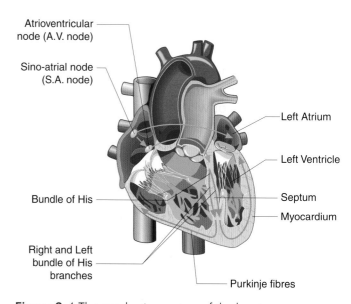

Figure 2.4 The conduction system of the heart

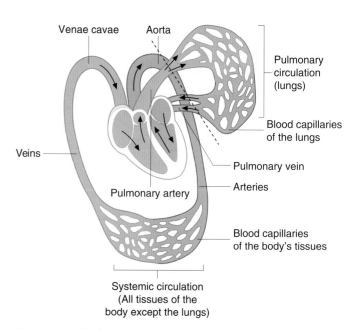

Figure 2.5 The heart as a dual-action pump

The cardiac cycle

The cardiac cycle refers to the process of cardiac contraction and blood transportation through the heart. The cardiac cycle explains the sequence of events that takes place during one complete heartbeat. This includes the filling of the heart with blood (diastole phase) and the emptying of the blood into the arterial system (systole phase).

Each cycle takes approximately 0.8 seconds and occurs on average 72 times per minute. There are four stages to each heartbeat:

1 atrial diastole:
2 ventricular diastole; $\Big\}$ 0.5 sec.
3 atrial systole:
4 ventricular systole. $\Big\}$ 0.3 sec.

Each stage depends on whether the chambers of the heart are *filling* with blood while the heart is relaxing (diastole) or whether they are *emptying*, which occurs when the heart contracts (systole), forcing blood from one part of the heart to another, or into the arterial system, and subsequently to the lungs and the body.

> **Key terms**
>
> **Diastole:** The phase of the cardiac cycle that sees the heart relax and fill with blood.
> **Systole:** The phase of the cardiac cycle when the heart contracts. During systole, blood is ejected from the heart or forced from one chamber of the heart to another.

The first stage of the cardiac cycle is atrial diastole. The upper chambers of the heart are filled with blood returning from:

● the body via the venae cavae to the right atrium;
● the lungs via the pulmonary vein to the left atrium.

At this time, the atrioventricular valves are shut, but as the atria fill with blood, atrial pressure overcomes ventricular pressure. Since blood always moves from areas of high pressure to areas of low pressure, the atrioventricular valves are forced open, and ventricular diastole now takes place. During this stage, the ventricles fill

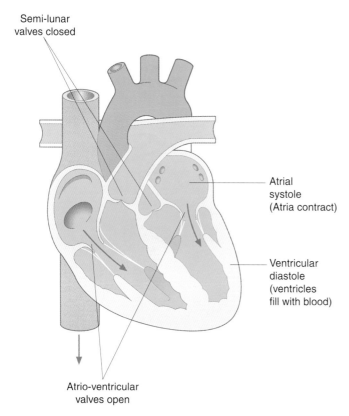

Semi-lunar valves closed

Atrial systole (Atria contract)

Ventricular diastole (ventricles fill with blood)

Atrio-ventricular valves open

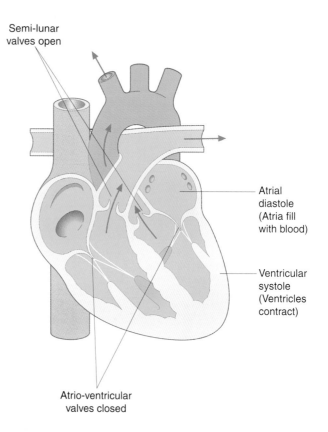

Semi-lunar valves open

Atrial diastole (Atria fill with blood)

Ventricular systole (Ventricles contract)

Atrio-ventricular valves closed

Figure 2.6 Stages of the cardiac cycle

with blood and the semilunar valves remain closed. The atria now contract, causing atrial systole, which ensures that all the blood is ejected into the ventricles. As the ventricles continue going through diastole, the pressure increases, which causes the atrioventricular valves to close. Ultimately, the ventricular pressure overcomes that in the aorta and the pulmonary artery. The semilunar valves open and the ventricles contract, forcing all the blood from the right ventricle into the pulmonary artery, and the blood from the left ventricle into the aorta. This is ventricular systole, and, once this is completed, the semilunar valves snap shut. The cycle is now complete and ready to be repeated.

Generally, the complete diastolic phase takes approximately 0.5 seconds, and the complete systolic phase lasts 0.3 seconds. However, it is interesting to note that trained athletes have been reported to have a longer diastolic phase

of the cardiac cycle, enabling a more complete filling of the heart. In this way, the trained athlete can increase venous return and therefore stroke volume (refer to Starling's law of the heart) during resting periods, which accounts for the decreased resting heart rate (known as bradycardia) often experienced by trained athletes. Take a moment to study Figure 2.6, which illustrates the stages of the cardiac cycle.

Activity 2

You should appreciate by now that the conduction system of the heart and the cardiac cycle are inextricably linked. Figure 2.7 shows the link between the cardiac cycle and the conduction system of the heart, but the stages have been muddled up. Can you identify the correct sequence? Assume that the first box is correct.

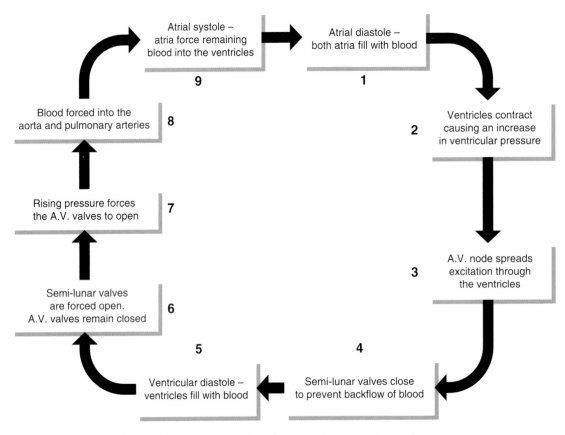

Figure 2.7 The interaction of the conduction system of the heart and the cardiac cycle

1 Describe how the blood travels through the heart in the following stages of the cardiac cycle:

- diastole;
- atrial systole;
- ventricular systole.

2 While exercising, a greater volume of blood is ejected during ventricular systole. Why is this beneficial to performance?

The control and regulation of the heart

The heart is governed by the autonomic nervous system (ANS), which operates without us having to think about it. In respect to the heart, it is the ANS which determines the rate at which the pacemaker (SA node) sends out impulses. The sympathetic and parasympathetic nervous systems are the two subdivisions of the autonomic nervous system which determine the actions of the cardiac control centre (CCC) in the medulla oblongata of the brain. They are fundamental to the regulation of the heart and work antagonistically as follows:

1 The sympathetic nervous system increases the heart rate by releasing adrenaline and noradrenaline from the adrenal medulla. Adrenaline increases the strength of ventricular contraction, and therefore stroke volume, while noradrenaline (a transmitter substance) aids the spread of the impulse throughout the heart, and therefore increases heart rate.

2 The parasympathetic nervous system, on the other hand, releases acetylcholine, which slows the spread of impulses and therefore reduces heart rate, returning it to the normal resting level.

Key terms

Sympathetic nervous system: One of the two subdivisions of the autonomic nervous system which is primarily responsible for increasing heart rate, particularly during exercise.

Key terms

Parasympathetic nervous system: The second of the two subdivisions of the autonomic nervous system. Its actions oppose those of the sympathetic nervous system and it is primarily responsible for returning the heart and respiratory rate to normal resting levels following exercise.

Key terms

Cardiac control centre: Located in the medulla oblongata within the brain, the cardiac control centre (CCC) is primarily responsible for controlling the heart rate.

Essentially, there are three main factors that determine the action of the cardiac control centre:

1 Neural factors – Once exercise begins, proprioceptors and mechanoreceptors within the muscles, tendons and joints relay messages to the cardiac centre, informing it that the amount of movement has increased and therefore muscles will require a greater supply of blood. Chemoreceptors located in the aorta and carotid arteries inform the centre of changes to the chemical composition of the blood, in particular reacting to increased levels of carbon dioxide. The cardiac centre increases

Table 2.1 The autonomic nervous system and cardiac function

The sympathetic function	The parasympathetic function
Increased heart rate	Decreased heart rate
Increased strength of contraction	Decreased strength of contraction
Vasodilation of arteries supplying the muscles and the heart	Vasoconstriction of arteries supplying the muscles and the heart
Some vasoconstriction of arteries of the abdomen, kidneys and skin	Vasodilation of arteries of the abdomen, kidneys and skin

the heart rate in order to speed up carbon dioxide removal. Baroreceptors, meanwhile, respond to changes in blood pressure as a result of increased activity.

2   Hormonal factors – Once stimulated, the sympathetic nerves cause the release of adrenaline and noradrenaline, which increases the strength of ventricular contractions of the heart and increases heart rate, which together greatly increase cardiac output. In addition, these hormones help to control blood pressure and assist in the redistribution of blood to the working muscles through vasoconstriction and vasodilation of arterioles.

3   Intrinsic factors – When exercise commences there is an increase in body temperature, which helps increase the flow of blood round the body (as blood becomes less viscous) and helps raise heart rate by increasing the speed of nerve impulse transmission.

Activity 3

Place the following stages in the control of heart rate in the correct order:

- Sympathetic nerves release adrenaline/noradrenaline.
- Parasympathetic nerves emit impulses and release acetylcholine.
- Proprioceptors (e.g. muscle spindles) detect changes in motor activity.
- Increases the activity of the SA node and causes an increase in heart rate.
- Chemoreceptors detect changes in carbon dioxide and the pH of the blood.
- Once exercise ceases, baroreceptors detect elevated blood pressure in the aorta and carotid arteries.
- Decreases the activity of the SA node and reduces heart rate slowly, back to resting levels.

Key terms

Chemoreceptors: Sensory cells situated in the aorta and the carotid arteries which monitor the level of acidity of the blood. They are particularly sensitive to changes in the carbon dioxide content of the blood and cause the cardiac control centre to adjust heart rate accordingly.

Key terms

Mechanoreceptors: These are sensory cells that provide feedback to the central nervous system of the body about any mechanical movement that takes place.

Key terms

Baroreceptors: These are sensory cells situated in the aorta, venae cavae and atria. These respond to changes in blood pressure. The cardiac control centre and vasomotor centre will respond to changes in blood pressure by adjusting the heart rate and blood vessel diameter accordingly.

Regulation during exercise

At rest, the parasympathetic system overrides the sympathetic system, and keeps the heart rate down. However, once exercise begins, the sympathetic system increases its activity and the parasympathetic system decreases activity, so heart rate is allowed to rise. Increased metabolic activity causes an increased concentration of carbon dioxide and lactic acid content in the blood, which increases acidity and decreases blood pH. These changes are detected by chemoreceptors sited in the aortic arch and carotid arteries. They inform the sympathetic centre in the upper thoracic area of the spinal cord to increase the heart rate in order to transport the carbon dioxide to the lungs, where it can be expelled. Messages from the sympathetic centre are sent to the SA node via accelerator nerves, which release adrenaline and noradrenaline on stimulation.

Adrenaline and noradrenaline released from the adrenal medulla (situated at the top of the kidneys) generally have the same effect – increasing heart rate and increasing the strength of contraction. They also help to increase metabolic activity, convert glycogen into its usable form, glucose, make glucose and free fatty acids available to the muscle, and redistribute blood to the working muscles.

Other factors which increase heart rate during exercise include:

- increased body temperature – and therefore decreased blood viscosity (the relative 'thickness' of the blood);
- increased venous return (a result of the increased action of the muscle pump).

Both these factors will result in greater cardiac output.

Once exercise ceases, sympathetic stimulation decreases and the parasympathetic system takes over once again. The parasympathetic system responds to information from baroreceptors – the body's inbuilt blood pressure recorders. When blood pressure is too high, messages are sent from the cardiac inhibitory centre to the SA node via the vagus nerve. The parasympathetic nerve then releases acetylcholine, which decreases the heart rate.

This continuous interaction of the sympathetic and parasympathetic systems ensures that the heart works as efficiently as possible, and enables sufficient nutrients to reach the tissue cells to ensure effective muscle action.

Activity 4

1   Fill in the missing gaps:

The _____ is a bundle of specialised cardiac muscle cells which generate action potentials and govern the heart rate. Impulses are spread across the atria and reach the _____, which delays the action potentials from spreading through the ventricles.

2   Describe the structure and function of the heart's conducting system.

3   Explain the role of the autonomic nervous system before, during and after embarking on a distance run.

Cardiac dynamics – the relationship between heart rate, stroke volume and cardiac output

The performance of the heart is largely dependent on two variables, which work together to optimise cardiac functioning:

● stroke volume;
● heart rate.

Stroke volume

Stroke volume is the volume of blood pumped out of the heart per beat. It usually refers to the blood ejected from the left ventricle and is measured in millilitres (ml) or cm^3. A typical resting value of stroke volume is about 75ml, but this can increase significantly in a trained athlete.

Stroke volume is determined by several factors:

● Venous return – the volume of blood returning to the right atrium. The greater the venous return, the greater the stroke volume, since more blood is available to be pumped out.
● The elasticity of cardiac fibres (sometimes referred to as pre-load) – this refers to the degree of stretch of cardiac tissue just prior to contraction. The greater the stretch of the cardiac fibres, the greater the force of

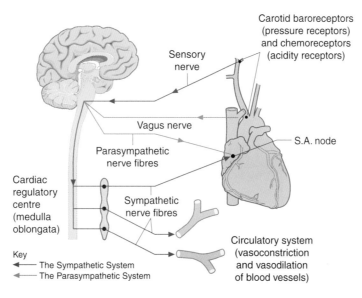

Figure 2.8 The regulation of heart rate

contraction, which can further increase the stroke volume. This is also known as the Frank-Starling mechanism (Starling's law).

- The contractility of cardiac tissue – with increased contractility, a greater force of contraction can occur, which can cause an increase in stroke volume. This is partly due to an increased ejection fraction. The ejection fraction is the percentage of blood actually pumped out of the left ventricle per contraction. It is determined by dividing the stroke volume by the end-diastolic volume and is expressed as a percentage. At rest, the ejection fraction is about 60 per cent (meaning that 40 per cent of blood that enters the heart remains in it), but this can increase to over 85 per cent during exercise.

Heart rate

The heart rate represents the number of complete cardiac cycles, and therefore the number of times the left ventricle ejects blood into the aorta, per minute. The average resting heart rate of a human is 72 beats per minute, but this can vary tremendously depending on levels of fitness. We might expect an elite endurance athlete, for example, to have a resting heart rate of below 60 beats per minute. When this happens, bradycardia is said to have taken place.

Figure 2.9 Michael Indurain is reported to have a resting heart rate of 28 beats per minute

It is possible to measure your heart rate by palpating your radial or carotid arteries. This is referred to as your pulse rate.

IN CONTEXT

Five times winner of the Tour de France, Miguel Indurain, is reported to have a resting heart rate of 28 beats per minute, one of the lowest human rates ever recorded.

Cardiac output

Cardiac output is the volume of blood that is pumped out of the heart, from one ventricle, per minute. Cardiac output is generally measured from the left ventricle, and is equal to the product of stroke volume and heart rate. The relationship between these variables is summarised below:

Cardiac output = Stroke volume × Heart rate
Q = SV × HR

- The stroke volume is the volume of blood ejected into the aorta in one beat.
- The heart rate reflects the number of times the heart beats per minute.

On average, the resting stroke volume is 75ml per beat, and the resting heart rate for a person is 72 beats per minute. Therefore, cardiac output at rest is:

Q = SV × HR
= 75ml × 72bpm
= 5,400ml/min (5.4L/min)

However, during exercise, cardiac output may rise to 30L/min – a sixfold increase!

Cardiac dynamics during exercise

During exercise, the body's muscles demand more oxygen. Consequently, the heart must work harder in order to ensure that sufficient oxygen is delivered by the blood to the working muscles, and that waste products such as carbon dioxide and lactic acid are removed. We have just seen that:

Cardiac = Stroke volume (SV) × Heart rate (HR)
output (Q)

It is now necessary to consider what happens to each of these variables during exercise.

Heart rate response to exercise

You will be aware that when we exercise our heart rate increases, but the extent of the increase is largely dependent on exercise intensity. Typically, heart rate increases linearly, in direct proportion to exercise intensity, so that the harder you are working, the higher your heart rate will be. This proportional increase in heart rate will continue until you approach your maximum heart rate (you should recall that this can be calculated by subtracting your age from 220). However, we do not always perform exercise of increasing intensity. During submaximal exercise, where exercise is performed at constant intensity over a prolonged period of time, such as a 1,500m swim, you might expect heart rate to plateau into a steady state for much of the swim. This steady state represents the point where oxygen demand is being met by oxygen supply, and the exercise should therefore be relatively comfortable. Figure 2.12 (on page 67) illustrates typical heart rate curves for maximal and submaximal exercise. Make sure that you are able to draw and label these curves. You will note that just prior to exercise, heart rate increases, even though the exercise has yet to commence. This phenomenon is known as the anticipatory rise and represents the heart's preparation for the forthcoming activity. It results from the release of hormones such as adrenaline, which cause the SA node to increase the heart rate. You will also note that following exercise the heart rate takes a while to return to its resting level; this represents the body's recovery period. During this phase, the heart rate must remain slightly elevated in order to rid the body of waste products such as lactic acid.

Stroke volume response to exercise

You will recall that stroke volume is the volume of blood pumped out of the heart with each contraction. As with heart rate, stroke volume increases linearly with increasing intensity, but only up to 40–60 per cent of maximum effort. After this point, stroke volume plateaus (see Figure 2.10 on page 66). One reason for this is the shorter diastolic phase (ventricular filling) that results from the significantly increased heart rate near maximal effort.

Stroke volume is able to increase during exercise for two reasons:

- Increased venous return – this is the volume of blood that returns from the body to the right side of the heart. During exercise, the venous return significantly increases due to a mechanism called the muscle pump, where skeletal muscles squeeze blood back towards the heart. (This will be explained a little later in this chapter.)
- The Frank-Starling mechanism – this mechanism basically suggests that when the heart ventricles stretch more, they can contract with greater force and therefore pump more blood out of the heart. With increased venous return, more blood enters the ventricles during the diastolic phase, which causes them to stretch more and thus contract more forcefully. The reduced heart rate that is experienced by the trained athlete also allows greater time for the ventricles to fill with blood, increasing the degree of stretch by the cardiac tissue and therefore causing the stroke volume of these trained individuals to increase.

Cardiac output response to exercise

We have seen that cardiac output is the volume of blood pumped out of the heart per minute and is the product of stroke volume and heart rate:

Cardiac output (Q) = Stroke volume (SV) × Heart rate (HR)

As such, the response of cardiac output during exercise is easy to predict. You have just discovered that during exercise both heart rate and stroke volume increase linearly with increasing exercise intensity. Consequently, the pattern of cardiac output during exercise is the

Table 2.2 Stroke volume values at rest and during exercise for trained and untrained subjects

	Resting stroke volume	Submaximal exercise	Maximal exercise
Trained	80–110ml	160–200ml	160–200ml
Untrained	60–80ml	100–120ml	100–120ml

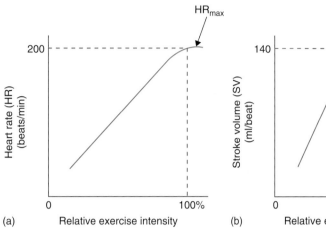

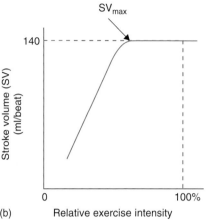

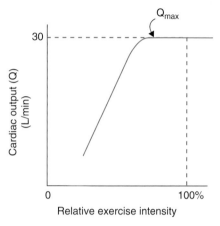

Figure 2.10 (a) Heart rate response (b) Stroke volume response

Figure 2.11 Cardiac output response

Table 2.3 Cardiac output values at rest and during exercise for trained and untrained subjects (approximate values)

	Resting cardiac output	**Submaximal exercise**	**Maximal exercise**
Trained	5L/min	15–20L/min	30–40L/min
Untrained	5L/min	10–15L/min	20–30L/min

same and will continue to increase linearly until maximum exercise capacity, where it will plateau. This is shown in figures 2.10 and 2.11.

Cardiac output represents the ability of the heart to circulate blood in the body, delivering oxygen to the working muscles. During maximum

exercise, cardiac output may reach values of between four and eight times resting values and is therefore a major factor in determining endurance capacity.

Activity 5

Using the text and Figure 2.12, complete the table below. Note: Don't forget the units!

Variable	Definition	Approximate resting value	Approximate exercise values
Heart rate			
Stroke volume			
Cardiac output			

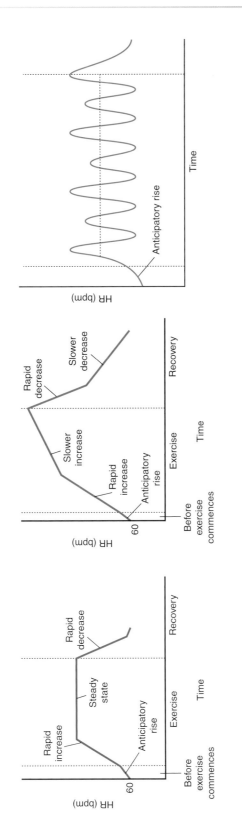

a) Low intensity (sub-maximal) exercise

(b) High intensity (maximal) exercise

(c) Heart rate response to fluctuating intensities of exercise

Figure 2.12 Expected heart rate curves for different intensities of exercise

Exam-style questions

A cyclist is completing a 10-mile training ride.

1   Draw a graph to show how the cyclist's cardiac output changes in the following phases of the aerobic training session: prior to exercise, during exercise, recovery period.

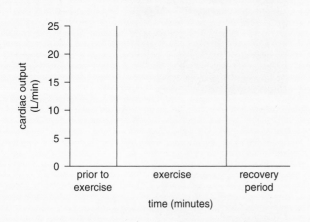

2   Draw and label a diagram to show how the blood flows through the pulmonary and systemic networks of the cyclist's body during the training ride.

3   Stroke volume is an important factor during aerobic performance. Define stroke volume and give a maximal value for an aerobic athlete.

The pulse

The pulse is a pressure wave which is generated from the heart each time the left ventricle pumps blood into the aorta. The increased pressure causes slight dilation of the arteries as the blood travels through them around the body, and this can be felt at various sites on the body. The most common sites where the pulse can be palpated are as follows:

- radial artery;
- carotid artery;
- femoral artery;
- brachial artery;
- temporal artery.

Activity 6

1   Record your pulse for a 10-second count at each of the following sites:
   - carotid artery;
   - radial artery;
   - brachial artery.
   Remember to start counting from zero.
2   Multiply your scores by six to achieve your heart rate score in beats per minute.
3   Account for any differences in your heart rate scores at the different sites.
4   Why should you never use your thumb to measure your pulse?

Activity 7

You are going to carry out an investigation to examine heart rate response to varying intensities of exercise. You will need a stopwatch, a gymnastics bench and a metronome.

1   Record resting heart rate for a 10-second count at the beginning of the class.
2   Record heart rate for a 10-second count at the carotid artery immediately prior to exercise.
3   Start exercising by stepping on and off the bench at a low intensity, keeping time with the metronome.
4   Record your pulse after one, two and three minutes of exercise. After the third minute of exercise, stop the test. Continue to record your pulse each minute during recovery.
5   Once your heart rate has returned to its resting value (or within a few beats), repeat the test at a medium intensity. Record your results as before.
6   Repeat the exercise for a third time, but at a very high intensity. Once again, record your results.
7   Convert your heart rate scores into beats per minute by multiplying by six.
8   Now use your results to plot a graph for each of the three workloads. Plot each graph using the same axes, placing heart rate along the Y axis and time along the X axis. Don't forget to show your resting heart rate values on the graph.
9   For each of your graphs, explain the heart rate patterns prior to, during and following exercise.

Time	Exercise intensity		
	Low	**Medium**	**High**
Resting HR			
HR prior to exercise			
Exercise 1 min			
Exercise 2 min			
Exercise 3 min			
Recovery 1 min			
Recovery 2 min			
Recovery 3 min			
Recovery 4 min			
Recovery 5 min			
Recovery 6 min			
Recovery 7 min			

Activity 8

Using Figure 2.12, account for the different patterns in heart rate for submaximal and maximal exercise.

Activity 9

Wearing a heart rate monitor, participate in an invasion game of your choice (e.g. netball, football, basketball) for at least 15 minutes. Don't forget to record your resting heart rate and your heart rate immediately prior to the start.

At a maximum of three-minute intervals, record your heart rate for the duration of the game. Note: The longer you participate in the game, the better!

Copy out and complete the table and graph below.

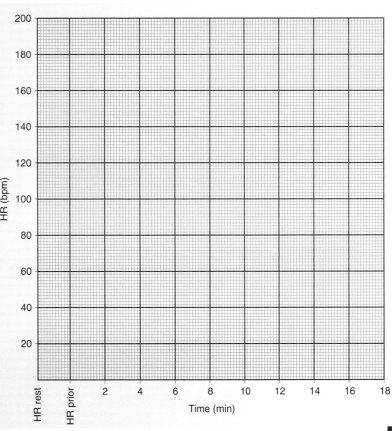

Time	Heart rate
Rest	
Prior to exercise	
1	
2	
3	
4	
5	
6	
7	
8	
9	
10	
11	
12	
13	
14	
15	

Explain the pattern of heart rate illustrated by the graph.

The trained heart

We have examined how the heart responds and adjusts to exercise in a short exercise session. Let us now turn our attention to the effects of long-term training on the heart.

As mentioned above, the heart of an athlete is larger than that of a non-athlete and often displays greater vascularisation. Cardiac hypertrophy is characterised by a larger ventricular wall and a thicker myocardium. Endurance athletes tend to display larger ventricular cavities, while those following high-resistance or strength-training regimes display thicker ventricular walls.

Cardiac hypertrophy is accompanied by a decreased resting heart rate. This can easily be demonstrated by comparing the resting heart rates of trained and untrained people. When the heart rate falls below 60 beats per minute, bradycardia is said to have occurred, and is due to a slowing in the intrinsic rate of the atrial pacemaker (SA node) and an increase in the predominance of the parasympathetic system acting on the pacemaker.

> **Key term**
>
> **Cardiac hypertrophy:** The enlargement of the heart due to the effects of training. Endurance athletes tend to display larger ventricular cavities, while those following high-resistance strength training will display thicker ventricular walls.

> **Key term**
>
> **Bradycardia:** Literally meaning 'slow heart', bradycardia is the term used to describe the reduction in resting heart rate that accompanies training (usually when resting heart rate falls below 60 beats per minute).

Some endurance athletes have recorded resting heart rates of below 30 beats per minute! Since the resting cardiac output for an athlete is approximately the same as that of a non-athlete, the athlete compensates for the lower resting heart rate by increasing stroke volume. This increased resting stroke volume is greatest among endurance athletes (as great as 200ml/beat), due to the increased size of the ventricular cavity. The increase can also be the result of improved contractility of the myocardium, which is highlighted by the increased ejection fraction reported by athletes. The ejection fraction represents the percentage of blood entering the left ventricle which is actually pumped out per beat. It is calculated by dividing the stroke volume by the volume of blood in the ventricles at the end of the diastolic phase (EDV). On average, this is approximately 60 per cent, but can reach 85 per cent following training (see Figure 2.13).

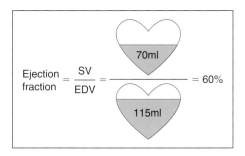

Figure 2.13 Calculation of the ejection fraction

Training signals an improvement in cardiac output during exercise, brought about by an increase in stroke volume, due to the larger volume of the left ventricle and the hypertrophy (enlargement) of the heart (sometimes referred to as athlete's heart). At rest, cardiac hypertrophy plays an important role, since increased stroke volume (which accompanies hypertrophy) allows the resting heart rate to decrease. This is known as bradycardia. The increased size of the ventricular cavity in trained athletes allows a longer diastolic phase, during which time the heart can fill up with more blood. This stretches cardiac fibres and increases the strength of contraction, with the resultant effect of increasing stroke volume. Consequently, cardiac output does not change at rest following training.

Figure 2.14 Lance Armstrong is reported to have a heart 30 per cent larger than the average

Key term

Starling's law: Starling's law states that stroke volume increases in response to an increase in the diastolic filling of the heart (which is dependent on venous return). The increased volume of blood stretches the ventricular wall, causing the cardiac muscle to contract more forcefully.

Key term

Ejection fraction: The proportion of blood actually pumped out of the left ventricle per contraction.

The vascular system

Having examined how the heart works to pump the blood into the network of blood vessels, we will now take a closer look at how the blood supports the functioning of the body and how the blood vessels ensure that sufficient blood reaches the body's tissues.

The blood

Blood consists of cells and cell fragments, surrounded by a liquid known as plasma. The average male has a total blood volume of 5–6L, and the average female blood volume is approximately 4–5L.

Functions of blood

The blood's functions are fundamental to life itself and include:

- transportation of nutrients such as glucose and oxygen;
- protection and fighting disease through interaction with the lymphatic system;
- maintenance of homeostasis, including temperature regulation and maintenance of the acid–base (pH) balance.

The blood is responsible for transporting oxygen to the body's cells and removing metabolites, such as carbon dioxide, from the muscle to the lungs. The blood also transports glucose from the liver to the muscle, and lactic acid from the muscle to the liver, where it can be converted back to glucose. Further functions include the transportation of enzymes, hormones and other chemicals, all of which have a vital role to play in the body, no more so than during exercise.

The blood protects the body by containing cells and chemicals which are central to the immune system. When damage to blood vessels occurs, the blood clots in order to prevent cell loss.

The blood is vital in maintaining the body's state of equilibrium; for example, through hormone and enzyme activity, and the buffering capacity of the blood, the blood's pH should remain relatively stable. In addition, the blood is involved in temperature regulation and can transport heat to the surface of the body where it can be released.

All these factors are particularly important during exercise, to ensure optimal performance.

Blood viscosity

Viscosity refers to the thickness of the blood and its resistance to flow. The more viscous a fluid, the more resistant it is to flow. The greater the volume of red blood cells, the greater the capacity to transport oxygen. However, unless it is accompanied by an increase in plasma, viscosity may also increase, and restrict blood flow. Viscosity may also increase when plasma content decreases, due to dehydration (which may accompany endurance-based exercise).

> ### Key term
>
> **Blood viscosity:** A term used to describe the relative thickness of the blood. If the blood is very viscous, it has a high amount of blood cells to plasma and consequently does not flow very quickly.

Training brings about an increase in total blood volume, and therefore an increase in the number of red blood cells. However, the plasma volume increases more than blood cell volume, so the blood viscosity decreases. This facilitates blood flow through the blood vessels, and improves oxygen delivery to the working muscles.

The circulatory system

The blood flows through a continuous network of blood vessels, which form a double circuit. This connects the heart to the lungs, and the heart to all other body tissues.

The double circulatory system

Pulmonary circulation transports blood between the lungs and the heart. The pulmonary artery carries blood low in oxygen concentration from the right ventricle to the lung, where it becomes oxygen-rich and unloads carbon dioxide. The pulmonary vein then transports the freshly oxygenated blood back to the heart and into the left atrium.

The blood returning to the left atrium is pumped through the left side of the heart and into the aorta, where it is distributed to the whole of the body's tissues by a network of arteries. Veins then return the blood, which is now low in oxygen and high in carbon dioxide concentration, to the heart, where it enters the right atrium via the venae cavae. This circuit is known as systemic circulation.

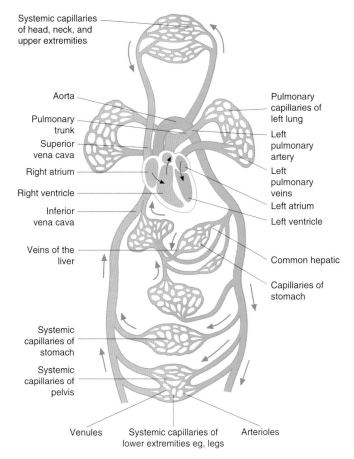

Figure 2.15 The double-circulatory system

Labels: Systemic capillaries of head, neck, and upper extremities; Aorta; Pulmonary trunk; Superior vena cava; Right atrium; Right ventricle; Inferior vena cava; Veins of the liver; Systemic capillaries of stomach; Systemic capillaries of pelvis; Venules; Systemic capillaries of lower extremities eg, legs; Arterioles; Pulmonary capillaries of left lung; Left pulmonary artery; Left pulmonary veins; Left atrium; Left ventricle; Common hepatic; Capillaries of stomach

Blood vessels

The vascular network through which blood flows to all parts of the body comprises arteries, arterioles, capillaries, veins and venules.

Arteries and arterioles

Arteries are high-pressure vessels which carry blood from the heart to the tissues. The largest artery in the body is the aorta, which is the main artery leaving the heart. The aorta constantly subdivides and gets smaller. The constant subdivision decreases the diameter of the vessel arteries, which now become arterioles. As the network subdivides, blood velocity decreases, which enables the efficient delivery and exchange of gases.

Arteries are composed of three layers of tissue:

1   an outer fibrous layer – the tunica adventitia or tunica externa;
2   a thick middle layer – the tunica media;
3   a thin lining of cells to the inside – the endothelium or tunica intima.

The tunica media comprises smooth muscle and elastic tissue, which enables the arteries and arterioles to alter their diameter. Arteries tend to have more elastic tissue, while arterioles have greater amounts of smooth muscle; this allows the vessels to increase the diameter through vasodilation, or to decrease the diameter through vasoconstriction. It is through vasoconstriction and vasodilation that the vessels can regulate blood pressure and ensure the tissues are receiving sufficient blood – particularly during exercise.

Arteries and arterioles have three basic functions:

● to act as conduits, carrying and controlling blood flow to the tissues;
● to cushion and smooth out the pulsatile flow of blood from the heart;
● to help control blood pressure.

> **Key terms**
>
> **Vasodilation:** A process by which blood vessels in the body (namely arteries and arterioles) become wider.
> **Vasoconstriction:** A process by which blood vessels in the body (namely arteries and arterioles) become narrower.

Veins and venules

Veins are low-pressure vessels which return blood to the heart. Their structure is similar to that of arteries, although they possess less smooth muscle and elastic tissue. Venules are the smallest veins and transport blood away from the capillary bed into the veins. Veins gradually increase in thickness the nearer to the heart they get, until they reach the two largest veins in the body, the venae cavae, which enter the right atrium of the heart.

The thinner walls of the veins often distend and allow blood to pool in them. This is also allowed to happen as the veins contain pocket valves which close intermittently to prevent backflow of blood. This explains why up to 70 per cent of total blood volume is found in the venous system at any one time, at rest.

Capillaries

Capillaries are the functional units of the vascular system. Composed of a single layer of endothelial cells, they are just thin enough to allow red blood cells to squeeze through their wall. The capillary network is very well developed as they are so small; large quantities are able to cover the muscle, which ensures efficient exchange of gases. If the cross-sectional area of all the capillaries in the body were to be added together, the total area would be much greater than that of the aorta.

Distribution of blood through the capillary network is regulated by special structures known as pre-capillary sphincters, the structure of which will be dealt with later in this chapter.

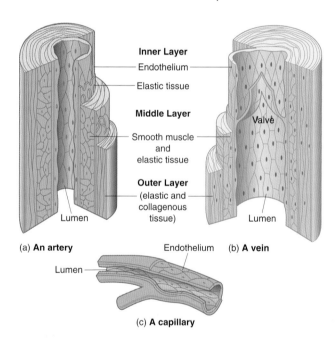

(a) **An artery**

Inner Layer
- Endothelium
- Elastic tissue

Middle Layer
- Smooth muscle and elastic tissue

Outer Layer
(elastic and collagenous tissue)

Lumen

(b) **A vein**

Valve

Lumen

Endothelium

Lumen

(c) **A capillary**

Figure 2.16 The structure of blood vessels

> **Key term**
>
> **Pre-capillary sphincters:** A ring-shaped band of muscle tissue located at the opening to the capillary bed which controls and regulates the volume of blood entering it.

> **Activity 10**
>
> Copy out the table below and write a short explanation in each box.
>
> | Vessel | Brief outline of structure | Function |
> |---|---|---|
> | Arteries/ arterioles | | |
> | Capillaries | | |
> | Veins/venules | | |

The venous return mechanism

Venous return is the term used for the blood which returns to the right side of the heart via the veins. As mentioned earlier, up to 70 per cent of the total volume of blood is contained in the veins at rest. This provides a large reservoir of blood which is returned rapidly to the heart when needed. The heart can only pump out as much blood as it receives, so cardiac output is dependent on venous return. A rapid increase in venous return enables a significant increase in cardiac output due to Starling's law.

> **Key term**
>
> **Venous return:** Blood returning to the right side of the heart.

There are several mechanisms which aid the venous return process:

- The muscle pump – As exercise begins, muscular contractions impinge on and compress the veins, squeezing blood towards the heart.
- Pocket valves inside the veins prevent any backflow of blood that might occur. This is illustrated in Figure 2.17.
- The respiratory pump – During inspiration and expiration, pressure changes occur in the thoracic and abdominal cavities which compress veins and assist blood return to the heart.

These mechanisms are essential at the start of exercise. As exercise commences, the muscles contracting squeeze the vast amount of blood within the veins back towards the heart, enabling stroke volume to increase and optimal delivery of nutrients to the working muscles.

Other factors that aid venous return include:

- smooth muscle within the walls and surrounding the veins which contracts and helps blood on its journey back to the heart;
- gravity, which helps the blood return to the heart from the upper body.

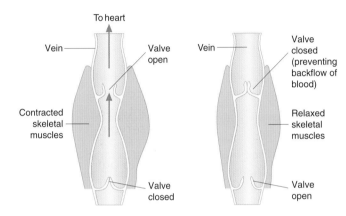

Figure 2.17 The muscle pump and venous return. The massaging action of the muscles when we exercise squeezes blood back towards the heart, increasing venous return and therefore cardiac output

Blood pressure

Blood pressure is the force exerted by the blood against the walls of the blood vessels. It is necessary to maintain blood flow through the circulatory system and is determined by two main factors:

1 Cardiac output – the volume of blood flowing into the system from the left ventricle.
2 Resistance to flow – the opposition offered by the blood vessels to the blood flow. This is dependent on several factors, including blood viscosity, blood vessel length and blood vessel radius.

Blood pressure = Cardiac output × Resistance

Therefore, blood pressure increases when either cardiac output or resistance increases.

Blood pressure in the arteries also increases and decreases in a pattern which corresponds to the cardiac cycle during ventricular systole. It is highest when blood is pumped into the aorta and lowest during ventricular diastole.

Blood pressure is usually measured at the brachial artery using a sphygmomanometer, and is recorded as millimetres of mercury (mmHg) of systolic pressure over diastolic pressure:

- Systolic pressure is experienced when the heart pumps blood into the system.
- Diastolic pressure is recorded when the heart is relaxing and filling with blood.

The typical reading for a subject at rest is:

$$\frac{120 \text{ mmHg}}{80 \text{ mmHg}} = \frac{\text{Systolic}}{\text{Diastolic}}$$

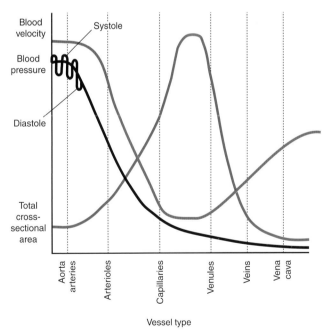

Figure 2.18 The relationship between blood vessel type, total cross-sectional area, blood velocity and blood pressure

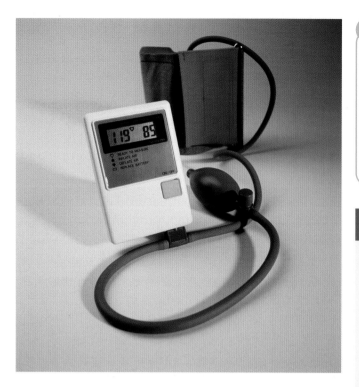

Figure 2.19 The ideal blood pressure reading is 120mmHg/80mmHg

Activity 11

You are going to investigate blood pressure, using a digital blood pressure meter, or sphygmomanometer.

1   Under the guidance of your teacher, wrap the cuff round the brachial artery.
2   Pump air into the cuff, up to approximately 190mmHg.
3   Slowly release the air inside the cuff by pressing the attachment on the bulb. The systolic pressure can now be read and recorded.
4   Continue to release air from the cuff until the diastolic pressure is displayed on the screen. Record your diastolic pressure.
5   Discover your blood pressure by placing the systolic reading over the diastolic reading:

$$\frac{\text{Systolic}}{\text{Diastolic}}$$

6   Follow the above procedure after completing two minutes of intense exercise.
7   Account for any differences in your readings.

Key terms

Blood pressure: The force exerted by the blood against the walls of the blood vessels.
Systolic pressure: The peak pressure in the arteries which occurs when the heart is contracting and emptying blood into the arterial system.
Diastolic pressure: The lowest pressure in the arteries which occurs when the heart is relaxing and filling with blood.

Exam-style questions

1   The skeletal pump mechanism is one way of helping to maintain venous return. Describe three other mechanisms involved in venous return.

2   Explain the importance of the skeletal pump mechanism during an active cool-down.

3   During exercise, more oxygen must be supplied to the working muscles. Describe the passage of oxygenated blood through the pulmonary and systemic networks, from the lungs to the working muscles.

4   Cardiac output is a determining factor during endurance activities. Describe how cardiac output is increased during endurance activities.

5   Large amounts of blood need to be circulated around the body during prolonged aerobic exercise. Identify the mechanisms of venous return that ensure a sufficient supply of blood is returned to the heart during exercise.

6   An increase in venous return leads to an increase in heart rate. Explain how this is achieved by intrinsic control.

During exercise, blood pressure change is dependent on the type and intensity of the exercise being performed. During steady aerobic exercise involving large muscle groups, the systolic pressure increases as a result of increased cardiac output, while diastolic pressure remains constant or, in well-trained athletes, may even drop, as blood feeds into the working muscles due to increased arteriole dilation. The increased systolic pressure associated with exercise is largely the result of increased cardiac output due to a greater intensity. This ensures that adequate blood

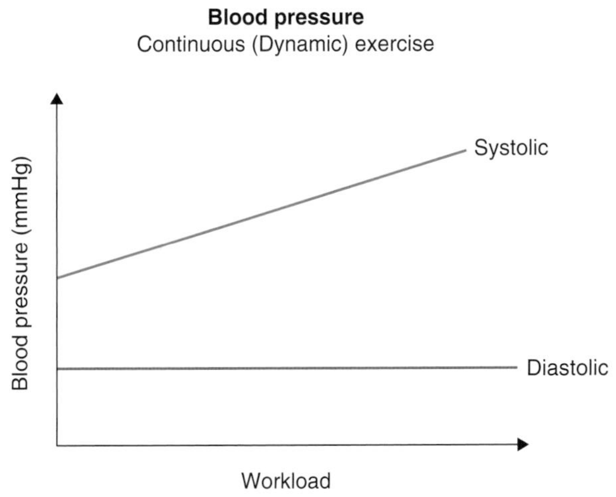

Blood pressure
Continuous (Dynamic) exercise

Blood pressure (mmHg)

Systolic

Diastolic

Workload

(a) Dynamic exercise

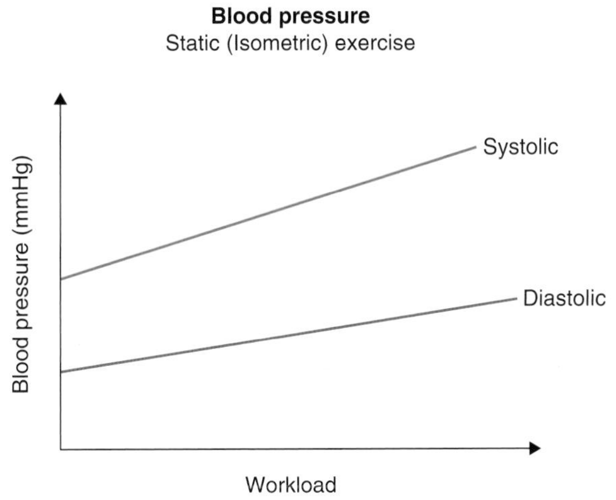

Blood pressure
Static (Isometric) exercise

Blood pressure (mmHg)

Systolic

Diastolic

Workload

(b) Static (Isometric) exercise

(c)

(d)

Figure 2.20 The effects of exercise on both systolic and diastolic blood pressure (a) Dynamic exercise (e.g. a marathon runner) (b) Static (isometric) exercise (c) marathon runner (d) weight-lifter

is supplied to the working muscle quickly. During high-intensity isometric and anaerobic exercise, both systolic and diastolic pressure rise significantly due to increased resistance of the blood vessels. This is a result of muscles squeezing the veins, increasing peripheral resistance, and an increase in intra-thoracic pressure due to the contraction of the abdominals. When weightlifting, for example, competitors often hold their breath during exertion, which causes a significant increase in both systolic and diastolic pressure.

It is essential that blood pressure is regulated and, where possible, at rest maintained within a normal range. High blood pressure can cause serious complications to the heart, brain and kidneys, whereas low pressure can result in insufficient oxygen and other nutrients reaching the muscle cells.

Blood pressure that is constantly above the 'normal' range is referred to as hypertension. This will be discussed in more detail below, in the section on 'Health-related considerations'.

The vasomotor control centre outlined in the following section is responsible for regulating blood pressure.

IN CONTEXT

The systolic blood pressure of a powerlifter such as Mariusz Pudzianowski, a former World's Strongest Man, may reach levels of 200mmHg or more when competing.

Figure 2.21 The systolic and diastolic blood pressure of former World's Strongest Man Mariusz Pudzianowski will increase dramatically during exercise

Activity 12

Explain the importance of blood pressure with regard to sporting activity.

The distribution of cardiac output at rest and during exercise

Blood flow changes dramatically once exercise commences. At rest, only 15–20 per cent of cardiac output is directed to skeletal muscle; the majority goes to the liver (27 per cent) and kidneys (22 per cent). During exercise, however, blood is redirected to areas where it is needed most. For example, during exhaustive exercise, the working muscles may receive over 80 per cent of cardiac output. This increased blood flow to the muscle results from a restriction of blood flow to the kidneys, liver and stomach. This process is known as the vascular shunt mechanism. Figure 2.22 illustrates the distribution of cardiac output at rest and during exercise.

Activity 13

If you have access to a programme such as Microsoft Excel®, use the data in Table 2.4 to construct a pie chart that shows the relative distribution of blood at rest and during maximal effort. (If you do not have access to such a programme, simply draw a pie chart.) Explain the changes shown in your pie chart.

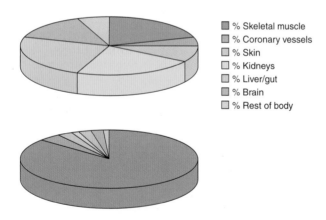

% Skeletal muscle
% Coronary vessels
% Skin
% Kidneys
% Liver/gut
% Brain
% Rest of body

Figure 2.22 (a) distribution of cardiac output at rest (b) distribution of cardiac output during exercise

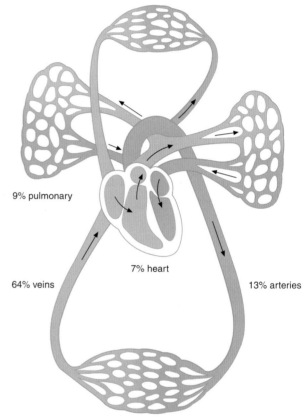

9% pulmonary

7% heart

64% veins

13% arteries

7% arterioles, capillaries

Figure 2.23 The distribution of blood in the body at rest

Table 2.4 Blood flow changes during exercise in cm³/min

Organ	At rest (cm³)	% Blood flow	Maximum effort (cm³)	% Blood flow
Skeletal muscle	1,000	20	26,000	88
Coronary vessels	250	5	1,200	4
Skin	500	10	750	2.5
Kidneys	1,000	20	300	1

Liver/gut	1,250	25	375	1.25
Brain	750	15	750	2.5
Whole body	5,000	100	30,000	100

Source: Clegg, *Exercise Physiology*, Feltham Press, 1995

Key term

Vascular shunt mechanism: The redistribution of blood in the body during exercise so that the working muscles receive an increased proportion. Through vasodilation and vasoconstriction of arteries and arterioles, the volume of blood reaching the working muscles can increase fourfold, from approximately 20 per cent to 88 per cent.

Vasomotor control

The redistribution of blood is determined primarily by the vasoconstriction and vasodilation of arterioles. It reacts to chemical changes of the local tissues. For example, vasodilation will occur when arterioles sense a decrease in oxygen concentration or an increase in acidity due to higher CO_2 and lactic acid concentrations. When embarking on a distance run, the increased metabolic activity increases the amount of carbon dioxide and lactic acid in the blood. This is detected by chemoreceptors, and sympathetic nerves stimulate the blood vessel size to change shape. Vasodilation will then allow greater blood flow, bringing the much needed oxygen and flushing away the harmful waste products of metabolism.

Sympathetic nerves also play a major role in redistributing blood from one area of the body to another. The smooth muscle layer (tunica media) of the blood vessels is controlled by the sympathetic nervous system, and remains in a state of slight contraction, known as vasomotor tone. By increasing sympathetic stimulation, vasoconstriction occurs and blood flow is restricted and redistributed to areas of greater need. When stimulation by sympathetic nerves decreases, vasodilation is allowed, which will increase blood flow to that body part.

Further structures which aid blood redistribution are pre-capillary sphincters. Pre-capillary sphincters are ring-shaped muscles which lie at the opening of capillaries and control blood flow into the capillary bed. When the sphincter

contracts, it restricts blood flow through the capillary and deprives tissues of oxygen; conversely, when it relaxes, it increases blood flow to the capillary bed. These are illustrated in Figure 2.24.

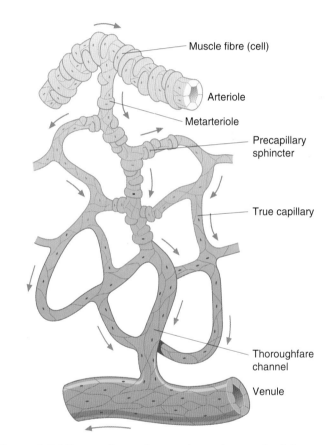

Muscle fibre (cell)

Arteriole

Metarteriole

Precapillary sphincter

True capillary

Thoroughfare channel

Venule

Figure 2.24 Pre-capillary sphincters lie at the mouth of the capillary bed

IN CONTEXT

For a triathlete such as world champion Tim Don, the vascular shunt mechanism will be in operation and will change according to the specific needs of the working muscles. To start with, the swim will require much blood to be redistributed to the shoulders (deltoids) and quadriceps group of the legs, reducing blood flow to the vital organs. During the cycle and run sections of the triathlon, a much greater proportion of the blood will be distributed to the quadriceps femoris and biceps femoris muscles of the leg.

Figure 2.25 Redistribution of blood is vital for effective performance in the triathlon

Activity 15

1   Name the major blood vessels in the body, beginning with those affecting the heart. In each case, state how the structure is suited to the function.
2   Explain how vasoconstriction and vasodilation function in the body, and how they can affect the athlete while exercising.
3   What are the major differences between the heart of a trained athlete and that of an untrained person?
4   Discuss how the vasomotor centre operates.

Activity 14

Copy the outline of the graph below. On your graph, draw two lines: one to show what happens to blood flow to skeletal muscle during exercise, and the other to illustrate blood flow to all other organs of the body while exercising. Make sure you label each of the lines and give a brief explanation for each one.

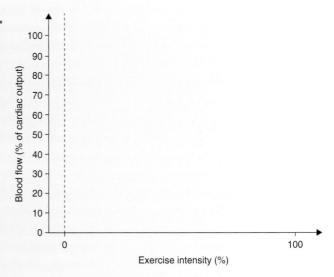

Activity 16

Copy and complete the table below showing the responses of the cardiovascular system to exercise, giving a brief explanation for each. The heart rate response has been completed as an example.

Factor	Increase/decrease	Explanation
Heart rate	Increase	During submaximal exercise, HR increases rapidly at first and then plateaus into a steady state, where oxygen demand is being met by supply. During maximal exercise, HR increases proportionally with exercise intensity until a maximum level is reached. This will also be the point of $\overline{V}O_2$ max. The release of hormones such as adrenaline and noradrenaline causes the increase in heart rate.

Stroke volume		
Cardiac output		
Blood pressure		
Blood flow to working muscles		
a–$\overline{V}O_2$ diff.		
Blood acidity		
Parasympathetic activity		
Sympathetic activity		

The transport of oxygen

Approximately 97 per cent of oxygen is carried by the red blood cells combined with haemoglobin – an iron-based protein, that chemically combines with oxygen to form oxyhaemoglobin.

Haemoglobin + Oxygen → Oxyhaemoglobin
Hb   + O_2 → HbO_2

Each molecule of haemoglobin can combine with four molecules of oxygen, which amounts to approximately 1.34ml. The concentration of haemoglobin in the blood is about 15g per 100ml; thus, each 100ml of blood can transport up to 20ml of oxygen (1.34 × 15). The remaining 3 per cent of oxygen is transported within the plasma component of the blood.

The impact of smoking on the transport of oxygen

A ban on smoking in enclosed spaces in Britain came into effect fully on 1 July 2007. It is a well-known fact that smoking can reduce levels of fitness, particularly aerobic fitness, which relies on the effective transport and utilisation of oxygen by the body. Smoking primarily reduces the amount of oxygen available in the body, which has a significant negative impact on physical performance.

The chief culprit for the reduced availability of oxygen to the tissues is the carbon monoxide contained in cigarette smoke. You will recall that once it leaves the lungs, oxygen is transported in the blood by attaching to the haemoglobin within red blood cells. Oxygen has a high affinity for haemoglobin. However, carbon monoxide's affinity for haemoglobin is about 250 times greater than that of oxygen, so it binds preferentially to haemoglobin. Therefore, as the levels of carbon monoxide increase in the blood, the level of oxygen transport and release decreases significantly. The net effect of this is to cause the heart to work harder in an attempt to compensate for the lack of oxygen reaching the muscles. This condition is prominent with the carbon monoxide accumulation that results from smoking.

The transport of carbon dioxide

Carbon dioxide produced in the body's tissues is also transported in the blood in various ways:

- approximately 8 per cent is dissolved in the blood plasma;
- up to 20 per cent combines with haemoglobin to form carbaminohaemoglobin;
- up to 70 per cent of carbon dioxide is dissolved in water as carbonic acid.

Removal of carbon dioxide from the body is necessary if effective performance is to be maintained.

IN CONTEXT

Smokers usually cannot compete with non-smokers. This is because the associated physical effects of smoking (e.g. rapid heartbeat, impaired circulation and shortness of breath) impair sports performance. Smoking also affects the body's ability to produce collagen, so common injuries, such as tendon and ligament damage, will take longer to heal in smokers than non-smokers.

Figure 2.26 Smoking can reduce the effectiveness of oxygen transport in the body

Exam-style questions

A marathon runner is taking part in a five-mile training run.

1. Describe how the conduction system of the marathon runner's heart controls the cardiac cycle to ensure enough blood is ejected from the heart during the training run.

2. Identify two ways in which oxygen is transported in the blood during the marathon runner's training run.

3. Identify two mechanisms of venous return which enable the marathon runner to deliver deoxygenated blood back to the heart during the training run.

The physiological effects of a warm–up and a cool-down on the cardiovascular system

In Chapter 1 we learned how a warm-up should be structured and the benefits a warm-up has on the musculoskeletal system. Take a few moments to review this information.

The following bullet points consider the effect a warm-up has on the vascular system:

- improves oxygen delivery to the muscles, due to an increase in heart rate and the strength of contraction through the release of adrenaline;
- increases venous return, and therefore stroke volume, through the action of the skeletal muscle pump;
- initiates the vascular shunt mechanism, which facilitates the redistribution of blood to the working muscles through the vasodilation and vasoconstriction of arterioles and pre-capillary sphincters;
- increased temperature reduces the viscosity of the blood, improving blood flow to the working muscles;
- delays the onset of blood lactate accumulation (OBLA), so performers can work harder for longer before fatigue sets in.

The reasons for performing a cool-down following exercise are well documented. The following bullet points consider the role the cardiovascular system plays in the cool-down process:

- maintains cardiorespiratory functioning, which helps to speed up the recovery process;
- keeps capillaries and other blood vessels dilated, enabling the muscles to be flushed through with oxygen-rich blood, which helps to remove fatiguing by-products, such as lactic acid and carbon dioxide, which can act on our pain receptors;
- maintains the venous return mechanisms of the skeletal and respiratory pumps, thereby preventing blood pooling in the veins, which can cause dizziness if the exercise is stopped abruptly.

Exam-style questions

1. It is recommended that a performer completes a warm-up prior to exercise. Give two effects of a warm-up on the vascular system.

2. A cool-down has a number of effects on the vascular system which aid the performer. One effect is the prevention of blood pooling. Identify two other effects.

3. One change to the vascular system during a warm-up is the ability of the haemoglobin to release oxygen quicker. Identify two other changes to the vascular system during a warm-up.

Figure 2.27 A cool-down helps to promote recovery following exercise

Health-related considerations – the role of exercise in maintaining a healthy and active lifestyle

It has long been known that exercise can lead to a healthier lifestyle. The following section seeks to illustrate how exercise and physical activity can be used for health-related reasons; in particular, how exercise can be used to prevent and control common health problems, including cardiovascular diseases such as coronary heart disease (CHD), arteriosclerosis, atherosclerosis and angina.

Exam-style questions

A long-distance runner completes a 60-minute submaximal training run.

1 Complete the graph below to show the changes in heart rate at the following three stages:

- before the run;

- during the run;

- for a 10-minute recovery phase.

2 Explain how the cardiac control centre (neural control) increases the heart rate.

3 During the training run, blood needs to be diverted away from non-essential organs to the working muscles. Explain how the vasomotor centre controls this distribution.

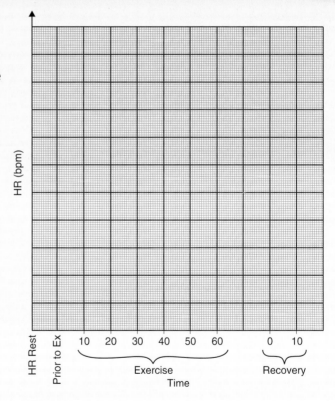

Cardiovascular disease

Cardiovascular disease is the main cause of death in the industrialised nations of western civilisation, and accounts for an estimated 40 per cent of all deaths in the United Kingdom. There are several forms of cardiovascular disease, which include:

● atherosclerosis – the deposition of fatty deposits in the arteries;
● coronary heart disease – the narrowing of coronary arteries, which can lead to angina pectoris or myocardial infarction (heart attack);
● stroke – a blockage of the arteries supplying the brain;
● hypertension – permanently high blood pressure.

Atherosclerosis is a degenerative disease. It is typified by a thickening and hardening of the arterial walls, as a result of atheroma or plaque being deposited.

By the laying down of atheroma, the lumen of the vessel is decreased in diameter. This is further narrowed by the formation of blood clots on the rough edges of the plaque. With continual deposition of atheroma, the walls of the arteries harden and lose their elasticity; this reduces their ability to vasoconstrict and vasodilate – two important mechanisms in regulating blood pressure. Consequently, blood pressure rises permanently, as the resistance to blood flow has increased; the body then suffers hypertension. This is clinically defined as blood pressure consistently above 160/100mmHg, and can increase the risk of stroke, heart attack and kidney failure.

When atherosclerosis occurs mainly in the coronary arteries (which supply the myocardium with blood), parts of the heart become deprived of oxygen and a heart attack may ensue. For severe cases of coronary heart disease, a heart bypass operation may be required, which enables blood to bypass the blocked part of the vessel and reach the oxygen-deprived tissue. Similarly, severe blockages of the cerebral arteries supplying the brain may cause oxygen deprivation, resulting in a cerebral infarction, or stroke.

The incidence and severity of the disease is dependent on the following independent and dependent risk factors.

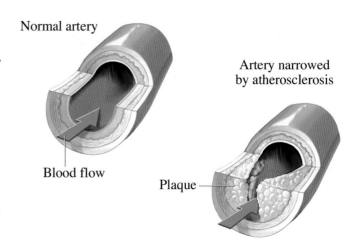

Figure 2.28 The development of atherosclerosis

Independent risk factors

Independent or primary risk factors are so called because the presence of any one of them can cause the development of such vascular diseases. These include smoking and a high fat intake.

1 Smoking increases the risk by up to 20 times and is a dose-related factor: the more you smoke, the greater the risk. However, ceasing smoking can reduce this risk greatly within a few years.
2 A high-fat diet can cause a greater risk, due to the deposition of cholesterol in the arteries.

Cholesterol is used by the body to form cell membranes and hormones. It is transported in the blood by protein molecules called lipoproteins. Generally, a high level of blood cholesterol is associated with an increased risk of coronary heart disease.

More important, however, is the type of lipoprotein that carries the cholesterol. The inflated risk is largely linked to a high proportion of low-density lipoproteins (LDL) to high-density lipoproteins (HDL). The quantity of LDL is increased when a diet high in saturated fats is followed. These lipoproteins have a tendency to deposit cholesterol in the arteries, whereas HDL act as waste disposal units – they remove cholesterol from the arterial wall and carry it to the liver, where it can be metabolised.

Consequently, a high proportion of HDL to LDL can substantially reduce the risk of atherosclerosis onset.

Dependent risk factors

Dependent risk factors are those which do not necessarily cause cardiovascular disease on their own, but which may substantially increase the risk when combined with other factors.

1   Heredity – there appears to be a genetic link in the development of cardiovascular diseases. The easiest way to determine if this factor is appropriate is to look at your family history for incidence of this disease.

2   Personality or stress is also widely accepted as a contributing factor. Although almost everybody will experience stress, how the individual deals and copes with that stress is the vital point. Type A personalities (characteristics of impatience, aggression and ambition) have a higher risk than type B individuals with the opposite characteristics.

3   Lack of exercise – studies show that people who habitually exercise at an intensity of 70 per cent of their predicted maximum heart rate have a much lower risk of heart and vascular diseases. (The reasons for this will be dealt with later in this chapter.)

4   Other factors that are uncontrollable, yet increase the risk, are increasing age (due to the progressive narrowing of arteries through atherosclerosis) and gender (men have historically had higher incidences of cardiovascular disease than women).

Atherosclerosis is not confined to the middle-aged. Research has found that fatty streaks can start appearing in the arteries of early teenaged children; by their mid twenties these may develop into fibrous plaques, and by their early forties, severe blockages of the arteries can start to occur. The rate at which the disease progresses is largely determined by the heredity factor and the lifestyles that individuals choose to follow.

The role of exercise in a healthy lifestyle

Numerous studies have been conducted into how exercise can prevent cardiovascular diseases. Following an exercise programme, together with stopping smoking, can go some way towards preventing such diseases and promoting a healthy lifestyle. Below is a summary of the major findings.

● Exercise tends to reduce the overall risk of developing some form of cardiovascular disease by about 30 per cent, largely due to the adaptation of the cardiovascular system. By exercising, improvements occur in the contractility of and blood supply to the heart. By causing blood vessels to vasoconstrict and dilate regularly, exercise can prevent the arteries from hardening and losing their elasticity, and so ward off the effects of atherosclerosis. This will also prevent hypertension and the associated dangers.

Figure 2.29 Exercise can help to maintain a healthy lifestyle and prevent the onset of cardiovascular diseases such as atherosclerosis and coronary heart disease

- Exercise can also reduce the level of fatty deposits in the blood and increase the proportion of HDL to LDL, as well as reducing overall cholesterol levels. The laying down of fatty deposits in the arteries is therefore significantly reduced.
- Exercise can also reduce body fat and decrease the strain on the circulatory system.
- The increased breakdown of blood glucose as a result of exercise reduces blood sugar content and decreases the incidence of adult-onset diabetes.
- Vigorous activity can also have a cathartic effect, reducing stress and generally instilling 'the feel-good factor'.

Activity 17

You have been asked to prescribe a 10-week exercise programme for a group of middle-aged men who have been relatively inactive for some years.

1 What factors do you need to consider in preparing the programme?
2 State the type of exercises you would include and give reasons for your choices.

Activity 18

Undertake some research on the following topic and draw up your conclusions: Critically evaluate the role of exercise in the prevention of cardiovascular diseases.

Key terms

Coronary heart disease: A narrowing of the small blood vessels that supply blood and oxygen to the heart (coronary arteries). The narrowing reduces the blood supply to the heart muscles and causes pain known as angina.

Angina pectoris: Angina pectoris is recurring acute chest pain or discomfort, resulting from decreased blood supply to the heart muscle.

Arteriosclerosis: A chronic disease in which thickening, hardening and loss of elasticity of the arterial walls results in impaired blood circulation.

Atherosclerosis: A process of progressive thickening and hardening of the walls of the arteries as a result of the deposition of fatty deposits on their inner lining.

What you need to know

* The structure of the heart is specially adapted to its function.

* Valves within the heart ensure a unidirectional flow of blood.

* The sounds of the heart are a result of these valves snapping shut. The 'lub' sound results from the closing of the atrioventricular valves, while the 'dub' results from the closure of the semilunar valves.

* Typically, the heart is composed of three layers: an outer pericardium, a thick muscular layer called the myocardium, and a smooth inner endocardium.

* Coronary arteries ensure that the heart receives an adequate supply of blood.

* The cardiac cycle explains the passage of blood through the heart. It consists of four stages: atrial diastole, atrial systole, ventricular diastole and ventricular systole.

* The heart is myogenic – it creates its own impulses.

* The impulse is emitted from the SA node and the surrounding fibres are innervated, causing the atria to contract. The impulse eventually arrives at the AV node, where it is dispersed down the bundle of His and throughout the Purkinje fibres, causing the ventricles to contract.

* The heart rate is governed by the parasympathetic and sympathetic nervous systems. The sympathetic nervous system increases heart rate by releasing adrenaline and noradrenaline, while the parasympathetic nervous system slows the heart down through the action of another hormone, acetylcholine.

* Increases in heart rate during exercise are largely the result of increased metabolic activity increasing the concentration of carbon dioxide.

* Cardiac output is the volume of blood pumped out of one ventricle in one minute. Stroke volume is the volume of blood pumped out of one ventricle in one beat. Heart rate is the number of times the heart beats per minute.

* Cardiac hypertrophy is the enlargement of the heart, often resulting from endurance training.

* Bradycardia is the reduction in resting heart rate (usually below 60 beats per minute) which accompanies cardiac hypertrophy.

* The vascular system encompasses the blood and blood vessels.

* The blood's main functions are the transportation of oxygen and the maintenance of homeostasis.

* Major blood vessels consist of arteries, arterioles, capillaries, venules and veins.

* The continuous network of blood vessels in the body is known as the circulatory system, which is composed of the pulmonary and systemic circuits.

* Blood returning to the heart via the veins is known as venous return. It is aided by the muscle and respiratory pumps.

* Blood pressure is the force exerted by the blood on the inner walls of the blood vessels. It is a product of cardiac output and resistance of the vessel walls.

* Blood flow is controlled by the vasomotor centre, which causes blood vessels to vasodilate and vasoconstrict, and determines the amount of blood reaching various parts of the body.

* The vascular shunt mechanism aids in the redistribution of blood during exercise.

* A warm-up helps to prepare the cardiovascular system for exercise by increasing heart rate, stroke volume and cardiac output. In addition, it increases body temperature and reduces blood viscosity, making it flow more easily. The warm-up also helps to speed up venous return and initiate the vascular shunt mechanism, which aids in the redistribution of blood during exercise.

* A cool-down following exercise maintains cardiorespiratory functioning. This helps to speed up the recovery process by keeping capillaries and other blood vessels dilated. This enables the muscles to be flushed through with oxygen-rich blood, which helps to remove fatiguing by-products, such as lactic acid and carbon dioxide, which can act on our pain receptors.

* Oxygen is transported in the blood by combining with haemoglobin.

* Smoking can impair the transport of oxygen since haemoglobin has a much higher affinity for carbon monoxide (found in cigarette smoke) than for oxygen.

* The majority (70 per cent) of carbon dioxide is transported as carbonic acid (dissolved in water); 20 per cent is transported by combining with haemoglobin, and 8 per cent is dissolved in blood plasma.

* Cardiovascular disease includes atherosclerosis, coronary heart disease, strokes and hypertension.

* Independent risk factors for cardiovascular disease include smoking and diet high in fat. These factors can cause the development of cardiovascular disease.

* Dependent risk factors include genetics, personality type, stress, inactivity, age and gender.

* Exercise can reduce the risk of cardiovascular disease by enhancing blood supply around the body, promoting HDLs, reducing body fat and inducing a feel-good factor.

Review questions

1 Describe the path that blood takes through the heart, from the point at which it enters via the venae cavae, to where it exits via the aorta.

2 When using a stethoscope, is it possible to hear the heart beating? What creates the heartbeat, and when do these sounds occur during the cardiac cycle?

3 Describe the action of the sympathetic and parasympathetic nervous systems on the heart, before, during and following exercise.

4 Outline the major functions of the blood. Explain the importance of blood when exercising.

5 Sketch and label a graph showing the heart rate pattern expected from an athlete completing a 400m run in a personal best time of 45 seconds, followed by a 15-minute recovery period. Account for these changes.

6 Outline the major factors which affect cardiac output during exercise.

7 During exercise, the return of blood to the heart is paramount. Explain how the body achieves this and relate it to Starling's law.

8 How is the redistribution of blood during exercise accomplished?

9 Explain what you would expect to happen to blood pressure in the following instances:

  1 an athlete undertaking a steady swim;

  2 an athlete completing a 100m sprint;

  3 a weightlifter performing a maximal lift;

  4 an athlete completing the cycling stage of a triathlon.

10 Endurance training results in significant benefits to the heart and vascular system. What are these benefits and how do they contribute to a 'healthier lifestyle'?

CHAPTER 3

The respiratory system – the maintenance of oxygen supply

Learning outcomes

By the end of this chapter you should be able to:

- outline the structure of the respiratory system;
- describe the process of external respiration;
- explain the mechanics of breathing at rest and the respiratory muscles involved;
- describe the changes in the mechanics of breathing during physical activity and the respiratory muscles involved;
- explain how the respiratory control centre regulates the mechanics of breathing, at rest and during physical activity;
- outline the process of gaseous exchange that takes place between the alveoli and blood, and between the blood and tissue cells;
- explain the changes in gaseous exchange that take place between the alveoli and blood, and between the blood and tissue cells, as a direct result of participation in physical activity;
- identify and explain the effect of altitude on the respiratory system and how it influences the performance of different types of physical activity;
- give a critical evaluation of the impact of different types of physical activity on the respiratory system;
- identify the impact of smoking on the respiratory system.

CHAPTER INTRODUCTION

During exercise, the body requires oxygen to produce energy to fuel muscular contraction. It is the role of the respiratory system, in conjunction with the cardiovascular system, to ensure that sufficient oxygen is taken into the body and transferred to the body's tissues to satisfy the demand. Likewise, the respiratory system is also responsible for ensuring adequate removal of waste products such as carbon dioxide and lactic acid.

This chapter examines the structure and function of the respiratory system, with a particular focus on the changes that occur from rest to exercise. Featured areas of study include the mechanics of breathing, the regulation of breathing, and the gaseous exchange that takes place between the alveoli and blood, and between the blood and tissue cells. We will also consider the effect that altitude plays on the performance of different types of activity, as well as evaluating the impact that training has on the respiratory system, and the effect of respiratory complications such as asthma and the effects of smoking.

External respiration

External respiration involves the movement of gases into and out of the lungs. The exchange of gases between the lungs and the blood is known as pulmonary diffusion.

On its journey to the lungs, air drawn into the body passes through many structures, as outlined below and illustrated in Figure 3.1.

Key term

External respiration: The process of moving respiratory gases into and out of the lungs.

Nasal passages

Air is drawn into the body via the nose. The nasal cavity is divided by a cartilaginous septum,

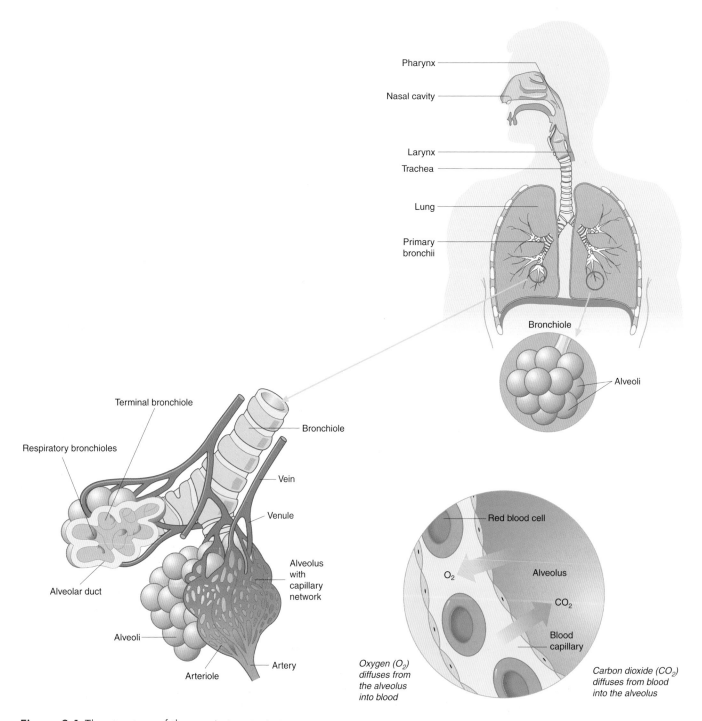

Figure 3.1 The structure of the respiratory system

forming the nasal passages. The interior structures of the nose help the respiratory process by performing the following important functions:

1   The mucous membranes and blood capillaries moisten and warm the inspired air.
2   The ciliated epithelium filters and traps dust particles, which are moved to the throat for elimination.
3   The small bones known as chonchae increase the surface area of the cavity to make the process more efficient.

The oral pharynx and larynx

The throat is shared by both the respiratory and alimentary tracts. Air entering the larynx passes over the vocal chords and into the trachea. In swallowing, the larynx is drawn upwards and forwards against the base of the epiglottis, thus preventing entry of food.

The trachea

The trachea, or windpipe, is approximately 10cm in length and lies in front of the oesophagus. It is composed of 18 horseshoe-shaped rings of cartilage, which are also lined by a mucous membrane and ciliated cells, which provide the same protection against dust as in the nasal passageways. The trachea extends from the larynx and directs air into the right and left primary bronchi.

The bronchi and bronchioles

The trachea divides into the right and left bronchi, which further subdivide into lobar bronchi (three feeding each lobe on the right, two feeding each lobe on the left). Further subdivision of these airways forms bronchioles, which in turn branch into the smaller terminal or respiratory bronchioles. The bronchioles enable the air to pass into the alveoli via the alveolar ducts, and it is here that pulmonary diffusion occurs.

Alveoli

The alveoli are responsible for the exchange of gases between the lungs and the blood. The alveolar walls are extremely thin and are composed of epithelial cells, which are lined by a thin film of water, essential for dissolving oxygen from the inspired air.

Surrounding each alveolus is an extensive capillary network, which ensures a smooth passage of oxygen into the pulmonary capillaries. The tiny lumen of each capillary surrounding the alveoli ensures that red blood cells travel in single file, and that they are squeezed into a biconcave shape, increasing the surface area and enabling the greatest possible uptake of oxygen. It has been estimated that each lung contains up to 150 million alveoli, providing a tremendous surface area for the exchange of gases. The alveoli walls also contain elastic fibres, which further increase the surface during inspiration.

The mechanics of breathing

The lungs are surrounded by pleural sacs containing pleural fluid, which reduces friction during respiration. These sacs are attached to both the lungs and the thoracic cage, which enables the lungs to inflate and deflate as the chest expands and flattens. The interrelationship between the lungs, the pleural sacs and the thoracic cage is central to an understanding of the respiratory processes of inspiration and expiration.

Inspiration

The process of inspiration is an active one. It occurs as a result of the contraction of the respiratory muscles, namely the external intercostal muscles and the diaphragm.

The external intercostal muscles are attached to each rib. When they contract, they cause the ribcage to pivot about thoracic vertebral joints and move upwards and outwards, much like the handle of a bucket as it is lifted. The diaphragm, a dome-shaped muscle separating the abdominal and thoracic cavities, contracts downwards during inspiration, increasing the area of the thoracic cavity. As the chest expands through these muscular contractions, the surface tension created by the film of pleural fluid causes the lungs to be pulled outwards, along with the chest walls. This action causes the space within the lungs to increase and the air molecules within to move further apart.

As pressure is determined by the rate at which molecules strike a surface in a given time, the pressure within the lungs (intrapulmonary pressure) decreases and becomes less than that outside the body. Gases always move from areas of higher pressure to areas of lower pressure, so that air from outside the body rushes into the lungs via the respiratory tract. This process is known as inspiration.

During exercise, greater volumes of air can fill the lungs, since the sternocleidomastoid, pectoralis minor and scaleni muscles help increase the thoracic cavity still further.

> ### EXAMINER'S TIP
>
> Gases always move from areas of higher pressures (or concentrations) to areas of lower pressures (or concentrations), until equilibrium is reached.

> ### EXAMINER'S TIP
>
> When determining which of the intercostal muscles are responsible for inspiration and expiration, think opposites: external intercostals are needed for inspiration, and internal intercostals are needed for expiration during exercise.

Expiration

The process of expiration is generally a passive process, and occurs as a result of the relaxation of the respiratory muscles used in inspiration. As the external intercostal muscles relax, the ribcage is lowered into its resting position, and the diaphragm relaxes and domes up into the thoracic cavity. The area of the lungs is thus decreased, and intrapulmonary pressure increases to an extent where it is greater than atmospheric pressure. Air inside the lungs is forced out to equate the pressure inside and outside the body.

During exercise, the process of expiration becomes more active as the internal intercostal muscles pull the ribs downwards to help increase the ventilation rate. These muscles are ably assisted by the abdominals and the latissimus dorsi muscles. Take a moment to study Figure 3.2, which illustrates the process of inspiration and expiration.

> ### EXAMINER'S TIP
>
> Make sure you can state the respiratory muscles used in inspiration and expiration, at rest and during exercise.

a) Inspiration

External intercostal muscles cause the rib cage to pivot on the thoracic vertebrae and move upwards and outwards.

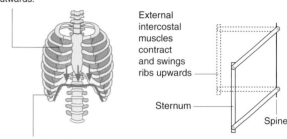

Diaphragm contracts downwards, increasing the 'depth' of the thoratic cavity.

b) Expiration at rest

Relaxation of respiratory muscles cause the rib cage to move downwards and inwards.

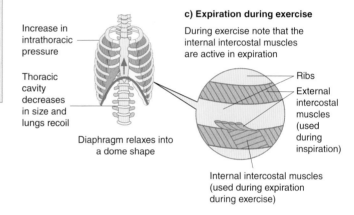

c) Expiration during exercise

During exercise note that the internal intercostal muscles are active in expiration

Increase in intrathoracic pressure

Thoracic cavity decreases in size and lungs recoil

Diaphragm relaxes into a dome shape

Ribs

External intercostal muscles (used during inspiration)

Internal intercostal muscles (used during expiration during exercise)

Figure 3.2 Action of the ribcage during (a) inspiration, (b) expiration and (c) expiration during exercise

Activity 1

Read the section above on 'The mechanics of breathing', then copy and complete the table below, naming the muscles responsible for inspiration and expiration, at rest and during exercise.

	Rest	**Exercise**
Inspiration		
Expiration		

Respiratory regulation – the respiratory control centre

Ventilation is controlled by the nervous system, and this enables us to alter breathing patterns without thinking about it consciously. The basic rhythm of respiration is governed and coordinated by the respiratory centre, situated in and around the medulla area of the brain. During inspiration, nerve impulses are generated and sent to the inspiratory muscles (external intercostals and diaphragm), causing them to contract. This lasts for approximately two seconds, after which the impulses cease and expiration occurs passively by elastic recoil of the lungs.

During exercise, however, when breathing rate is increased, the expiratory centre may send impulses to the expiratory muscles (internal intercostals), which speeds up the expiratory process.

It is the chemical composition of the blood, however, which largely influences respiration rates, particularly during exercise. The respiratory centre has a chemosensitive area, which is sensitive to changes in blood acidity. Chemoreceptors located in the aortic arch and carotid arteries assess the acidity of the blood and, in particular, the relative concentrations of CO_2 and O_2. If there is an increase in the concentration of CO_2 in the blood, the chemoreceptors detect this, and the respiratory centre sends nerve impulses to the respiratory muscles, which increase the rate of ventilation. This allows the body to expire the excess CO_2. Once blood acidity is lowered, fewer impulses are sent and respiration rates can decrease once again.

Other factors that help the control of breathing include:

- proprioceptors and mechanoreceptors, which inform the inspiratory centre that movement is taking place;
- thermoreceptors, which inform the respiratory centre that heat energy has been produced and the temperature of the blood increased;
- baroreceptors (located in the lungs), which send information to the expiratory centre concerning the state of lung inflation.

This regulation of breathing is aided by a series of stretch receptors in the lungs and bronchioles, which prevent overinflation of the lungs. If these are stretched excessively, the expiratory centre sends impulses to induce expiration – this is known as the Hering–Breur reflex.

Factors affecting the regulation of breathing are illustrated in Figure 3.3.

Key term

Hering–Breur reflex: A spontaneous response of the lungs that prevents overinflation.

IN CONTEXT

When a swimmer such as Ian Thorpe prepares to race, the contraction of the external intercostal muscles and the diaphragm initiate inspiration, while expiration remains a passive process through the relaxation of these muscles, as the swimmer remains at rest on the poolside. During the swim, however, both the rate and depth of breathing need to increase. This is controlled by the respiratory control centre in the medulla oblongata of the brain. The inspiratory centre responds to changes in the chemical composition of the blood (most notably an increase in CO_2, and a decrease in O_2 and pH), increases in blood temperature, and increased movement at the joints and contraction of the muscles. Consequently, the inspiratory centre calls on additional muscles to help expand the thoracic cavity further. These additional muscles include the sternocleidomastoid, the scaleni and the pectoralis major.

In order to help increase the rate of breathing, the expiratory centre responds to information from stretch receptors in the lungs, and enrols the help of the internal intercostal muscles and the abdominals to pull the ribcage down more quickly. In doing so, the process of gaseous exchange is facilitated and more oxygen can enter the swimmer's body, and more carbon dioxide can be expelled.

Activity 2

1   Explain the process of increased breathing rates during exercise.
2   Why do breathing rates remain high following exercise, even though exercise has ceased?

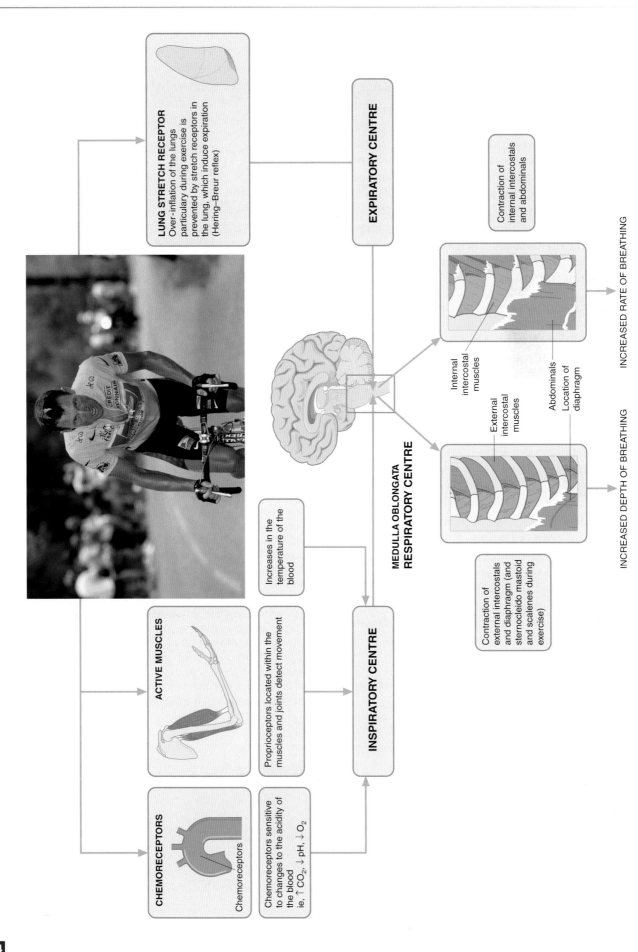

Figure 3.3 Respiratory regulation during exercise

Figure 3.4 Respiratory regulation enables a performer such as Ian Thorpe to remove excess carbon dioxide and supply the muscles with the necessary oxygen

Exam-style questions

1 Describe the mechanisms of breathing which allow a marathon runner to breathe in (inspiration) greater volumes of oxygen during a run.

2 Explain how the respiratory centre uses neural control to produce changes in the mechanics of breathing.

Pulmonary diffusion – gaseous exchange at the lungs

Pulmonary diffusion is the term used to explain the process of gaseous exchange in the lungs. It has two major functions:

1 to replenish the blood with oxygen where it can, then be transported to the tissues and muscles;
2 to remove carbon dioxide from the blood which has resulted from metabolic processes in the tissues.

IN DEPTH: Partial pressure of gases

Central to the understanding of gaseous exchange is the concept of partial pressure. The partial pressure of a gas is the individual pressure that the gas exerts when it occurs in a mixture of gases. The gas will exert a pressure proportional to its concentration within the whole gas. Thus the partial pressures of each individual gas within a mixture of gases should, when added together, be equal to the total pressure of the gas.

For example, the air we breathe is composed of three main gases: nitrogen (79 per cent), oxygen (20.9 per cent) and carbon dioxide (0.03 per cent). The percentages show the relative concentrations of each gas in atmospheric air.

At sea level, total atmospheric pressure is 769mmHg, which reflects the pressure that atmospheric air exerts. For example:

● The concentration of O_2 (oxygen) in the atmosphere is approximately 21 per cent.
● The concentration of nitrogen in the air is approximately 79 per cent.
● Together they exert a pressure of 760mmHg at sea level. Therefore, the pO_2 (partial pressure of oxygen) is calculated as:

$$pO_2 = \text{Barometric} \times \text{Fractional}$$
$$\text{pressure} \quad \text{concentration}$$
$$= 760 \quad \times 0.21$$
$$= 159.6\text{mmHg}$$

Partial pressure of gases explains the movement of gases within the body, and accounts for the processes of gas exchange between the alveoli and the blood, and between the blood and the muscle, or tissue.

Key terms

Partial pressure: The pressure exerted by an individual gas when it exists within a mixture of gases.
Diffusion: The movement of respiratory gases from areas of higher partial pressure to areas of lower partial pressure, until equilibrium is reached.

EXAMINER'S TIP

The units of measurement of pressure are millimetres of mercury (mmHg).

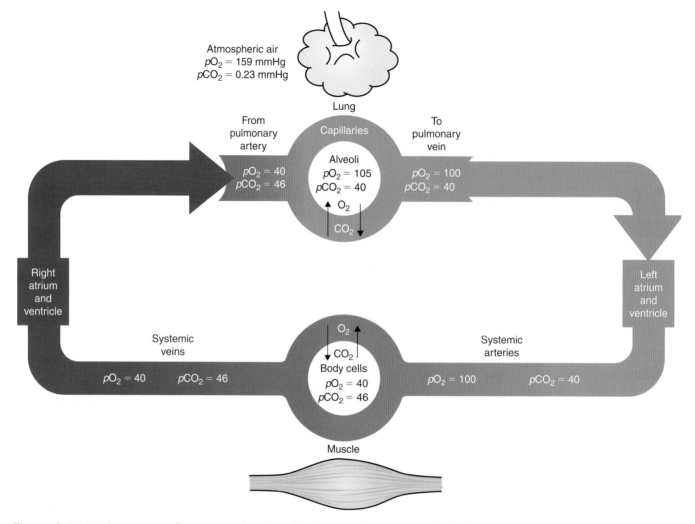

Figure 3.5 Partial pressures of oxygen and carbon dioxide at various sites in the body

Activity 3

Calculate the partial pressure in the atmosphere of:

- carbon dioxide (pCO$_2$);
- nitrogen (pN$_2$).

Gaseous exchange at the lungs

It is the imbalance between gases in the alveoli and the blood that causes a pressure gradient, which results in a movement of gases across the respiratory membrane (which facilitates this movement by being extremely thin, measuring only 0.5mm). This movement is two-way, with oxygen moving from the alveoli into the blood, and carbon dioxide diffusing from the blood into the alveoli. The partial pressure of oxygen (pO$_2$) in the atmosphere is approximately 159mmHg (0.21 × 760mmHg), which drops to

105mmHg in the alveoli, since the air combines with water vapour and carbon dioxide which is already present in the alveoli.

The diffusion gradient

Blood in the pulmonary capillaries which surround the alveoli has a pO$_2$ of 45mmHg, since much of the oxygen has already been used by the working muscles. This results in a pressure gradient of approximately 60mmHg, which forces oxygen from the alveoli into the blood, until such time that the pressure is equal on each side of the membrane.

In the same way, carbon dioxide moves along a pressure gradient, from the pulmonary capillaries into the alveoli. With a pCO$_2$ of 45mmHg in the blood returning to the lungs, and a pCO$_2$ of 40mmHg in the alveolar air, a small pressure gradient of 5mmHg results. This causes CO_2 to move from the pulmonary blood into the alveoli, which is later expired. Although the pressure gradient is relatively small, the CO_2 can cross the respiratory membrane much more rapidly than oxygen, as its membrane solubility is 20 times greater.

Endurance athletes, with larger aerobic capacities, will have greater oxygen diffusion ability (the rate at which oxygen diffuses into the pulmonary blood from the alveoli) as a result of increased cardiac output, increased alveoli surface area and reduced resistance to diffusion.

Activity 4

Discuss why the diffusion gradient is relatively small at rest and increases during exercise.

EXAMINER'S TIP

A diffusion gradient can be calculated by subtracting the partial pressure of the gas on one side of the respiratory membrane from the partial pressure of the gas on the other side of the respiratory membrane.

Activity 5

1   Explain what is meant by the partial pressure of a gas.
2   State how this affects gaseous exchange around the body.
3   What happens to the partial pressure of oxygen (pO_2) and carbon dioxide (pCO_2) in the muscle cell during exercise?

The effect of altitude on the respiratory system

With altitude there is a decrease in atmospheric pressure, but the percentages of gases within the air remain identical to those found at sea level (nitrogen 79 per cent, oxygen 20.9 per cent, carbon dioxide 0.03 per cent). However, it is the partial pressure of the gases that changes in direct proportion to an increase in altitude.

For example, at rest, the pO_2 of arterial blood is approximately 100mmHg, while in resting muscles and tissues it is 40mmHg. The difference between the two indicates the pressure gradient, and ensures an efficient movement of oxygen from the blood into the muscle. The pO_2 of arterial blood at an altitude of 8,000 feet drops significantly, to approximately 60mmHg, while that in the muscles remains at 40mmHg, causing the pressure gradient to fall to 20mmHg at altitude. This dramatic reduction in the pressure gradient reduces the movement of oxygen into the body's muscles, and performance decreases.

Many endurance athletes often undertake a period of altitude training before major events. The benefits of such training are summarised below.

Altitude training

Altitude training is a method of training based on the principle that with an increase in altitude, the partial pressure of oxygen (pO_2) in the atmosphere decreases by about a half, causing the body to adapt by increasing red blood cell mass and haemoglobin levels to cope with a lower pO_2. It is widely used by endurance athletes to enhance their oxygen-carrying capacity; when athletes return to sea level these increases remain, yet the pO_2 has increased, which means that the body can transport and utilise more oxygen, giving improved endurance performance. However, there appears to be contradictory evidence concerning the benefits of altitude training, and recent evidence suggests that living at altitude and training at sea level produces the greatest endurance performance, and that in doing this, athletes can increase the oxygen-carrying capacity of the blood by up to 150 per cent. Indeed, some athletes live in special cabins at sea level that mimic the conditions of altitude, so that they do not actually have to travel abroad.

There are, however, some disadvantages associated with altitude training. As well as being expensive, many athletes have found that training at altitude can cause altitude sickness, and as a consequence they cannot train at the same intensity as they would at sea level, and so actually suffer from detraining.

Table 3.1 Benefits and drawbacks of altitude training

Perceived benefits	Likely drawbacks
• Increased haematocrit (concentration of red blood cells) • Increased concentration of haemoglobin • Enhanced oxygen transport	• Expensive • Altitude sickness • Due to the lack of oxygen, training at higher intensities is difficult • Detraining • Any benefits are soon lost on return to sea level

Key term

Altitude training: A form of training based on the principle that with an increase in altitude, the partial pressure of oxygen in the atmosphere decreases proportionally.

EXAMINER'S TIP

Typically, prolonged exposure to altitude can cause adaptation, such as an improvement in the oxygen-carrying capacity of the blood.

IN CONTEXT

At the 1968 Olympics, held in Mexico City, Bob Beamon jumped 8.90m, shattering the long jump world record at the time by over 0.5m. The record lasted for almost 23 years, until 1991, when Mike Powell jumped 8.95m at the Tokyo World Championships. Beamon never repeated his performance of 1968. His personal best, excluding this jump, remained at 8.33m. So what can account for this extraordinary performance? Many put it down to the 'thinner air', or reduced atmospheric pressure experienced in Mexico City, which sits 7,349ft (2,240m) above sea level. In fact, this was not the only world record set during these games. Many records were set in both men's and women's athletic events up to 1,500m, but, surprisingly, none in the more aerobic-based events beyond this distance. So it appears that competing at altitude may positively benefit the more explosive, anaerobic-type activities such as the long jump, but may seriously hinder aerobic performances such as the marathon, due to the reduced availability of oxygen at altitude.

Figure 3.6 Altitude could have contributed to Bob Beamon's mammoth long jump at the 1968 Mexico City Olympics

Activity 6

Discuss the relative merits of altitude training compared to living at altitude and training at sea level.

Exam-style questions

The diagram below shows a cyclist completing a 10-mile training ride.

1   With reference to the mechanics of breathing, describe how the cyclist is able to inspire greater amounts of oxygen during the training ride.

2   Describe how carbon dioxide is diffused from the blood into the alveoli during the training ride.

3   Give reasons why the cyclist's performance would decrease when performing at altitude.

4   During endurance activities at altitude there may be a reduction in performance. Why do the changes in air pressure at altitude reduce performance?

The transport of oxygen and the oxyhaemoglobin dissociation curve

We established in Chapter 2 that the majority of oxygen is carried by the red blood cells combined with haemoglobin; this is an iron-based protein which chemically combines with oxygen to form oxyhaemoglobin.

Haemoglobin + Oxygen → Oxyhaemoglobin
Hb   + O_2 → HbO_2

Each molecule of haemoglobin can combine with four molecules of oxygen, which amounts to approximately 1.34ml. The concentration of haemoglobin in the blood is about 15g per 100ml; thus, each 100ml of blood can transport up to 20ml of oxygen (1.34×15). However, the amount of oxygen that can combine with haemoglobin is determined by the partial pressure of oxygen (pO_2). A high pO_2 results in complete haemoglobin saturation; while at a lower pO_2, haemoglobin saturation decreases.

Haemoglobin is almost 100 per cent saturated with oxygen, at a pO_2 of 100mmHg (which is the pO_2 in the alveoli). Therefore, at the lungs, haemoglobin is totally saturated with oxygen, and even if more oxygen were available, it could not be transported. As the pO_2 is reduced, haemoglobin saturation decreases accordingly. This is largely due to the increased acidity of the blood (decrease in blood pH), caused by an increase in CO_2 content or lactic acid, and the increase in body temperature, which causes a shift to the right in the haemoglobin saturation curve.

This is known as the Bohr shift, and explains how oxygen is dissociated from haemoglobin at lower pH values in order to feed the tissues.

During exercise, increased CO_2 production causes a greater dissociation of oxygen due to the decrease in muscle pH. A further cause is the increase in body temperature that accompanies exercise; as oxygen unloading becomes more effective, the dissociation curve shifts to the right.

To summarise, endurance performance is reliant on the quick and effective dissociation of oxygen from haemoglobin, which in turn is dependent on four factors:

1   a fall in the pO_2 within the muscle;
2   an increase in blood and muscle temperature;
3   an increase in the pCO_2 within the muscle;
4   a fall in pH due to the production of lactic acid.

IN CONTEXT

The overall efficiency of oxygen transport is dependent on haemoglobin content, and many athletes have sought to increase haemoglobin content through the illegal practice of **blood doping**. By removing blood, which is subsequently replaced by the body, the athlete reinfuses it, to increase blood volume and, more importantly, haemoglobin content. Results of research on the practice of blood doping are conflicting, and it should always be remembered that it is illegal under the current Olympic Committee doping rules.

More recently, the preferred cheater's drug has been **EPO** – a synthetic version of **erythropoietin**, a glycoprotein that occurs naturally in the body and stimulates the production of red blood cells. The drug's advantages are that it can increase the oxygen-carrying capacity of the blood and therefore improve endurance performance. But EPO has potentially fatal effects, as well as being illegal for competition (and very expensive). Several top cyclists have died following misuse of the drug. Thankfully, a new test has recently become available to detect the use of this dangerous drug.

Key term

Bohr shift: A shift in the oxyhaemoglobin dissociation curve to the right that is caused by increased levels in carbon dioxide and the subsequent increase in blood acidity.

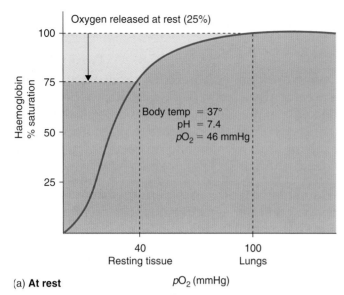

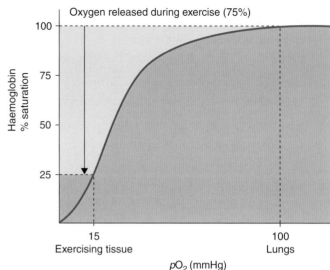

(a) At rest

At rest the pO_2 in the alveoli is approximately 100 mmHg. At this point the haemoglobin is almost 100% saturated with oxygen. In resting muscles and tissues the pO_2 is approximately 40 mmHg. At this point haemoglobin is only 75% saturated with oxygen. This means that 25% of the oxygen picked up at the lungs is released into the muscle to help in energy production

(b) During exercise

During exercise the pO_2 in the alveoli remains at approximately 100 mmHg with almost 100% haemoglobin saturation. In working muscles the pO_2 can be greatly reduced when compared to resting figures. The diagram shows a pO_2 in working muscles of 15 mmHg. This represents an oxy-haemoglobin saturation of 25% meaning that 75% of the oxygen picked up at the lungs is released into the muscle to help meet the extra energy demands.

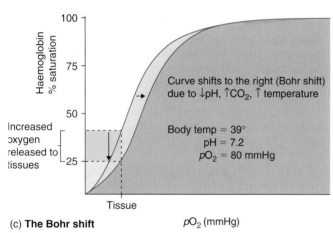

(c) The Bohr shift

During exercise there is an increase in the production of carbon dioxide in the muscle cell raising the pCO_2. As a result of this and increases in the concentration of lactic acid, blood acidity increases causing a fall in the pH. Energy produced in the muscle cell increases temperature. These factors cause a shift in the curve to the right (known as the Bohr shift) which results in an increased release of oxygen.

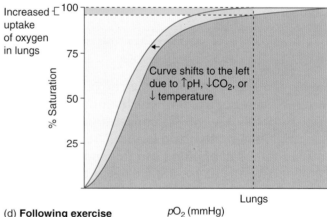

(d) Following exercise

Once exercise ceases we see an increase in blood pH, a decrease in pCO_2 and a decrease in temperature in the lungs. The curve shifts to the left returning to its resting position. It results in an increased ability of haemoglobin to pick up oxygen at the lungs.

Figure 3.7 The oxygen–haemoglobin dissociation curve

Activity 7

1 During resting conditions, approximately 5ml of oxygen is transported to the tissues in each 100ml of blood. We know from earlier discussions that cardiac output at rest is approximately 5,000ml/min. Calculate how much oxygen is delivered to the tissues each minute.

2 During exercise, the oxygen transport can be increased by up to three times, due to the greater release of oxygen from haemoglobin. In addition, the rate of oxygen transport can increase fivefold, due to the increase in cardiac output while exercising. Calculate how much oxygen can now be delivered to the tissues when exercising.

Activity 8

1 Explain how the oxyhaemoglobin disassociation curve can aid our understanding of gaseous exchange. How might increases in blood acidity affect the curve?

2 Outline how CO_2 is transported in the body. What is the role of the bicarbonate ion in this process?

Activity 9

Draw diagrams to show how and why gases move between:

● the alveoli and the pulmonary capillaries;

● the systemic capillaries and the muscle.

EXAMINER'S TIP

Don't forget that an increase in blood acidity amounts to a decrease in the pH of the blood.

IN CONTEXT

Paula Radcliffe's record as an endurance performer speaks for itself. The defining factor that determines successful performance in activities such as a marathon run is undoubtedly the availability of oxygen to the runner's muscles. The marathon runner's body has adapted to increase the supply of oxygen to the working muscles. We already know that during exercise, the oxyhaemoglobin curve shifts to the right (the Bohr shift), which facilitates the dissociation of oxygen from haemoglobin. This shift to the right arises due to the following factors:

1 A fall in the pO_2 inside the muscle cell, due to an increased oxygen uptake by the muscles. This increases the oxygen diffusion gradient.

2 An increase in pCO_2 inside the muscle cell. Carbon dioxide is produced when the body releases energy from our food fuels. This increases the carbon dioxide diffusion gradient.

3 A fall in blood pH (increased acidity), resulting from both carbon dioxide and lactic acid production in the muscle cell.

4 An increase in body temperature, which arises from the heat energy produced during the increased muscle contractions that accompany physical activity.

Together, these four factors ensure that the muscles of the runner receive the necessary oxygen to complete the marathon, delaying fatigue and increasing the intensity of the performance.

Figure 3.8 The marathon runner's body has adapted to increase the supply of oxygen to the working muscles

Exam-style questions

1 The diagram below shows oxygen diffusing into the bloodstream and being transported in the blood to the working muscles.

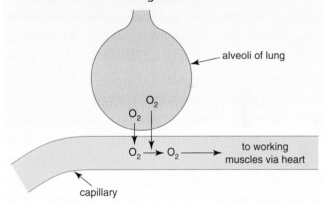

(a) Explain how gas exchange is increased at the lungs to ensure that a greater amount of oxygen is diffused into the blood during exercise.

(b) How is oxygen transported in the blood to the working muscles?

2 A marathon runner is taking part in a five-mile training run.

(a) Identify two ways in which oxygen is transported in the blood during the training run.

(b) How is oxygen exchange increased at the muscle tissues (gas diffusion) during the training run, and why is this beneficial to performance?

(c) Describe how the mechanics of breathing ensure that carbon dioxide is expired during the training run.

Gas exchange at the muscles and tissues

We have seen how oxygen is brought into the lungs and transported to the capillary beds on the muscles. We now need to turn our attention to how the oxygen can enter the muscle cell.

The process is similar to the exchange of gases at the lungs: the partial pressure of the gases in the blood and tissues determines the movement of oxygen and carbon dioxide into and out of the tissue cells. The high partial pressure of oxygen in the arterial blood, and the relatively low pO_2 in the muscles, causes a pressure gradient which enables oxygen to dissociate from haemoglobin and pass through the capillary wall and into the muscle cytoplasm. Conversely, the high pCO_2 in the tissues and low pCO_2 in the arterial blood causes a movement of carbon dioxide in the opposite direction. In fact, the production of carbon dioxide stimulates the dissociation of oxygen from haemoglobin (as we saw above), and this, together with greater tissue demand for oxygen, increases the pressure gradients during exercise.

Once oxygen has entered the muscle cell, it immediately attaches to a substance called myoglobin, which is not dissimilar to haemoglobin and transports the oxygen to the mitochondria, where aerobic respiration can take place. The concentration of myoglobin is much higher in the cells of slow-twitch muscle fibres, as these are more suited to aerobic energy production. Myoglobin has a much higher affinity for oxygen than haemoglobin, and also acts as an oxygen reserve, so that when demand for oxygen is increased, as for example during exercise, there is a readily available supply.

The arterial–venous oxygen difference (a–$\bar{V}O_2$ diff.) is the difference in oxygen content between the arterial blood and venous blood, and can measure how much oxygen is actually being consumed in the muscles and tissues. At rest, only about 25 per cent of oxygen is actually used. This increases dramatically during intense exercise, however, to as much as 85 per cent. Figure 3.9 illustrates the a–$\bar{V}O_2$ diff. at rest and during intense exercise.

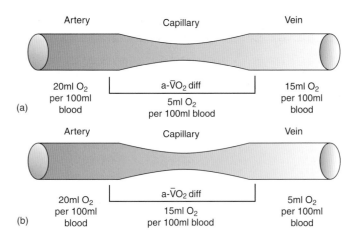

Note: During intense exercise (b) more oxygen has been extracted and used by the working muscles increasing the a-$\bar{V}O_2$ diff up to 15 ml O_2/100 ml blood

Figure 3.9 The arterial–venous oxygen difference a) at rest and b) during intense exercise
Note: During intense exercise (b), more oxygen has been extracted and used by the working muscles, increasing the a–$\bar{V}O_2$ diff up to 15ml O_2/100ml blood

Key terms

Myoglobin: A respiratory pigment that binds to oxygen in the muscle cell. As well as acting as an oxygen store, it transports oxygen to the mitochondria.

Mitochondria: Specialised cells in the body's tissues that use the inspired oxygen to produce energy.

Aerobic respiration: The process of energy creation through the oxidation of food fuels. As well as energy, carbon dioxide and water are produced.

a–$\bar{V}O_2$ diff.: The arterial–venous oxygen difference is the difference in oxygen content of the blood in the arteries and the veins. It is a measure of the amount of oxygen consumed by the muscles.

Minute ventilation

During normal, quiet breathing, we inspire approximately 500ml of air; the same amount is exhaled during the process of expiration. This volume of air inspired or expired is known as tidal volume. Of this 500ml, only about 350ml makes its way to the alveoli. The other 150ml remains in the passageways of the nose, throat and trachea, and is known as dead space. The volume of air which is inspired or expired in one minute is called minute ventilation, and is calculated by multiplying tidal volume by the number of breaths taken per minute. On average, we breathe 12 to 15 times per minute, so our resting minute ventilation can be calculated as follows:

Minute ventilation (VE)
= Tidal volume (TV) × Frequency (breaths/min) (f)
= 500ml   × 15
= 7,500ml/min (7.5L/min)

> **Key term**
>
> **Minute ventilation:** The total volume of air taken into the lungs per minute. It is the product of tidal volume and the number of breaths taken per minute. At rest, this volume should be between 6,000 and 7,500ml per minute.

EXAMINER'S TIP

When asked to calculate minute ventilation, be sure to state the correct units – ml/min or L/min.

Exam-style questions

1   Minute ventilation is defined as the volume of air inspired or expired in one minute. Sketch a graph below to show the minute ventilation of a swimmer completing a 20-minute submaximal swim. Show minute ventilation:

   ● prior to the swim;

   ● during the swim;

   ● for a 10-minute recovery period.

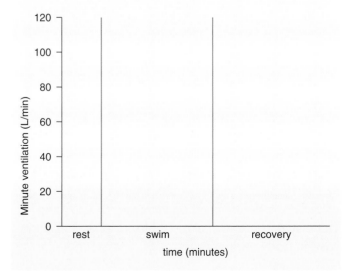

2   Lung volumes can be a good indicator of aerobic fitness. Define minute ventilation and give an average value during maximal exercise.

3   What happens to the inspiratory reserve volume as an athlete moves from rest to exercise?

Ventilation during exercise

During exercise, both the depth and the rate of breathing increase. The tidal volume and the frequency of breathing increase during exercise, causing minute ventilation to rise dramatically – values up to 180L/min have been recorded for trained endurance athletes.

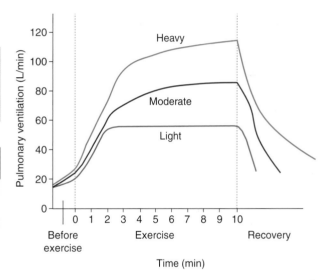

Figure 3.10 Respiratory response to varying intensity of exercise
Note: Remember the anticipatory rise prior to exercise and the continual increase in ventilation during intense exercise

	Tidal volume (TV) × Frequency (breaths/min)	**= Minute ventilation**
Rest	500ml (0.5L) × 15	= 7.5L/min
Maximal work	4,000ml (4.0L) × 50	= 200L/min

Changes in ventilation occur before, during and after exercise, as shown in Figure 3.10. Before exercise starts, there is a slight increase in ventilation; this is called the anticipatory rise and is the result of hormones, such as adrenaline, stimulating the respiratory centre. Once exercise begins, there is a rapid rise in ventilation caused by nervous stimulation. During submaximal exercise, this sudden increase in ventilation begins to slow down and may plateau into what is known as the steady state. This assumes that the energy demands of the muscles are being met by the oxygen made available, and that the body is expelling carbon dioxide effectively. During maximal exercise, however, this steady state does not occur, and ventilation continues to increase until the exercise is finished. This is thought to be due to the stimulation of the respiratory centre by carbon dioxide and lactic acid, and suggests that it is the body's need to expel these metabolites, rather than its desire for oxygen, which determines the pattern of breathing. If exercise intensity continues to increase to a point near the athlete's $\bar{V}O_2$ max. (the maximum amount of oxygen that can be taken in, transported and utilised in one minute), then the amount of oxygen entering the body is not sufficient to meet the demands of the working muscles. Because the athlete is working at maximal levels, s/he is unable to meet the body's requirements and may need to stop exercising or, at the very best, significantly reduce the intensity of the exercise. In this way, oxygen supply can once again meet the demands imposed by the body.

During recovery from exercise, ventilation drops rapidly at first, followed by a slower decrease. The more intense the preceding exercise, the longer the recovery period and the longer ventilation remains above the normal resting level. This is largely due to the removal of by-products of muscle metabolism such as lactic acid.

Key terms

$\bar{V}O_2$ **max. (maximal oxygen uptake):** The maximum volume of oxygen that can be taken in, transported and utilised by the working muscles per minute.

Steady state: The plateau demonstrated in pulmonary ventilation that represents a situation where oxygen demand is being met by oxygen supply.

Activity 10

You are going to carry out an investigation to estimate total lung capacity, using a handheld spirometer.

1. Take a deep breath and exhale.
2. Take another deep breath until you cannot take in any more air.
3. Place your mouth tightly around the spirometer and expel all air possible. (If you bend forwards slightly towards the end of exhalation, you will be able to force all air out of the lower area of the lungs. This represents your vital capacity (VC).)
4. Record your results.
5. Now calculate and record your residual volume:

   Males: Residual volume $= 0.24 \times VC$

   Females: Residual volume $= 0.27 \times VC$
6. If Total lung capacity = Vital capacity + Residual volume, calculate your total lung capacity.

Activity 11

Copy and complete the table below, showing the responses of the respiratory system to exercise. The first factor has been completed for you.

Factor	Increase/decrease	Explanation
Respiratory rate	Increase	The respiratory rate increases directly in proportion to exercise intensity. Initially, there is a rapid rise in the rate of breathing. This is largely due to proprioceptive feedback from skeletal muscles. There then follows a more gradual increase, or sometimes a plateau, in respiratory rate, depending on exercise intensity. This is determined by increases in CO_2 and the lactic acid content of arterial blood, as well as an increase in body temperature.

Expiratory reserve volume		
Oxygen content of arteries		
Minute ventilation		
Tidal volume		
Oxygen consumption		
Max. oxygen consumption		
a–$\overline{V}O_2$ diff.		
Action of respiratory muscles		
Transport of carbon dioxide		

EXAMINER'S TIP

Minute ventilation at rest is typically between 6,000 and 7,500ml per minute, and is dependent on age, sex, body size and levels of fitness.

Respiratory complications

It is likely that many of us either have asthma ourselves or know someone who does. Asthma causes constriction of bronchial airways and inflammation of mucous membranes, which results in shortness of breath and restriction to ventilation. However, asthma should not prevent asthmatics from participating in an exercise programme. In fact, many past Olympic athletes have asthma and have competed at the top level. What is important is that asthmatics follow a few simple rules before and during their exercise sessions.

Medication is obviously vital. The purpose of asthma medicines is to control asthma so that individuals can undertake fully what they wish to do, without allowing their asthma to get in the way, and this includes exercising. There are two main types of asthma medicine:

- bronchodilators, which relieve the symptoms of asthma;
- anti-inflammatories, which help prevent asthma attacks.

Assuming that medication is used correctly, it should enable individuals to participate fully in exercise programmes.

Here are some exercise tips for people who have asthma:

- Do not start exercising if you are experiencing symptoms of your asthma.
- Follow appropriate warm-ups prior to exercise and appropriate cool-downs afterwards.
- Stop exercising if an asthma attack develops.
- In cold or damp conditions, try to exercise indoors.
- Always train with a partner in case an attack develops.

If these tips are followed, asthmatics should benefit fully from their exercise programme, and it may actually help to control their symptoms too.

IN CONTEXT

Peak flow is a measure of how fast you can expel air from your lungs. It measures how wide the respiratory airways are. Average measures for 16-year-olds range between 500 and 600L/min. Asthmatics will often use peak flow to assess the state or impact of their asthma on a particular day. In extreme cases, peak flow may reach levels as low as 70L/min.

Figure 3.11 Peak flow is used by asthmatics to determine the severity of asthma on any particular day

Activity 12

Use a peak flow metre to measure your peak flow, and compare your score to others in your class. What reasons can you suggest for the individual differences in results?

The impact of smoking on the respiratory system

In Chapter 2, we considered the impact of smoking on the transport of oxygen and the role it plays in the development of cardiovascular disease. The case for not smoking due to respiratory complications is twofold:

1   Impaired transport of oxygen in the blood – the high levels of carbon monoxide found in cigarette smoke reduce the amount of oxygen absorbed into the blood from the lungs, and the amount released to the tissues from the blood. This factor alone reduces physical endurance capacities and can reduce $\bar{V}O_2$ max. (maximal oxygen uptake) by up to 10 per cent.

2   Greater airway resistance through the narrowing of the air passages. The act of inhaling cigarette smoke can increase resistance of the airways immediately, by causing swelling of the mucous membranes which line them. Tar contained within cigarettes can also coat the airways and lungs, reducing the elasticity of the alveoli, hampering gaseous exchange and resulting in reduced lung volumes and less oxygen reaching the bloodstream. Pollutants from cigarettes (which contain at least 400 toxic

Figure 3.12 Smoking can lead to shortness of breath and impaired circulation

substances) can irritate the bronchial tubes and lungs, causing increased mucous secretion, phlegm and coughing – a problem that is only exacerbated when exercising.

If you want to maintain a healthy lifestyle and lifelong participation in sport and physical activity, the message is quite clear – DO NOT SMOKE!

IN CONTEXT

People who smoke usually cannot compete with their non-smoking peers. This is because the associated physical effects of smoking, such as a rapid heartbeat, impaired circulation and shortness of breath, impair sports performance. Smoking also affects the body's ability to produce collagen, so common sports injuries, such as tendon and ligament damage, will take longer to heal in smokers than non-smokers.

The adaptive responses of the respiratory system to training

Training signals an improvement in lung function. This is due to the following factors:

1   Small increases in lung volumes:
   ● Tidal volume remains unchanged at rest and during submaximal exercise, but does appear to increase during high-intensity, maximal exercise. This ensures as much oxygen as possible is being taken into the lungs with each breath, and as much carbon dioxide expelled.
   ● Vital capacity also increases slightly, which causes a small decrease in the residual volume.
   These increases in lung volumes result from the increased strength of the respiratory muscles following training.

2   Improved transport of respiratory gases:
   ● Training can signal an increase in the total volume of the blood (primarily due to an increase in blood plasma volume), and an increase in the number of red blood cells (erythrocytes), which leads to an increase in the content of haemoglobin. These changes provide for increased oxygen delivery to the working muscles and improved removal of carbon dioxide.
   ● The increase in blood plasma volume also means that the viscosity of the blood is reduced. Reduced blood viscosity means that

there is less resistance to blood flow, allowing the blood to flow more freely and improving the blood supply to the working muscles.

3   Enhanced gaseous exchange at the alveoli and the tissues:
  ● Capillary density surrounding the alveoli and muscle tissue increases substantially following endurance training, which provides for greater gaseous exchange. This therefore enhances the supply of oxygen to, and the removal of carbon dioxide from, the working muscle.
  ● Endurance athletes also appear to have enhanced blood flow to the lungs (pulmonary blood flow), which, together with an increase in maximal minute ventilation, causes a significant increase in pulmonary diffusion (i.e. gaseous exchange at the alveoli), once again ensuring maximum exchange of oxygen and carbon dioxide.

4   Greater uptake of oxygen by the muscles:
  ● Endurance training improves the ability of skeletal muscle to extract oxygen from the blood. This is largely the result of increased myoglobin and mitochondrial density within the muscle cell, which will cause an improvement in an athlete's maximum oxygen uptake, or $\bar{V}O_2$ max., by about 10–20 per cent.
  ● The enhanced oxygen extraction by skeletal muscle also causes an increase in the arterial–venous oxygen difference (a– $\bar{V}O_2$ diff.), which is a measure of the amount of oxygen actually consumed by the muscles.

IN CONTEXT

Elite rowers, such as Matthew Pinsent and James Cracknell, are some of the fittest athletes around. Their bodies have adapted to cope with the demands of their excessive training regimes. Matthew Pinsent is reported to have a vital capacity of 8.5L, compared to the average male score of 5.5L. Not surprisingly, he is also reported to have one of the highest $\bar{V}O_2$ max. scores ever recorded in the UK, at 8.5L/min.

Figure 3.13 Elite rowers, such as Matthew Pinsent, have some of the greatest aerobic capacities

What you need to know

* Respiration can be divided into external and internal respiration.
* External respiration is the process of getting air into and out of the lungs.
* Inspiration occurs when the respiratory muscles contract, lifting the ribcage upwards and outwards, and lowering the diaphragm. The resultant pressure differential causes air to rush into the lungs.
* Expiration at rest is a passive process, simply a result of the intercostals and diaphragm relaxing. This causes a pressure differential and air is forced out of the lungs.
* Respiration is governed by various levels within the brain. The main regulatory mechanism is performed by chemoreceptors within the aortic arch and carotid arteries. These assess the concentration of carbon dioxide within the blood.

* Oxygen enters the bloodstream at the alveoli, through the process of diffusion.

* Diffusion of gases at the alveoli is facilitated by several structural features of the respiratory system:
  * The respiratory (alveolar-capillary) membrane is very thin, which means that the diffusion distance between the air in the alveoli and the blood is very short.
  * The numerous alveoli create a very large surface area over which diffusion can take place.
  * The alveoli are surrounded by a vast network of capillaries, which further provides a huge surface area for gaseous exchange.
  * The diameter of the capillaries is slightly narrower than the area of a red blood cell, which causes the blood cell to distort, increasing its surface area and ensuring the blood cells travel slowly in single file, maximising oxygen absorption.

* The efficiency of the respiratory system is reduced at altitude and therefore performance in aerobic events may suffer. The reduced atmospheric pressure may be more beneficial to anaerobic or explosive activities, due to the 'thinner air'.

* Gaseous exchange occurs as a result of differences in concentration of oxygen and carbon dioxide round the body.

* The partial pressure of a gas is the individual pressure the gas exerts when in a mixture of gases, and this explains the movement of gases in the body.

* Oxygen is transported round the body by combining with haemoglobin to form oxyhaemoglobin.

* During exercise, oxygen dissociates more easily from haemoglobin due to the increase in body temperature, a reduced pO_2, an increased pCO_2 and a lower blood pH (increased acidity). This is illustrated by a shift to the right in the oxyhaemoglobin dissociation curve, and is known as the Bohr shift.

* During exercise, both the rate (frequency) and depth (tidal volume) of breathing increases in direct proportion to the intensity of the activity.

* The ventilatory response to exercise (including changes from submaximal exercise to maximal exercise) mirrors that of the heart.

* Smoking and asthma can seriously impair respiratory functioning.

* Training improves respiratory and lung function due to:
  * small increases in lung volumes and capacities;
  * improved transport of the respiratory gases;
  * more efficient gaseous exchange at the alveoli and tissues;
  * improved uptake of oxygen by the muscles.

Review questions

1 Trace the path of inspired air, outlining the structures it passes on its journey from the nasal cavity to the alveoli.

2 Identify the muscles used in respiration, at rest and during exercise.

3 Sketch a graph to show what happens to oxygen consumption (VO_2) during an exercise session that gets progressively harder (e.g. the multi-stage fitness test).

4 Outline the reasons why some athletes will undertake a period of altitude training prior to competition. Why might others choose not to?

5 To what extent do you agree with the view that any records set at altitude should not be validated. Justify your argument.

6 Identify and explain four factors that influence the efficiency of gaseous exchange between the lungs and the pulmonary capillaries.

7 Explain the importance of the partial pressure of gases in the respiratory process.

8 How are oxygen and carbon dioxide transported in the body?

9 What is asthma, and what precautions might an individual who has asthma need to take before participating in exercise?

10 What factors influence the respiratory system during exercise?

11 How does the body combat increases in blood acidity resulting from intense exercise?

12 What factors account for the enhanced respiratory functioning that accompanies training?

Since the second half of the twentieth century the status of sport and physical education within society has increased tremendously. This has been linked, in the main, to developing media, commercial and political interest and has resulted in increased pressure and demands being placed on sports performers. While this in turn has led to major improvements in both technological and physiological preparation it has also meant that more recognition has been given to the need to prepare performers psychologically.

It has long been recognised that even if a performer is physically trained to near perfection and supported by the best equipment and technology available, this does not guarantee an excellent performance or victory. Since the early 1960s research has been carried out by sports psychologists in order to help us to:

● understand – learning/behaviour/performance and situations in sport
● explain – learning/behaviour/performance or factors that influence performance/events in a systematic manner
● predict – potential learning/behaviour/events or outcomes/performance
● influence/control – potential learning/ behaviour/performance or events.

When observing sport, commentators and the media often use simplistic terms to explain why certain things happen. Phrases like 'there has been a psychological shift in the game', a performer is 'coping with pressure', a performer has been 'psyched out of the game', a performer has the 'wrong temperament' are all used, along with many others, to explain variations in performance.

Although such phrases are used often without a real understanding of what they mean, they do at least indicate the importance and influence of psychological factors within the context of sport and physical education. During this section of your studies you will begin to gain a clearer understanding of the various strategies that sports psychologists have used to help develop and prepare performers individually or in groups (teams) to cope with the increased pressures of modern sport. It is generally recognised that the traditional approach to sport psychology (the pre-competition 'rousing pep-talk', the 'up and at them' approach) is of very little 'real' long-term value and in some cases could even be considered counterproductive, perhaps leading to poor performance in the short term.

In the same way that an athlete's physical and skills preparation cannot be developed overnight, psychological preparation needs to be developed over a prolonged period of time in order to be effective and retain long-term value. Developing your knowledge of sports psychology should give you a better understanding of the 'causes' and 'effects' of various psychological phenomena which underpin learning and performance in sport.

After reading this section on skill acquisition and sports psychology you will begin to gain a better understanding of:

1 The variety of factors, principles and theories that can affect the learning process during skill development
2 The factors that determine how a performer interprets information and produces skilled movement
3 Strategies that can be employed to develop and refine skill.

Classification of motor skills and abilities

Learning outcomes

By the end of this chapter you should be able to:

- understand the term 'skill';
- understand different skills and explain how they influence performance;
- explain the different classifications of skills; identify specific sporting examples and justify your decisions for placing them on a specific continuum;
- understand the term 'ability' and explain its characteristics;
- explain the difference between 'gross motor abilities' and 'psychomotor abilities';
- identify sporting examples where specific gross motor abilities and psychomotor abilities are required, and justify your decisions;
- outline the relationship between 'skill' and 'ability';
- explain the various types of practice, including part and whole practice, progressive part practice and whole-part-whole practice;
- outline specific types of skills which can be developed most effectively by each practice method, and justify your decisions;
- evaluate the effectiveness of each type of practice in its contribution to skill development.

Nature of skilled performance

The terms 'skill' and 'ability' are frequently used to describe sporting performance, but are their full meanings understood and used in the correct context?

As a sporting performer, you will have developed numerous skills and experienced a variety of practice methods to refine those skills in a sporting situation. If skills are to be maximised, both performer and coach must understand the different nature of skills, the abilities required to execute particular skills, and the different methods of manipulating practice sessions to allow for the effective use of time and the refinement of those skills.

We have learned and developed a wide range of skills which we use daily without consciously thinking about it. For example, writing your name, using a mobile phone to send text messages and using money to pay for goods. All these are skills which have developed through practice over time. The aim of every sports performer is to refine their skills, allowing them to execute these with precision and consistency whenever the situation demands it. This can only be achieved through practice. Your aim by the end of this chapter should be to answer the question: What makes one performer more skilled than another, and how can we recognise high quality skills?

What is a skilled performance?

In discussion with your fellow students you will all have been able to suggest various examples of skilled performances, perhaps identifying similar points to the following:

- A concert pianist may be said to be performing skilfully.
- A ballet dancer's coordination and timing are skilful.
- A perfect pass by a quarterback in American football is skilful.
- A long-range three-point score in basketball is skilful.
- A well-executed off drive in cricket is skilful.
- A gymnast performing a vault in the Olympic Games is skilful.
- A pole-vaulter completing a vault is skilful.
- A potter using a potter's wheel is skilful.

In other words, we can all recognise the outcome or the end product of a skilful performance. However, as students of physical education and sport you need to know:

- how this end product comes about;
- what process underlies the acquisition of skill and control of movement;
- how skill is acquired;
- what factors influence the attainment of skill and how it is retained.

There are no right or wrong ways to learn skills, as every performer is different and will respond accordingly. The skill of the coach or teacher is to recognise individual characteristics and to structure the learning environment to maximise the chance of learning taking place. Think about your own experiences when attempting to learn a new skill; some methods may have worked while others have failed. Why is this?

Using the term 'skill'

You may have noticed in the list of examples given above (or in your own discussions) that the word 'skill' can be used in two slightly different ways. We can use the word when referring to skill as an act or task, such as a rugby player converting a penalty or an athlete hurdling. It can also be used as an indicator of quality of performance, such as a gymnast completing a floor routine, or when comparing the performance of one hockey player to another during a game.

Skill as an act or task

In this context, the word is used to denote an act or a task which has a specific aim or goal; for example, a gymnast performing a vault. Further examples are shown in Figures 4.1, 4.2 and 4.3.

Figure 4.1 Taking a penalty flick in hockey

Figure 4.2 Shooting a free shot after a foul in basketball

Figure 4.3 Serving in tennis

If we were to observe players engaged in any of these examples on a regular basis, and they were achieving a high percentage success rate, we would consider them skilful players. The use of the word in this context refers to a physical movement, action or task that a person is trying to carry out in a technically correct manner, involving some or all of the body. Thus skill can be seen as goal-directed behaviour.

Skill as an indicator of quality of performance

The word in this context is probably a little more ambiguous than skill as an act or task. The word 'well' added to the description of the skill infers a qualitative judgement (by you as the observer) of the skill being made. For example, you might remark on a well-executed off drive during a cricket match. Very often we make judgements by comparing players' performances, looking at players' achievements in the context of the class or school team, or against set criteria. Thus we measure or assess in either relative or absolute terms. However, what we need to understand is what makes it a *well*-performed skill.

> **Key term**
>
> **Qualitative:** An opinion or judgement of an individual, which is not supported by facts or data.

Acquisition of skill

In the phrase 'acquisition of skill', the word 'acquisition' implies that skill is something which you can gain, as opposed to something you already have.

Skill is said to be gained through learning. Skill is said to be learned behaviour! (B. Knapp)

> **Activity 2**
>
> 1 Select two well-known performers from different sports, or watch a video clip of a sporting event. List five words to describe the athletes' performance. Compare lists with other students.
> 2 Consider your own performance compared to the performers you have analysed. What are the differences between you? Are they more 'skilled' than you? Justify your answer.

Definitions and characteristics of skill

You will have a better understanding of the nature of skill if you consider a variety of definitions and see how these have developed. There are numerous definitions of the term 'skill', several of which are outlined below. As you read each one, try to highlight similar characteristics to those you identified in Activity 2 (above).

> Skill is the learned ability to bring about predetermined results with maximum certainty, often with the minimum outlay of time or energy or both. (B. Knapp)

> Skill is an organised, coordinated activity in relation to an object or situation which involves a whole chain of sensory, central and motor mechanisms. (A.T. Welford)

> While the task can be physical or mental, one generally thinks of skill as some type of manipulative efficiency. A skilled movement is one in which a predetermined objective is accomplished with maximum efficiency with a minimum outlay of energy. A skilful movement does not just happen. There must be a conscious effort on the part of the performer in order to execute a skill. (M. Robb)

> **EXAMINER'S TIP**
>
> You will not be expected to remember definitions, but you must be able to explain the terms using relevant examples to support your answer.

Using the definitions set out above, and your own discussions, we can say that the characteristics of skill are:

- *excellent performance* – high quality;
- *goal-directed* – the intention to do it (it is not just luck – there must be a conscious decision and effort);
- *learned* – learning through practice and experience to use the appropriate innate abilities;
- *predetermined* – you have an aim to achieve;
- *consistent* – you are able to execute the action with maximum certainty depending on the environmental conditions;
- *efficient* – there is a minimum outlay of time and energy;
- *aesthetic* – it looks pleasing to the eye, appearing controlled and effective;
- *recognisable* – often the technique can be named and compared either to set criteria or other performers.

The performance of skilled movement involves:

- *sensory mechanisms* – taking in information via the various receptor systems (e.g. senses);
- *central mechanisms* – brain (interpretations and decision making);
- *motor mechanisms* – nerves and muscle systems being used to create movement.

Basically, skills involve the use of the senses to detect and take in information; the brain to interpret the information and make decisions according to what you know about the situation; and the nervous system, together with muscles, to work the various parts of the body in order to carry out the action.

Types of skill

Psychologists have considered different types of skill, trying to differentiate between motor skills and verbal skills, for instance. Examples of three different types of skill are:

1 Intellectual skills or cognitive skills – skills which involve the use of a person's mental powers, for example, problem solving, verbal reasoning (verbal skill). Within a sporting context, this may involve planning strategies and tactics to outwit an opponent, or calculating the split times required to run a race in a certain time.
2 Perceptive skills – interpreting and making sense of information coming in via the senses.

For example, during a basketball match a player will have to analyse their own location and that of other players on court, the flight of the ball, the options available and the rules before making a decision on which skill to attempt.

3 Motor skills – smoothly executing physical movements and responses, for example, the completion of a pass, dribble or shot resulting in a successful basket or defensive play.

> **Key terms**
>
> **Cognitive skill:** Skill which involves thought process and intellectual ability.
> **Perceptual skill:** Skill which involves the detection and interpretation of information from the environment.
> **Motor skill:** Skill which involves physical movement and muscular control.

When National League basketball players are performing a 'skilful' dribble and 'driving' the basket, not only are they showing technically good movements (i.e. showing motor skill), but in carrying out the action the player has also had to make many decisions, including:

- whether to dribble or pass;
- how to dribble;
- position of opposition;
- position of own teammates;
- context of game;
- situation in game (winning or losing);
- time in game (how long to go?);
- whether to score or keep the ball;
- the odds of making the dribble, drive and possible shot.

This obviously involves a whole host of cognitive and perceptual skills. Only after taking into account all the information (cues, signals, stimuli) being received from around them can a basketball player carry out the necessary motor skill successfully. Therefore, from a sporting point of view, when we talk of 'skill', we usually mean a combination of all three areas. Skill is more than just technical excellence. (In your further reading around this topic you will come across the phrase 'perceptual motor skills', or very often just 'motor skills' – the perceptual or cognitive involvement is usually implied.)

Figure 4.4 A basketball player has to master numerous skills

Classification of skills

In order to maximise the opportunity for learning and refining skills, classification systems are often used to group together different types of skills with similar characteristics. This will allow the most appropriate training or practice method to be used. By classifying skills that are involved in sporting activities:

● a teacher or coach is able to generalise across groups of skills and apply major concepts, theories and principles of learning to types of skills;
● a teacher or coach will not necessarily have to consider each specific skill in a unique way;
● a teacher or coach will be able to select the appropriate starting point for a learner;
● the identification of appropriate types of practice conditions (e.g. whole, part, whole, massed or distributed – see page 123, The application of classification to the organisation and determination of practice) will be easier – similar methods can be applied to skills within the same groupings;
● the timing and types of instruction to be given are clarified (e.g. verbal feedback, ongoing or terminal);
● the detection and solving of any problems the learner may be facing is made easier;
● a teacher or coach would probably not use the various classifications in isolation, but would move from one to another, or combine aspects of all of them at the appropriate time.

Classification systems

Several different ways of classifying or grouping skills have been developed to assist in our understanding of motor skills. In order to solve the problem of listing skills under certain headings, which could lead to confusion over where to list skills made up of several different aspects, the use of a continuum was devised. This allows for skills to be analysed and placed between two given extremities, according to how they match the analysis criteria being applied.

Criteria   Criteria

A   B

Many skills have components which may fall into either end of a particular continuum. In such cases, it is advisable to view the skill as a whole movement rather than attempting to identify sub-routines, which can lead to misunderstanding. For example, the entire bowling action of a cricketer should be classified, rather than just the wrist action during the release of the ball.

Key term

Continuum: A continuum is an imaginary line between two extremes.

EXAMINER'S TIP

When classifying a skill, always use a specific example (e.g. do not simply say 'basketball' – name the actual skill, such as the 'lay-up shot').

Exam-style question

1　A continuum is used to classify skills. The continuity continuum contains three elements — discrete, serial and continuous — whilst the environmental continuum contains open and closed skills.

Use practical examples to explain each of these elements.

(5 marks)

The muscular involvement (gross–fine) classification

This classification is based on the degree of bodily involvement, or the precision of movement needed to execute the skill.

Activity 3

Using the gross–fine classification (see Table 4.1), place darts, spin bowling and badminton along a continuum, according to how they match the criteria being applied.

Gross　　　　　　　　　Fine

As you can see from Table 4.1 below, some skills do not fall easily into specific categories; nor can they be listed exclusively under exact headings. Darts, spin bowling and serving in a game of badminton all involve wrist and finger speed and dexterity, along with aiming accuracy, which suggests that they should be taught as a fine skill. In order for these small movements to be made, however, larger movements – particularly in spin bowling – have also had to take place, which suggests that they should be taught as a gross skill.

EXAMINER'S TIP

When classifying a skill, always justify your answer. Do not simply state where you think the skill should be placed on a continuum.

Table 4.1 Gross–fine skill classification

Gross skills	Fine skills
Involve large muscle movements	Involve small muscle movements
Involve large muscle groups	Involve small muscle groups
Major bodily movement skills associated with: ● strength ● endurance ● power	Small bodily movement skills associated with: ● speed ● efficiency ● accuracy
For example, walking, kicking a football, jumping, running	For example, shooting, throwing a dart, a snooker shot, release of the fingers in archery
? ← Darts → ?	
? ← Spin bowling → ?	
? ← Badminton → ?	

The environmental influence (open–closed) classification

This classification is based on the stability of the environment or situation in which the skill is being performed. A performer may only have to focus on their own technique if they are involved in an event in which they are competing individually and the conditions remain virtually the same on each occasion (e.g. a javelin thrower). However, team players may have to take into account the positions of others, the flight path of a ball and the playing surface before adapting and executing an existing skill.

Table 4.2 The open–closed continuum

Closed skills	Open skills
Not affected by the environment	Very much affected by the unstable, changing environment
Stable, fixed environment (space/time) predictable	Externally paced environment
Internally/self paced predominantly habitual stereotyped movements (e.g. headstand in gymnastics/weightlifting)	Predominantly perceptual movement patterns require adjustment (adaptation)
	Very often rapid adjustments, variations of skill needed (e.g. passing/receiving in netball or basketball/ tackling in rugby)

Activity 4

Draw an open–closed continuum and place the following skills on it:
- free shot in basketball;
- serve in tennis;
- serve in badminton;
- dribbling in a game of football;
- rugby tackle;
- running a 1,500m race;
- sailing;
- backhand defensive shot in table tennis;
- judo.

The continuity (discrete–serial–continuous) classification

This classification is made on the basis of the relationship between sub-routines, and how clearly defined the beginning and end of the skill are to observers.

Figure 4.5 The javelin throw is a closed skill

Figure 4.6 The rugby tackle is an open skill

Table 4.3 The discrete–serial–continuous continuum

Discrete skills	Serial skills	Continuous skills
Criteria	Criteria	Criteria
Well-defined beginning and end	A number of discrete skills put together to make a sequence or series	Poorly defined beginning and end
Usually brief in nature – a single specific skill	Order in which the distinct elements are put together is very important	Activity continues for an unspecified time (ongoing)
If skill is repeated, have to start at beginning (e.g. a basketball free throw/kicking a ball/hitting, catching/diving/vaulting)	Each movement is both stimulus and response (e.g. gymnastic routine/triple jump/high jump)	End of one movement is beginning of next repetition (e.g. swimming/running/cycling)

Figure 4.7 A cricket shot is a discrete skill

Figure 4.8 A triple jump is a serial skill

Figure 4.9 Cycling is a continuous skill

Activity 5

Using the information in Table 4.3, decide where the following activities fit on the continuum, making sure you can justify your decision in each case:

● hockey pass;
● serve in tennis;
● throw-in in football;
● long jump;
● throwing a javelin;
● penalty flick in hockey;
● dance routine;
● skiing;
● aerobics;
● 1,500m run;
● trampoline routine;
● penalty corner routine in hockey.

The pacing (externally paced–self-paced) classification

This classification is based on the degree of control the performer has over the movement or skill being carried out (i.e. not governed by the actions of others). It refers to the amount of control for both the timing and the speed of the movement. This classification is synonymous with the open and closed classification.

Table 4.4 The pacing continuum

Self-paced/internally paced skills	Externally paced skills
Performer controls the rate at which the activity is carried out	Action is determined by external sources
Performer decides when to initiate movement	
Involves pro-action	Involves the performer in reaction
More closed skill (e.g. shot put/ forward roll)	More open skill (e.g. white-water canoeing/receiving a serve in tennis)

Figure 4.10 Shot put is a self-paced skill

Figure 4.11 White-water rafting is an externally paced skill

The difficulty (simple–complex) classification

This classification is based on the complexity of the movement, depending on the amount of information to process, the time available to make a decision, the number of sub-routines and the use of feedback during performance.

Figure 4.12 Swimming is a simple skill

Table 4.5 The simple–complex continuum

Simple skills	Complex skills
Not affected by the environment	Very much affected by the unstable, changing environment
Few sub-routines	Numerous sub-routines which must be performed in the correct sequence and at the right time
Little information to process	Large amount of information to process
Time to evaluate the situation	Short amount of time to evaluate the situation
Feedback is not essential	Feedback aids the performance
(e.g. swimming/sprinting)	(e.g. gymnastic routine/ tennis serve)

Figure 4.13 A gymnastic routine is a complex skill

The organisation (low–high) classification

This classification is based on the relationship between the sub-routines of the specific skill.

Table 4.6 Low and high organisation skills

Low organisation skills	High organisation skills
Sub-routines can be identified easily and isolated from the overall movement	Sub-routines are difficult to identify and isolate from the overall movement
Sub-routines can be practised and developed to improve overall performance (see whole-part-whole learning, below)	Sub-routines have to be practised as part of the whole movement
(e.g. swimming/ trampoline routine)	(e.g. sprint start/golf swing/somersaults)

Activity 6

Analyse each of the skills listed below, with reference to their complexity and organisation:

- hockey penalty flick;
- rugby set play;
- swimming front crawl;
- badminton serve;
- basketball free throw;
- cricket shot;
- sprint start;
- high jump;
- cycling race;
- gymnastic floor routine.

Exam-style question

1 Performers aim to execute skilled movements.

(a) What are the characteristics of a skilled performance?

(b) Explain the difference between the terms 'skill' and 'ability' and outline the relationship between them.

(5 marks)

Application of classification to the organisation of practice

When deciding how best to develop particular skills, the classification systems discussed above are a good starting point to identify the common characteristics which lend themselves to the most appropriate method of presentation. This will depend on the nature of the skill, its complexity, the relationship of the sub-routines, the experience of the performer and the practice environment, which should replicate the competitive environment as closely as possible.

Therefore, when considering the practice, a coach/teacher would carry out a task analysis and ask themselves:

- Is it a simple or complex task?
- Is it an organised or unorganised task?
- What is the classification?
- Is transfer possible?

A knowledge of task complexity and task organisation will help the coach/teacher to decide if a skill is best taught in the 'whole' or 'part' method.

IN CONTEXT

When devising the most suitable method to develop skill, the coach must always aim to improve performance and maintain motivation. For example, if you are being taught a new skill (e.g. a somersault on the trampoline), you must feel safe and experience success initially. If not, you may become demotivated and give up.

Complex or simple tasks

When deciding on the degree of complexity of a skill or task, a teacher/coach will consider the difficulties it could present to the beginner. These difficulties are generally associated with the amount of information the performer has to cope with when trying to complete the skill or task (cognitive involvement).

Complex tasks have a high degree of cognitive involvement and require a great deal of 'attention' to the skill. Simple tasks have a low level of cognitive involvement and require a lower level of attention. By being aware of the information-processing and memory demands placed on a learner, a teacher/coach can try to structure practices in order to reduce the complexity of skills.

One way of achieving this is for the teacher/coach to break down the main skill or task into various parts, reducing the amount of information (cognitive involvement) the performer has to cope with. As the performer moves through the various stages of learning (see Chapter 5), the amount of information they have to deal with can be increased.

Organisation of a skill/task

Having suggested that complex skills can be broken down into their constituent parts to simplify them, some skills/tasks are, by their very nature, difficult to break down into sub-routines and therefore have to be taught as a 'whole' movement. Skills or tasks that are difficult to break down are said to be highly organised: there is a very strong relationship between the components of the skill.

If a skill/task is said to be low in organisation, this means that it can be broken down easily into sub-routines. These sub-routines can be practised in isolation, as they are relatively independent of each other, and then joined together in various ways to make up the 'whole' skill.

- Some skills can be high in complexity and low in organisation (e.g. gym/trampoline sequence).
- Some skills can be low in complexity and high in organisation (e.g. simple jumping, throwing, batting or hitting).

Whole or part method of practice

The whole method of learning is when the activity or skill is presented in total and practised as a full/entire skilled movement or activity.

The part method of learning is when the activity or skill is broken down into its various components or sub-routines, and each sub-routine is practised individually.

Additional variations have been developed whereby whole-part, part-whole and progressive part methods have been used. Whether it is more effective to teach a skill as a whole or to break it down into its various sub-routines depends very much on the answers to several questions:

1 Can the skill/task be broken down into its sub-routines without destroying or changing it beyond all recognition?
2 What is the degree of transfer from practising the parts (sub-routines) back to the main skill or activity?
3 What is the performer's level of experience or stage of learning?

Whole approach

It is argued that if a whole approach is used, a learner is able to develop their kinaesthetic awareness, or total feel for the activity. The learner is usually given a demonstration or explanation of what is required, builds up a cognitive picture and then becomes acquainted through practice with the total skill. They are then able to positively transfer the actions/skills more readily to the competitive or 'real' situation. By being able to link the essential spatial and temporal elements of the skill, the activity/skill quickly becomes meaningful to the performer.

This approach is seen as a more effective use of time when skills have:

- low levels of complexity;
- high levels of organisation;
- rapid movement patterns (discrete or ballistic in nature).

Although it might be possible to break down the parts, they are usually very much interrelated, so breaking the skill down would change it out of all recognition – with possible negative effects on transfer (e.g. hitting a soft ball).

When a skill is complex, highly organised and thus difficult to break down, an easier way to present it to beginners often has to be found. Simplifying the activity/task enables the performer to experience the whole activity, but with less information and decision making to deal with. Equipment is very often made lighter or bigger/smaller, and less technical rules are imposed, or fewer physical demands and dangers (e.g. uni-hoc, mini hockey, short tennis).

In general, this method is better with:

- experienced performers;
- motivated performers.

Figure 4.14 The long jump can be taught using the whole method

Part approach

This approach is seen as a more effective use of time when skills have:

- high levels of complexity;
- low levels of organisation;
- elements of danger.

Skills which are very complex, but low in organisation, lend themselves to being practised and learned more effectively by the part method. An additional consideration, again, is how interrelated or independent the various sub-routines are. Just because sub-routines are easily separated does not mean that they have to be practised by themselves. The part method, while allowing teachers and coaches to work on areas of the skill that a beginner finds difficult, also tends to be more time-consuming.

Activities such as front crawl in swimming, which are not too complex, and low in organisation, lend themselves to being taught by the part method. The arm action, leg action, breathing pattern and body position can all be analysed and taught individually. While each can be (and usually is) practised independently, allowing the performer to experience success and thus gain confidence, it is important that the performer is able to practise synchronising the various sub-routines. If the beginner does not experience the whole stroke, there is a possibility that the kinaesthetic feel for the entire action could be lost (e.g. the timing of breathing in coordination with the arm action). In breaststroke, where the kick, glide and pull have to be synchronised exactly, this is even more important.

When teaching the skills of passing in major team games, such as football, rugby and hockey, it is essential that they are not taught in isolation. The beginner needs time for the interrelated units or sub-routines to be practised together so that they can make the natural link between the parts. Therefore, this becomes a more progressive part method, with combinations of the whole.

In general, this method is better with:

- inexperienced performers;
- performers with a limited attention span or low motivation.

Figure 4.15 Swimming can be taught using the part method

The progressive part method

The progressive part method involves the learner being taught complex skills by gradually linking one part of the skill to another. This approach is seen as a more effective use of time when skills are:

- complex;
- serial;
- potentially dangerous.

Once one stage has been mastered, the next can be added. For example, a coach trying to develop a gymnast's routine would often follow a progressive part method. All the relatively complex but independent parts of the routine (e.g. handstand, cartwheel, handspring, somersault) are learned and practised in isolation, then joined together in small units so that the gymnast can experience and learn how to fluently link (sequence) the individual skills. These blocks

of skills are then linked again, until the various parts of the action have been built up into the whole routine (the chain is completed).

This method is generally effective when:

- performers are novices (giving them a sense of achievement);
- performers have limited attention span.

However, this method can be time-consuming, and the performer may become overly concerned with mastering one particular sub-routine rather than viewing the skill in its overall context.

Whole–part–whole method

A variation on the whole and the part methods is the whole-part-whole practice. The teacher/coach introduces the complete skill, highlighting the important elements. The performer then attempts to carry out the skill. As a result of any problems or faults observed, the teacher breaks down the whole skill into various sub-routines to allow the learner to practise appropriate areas of difficulty.

Figure 4.17 A high jumper could use the whole-part-whole method

Figure 4.16 A gymnast completing a floor routine would use the progressive part method

The isolation of the difficult elements may differ for individuals. Once the teacher is satisfied that the problem areas have been mastered, the parts are integrated back into the whole skill. For example, a high jumper may be experiencing a problem with their lay-out position while passing over the bar. The coach would isolate this aspect of the skill and develop a particular practice to rectify the fault; then the athlete would attempt to incorporate the new lay-out position into the full jumping technique.

Teaching by any specific method is not guaranteed to work and the best teachers and coaches are generally flexible, using various combinations of the different methods at different times. Many teachers begin an activity by allowing the beginner to experience the sequencing of the whole movement. They will then analyse strengths and weaknesses, enabling them to develop a part method to deal with any problem areas. Then a progressive part process may develop, where chunks or units of actions are practised together in a simplified task or small-sided game. The performer is then allowed to return to the whole movement. Small problem areas may continue to be practised in isolation in order to refine technique. Complete adherence to one or other method is not advisable or useful.

Table 4.7 Summary of methods of practice

Whole method	Part method	Progressive part method
<ul><li>Low level of complexity/simple task</li><li>High levels of organisation</li><li>Interrelated sub-routines</li><li>Discrete skills</li><li>Short duration/rapid ballistic</li><li>Lacks meaning in parts</li><li>Allows coordination of important spatial/temporal components</li></ul>	<ul><li>High levels of complexity</li><li>Low levels of organisation</li><li>Independent sub-routines</li><li>Serial tasks</li><li>Slow tasks</li><li>Lengthy or long duration</li><li>Dangerous skills</li></ul>	<ul><li>Complex task</li><li>Helps 'chaining' of complex skills learned independently</li><li>Allows for attention demands to be limited</li><li>Allows for coordination of spatial/temporal components to be experienced</li><li>Helps with transfer to whole</li></ul>
	Performer is:	
<ul><li>experienced;</li><li>someone with high levels of attention;</li><li>in the later stages of learning;</li><li>older;</li><li>highly motivated;</li><li>using distributed practice.</li></ul>	<ul><li>a beginner;</li><li>someone with a limited attention span;</li><li>in the early stages of learning;</li><li>having problems with a specific aspect of skill;</li><li>someone with limited motivation;</li><li>using massed practice.</li></ul>	

Table 4.8 Advantages of whole and part method

Whole method	Part method
<ul><li>Wastes no time in assembling parts</li><li>Useful for quick, discrete skills where a single complete action is required</li><li>Better for time-synchronised tasks if the learner can cope with the level of the skill (e.g. swimming stroke)</li><li>The learner can appreciate the end product</li><li>The movement retains a feeling of flow/kinaesthetic sense</li><li>The movement can be more easily understood (the relationship between sub-routines)</li><li>The learner can develop their own schema/motor programme through trial-and-error learning</li><li>Transfer from practice to real situations is likely to be positive</li><li>Good for low organisational tasks which can be broken down easily</li></ul>	<ul><li>Allows serial tasks to be broken down and learned in components (e.g. gymnastic movement)</li><li>Reduces the demand on the learner when attempting complex skills</li><li>Allows confidence and understanding to grow quickly or be built up gradually with more complex skills</li><li>Helps to provide motivation to continue if progress can be seen to be being made</li><li>Especially important with skills which can be seen as potentially dangerous (e.g. some gymnastic skills)</li><li>Can reduce fatigue in physically demanding skills</li><li>Allows the teacher to focus on a particular element and remedy any specific problems</li><li>Provides stages of success</li><li>Good for low organisational tasks which can be broken down easily</li></ul>

Table 4.9 Disadvantages of whole and part method

Whole method	Part method
<ul><li>Ineffective with complex tasks</li><li>Not appropriate in tasks with an element of danger</li><li>Not always appropriate if group/performer has very little experience</li><li>May overwhelm a performer and produce little success at first</li><li>Could lead to learner losing confidence</li></ul>	<ul><li>Transfer from part to whole may be ineffective</li><li>Highly organised skills are difficult to break down into parts</li><li>Loss of awareness of end product</li><li>Loss of continuity/feel of flow</li><li>Loss of kinaesthetic sense</li><li>Can have a demotivating effect when not doing full movement</li><li>Can be time-consuming</li></ul>

Activity 7

Explain how you would introduce the skills listed below to a group of inexperienced performers, justifying your answer in each case:

- sprint start;
- basketball lay-up;
- triple jump;
- netball shot;
- tennis serve;
- cricket bowling action;
- rugby tackle;
- hockey dribble;
- gymnastic vault;
- volleyball spike/smash;
- golf shot;
- paddling a kayak.

Exam-style question

1 Discuss the advantages and disadvantages of using the whole and part methods of practice when developing a sports skill.

(10 marks)

Classification of abilities relating to movement skills

Using the term 'ability'

It is important at this stage to consider another term which is very often used synonymously with the word 'skill', and is frequently used in definitions of skilled behaviour: *ability*.

In your discussions of what constitutes skill, the term 'ability' may well have been used in the wrong context. In a variety of sports, players from abroad are commonly referred to as having higher levels of ability than our 'home' players, when what we mean is that their skills in terms of technique are of a higher quality. It is the word 'ability' which is being used in the wrong context here. We tend to talk of players having 'lots of ability', when what we mean is that they have developed high levels of skill.

Definitions and characteristics of ability

It is important to understand the differences between skill and ability. Below are three definitions of ability:

> An inherited, relatively enduring trait that underlies or supports various kinds of motor and cognitive activities or skills. Abilities are thought of as being largely genetically determined. (R. Schmidt)

> Motor abilities are relatively enduring traits which are generally stable qualities or factors that help a person carry out a particular act. (E. Fleishman)

> Motor abilities are innate inherited traits that determine an individual's coordination, balance, agility and speed of reactions. (R. Arnot and C. Gaines)

We can therefore identify particular characteristics of abilities. Abilities are:

- stable and enduring capacities or qualities;
- genetic/innate, inherited traits;
- crucial to underpinning skills – abilities combine to allow specific skills to be performed.

A person trying to perform a sporting activity will learn to use these underlying innate qualities or characteristics in an organised way in order to carry out coordinated movement. It is probably true to say that your innate level of ability will be a major determining factor in your sporting success. For example, if you possess speed and leg power you may be suited to the long jump, but might lack the required slow-twitch fibres and aerobic capacity to excel at endurance-based events.

Types of abilities

Numerous attempts have been made to classify abilities. One of the most common is that proposed by E. Fleishmann, who subdivided abilities into two categories:

- gross motor abilities (physical proficiency abilities) – which involve movement and are often linked to fitness;
- psychomotor abilities (perceptual motor abilities) – which involve information processing and implementing the selected movement.

Psychomotor abilities

These include:

1 *limb coordination* – the ability to coordinate the movement of a number of limbs simultaneously;
2 control precision – the ability to make highly controlled and precise muscular adjustments where large muscle groups are involved;
3 *response orientation* – the ability to select rapidly where a response should be made, as in a choice reaction time situation (see Chapter 6);
4 *reaction time* – the ability to respond rapidly to a stimulus when it appears;
5 *speed of arm movement* – the ability to make a gross, rapid arm movement;
6 *rate control* – the ability to change speed and direction of response with precise timing, as when following a continuously moving target;
7 *manual dexterity* – the ability to make skilful, well-directed arm/hand movements, when manipulating objects under speed conditions;
8 *finger dexterity* – the ability to perform skilful, controlled manipulations of tiny objects, primarily involving the fingers;
9 *arm/hand steadiness* – the ability to make precise arm/hand-positioning movements where strength and speed are minimally involved;
10 *wrist/finger speed* – the ability to move the wrist and fingers rapidly, as in a tapping task;
11 *aiming* – the ability to aim precisely at a small object in space.

> **Key term**
>
> **Gross motor ability:** This usually involves movement and is related to fitness.

> **Key term**
>
> **Psychomotor ability:** This usually involves the processing of information and the formation of a decision which is executed as a skill.

Gross motor abilities

These include:

1 *static strength* – maximum force exerted against an external object;
2 *dynamic strength* – muscular endurance in exerting force repeatedly (e.g. pull-ups);
3 *explosive strength* – the ability to mobilise energy effectively for bursts of muscular effort (e.g. high jump);
4 *trunk strength* – strength of the trunk muscles;
5 *extent flexibility* – the ability to flex or stretch the trunk and back muscles;
6 *dynamic flexibility* – the ability to make repeated, rapid, trunk-flexing movements, as in a series of stand and touch toes, stretch and touch toes;
7 *gross body coordination* – the ability to coordinate the action of several parts of the body while it is in motion;
8 *gross body equilibrium* – the ability to maintain balance without visual cues;
9 *stamina* – the capacity to sustain maximum effort requiring cardiovascular exertion (e.g. a long-distance run).

> **EXAMINER'S TIP**
>
> When asked to outline the abilities required for a specific skill, always justify why they are needed.

Ability is task–specific

Certain skills may use different sets of abilities, or they may use the same abilities put together in a different order. Abilities are not necessarily linked or related; for example, a person having high levels of trunk strength may not have high levels of explosive strength. If a person is good at throwing a cricket ball, there is no guarantee that they will be good at throwing a basketball or a javelin. In other words, the fact that a person does not have the level of abilities necessary to succeed at one activity does not mean that they do not have the potential to succeed in another activity, requiring slightly different abilities or levels. Performers learn to combine and use abilities in specific situations and for carrying out specific skills. For example, high jumpers need high levels of explosive strength.

Activity 8

Using the lists of abilities set out above, make a list of the abilities required for the following activities:
- badminton;
- hockey;
- gymnastics;
- table tennis;
- weightlifting;
- swimming;
- high jump.

Compare lists with a partner and try to decide on the ability level needed in order to excel in each activity:
- high level;
- reasonable level;
- basic level.

It is important to understand that all individuals possess all the abilities identified above, but we do not possess them at equal, or even similar levels. If a person does not possess the appropriate levels of specific abilities needed for a particular sport, then the odds against them making it to the top in that sport may be high. But this does not mean that such a person has to give up altogether. Practically no one is born with a package of superior abilities large enough to make for an overall athletic ability. Although researchers have tried to identify the possibilities of an 'all-round, general athletic ability', results have tended to support the view that specific skills require specific abilities. However, while we are born with certain levels of abilities, these can be trained and improved in specific situations.

While there is a certain degree of overlap between the requirements of different activities (e.g. strength, coordination and speed), when you analysed the level and type of abilities required you will have seen that they became much more specific to the sport being considered (e.g. different types of strength). Dynamic strength is used in weightlifting, but explosive strength is employed in the high jump.

The implications for teaching and coaching

1   We have to ensure that we do not assume from the above that two people cannot achieve similar standards of performance in a physical activity because of different levels of genetically determined abilities. If one person (possibly with lower levels of specific abilities) is given the opportunity at an early age to use their abilities (e.g. parents take them to the local sports club) and they are prepared to work hard, learning to use their abilities in an appropriate manner, they could achieve a level of proficiency similar to a person who has not had the opportunity or is unwilling to develop innate abilities to higher levels.

2   By analysing the types of abilities needed for specific sports, teachers and coaches could ensure that their students experienced the types of practice necessary for these abilities to be developed more fully. Since balance is an essential ability, required for the successful completion of a wide variety of complex or difficult skills, it would appear relevant for a PE programme in infant and junior schools to provide the opportunity for children to develop their balance ability in a variety of situations.

3   Teachers and coaches should ensure that children who show a high inherited potential for sports are not disadvantaged from an early age as a possible result of their personality and social environment. Some young children appear to display natural athletic tendencies, often as a result of being bigger and stronger early on. This can result in early success, greater motivation, higher teacher expectations and further development. However, without early success, even children with higher levels of innate ability will avoid continued participation in sport, thus building up what has been termed a skill deficit. This has obvious sociocultural implications for a child's future interest in sport.

4   The role of ability identification as a predictor of potential achievement in learners has to be considered carefully. Think of the implications, both good and bad, if we were able to measure a beginner's abilities and then channel them into the appropriate sport. Prediction studies have shown that abilities which are important at the early stages of learning (cognitive phase) are not necessarily the same as those which are important at more advanced stages of learning (autonomous phase).

5   The ability to take in information and make sense of it, in other words, perceptual ability – involving cue selection, concentration and attention, and vision spatial orientation – is more important at the early stages of learning than later, when learning is replaced more by kinaesthesia.

What you need to know

* Skills are learned behaviour and are refined through practice.
* Skills are consistent, appear effortless, involve decision making and have a predetermined objective.
* Skills can be cognitive (thinking), perceptual (interpreting and analysing) and motor (movement). Sports skills are often referred to as psychomotor skills.
* Classification systems consider the common characteristics of skills.
* A continuum is a more effective tool in classifying skills.
* Abilities are innate, enduring qualities or capacities.
* Abilities are task-specific. Specific skills need different abilities.

* Abilities underpin skill development.

* Gross motor abilities involve movement and are linked to fitness.

* Psychomotor abilities involve processing information and executing the movement.

* When deciding on whole or part practice, the complexity and organisation of a skill/task needs to be analysed in relation to the individual needs of the learner and the situation.

* Whole practice involves experiencing the entire skill.

* Part practice involves developing one or more parts of the skill in isolation.

* Progressive part and whole-part-whole practice involve manipulating the sub-routines to address weaknesses before attempting the whole skill.

Review questions

1 What are motor skills and perceptual skills?

2 What are cognitive skills?

3 What are complex skills and simple skills?

4 What is an ability?

   1   What is a psychomotor ability?

   2   What is a gross motor ability?

5 Explain the relationship between skill and ability.

6 Identify three gross motor abilities required for badminton. Justify your answers.

7 Identify three perceptual abilities required for volleyball. Justify your answers.

8 What is meant by classification of skills?

9 Why do we classify skills?

10 What is a continuum and why is it used?

11 Differentiate between gross and fine skills. Give examples.

12 What are discrete, continuous and serial skills? Give examples.

13 What are self-paced and externally paced skills? Give examples.

14 What are high and low cognitive skills? Give examples.

15 What are open and closed skills? Give examples.

16 What is the relationship between classification of skill and methods of practice?

17 What is the purpose of a coach/teacher carrying out a task analysis?

18 Select a specific skill/technique and carry out an in-depth task analysis.

19 Explain the term 'whole approach'.

20 Why might the whole-part-whole approach be advantageous to a long jumper in the associative phase of learning?

21 Outline when use of the part approach method of presentation would be advisable and beneficial in terms of the performer and the task.

22 Suggest two advantages of the whole approach method of presentation.

23 Outline when use of the whole approach method of presentation would be advisable and beneficial in terms of the performer and the task.

24 Suggest two advantages of using the progressive part approach.

25 Why should a coach be flexible in their method of presentation?

CHAPTER 5

Development of motor skills and the use of different practice methods

Learning outcomes

By the end of this chapter you should be able to:

- explain the terms 'learning' and 'performance';
- outline the stages and characteristics of the cognitive, associative and autonomous stages of learning;
- understand the term 'guidance' and explain the advantages and disadvantages of each method;
- identify the most appropriate type of feedback and guidance for each stage of learning;
- understand the term 'plateau'; identify possible causes of plateaus and strategies to overcome their occurrence;
- explain the terms 'massed practice', 'distributed practice', 'fixed practice' and 'varied practice';
- identify situations where each type of practice would maximise the development of skilled movement;
- explain the term 'mental rehearsal' and discuss how it can be used effectively;
- compare the effectiveness of mental practice and physical practice.

CHAPTER INTRODUCTION

All human beings have tremendous capabilities for learning. As a student of physical education and sport, it is not enough simply to recognise that learning has or has not taken place (the end result or outcome); you should have a more in-depth understanding of the theories and principles associated with the underlying learning process and be able to apply this understanding to the practical learning situation.

It would be very convenient to have a list of absolute truths about the learning and teaching of specific motor skills related to every possible sports performance. However, your own experiences should help you realise that there are no conclusive statements and guarantees that learning will take place.

Learning and performance

Definitions of learning

As we discussed in Chapter 4, implicit in the understanding of the term 'skill' is the notion that learning has taken place, that skill is learned behaviour. Becoming skilful involves a person's performance changing in line with certain criteria and characteristics associated with skill.

It is generally accepted that for learning to have taken place there has to be a recognisable change in behaviour, and that this change must be permanent. Thus, the performance improves over time as a result of practice and/or experience becoming more consistent in terms of its:

- accuracy;
- efficiency;
- adaptability.

Learning has been defined as:

> the more or less permanent change in behaviour that is reflected in a change in performance. (B. Knapp)

> a change in the capability of the individual to perform a skill that must be inferred from a relatively permanent improvement in performance as a result of practice or experience. (R. Magill)

> a relatively permanent change in behaviour due to past experience. (D. Coon)

> a set of processes associated with practice or experience leading to relatively permanent changes in the capability of skilled performance. (R. Schmidt)

Activity 1

In discussion with other students in your group, consider the four definitions provided here and select the main characteristics of these.

In your discussion of the four definitions you should have concluded, and psychologists generally agree, that:

- learning is *not* a 'one-off' lucky effort/performance;
- learning is *relatively* permanent (this does not mean, however, that the skill is performed 100 per cent correctly each time; it does mean that

a learner's capability of performing a particular skill consistently has increased);
- learning is due to past experience and/or practice.

How do we judge if a skill has been learned?

There are various methods of assessing a performance in order that more accurate inferences can be made about learning. The general methodology would be to:

- observe – behaviour/performance;
- measure/test – behaviour/performance;
- evaluate – behaviour/performance;
- translate – the information gained into meaningful conclusions;
- infer – that learning has or has not taken place.

Reasons for evaluating if learning has occurred

These include the following:

- To give the learner/performer accurate/meaningful feedback.
- To assess whether goals/targets have been achieved.
- To assess the effectiveness of teaching/coaching strategies.
- To record progress/achievement over time.
- To assess performance potential.
- To carry out match/performance statistical analysis (e.g. accuracy, technique, timing, errors, amount, frequency).

Evaluations can be:

- formative (ongoing – helps to provide feedback);
- summative (provides a summary over time).

IN DEPTH: Types of learning

As you will have realised in your earlier discussions about types of skill, in order to carry out motor skills at the highest levels, more than just pure physical movement is involved. There is usually some degree of cognitive and perceptual involvement, depending on the skill being carried out. In the same way that motor skills involve more than purely the physical movement of muscles, limbs, and so on, learning can occur in more than just a physical way. There have been many different approaches to the analysis of what form learning can take in relation to the types of skills or situations being experienced.

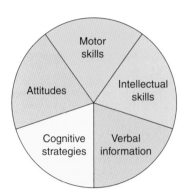

Figure 5.1 The categories of learning

Robert Gagné (1977) suggested that there are five main categories of human performance which may be developed by learning, and that any learned capability, whatever it is called (history, geography, physics, football, swimming, etc.), has characteristics from one or more of these categories:

1 Intellectual skills – Dealing with the environment in a symbolic way (e.g. reading, writing mathematical symbols).
2 Verbal information – Learning to state or tell ideas or information by using oral, written or body language (i.e. communication).
3 Cognitive strategies – Learning to manage one's own learning (i.e. use of memory, thinking, problem solving and analysis).
4 Attitudes – Acquiring mental states which influence choices of personal actions (e.g. choosing badminton rather than hockey as a preferred recreation).

5 Motor skills – Learning to execute movement in a number of organised ways, either as single skills or actions (e.g. catching a ball) or as more comprehensive activities (e.g. playing netball or basketball).

A more simplistic view of learning experienced within physical education and sport can be seen in Table 5.1. When asked to comment on the types of learning experienced within sport and PE, you would need to refer to cognitive, affective and effective.

In dealing with motor learning, it is often difficult to separate the various aspects, as all these will contribute in some way, at some time, to the level of skill. It is therefore necessary to develop all areas in order to make the learning process more meaningful. For example, a sensitive teacher or coach might find that in order to develop a student's high-jumping technique (effective learning), they might have to help the student understand the basic biomechanics of the movement and link this to their ability to analyse their own movement (cognitive learning). In addition, positive attitudes may be needed with regard to specific physical training and psychological aspects, such as confidence and focusing, and holding the moral belief that the use of drugs is cheating (affective learning).

The nature of performance

While 'learning' is said to be a permanent change in behaviour, as a sports performer it is not always possible to execute each skill correctly every time. This may be due to any number of factors, including over-arousal, interference from opponents, injury and distractions from the crowd, to name just a few. The aim will be to complete the movement as skilfully as possible, but as you will no doubt have

Table 5.1 The three types of learning

Cognitive	Affective	Effective
To know	To feel	To do
Mental processes, such as: ● tactical awareness; ● strategies; ● problem solving.	Attitudes and values, such as: ● ethics; ● sportsmanship.	Motor learning, such as: ● physical; ● catching; ● passing.
(inclusive of Gagné's categories 1, 2, 3)	(Gagné's category 4)	(Gagné's category 5)

experienced yourself, this is not always possible. The term associated with the execution of a skill at any given time is 'performance'.

Stages of motor skill learning

Just as there are different types of learning associated with the learning of motor skills, so there are different stages or phases of the learning process. In order to gain a clearer understanding of the learning process, there have been many attempts to identify the various phases, or stages, that students go through when learning motor skills. It has been agreed that whatever the number and names of the phases identified, these are not separate or distinct, but they gradually merge into each other as a person moves from being a novice to becoming proficient.

Having a better understanding of what is happening and what the learner is experiencing during each phase should help you in developing appropriate teaching and coaching strategies to ensure that the learning process is efficient and successful.

EXAMINER'S TIP

Be careful not to confuse the three *types* of learning with the three *stages* of learning.

Three-stage model

Paul Fitts and Michael Posner (1967) identified one of the better-known models, which in its turn has been expanded by others. The three phases identified are:

1 Cognitive;
2 Associative;
3 Autonomous.

While each of these phases has certain characteristics associated with it, movement from one phase to the other is seen as developmental and gradual, along a continuum. The rate at which a performer progresses through the phases is different for each individual.

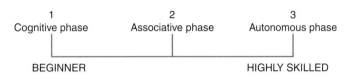

Cognitive phase

This is the initial phase in the learning process when, as a beginner faced with a new skill or set of skills to learn, you want to be told what you need to know. For example:

● What is required of you?
● What task is to be performed?
● What are the basic rules?

The beginner is trying to get to grips with the basics while dealing with lots of visual, verbal and kinaesthetic information in the form of:

● demonstrations from the teacher or fellow students (visual guidance/mental picture);
● instructions and explanations (verbal guidance to help sequencing);
● initial trials/practice in the form of basic trial/error (kinaesthetic picture).

The emphasis in this phase is very much on early understanding or cognitive involvement (internalising information), allowing a mental picture to be created so that initial plans of action can be formulated. Beginners are directed towards important aspects of the new skill by paying attention to verbal cues. These cues may be highlighted or intensified in order to help concentration (e.g. bigger or brighter bats and balls are often used), and any initial success is reinforced enthusiastically. The length of this phase varies according to the beginner and the strategies being used, but it is generally a relatively short phase.

Key term

Kinaesthetic: The feeling created during a movement. Proprioceptors located in the muscles detect force and speed of movement, which is transferred to the brain, allowing adjustments to be made.

Figure 5.2 In the cognitive phase it is important to keep information clear and simple

Problems linked to the cognitive phase

- Beginner has difficulty deciding what to pay attention to (selective attention).
- Beginner has difficulty processing information (potential overload).
- Gross errors made (often uncoordinated movements).

Children do not always understand adult words and descriptions. Explanations are too complex for the learner. Therefore teaching/guidance needs to be simple, clear and concise. Demonstrations (visual guidance) are generally seen as being more effective than lots of verbal input at this stage.

As the learner has little idea of what constitutes correct performance, the teacher may have to use manual guidance and physically manipulate the learner's limbs into the correct position.

Associative phase

This intermediate or practice phase in the learning process is generally significantly longer than the cognitive phase, with the learner taking part in many hours of practice. The characteristics of this phase are:

- The fundamental basics of the skill required have generally been mastered and are becoming more consistent.
- The mental or early cognitive images of the skill have been associated with the relevant movements, enabling the coordination of the various parts of the skill (sub-routine) to

become smoother and more in line with expectations.

- Motor programmes are being developed.
- Gross error detection and correction is practised.
- The skills are practised and refined under a wide variety of conditions.
- There is a gradual change to more subtle and detailed cue utilisation.
- More detailed feedback is given and used.
- There is greater use of internal/kinaesthetic feedback (comparison to ideal by performer).

While the skills are not yet automatic or consistently correct, there is an obvious change in the performance characteristics.

Figure 5.3 To remain in the autonomous phase, regular reference back to the associative phase is essential, even for highly skilled professionals, in order to reinforce motor programmes

Autonomous phase

After much practice and variety of experience, the learner moves into what is considered the final phase in the learning process, the autonomous phase. The characteristics of this phase are as follows:

- The performance of the skill has become almost automatic.
- The skill is performed relatively easily and without stress.
- The skill is performed effectively, with little if any conscious control – it is habitual.
- The performance is consistent with highly skilled movement characteristics.
- Skills can be adapted to meet a variety of situations.

The performer is able to:

- process information easily, helping decision making;
- concentrate on the relevant cues and signals from the environment;
- concentrate on additional higher-level strategies, tactics and options available;
- detect and correct errors without help.

Once a player has reached this phase of learning, it does not mean that learning is over. Although the performer is very capable, small improvements can still be made in terms of style and form, and the many other factors associated with psychological aspects of performance, which can help develop learning even further; for example:

- self-evaluation of performance;
- mental practice;
- stress management;
- personal motivation.

Figure 5.4 In the autonomous phase, skilled soccer players can dribble the ball habitually, enabling their attentional capacities to consider other aspects of the game at the same time, such as the movements of other players and the options available

Activity 2

Use the criteria for each phase given above to judge your own level of learning. Place on the continuum where you would classify yourself in relation to your performance of the following skills:

- headstand;
- throwing a cricket/rounders ball;
- kicking a ball;
- shooting a netball;
- jogging;
- backward roll in gymnastics;
- dribbling in hockey.

Cognitive   Associative   Autonomous

Make sure you can justify your placements.

The relationship between learning and performance

As we have already stated, occasional good or 'one-off' performances are not a true indication of learning having taken place. There has to be a relatively permanent change in performance over time, as a result of practice and/or experience. One of the more traditional ways of gathering evidence in order to discover if learning has taken place or not is by comparing practice/performance observations. Performance levels over a certain length of time are recorded and the results are plotted on a graph, producing performance curves. Very often, these curves of performance are referred to inaccurately as learning curves. This is based on the assumption that changing levels of skill closely parallel performance scores. However, it is performance, not learning, that is being measured. By keeping records of skill performance over a period of time (e.g. a lesson, one hour, a term, a season), an individual's, but more often a group's, progress can be plotted. This will provide a graphical representation of the specific aspect of performance being tested. Thus a picture of the relationship between practice and performance is presented, from which inferences can be drawn.

It has been suggested that the validity of performance curves as true representations of learning is problematical, due to the many variables which may have an effect. However, as long as they are not used in total isolation, such curves do act as useful indicators of general trends in learning. Although they may be employed to show changes in an individual's performance of a particular motor skill or skills, performance curves tend to be more widely used to represent composite or group performance.

A performance curve consists of three areas:

- The vertical y-axis of the graph, showing the level of performance being measured.
- The horizontal x-axis of the graph, indicating the amount of time over which the performance has been measured.
- The shape of the curve, from which inferences can be made about the amount of learning taking place.

IN DEPTH: Types of performance curves

When analysing performance curves, it has been found that graphs are made up of several different shapes within the overall context of the general performance curve. The curves shown in Figures 5.5–5.9 are termed 'smooth curves'. However, as you will have noticed from your own graphs and further reading, curves found in research studies are usually erratic in nature.

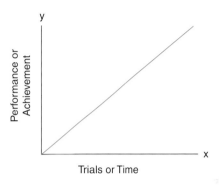

Figure 5.5 Linear curve of performance

Activity 3

You are going to undertake a learning experiment in a new skill. It could be a badminton serve with your non-dominant hand, or one-handed ball juggling. You decide on a suitable task. No practice is allowed beforehand or in between attempts.

1 Divide yourselves into pairs.
2 Have ten consecutive attempts at each skill.
3 Count the number of successful attempts each person can manage each time.
4 Log the results on a table, as shown below:

Attempts	1	2	3	4	5	6	7	8	9	10
Success										

5 Plot your own performance and that of a partner on two graphs and compare these.
6 Average out your two scores and draw another graph.
7 Average out all the scores of the members of your group and draw a composite graph for the whole group.
8 What inferences can be drawn from this final graph?
9 What variables may have affected the individual and group performances? How could you make this experiment scientifically more valid?
10 What did you notice with regard to the shape of the curves as you averaged out more by adding more results?
11 A further way to develop your performance curves would be to treat the ten attempts as a block of trials and average this out. Then, over a period of time, repeat the block of ten attempts on a regular basis. This could be done with various skills (e.g. basketball free throws, serving in tennis, target shooting in hockey or football, shooting in netball).

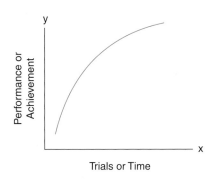

Figure 5.6 Negatively accelerated curve of performance

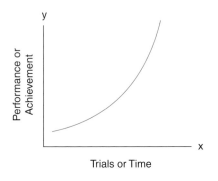

Figure 5.7 Positively accelerated curve of performance

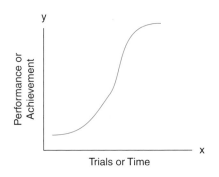

Figure 5.8 Ogive or S-shaped curve of performance

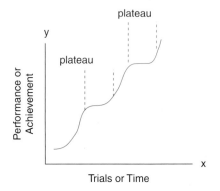

Figure 5.9 Plateau in performance

Figure 5.5 indicates that performance improves directly in proportion to the amount of time or number of trials. In Figure 5.6, the curve of decreasing gain indicates that a large amount of improvement occurred early on in practice; then, although improvement usually continues, it is very slight in relation to the continued amount of time or trials. The inverse curve of increasing gain in Figure 5.7 indicates small performance gains early on in practice, followed by a substantial increase later in practice. Figure 5.8 is a combination of the previous types of curve. The plateaus in Figure 5.9 indicate that during certain periods of practice, or from one particular trial to another, there was no significant improvement in performance.

Plateaus The levelling off in performance preceded and followed by performance gains has been called a plateau. Think of experiences you have had when trying to learn particular skills. There must have been times when initial success was followed by a period when, however hard you tried, no apparent improvement was achieved. Then, all of a sudden, everything 'clicked' and now you cannot even remember what the problem was.

While we may experience plateaus in practice and performance, it has been argued (F.S. Keller 1958) that learning continues, or at the very least that plateaus do not necessarily mean that learning has also plateaued. In terms of learning development, it is generally agreed that if plateaus do exist, they are something that should be avoided, as they can lead to stagnation in performance and a possible loss of overall interest.

Possible causes of plateaus It has been suggested that the following factors have to be considered as possible causes of plateaus:

1   Movement from learning lower-order or simple skills to higher-order or more complex skills may create a situation in which the learner needs to take time to assimilate more involved information and attend to correct cues and signals (transitional period).
2   Goals or targets are set too high or too low.
3   Fatigue/lack of physical preparation.
4   Lack of variety in practice.
5   Lack of motivation/interest due to problems associated with the above.
6   Lack of understanding of plateaus.

7   Physical unreadiness for new skill or next stage.
8   Low level of aspiration.
9   Lack of ability to adapt skills.
10 Bad technique.

Combating the performance plateau effect A coach/teacher may have to consider the following strategies to reduce the effect of plateaus:

- ensure that the performer/learner is capable of performing the skill;
- break the practice into shorter/distributed periods;
- re-set goals with agreement of performer;
- offer extrinsic rewards/encouragement;
- use mental rehearsal in practice;
- use appropriate feedback;
- arrange relevant competition against realistic opposition;
- ensure performer pays attention to appropriate cues (selective attention);
- emphasise role in team – enjoyment;
- change role/position/responsibility.

Activity 4

1   Select a skill which you have mastered, but with which you have experienced a plateau during its development.
2   Consider the possible causes of the plateau and list the practical suggestions made by your teacher or coach to help you progress.
3   Outline what you could have done differently to improve your performance.
4   Present your suggestions to the class and compile a full list of suggestions and strategies.

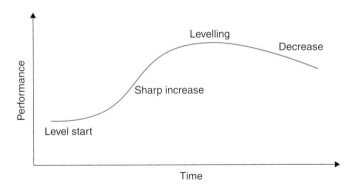

Figure 5.10 Example of a beginner completing a massed practice of given simple, closed sports skill

Figure 5.10 demonstrates the performance curve of a beginner:

- The graph starts at a low level because the beginner has a low skill level.
- At first, progress is slow (shallow slope). The learner is still working out the requirements of the task.
- Early practice produces a sharp increase in performance level.
- The upper level is achieved due to either optimum performance or decreased motivation.
- Levelling out can also be caused by poor coaching/lack of information on how to improve skill level, or fatigue.
- The fall in performance is due to lack of motivation/boredom/fatigue/distraction/faulty technique.

As you can see from your earlier experiment, discussions and reading, there is no one curve of performance. The appearance of these curves is the function of a combination of variable factors. It is important when you interpret the curves and make certain inferences that you are aware of the many factors which can influence learning. If any of these is seen to be a problem in the learning process, the reasons or causes can be recognised, isolated and dealt with in the appropriate manner.

Considerations in motor learning

There are many different factors called learning variables which you have to be aware of, understand and consider. These can influence the effectiveness of the learning process.

There are four main categories of learning variables. In considering these categories you may come across unfamiliar terms; these are explained in later sections.

Category 1: variables associated with the learning process

The basic process that learners go through when faced with a new situation to which they have to respond is usually similar for everyone. The learner will:

- observe the situation;
- interpret the situation;
- make decisions as to what they have to do;

- decide on plans of action;
- generate movement plans;
- take in further information (feedback) which becomes available in some form as the result of actions.

The learner can experience success or difficulty in any part of this process. Understanding it helps a teacher in the task of presenting useful information to the learner.

Category 2: variables associated with individual differences

A sensitive teacher or coach would try to develop good knowledge of the individual differences listed below, and consider how they might affect the learner, in order to help the learning process:

- ability;
- age (chronological and maturational);
- gender;
- physiological characteristics such as physique (size, shape, weight linked to maturity, fitness);
- psychological characteristics, such as motivation, attitudes, personality;
- previous experience;
- sociological aspects.

Category 3: variables associated with the task

A teacher would need to consider:

- the complexity of the task (e.g. simple or complex?);
- the organisation of the task (e.g. high or low?);
- the classification of the task (e.g. open/closed? fine/gross?);
- the transfer possibilities.

An understanding of task analysis is essential in order that the appropriate teaching strategies can be developed.

Category 4: variables associated with the instructional conditions

Teachers and coaches can manipulate the learning environment in a variety of ways:

- through styles of teaching;
- through mode of presentation;
- by using different forms of guidance;
- by choosing appropriate types of practice.

All the above approaches will have a considerable effect on the learning experience of the individual or group.

Exam-style question

Outline the stages of learning and explain how a coach can help a performer progress through each stage. Explain how a coach can evaluate that learning takes place.

Types of guidance

Guidance is information given to the learner or performer in order to help them limit possible mistakes (incorrect movement), thus ensuring that the correct movement patterns are carried out more effectively. While guidance or instructions are usually given to beginners when skills/tasks are unfamiliar, they are obviously used continually in various forms at all stages of learning and performance. The form of guidance given, together with its effectiveness, will depend on several aspects:

- the learner – motivation; stage of performer's experience/learning linked to their information-processing capacities and capabilities;
- the type/nature of the skill/task;
- the environment or situation.

In order to facilitate the acquisition of skill, formal guidance can take several forms:

- visual guidance;
- verbal guidance;
- manual/mechanical guidance.

If formal guidance does not serve to improve performance through the long-term retention of learning, it cannot be called guidance.

Visual guidance

Visual guidance can be given in many different ways in order to facilitate the acquisition of skill:

- demonstration;
- video/film/TV/slow motion;
- posters/charts;
- OHTs/slides;
- modify the display (see page 152 for a discussion of the term 'display').

Figure 5.11 A coach uses visual guidance to demonstrate the correct technique

Visual modes of receiving information are valuable at all levels. Visual guidance is particularly useful, however, in the early stages of learning (cognitive phase), by helping the learner establish an overall image or framework of what has to be performed. This modelling of the elements involved in skills is an important aspect of skill acquisition. However, when presenting the learner, particularly a beginner, with effective visual guidance, it is important that:

- accurate/correct models of demonstration are used/given (usually provided by the teacher or an experienced performer);
- attention be directed in order that major aspects of the skill are emphasised/reinforced;
- demonstrations/models should not be too complex/lengthy (usually whole skill first, then parts later);
- demonstrations/models should be realistic/appropriate;
- demonstrations must be repeated or referred back to;
- demonstrations can be combined with verbal guidance to highlight key points.

There are considerable differences of opinion with regard to the long-term effectiveness of visual guidance. However, for the more advanced performer, specific and complex information can generally be provided more readily by modern technology, such as biomechanical analysis and use of slow-motion playback.

Visual guidance can also be used to highlight certain cues or signals from the display, helping

the selective attention processes of beginners in particular. Equipment in infant and junior schools is often brighter or bigger in order to help performers to 'see things' more clearly.

The teacher or coach can modify the display more specifically by highlighting areas of the court or pitch that shots should be played into, or by making target areas bigger. Routes of movement can also be indicated by markers, and so on.

It is very difficult in reality to consider visual guidance in isolation, as verbal explanations very often have to accompany the demonstration or visual image being presented.

The disadvantages of visual guidance are:

- It depends on the coach's ability to demonstrate the correct model.
- It can be dependent on expensive equipment (e.g. video).
- It has limited value to a group coaching situation regarding technical skill.
- It is dependent on the coach's ability to demonstrate problems within skills.
- Some skills may be too complex to be absorbed by the performer.
- Some information presented may not be relevant.
- Some images may be rather static and therefore give little information about movement patterns.
- It is difficult to use in isolation.

Verbal guidance

Verbal guidance is another common form of guidance used by teachers or coaches and can be either very general or specific. A teacher may talk through a particular strategy in team games in order to give players a general picture of what is required before putting the move into practice. It is also useful to draw learners' attention to specific details of certain movements by giving verbal cues alongside visual demonstrations. Verbal labelling of specific aspects of a movement by a performer is also thought to facilitate learning. A teacher may help the beginner to link their visual image of the task to certain verbal cues.

It is important that the learner does not become too heavily reliant on verbal guidance, thus

Figure 5.12 A coach uses verbal guidance to highlight key points to the players

reducing their ability to pay attention to aspects of performance, process information, make decisions and solve their own problems when guidance is removed.

Verbal guidance is thought to be more effective with advanced performers who, because of increased experience and wider movement vocabulary, are able to translate verbal comments into visual images more readily. Teachers or coaches may therefore find it difficult to simply describe certain movements to beginners, particularly those involving more complex or highly organised skills. They will have to use a combination of both visual and verbal guidance in order to help the learner internalise the information being presented.

When considering verbal guidance, it is important that it is:

* clear/precise;
* relatively short;
* appropriate to the level of the learner;
* not overused.

It is important not to overload the learner. Only a few important points will be taken in during the first few attempts. Children have very short attention spans.

It is also useful to note that when giving verbal guidance:

* everybody should be able to hear;
* the pitch and tone of the voice should be varied in order to encourage or emphasise a specific point;
* a sense of humour is a great help.

The disadvantages of verbal guidance are:

* It is heavily dependent on the coach's ability to express the necessary information.
* It is less effective in early stages of learning.
* It is dependent on the performer's ability to relate the verbal instruction/information to the skill under practice.
* Some techniques are very difficult to describe verbally.
* Verbal guidance can become boring if it is too lengthy.

Activity 5

In discussion with a partner, try to think of ways you could verbally guide a performer through learning a gymnast vault.

Manual/mechanical guidance

This type of guidance involves trying to reduce errors by physically moving (forced response) or restricting/supporting (physical restriction) a performer's movements in some way.

This form of guidance is particularly useful in potentially dangerous situations. A performer may need physical or mechanical support initially in order to develop the confidence necessary to perform the skill themselves. In trampolining, a coach may stand on the bed and physically support the beginner through the stages of a somersault. With more advanced performers they may also use a twisting belt, which would provide mechanical guidance by physically restricting the performer.

Figure 5.13 A coach uses manual guidance to develop the correct movement patterns

A performer may have their response or actions forced by the coach or teacher. In taking a performer through an action in tennis, for example, a coach will very often take hold of the racket arm, forcing the performer to carry out certain movements (e.g. a backswing for early preparation).

While in the initial stages of learning, mechanical aids, such as floats and armbands in swimming, serve a very useful purpose, although it is important that beginners do not become over-reliant on them and lose their own kinaesthetic feel for the movement. There has to come a time, in gymnastics for example, where support for the learner is gradually removed, once the teacher or coach is sure that the performer is safe.

By producing his or her own movements, and not relying on what has been termed a 'crutch', the performer can develop their own kinaesthetic awareness. This will help in reducing possible bad habits (negative transfer), and by increasing confidence should serve to develop the performer's motivation and self-confidence.

The disadvantages of mechanical guidance are:

- It has limited use in group situations.
- It has limited use in fast/complex movements.
- The 'feel' of the movement is not experienced by the performer to the same extent as in an unaided movement.
- Kinaesthetic awareness can be limited.
- The performer may become reliant on the support.
- There is the risk of implied sexual misconduct.

Figure 5.14 Mechanical guidance is often used when trampolining

Activity 6

For each of the activities listed below suggest the most appropriate forms of guidance to use when introducing the skills to a group of novices. Justify your answers.

- High jump
- Back crawl in swimming
- Set plays in rugby
- Badminton smash shot
- Gymnast vault

Exam-style question

1 Guidance is often used to enhance learning and understanding.

(a) Explain the term 'guidance'.

(b) Outline the advantages and disadvantage of using manual or mechanical guidance.

(5 marks)

Types, structure and presentation of practice

In deciding how to use their allotted time to benefit learners effectively, teachers and coaches need to make decisions about when to practise, and how often. In making these decisions they should consider whether practice is better all at once (massed) or whether breaks are required (distributed). Within these blocks of practice they will consider whether the skill should be taught as a whole, in parts or in various combinations. The question of mental practice or rehearsal also needs to be considered.

As ever, there are no easy answers. Decisions regarding questions as to which type of practice will be most effective depend on the:

- individual's stage of learning;
- nature of the task;
- nature of the specific situation;
- time available.

Massed and distributed practice

The two main forms of practice available for a coach to use are massed and distributed practice. Massed practice is seen as being almost continuous practice, with very little or no rest between attempts or blocks of trials. Distributed practice is seen as practice with relatively long breaks or rest periods between each attempt or block of attempts.

Other forms of practice may include fixed and variable practice. Fixed practice involves repetition of the same skill to reinforce learning. Varied practice involves using a mixture of massed and distributed practice within one session.

Practice and the learner

Although massed practice may appear to save time, as the teacher or coach does not have to spend time after long breaks either reintroducing the performer to the task or reducing psychological barriers (fear, anxiety, etc.), this may be a short-sighted policy, as distributed practice is seen as being a more effective learning process for beginners.

The length of the practice session should be appropriate to both the physical and the psychological maturity of the performer. Beginners are more likely to be affected by a lack of attention/concentration and a lack of appropriate physical and mental fitness to sustain long periods of practice. Therefore, distributed practice with beginners, allowing for greater variation of practice, is seen as essential, as it not only allows for better schema developments and transfer possibilities, but also helps to maintain motivation. Random practice is seen as being more effective than ordered practice.

There is evidence to support the view that for the more experienced/older/fitter performer, massed practice is more effective.

Practice and the task

Practice sessions need to be long enough to allow for improvement, but should not be overly long. While the effect of fatigue in relatively dangerous situations (gymnastics, outdoor pursuits) could be potentially serious, the effect of fatigue in massed practice can hinder performance in the short term, although not necessarily skill learning in the long term.

Table 5.2 Practice and the individual

Massed practice	Distributed practice
Better when the individual is: • experienced; • older; • fitter; • more motivated.	Better when the individual is: • a beginner; • less experienced; • limited in their preparation (physical/mental); • less motivated.

Alternatively, distributed practice for discrete skills may lead to a lack of motivation due to the performer's frustration at having delays between attempts. Group or team activities can be practised for longer than individual tasks as players can have rests in between, thus lessening fatigue and frustration. At the same time, groups should not be so big that rest intervals or waiting times become too long, thus demotivating learners or allowing opportunities for ill discipline.

The use of rest periods or intervals needs to be considered within distributed practice. They can be used for the following:

• to reduce fatigue;
• to reduce short-term inhibition;
• to give feedback (knowledge of results and knowledge of performance);
• to offer an alternative activity/novelty game (must ensure no negative transfer);
• to develop positive transfer;
• to re-motivate;
• to offer mental practice/rehearsal (see page 147).

Table 5.3 Practice and the task

Massed practice	Distributed practice
Better when the task is: • discrete, brief in nature (e.g. hitting a golf ball, shooting baskets); • simple.	Better when the task is: • continuous, requiring repetition of gross skills (e.g. swimming, cycling, running); • complex – precision-orientated; • dangerous.

Exam-style question

1 Massed practice and distributed practice are commonly used to aid learning.

   (a) Outline the meaning of each type of practice.

   (b) Suggest situations when a coach might use distributed practice and explain the advantages for the performer.

(5 marks)

Variability of practice

Repetition of skills is important in order to reinforce the correct movement patterns, particularly at the early stages of learning and with closed skill, that is, fixed practice. However, the nature of the skill should be considered. If a skill is classified as an 'open' skill, it would be better to vary the practice to allow a performer to become familiar with the demands of executing the skill in a situation similar to that found in the competitive situation.

The characteristics of varied practice are:

- skills practised in new/different situations;
- useful for open skills;
- helps development of schema (see page 173);
- helps performer successfully adapt to meet the demands of the situation;
- practice should be similar to 'real game' situation;
- practice should be meaningful;
- variety of massed and distributed practice;
- will maintain motivation.

Mental practice

The definition of mental practice is the mental or cognitive rehearsal of a skill without actual physical movement.

When looking at the various types of practice available for a teacher or coach to use, mental practice or mental rehearsal is an area frequently overlooked. We have mentioned already that time intervals or rest periods between practice can be used for mental practice.

Mental practice or rehearsal is seen as being very beneficial. In the early stages of learning (cognitive phase), mental rehearsal is seen as the learner going through a skill/task and building up a mental picture of the expected performance in their mind (a cognitive process). This may involve an individual deciding how to hold a hockey stick,

or a gymnast going over the sequence of a simple vault in their mind. More advanced performers can use mental practice to rehearse possible alternative strategies or complex actions/ sequences, almost pre-programming their effector systems and possibly helping with response preparation, reactions and anticipation.

Mental practice can be a powerful tool in the preparation of the highly skilled performer. Top-class skiers regularly use it to rehearse turns, and to imagine the approach to gates and certain aspects of the terrain. A traditionally held view is that through mental practice a performer can slightly stimulate (below optimum threshold) the neuromuscular systems involved in activities and thus simulate (practise) the movement. In addition, mental practice is used regularly by more experienced performers in learning to control their emotional states. Optimum levels of arousal can be reached and maintained for effective performance. Wider developments in sports psychology have meant that mental rehearsal is being used increasingly to reduce anxiety and increase confidence, by getting the performer to focus their attention on winning or performing successfully.

Although mental rehearsal is now seen as an important element of practice (better than no practice at all) (see Figure 5.15), it is not seen as a type of practice to be used exclusively; rather, it is much more effective when used in conjunction with physical practice. In being aware of the effects of mental rehearsal, it is important that

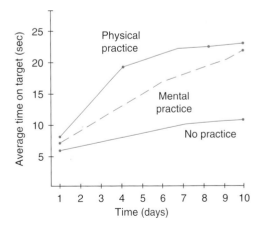

Figure 5.15 Comparison of effects of mental and physical practice on performance
Source: Rawlings, Rawlings, Chen Yilk, The facilitating effects of mental rehearsal in the acquisition of rotary pursuit tracking, (1972) *Psychonomic Science* 26, p.71 (Copyright 1972 Psychonomic Society Inc.)

teachers and coaches not only plan their sessions to allow time for it to take place, but also that they teach performers how and when to use it effectively. Practice is essential.

The use of mental practice prior to performance

The performer needs to be advised to seek out a relatively quiet situation where they can focus mentally on the task. This will probably involve moving away from the competitive or performance situation. The learner or performer needs to:

- go somewhere quiet;
- focus on the task;
- build a clear picture in their mind;
- sequence the action;
- imagine success;
- avoid images of failure;
- practise regularly.

The use of mental practice between practices

When used in between physical practices, a performer must try to recreate the kinaesthetic feeling and mental image they have successfully experienced (remembering what was good). Equally, when a performer makes a mistake, stopping for a few seconds to reason why and then rehearsing a good performance may have a positive effect on future performances.

This mental review of good and bad practice both during and after performance will help in building up positive images. A golfer, when playing a practice swing, is very often mentally rehearsing the positive feel for the shot, imaging distance, angles of trajectory and power needed.

As we have seen already, more experienced performers can plan ahead, particularly in situations requiring adaptation or performance strategies. Questions (Where…? What if…?) can be considered, determined and possibly prepared for.

Mental practice within the associative phase (motor stage) can enhance learning, helping the performer to develop the decision-making and conceptual aspects of the skill which link to the specific skills being taught. Tactics and strategies can be combined with the sequencing of skills. It can also be used to help create effective random practice.

The uses of mental rehearsal in sport and physical education

- Mental rehearsal creates a mental picture of what needs to be done.
- Mental rehearsal evaluates possible movements and can mentally experience their outcomes (success/failure).
- Mental rehearsal can build self-confidence.
- Mental rehearsal can be used as a mechanism to focus attention.
- It has been proved that mental rehearsal produces small muscle contractions, simulating actual practice.
- Performers at the cognitive stage of learning can use mental rehearsal to focus on the basics of a skill/the whole movement.
- Performers in the autonomous stage of learning can use mental rehearsal to control arousal level/to focus attention on immediate goals.
- Mental rehearsal provides mental warm-up.
- Mental rehearsal must be practised regularly in order to be useful.
- Mental rehearsal can be used before competition and in rest periods during competition.
- Mental rehearsal must be as realistic as possible in order to be effective.
- The performer can use all the senses during mental rehearsal.
- The performer can use mental rehearsal to envisage images of both success and failure.
- Mental rehearsal may be used in rest periods during distributed practice.
- Mental rehearsal may prevent physical wear and tear (e.g. triple jumpers use mental rehearsal to save joints).

Activity 7

1   Divide your group into three and record the results of ten attempts of a skill. The skill can be anything you wish (e.g. a basketball shot, volleyball serve or badminton serve).

2   After the first round of trials, each group experiences a different form of practice:

   ● Group A – mentally practise the skill for five minutes.

   ● Group B – no practice, actually perform a totally different skill.

   ● Group C –practise the same skill for five minutes.

3   Complete a second set of trials and record the results.

4   Calculate the average scores for each set of trials, sketch a graph and discuss the results.

What you need to know

   ∗   Learning is relatively permanent.

   ∗   Learning is due to practice or experience.

   ∗   Learning is inferred.

   ∗   There are different types of learning (cognitive, affective, effective).

   ∗   There are different phases of learning (cognitive, associative, autonomous).

   ∗   Learning develops along a continuum.

   ∗   There are different types of performance curves.

   ∗   Plateaus are to be avoided.

   ∗   Learning is affected by many variables.

   ∗   Teachers or coaches can adapt a variety of guidance techniques appropriate to the individual needs of the learner. Visual, verbal and mechanical/physical are the main types of guidance.

   ∗   Practice over an extended period, with short practice periods and limited rest periods, is generally found to be most effective.

   ∗   The effectiveness of massed or distributed practice depends on the type of task, the level of the learner and the situation.

   ∗   Sticking rigidly to one method of either whole or part practice is generally not advised. A combination is often more effective.

   ∗   Research studies have shown that learners can benefit greatly from mental practice. The effectiveness of mental practice is increased considerably if used in conjunction with, rather than instead of, physical practice.

   ∗   It is important that learners are taught how to use mental practice effectively.

Review questions

1 Explain the difference between performance and learning.

2 Why can we only infer if learning has or has not taken place?

3 What are the characteristics associated with the three stages of Fitts and Posner's model of learning?

4 In what ways does a performer in the autonomous phase differ from a performer in the cognitive phase?

5 How is the notion of a continuum related to learning development?

6 Why is the term 'performance curve' used rather than 'learning curve'?

7 What is a plateau in a performance curve? What do you think it would feel like to experience it?

8 Should we infer that plateaus in performance mean learning is not taking place?

9 How might you learn from performing wrongly?

10 What factors may cause plateaus in performance?

11 Consider an ogive-shaped curve of performance for a beginner and explain the reasons behind the shape.

12 What are the four categories of variable factors that need to be considered by a teacher before they can develop an effective learning environment?

13 What are the various types of guidance a teacher can give to a learner?

14 What are the advantages and disadvantages of using visual aids?

15 What problems may be caused by a lengthy set of instructions prior to practice?

16 When a demonstration is given, what important factors must a teacher consider?

17 Why is distributed practice more appropriate for a beginner?

18 What type of practice might suit a more advanced performer, and why?

19 Is it possible to learn a skill by mental practice? Support your answer.

20 In what ways can a teacher help a learner to use mental practice more effectively?

6

Information processing during the performance of skills in physical activity

Learning outcomes

By the end of this chapter you should be able to:

- explain the stages of Welford's and Whiting's models of information processing;
- identify the stages of information processing with reference to practical examples;
- outline the stages of the multi-store memory model;
- explain the characteristics and functions of the short-term sensory store, short-term memory and long-term memory;
- suggest strategies to improve all stages of the memory process;
- define the terms 'reaction time', 'response time' and 'movement time';
- discuss the impact of reaction time on performance and outline the factors which contribute to a performer's reaction time;
- explain the terms 'psychological refractory period', 'single-channel hypothesis', 'choice reaction time', 'Hick's law' and 'anticipation'.

CHAPTER INTRODUCTION

Information processing is a key topic and is central to your understanding of many other areas of your course. A sports performer uses information from the current situation, previous experience and their memory systems in order to reduce uncertainty and help them to decide how to act. Information processing is an approach which sees the development of human motor behaviour (motor learning) as a process rather than a specific stimulus-and-response relationship. It has developed under the umbrella of cognitive psychology.

Much of the terminology used in the various models is reflective of the post-war computer age in which it developed. The models appear to make comparisons between the ways in which computers function and process information, and the ways in which humans 'achieve, retain and transform knowledge' (Bruner 1972). Although research and the many models produced tend to suggest that the process learners go through is

basically the same, the information-processing approach recognises the individuality of the learner.

Traditionally, the information-processing approach has been based on two assumptions:

1 That the processing of information can be broken down into various sub-processes or components/stages.
2 That each of these components has limitations in terms of capacity or duration which affect the amount of information that can be processed.

Information processing emphasises that the following all play an important part in the overall learning process:

- perception;
- attention;
- memory;
- decision making;
- feedback.

Information-processing models

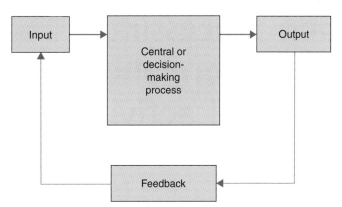

Figure 6.1 Simplistic information-processing model

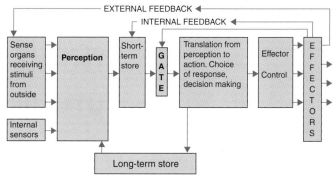

Figure 6.2 Welford's information-processing model
Source: Adapted from A.T. Welford (1968) *Fundamentals of Skill*, Methuen

Various psychologists have put forward graphical representations (models) of how they see the various parts of the cognitive process relating to each other. These models are intended to aid understanding by helping teachers/coaches in their task analysis. The learning process, however, is a changing, complex and multidimensional one, and such models must be seen as hypothetical and flexible. Two of the better-known models which are generally referred to are Welford's and Whiting's, and can be seen in Figures 6.2 and 6.3.

Although they use slightly different terminology, both models reflect basically the same process:

- Stimulus identification stage/input stage.
- Response identification/selection stage/ central stage.
- Response programming stage/output stage.

Stimulus identification stage (input)

This stage is mainly a sensory stage where the stimulus (e.g. a ball) is detected, along with speed, size, colour, direction of movement, and so on, from the display.

The display

This is the physical environment in which the learner is performing. The display for the player shown in Figure 6.4 would be her own teammates, the opposition, the pitch, the ball, the goal posts, the crowd and whatever else is going on in the vicinity of the game, whether important or not.

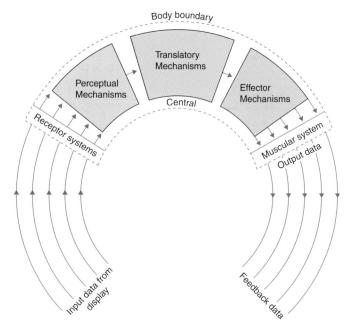

Figure 6.3 Whiting's model is a well-known illustration of the information-processing theory
Source: Adapted from H.T.A. Whiting (1969) *Acquiring Ball Skill*, Bell & Son

Figure 6.4 The stimulus identification stage: a player hears her teammates call, sees the ball, feels her grip on the stick and braces her legs in ready position to receive the ball

Stimuli and cues

These are specific aspects of the display that are being registered by the learner's sense organs (e.g. a ball being passed to them, or players calling for the ball).

Sense organs, sensory systems and receptors

These are the receptors which take in the sensory information. There are three types or categories of receptors:

1   Exteroceptors – receive extrinsic information from outside the body (from the display):
    ● visual;
    ● auditory;
    ● touch;
    ● smell;
    ● taste.
2   Proprioceptors – nerve receptors within the body in muscles, joints, and so on, providing intrinsic information regarding what class of movement is occurring. Kinaesthetic information is also provided about the feel or sense of movement. The inner ear also provides proprioceptive information (e.g. are you balanced?).
3   Interoceptors – information from the internal organs of the body (heart, lungs, digestive system, etc.). This information (e.g. how fast the heart is beating, register fatigue) is passed to the central mechanism of the brain via the body's sensory nervous system.

Activity 1

1   Play an invasion game of your choice, but alter the amount and type of information entering the sensory system to limit the amount of information received. For example, wear earplugs, an eye-patch, blinkers, thick gloves, and so on. Do not restrict all your senses at once!
2   Change the type of sensory inhibition after several minutes. Discuss the effects and implications on performance with a partner.

Activity 2

For each of the major sensory exteroceptors (vision, auditory and touch), suggest ways in which the intensity of the stimulus may be altered to aid the detection of the stimulus and processing of information.

Perception

This process involves the interpretation of the sensory input, along with discrimination, selection and coding of important information that may be relevant to the decision-making process. The process of selective attention and use of memory are important at this stage.

> **Key term**
>
> **Perception:** 'the process of assembling sensations into usable representations of the world.' (D. Coon 1983)

Response selection stage (central stage)

Having identified information from the display, this stage involves deciding on the necessary movement in the context of the present situation (e.g. does the hockey player receive the ball and pass, change direction and dribble, or hold the ball?).

Translatory/decision-making mechanism

This involves an individual having to use the coded information received to recognise what is happening around them in order to decide on and select the appropriate motor programme to deal with the situation. Perception, selective attention short-term memory and long-term memory are all involved.

> **Key term**
>
> **Selective attention:** A process that filters irrelevant information which has been gathered by the sensory system. Information is prioritised, which can help speed up the decision-making process.

Response programming stage (output)

In this final stage the motor systems are organised in order to deliver the chosen plan of action.

Effector mechanisms/effector control

Motor programmes or schemas (plans of action; see page 169) are selected and developed, involving short-term and long-term memory. These plans, in the form of coded impulses, are sent via the body's effector or motor nerves to the appropriate muscles, telling them what action to perform.

Muscular system/effectors

The muscles receive the relevant 'motor programme' or plan of action in the form of coded impulses; they initiate the movement and the action is performed.

Feedback

As a result of whatever action has been carried out, the receptor systems receive information in various forms. There are many different types of feedback, but it can be either extrinsic (from outside the body) or intrinsic (from within the body).

It can be seen that the body's control system (brain), through a series of receptors and effectors, controls our physical movements by evaluating the need for action and then executing it when and where it deems necessary. How effective this processing of information is depends on many variable factors, which we will discuss in this chapter.

Memory

The memory is seen as a critical part of the overall learning process. It is central to our ability to receive the relevant information, interpret it, use it to make decisions and then pass out the appropriate information via the body's effector systems.

There has been much debate about the structure, organisation and capacity of the memory process,

with many modifications being suggested to the basic 'two-dimensional process' or 'multi-store' model of memory as described by Atkinson and Shiffrin (1968). It is generally suggested, however, that there are two main aspects of memory: short-term memory (STM) and long-term memory (LTM). These two parts of memory are in some way preceded by a third area, known as the sensory system or short-term sensory store (STSS), which involves a selection and attention process.

The STSS receives all sensory information provided by sensory receptors. It can hold large amounts of information (it is virtually limitless). Information usually lasts in the STSS for a fraction of a second (maximum 1 second). Unless it is reinforced it will be lost – scanning is a way of reinforcing information.

Selective attention

Owing to the apparent limited neurological capacity of the short-term memory suggested by many single-channel models (e.g. Broadbent 1958; Norman 1969, 1976), it is acknowledged that there is some form of selection system in order to prioritise information, although there are disagreements about the positioning of this filtering system (see the gating process in Welford's model, Figure 6.2, page 152).

The process of selective attention is responsible for selecting relevant from irrelevant information from the display. This allows the tennis player, for example, to focus on the specific cues being presented by their opponent when receiving serve (the grip, throw-up of the ball, angle of racket, position in relation to service court, etc.) and to ignore other aspects of the environment

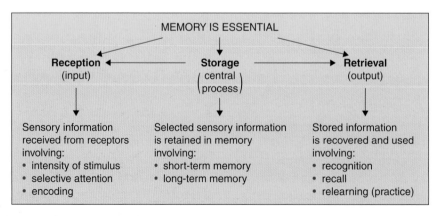

Figure 6.5 Memory is essential

(display) which may distract them (e.g. crowd, noise from the next court, ball boys), thus helping to prevent potential information overload. As well as increasing the time that a stimulus can remain in the STM, effective selective attention can help to reduce reaction time.

The efficiency of the short-term sensory store and the selective attention process is influenced by several factors:

- experience – an experienced tennis player will know what to look for when facing an opponent;
- arousal – the more alert you are, the more likely you are to choose the appropriate cues; in cricket, a batsman who is alert is able to pick up on the spin, speed and direction of the ball;
- quality of instruction – as a beginner, you do not always know what to respond to; the coach or teacher can direct your attention verbally, visually and mechanically;
- intensity of stimulus – the effectiveness of the senses (e.g. short-sighted, poor hearing) when

detecting speed, noise, size/shape, colour, and so on.

Selective attention can be improved by:

- lots of relevant practice;
- increasing the intensity of the stimulus;
- use of language associated with or appropriate to the performer in order to motivate and arouse;
- use of past experience/transfer to help explanations;
- direct attention.

Short-term memory

Because the short-term memory appears to function between the STSS and the LTM, receiving and integrating relevant coded information from both areas and passing on decisions via the body's effector systems (processing and storing information), it is often referred to as the 'working memory' or 'workspace' (Atkinson and Shiffrin 1971). The information in our STM at any one time is said to be our 'consciousnesses'.

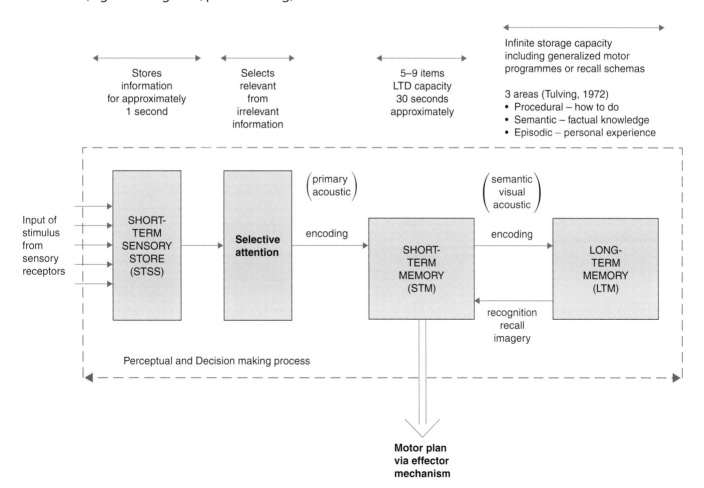

Figure 6.6 Memory stores

Capacity of STM

Compared with the other two aspects of memory, the STM has very limited capacity, hence the need for the process of selective attention (when only relevant information is encoded and passed to STM). Seven plus or minus two items (7 +/– 2) appears to be the maximum amount of information 'chunks' that any one person can hold. It has been suggested, however (Miller 1956), that by practising a process called 'chunking', or grouping together many items of information, a person can remember seven chunks of information rather than just seven individual items. Thus a games player, with practice, may be able to remember seven different tactical moves or options happening around them, rather than the seven aspects of a specific skill or strategy. In addition, a performer, by linking together various aspects of a particular skill, such as a tennis serve, will see it as a whole, once learned, rather than as the various sub-routines of the service, grip, stance, throw-up, preparation of racket, point of contact, follow-through and recovery.

Duration of STM

It is generally accepted that unless the 7 +/– 2 items of information within the STM are reinforced in some way by practice, repetition or rehearsal, they will only remain in the STM for a relatively short period of time: approximately 30 seconds. If 'attention' is directed away from the information being held in the STM, it tends to be forgotten. In order to keep information 'circulating' within the STM, research has suggested that it is more effective for a person to repeat it verbally. Visual imagery, although slower, can also be used. Important areas of information are passed on to the long-term memory for retrieval and use at a later date.

Activity 3

1 Compile a list of random numbers, the first comprising 4 digits, the next 5 digits, and so on, until there are 12 digits in the sequence.

2 Read each number in turn to your partner, who must recall and record the sequence immediately. Check the answers and then change roles, using a new set of numbers.

3 Compare your results – who has the best short-term memory?

Long-term memory

The long-term memory is what is generally thought of as someone's 'memory'. Information about past experiences is stored, including learned knowledge, perceptual skills, motor skills, and so on. In short, all classes of information associated with learning and experience are retained in the LTM.

Capacity of LTM

The long-term memory is thought to have unlimited capacity. It enables a performer to deal with present situations or tasks by using information (either behavioural or factual) that has been specifically learned, or information gained from general past experiences.

Duration of LTM

Information, once learned and stored in the long-term memory, is thought to be there indefinitely, perhaps permanently. The main problem with information stored in the long-term memory is one of retrieval. Once information has been rehearsed, reinforced and linked together in the appropriate manner within the STM (coding), it is passed to the LTM for storage. It is generally thought that once learned and stored in the LTM, motor skills in particular are protected from loss. There is evidence to suggest that retrieval is more effective with skills that have been 'over-learned' (practised continually) and have become autonomous. Skills that are linked or associated in a more continuous way (cycling, swimming), rather than individual skills (handstand, headstand), can also be retrieved more effectively.

Retrieval of information

Retrieval of information that has been stored in the LTM for future use can take several different forms. The more common forms are recognition, recall and relearning.

● Recognition: when a tennis player sees something familiar with regard to a style of serve by their opponent and has to adapt their own movement to it, or a defender in soccer sees several things happening in front of them and has to make up their mind which is the most dangerous, having 'recognised' certain cues or signals (retrieval cues).

- Recall: when a performer has to actively search their memory stores for certain previously learned skills or information that may help to solve a problem in the present.
- Relearning: if something has previously been learned and then forgotten, it may be easier to learn a second time round.
- Imagery: when a performer is able to 'hook' their present cognitive or motor situation onto some form of visual image of a previously well-performed situation, skill or strategy (mental rehearsal); movement memory is aided by verbal labels which can produce a mental image of the correct movement.

To ensure that important information stays in the LTM, a teacher/coach/performer will need to:

- rehearse/reinforce/repeat;
- link or associate information with familiar information;
- make information meaningful/relevant;
- make stimuli more recognisable/intense;
- group or 'chunk' information together;
- use imagery.

Activity 4

1 Draw a blank model of the memory process.
2 Select a skill you perform in a game situation.
3 Complete each stage of the model, using practical examples to explain how the final decision is made before it is passed to the effector mechanism.

Exam-style questions

Memory plays a vital role in the execution of motor skills.

1 Explain the memory process and suggest strategies to improve the capabilities of a performer's memory.

2 Use a practical example to illustrate your answer.

(10 marks)

Response time

In adopting an information-processing approach to analysing how a performer uses present information in the form of cues and signals from the environment (display), in conjunction with previously learned or experienced information or movement skills in order to carry out some form of response (decision making), you will have realised by now that this process takes time. Being able to select the correct plan of action (make a decision) quickly, is obviously critical in many sports, particularly those classified as using open skills, where adapting to continually changing situations is important (e.g. tennis, basketball, hockey). It therefore follows that the quicker a performer can go through the whole process, the greater advantage this should have for the motor action being carried out: anticipation becomes possible.

Response time is seen as an important performance measure, helping researchers to find out exactly what happens prior to a response being made (response preparation time) and what factors can affect the speed and effectiveness of the response.

- Reaction time is defined as 'the time between the onset of a signal to respond (stimulus) and the initiation of that response' (R.A. Magill). This is different to another time zone very often associated and sometimes confused with response time, namely 'movement time' response.
- Movement time is 'the time from the initiation of the first movement to the completion of that movement'.
- Response time is the time from the onset of a signal to respond (stimulus) to the final completion of the response or action (reaction time plus movement time).

Individuals differ considerably in their speed of reactions (reaction time – RT), or what has been termed 'response preparation time'. There are many important factors that can affect a performer's reaction time, usually associated with one of the following:

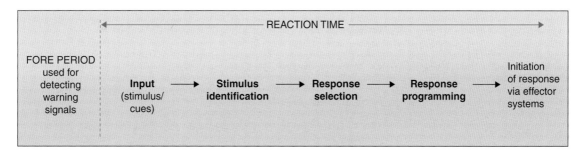

Figure 6.7 Reaction time

(a)

(b)

(c)

Figure 6.8 A sprinter in the blocks, and leaving the blocks after the gun has fired

Activity 5

Complete the missing labels in the diagram below.

```
       ◄── a) ──►◄── b) ──►◄─ c) ──►

       Starters            Swimmer              Swimmer
       gun/hooter          begins to            completes
                           leave blocks         50 m sprint


◄── d) ──►◄────── e) ──────►◄────────── f) ──────────►


          ◄─────────────────── g) ───────────────────►
```

a) _____ Identification   e) _____ _____ .

b) _____ Selection   f) _____ _____ .

c) _____ –   g) _____ _____ .

d) _____ Period

- stimulus (type or amount);
- individual performer;
- requirements of the task.

Response preparation time (decision making) can be affected by various factors associated with the amount of information and the number of decisions that have to be made.

Simple reaction time

This is a specific reaction to a specific stimulus (one stimulus – one response), such as reacting to a starter at the beginning of a race.

Choice reaction time

This is when there are a number of alternatives: either a performer has to respond correctly when faced with several stimuli all requiring a different response, or they have to respond correctly to a specific stimulus from a choice of several stimuli. Generally, the more choices a performer has to face with regard to either the number of stimuli there are to deal with, or, more importantly, the number of optional responses, the more information they have to process and the longer or slower the reaction time. This general rule of thumb is based on Hick's law (1952), which states that: 'Reaction time will increase logarithmically as the number of stimulus response choices increases.'

The linear relationship implies that response time increases at a constant rate every time the number of response choices is doubled. This has obvious implications for a performer when trying to outwit

an opponent. A bowler in cricket is better placed to dismiss a batsman if they have more types of delivery at their disposal and can use them at various times to create a feeling of uncertainty in the batsman's mind – RT can be increased by over 50 per cent.

Activity 6

For this activity you will need a pack of playing cards and a stopwatch. In pairs, one person records the time and the other completes the tasks below; then swap roles.

1 Divide the cards into two piles of red and black.
2 Divide the cards into four piles, one of each suit.
3 Divide the cards into eight piles, with picture cards and numbers of each suit.
4 Plot a graph and discuss the results. Compare your graph to that in Figure 6.9 showing Hick's law.

Psychological refractory period (PRP)

A performer using previous experience in order to help them anticipate certain moves or actions depends heavily on making the correct predictions in order to reduce the time needed to prepare a response. One way a performer can try to increase the RT of their opponent is by presenting false information – a certain stance or movement of the racket in tennis or stick in hockey which implies to the opponent that a certain shot or movement will occur (predicting). The opponent then processes this information in order to prepare and initiate a response. As the opponent's response to the first dummy or fake action is initiated, the player changes the move or shot, causing the opponent to re-evaluate the situation and react to the second set of stimuli. The processing of the new information (e.g. a drop shot in badminton rather than the anticipated overhead clear) takes time, creating a slight time delay. This delay in being able to respond to the second of two closely spaced stimuli is termed the psychological refractory period (PRP). In practice, if timed correctly, the opponent in tennis or badminton, or defenders in hockey or basketball, are made to look foolish as, by the time they have reorganised their movement to deal with the

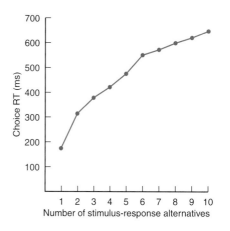

Figure 6.9 Response time curve

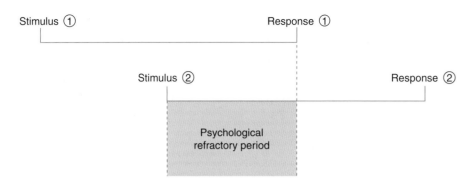

Figure 6.10 Psychological refractory period

second stimulus, the point has been won or they have been beaten by the attack.

Single-channel hypothesis

Theoretically, the delay is created by the increased processing time caused by a hold-up or 'bottleneck effect' within the response programming stage. Within this stage, it is suggested that the brain can only deal with the initiation of one action or response when presented with two closely following stimuli. This is known as the single-channel hypothesis. A PRP will only occur, however, if the fake or dummy move or action is significant enough to cause the opponent to think it is actually going to happen.

There must also be no lengthy delay in carrying out the second stimulus or 'real' action, as this may negate the whole significance of the PRP.

How to make use of 'deception' in sport

- Deception makes use of the psychological refractory period.

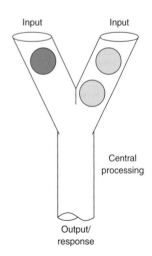

Figure 6.11 The single-channel hypothesis

- The response to one stimulus must be completed before the response to a second stimulus can begin.
- Therefore, by introducing a second stimulus before the response to the first stimulus is completed, the performer playing the dummy gains time.
- For example, when setting a dummy in team ball games, the ball player pretends to pass/run one way/direction; when the opponent responds to that movement, the ball player changes direction/passes the other way.
- More time is gained because the opponent must finish the first movement before reacting and readjusting to the second stimulus.
- Deception creates uncertainty/insecurity.

Activity 7

Copy and complete the diagram of the psychological refractory period (Figure 6.10) with a practical example you have experienced yourself.

Strategies to deceive opponents

- Delay movements as long as possible.
- Disguise relevant cues.
- Emphasise non-important cues.
- Present false information (e.g. fast early action, then soft contact – 'selling a dummy'):
  - This will create uncertainty.
  - The opponent will slow down if alternatives are presented (should s/he tackle/try to intercept a pass, etc.?).
  - Attention of opponent will be distracted by the uncertainty.
  - Reactions of opponent will be delayed by the second movement.

Anticipation

Anticipation is linked very closely to experience. Anticipation, where a performer is able to initiate movement programmes or actions with 'perfect timing', relies very much on them using signals and cues, and recognising certain stimuli early, thus predicting what is going to happen. The defender in hockey or football who always appears in the right place at the right time to make the tackle or intercept the attacking pass is using their previous experience.

An experienced tennis player receiving a second serve would have picked up on their opponent's angle of racket and subtle positioning of feet, and so on, to recognise that a top-spin serve, causing the ball to kick up high and wide to the forehand, was probably coming over the net. He or she then prepares accordingly; thus processing has begun earlier. An inexperienced beginner, on the other hand, would not understand what a top-spin serve can do to the ball or be able to recognise the warning signals/cues (selective attention). Thus they would be totally unprepared for the high bouncing ball when it arrived. Beginners need more processing time in order to organise, prepare and initiate a response.

Types of anticipation

Two types of anticipation have been recognised:

- Spatial or event anticipation is when a performer can judge or predict what is actually going to happen and therefore prepares appropriate actions accordingly, enabling the response to be initiated almost immediately the actual shot occurs (e.g. blocking in volleyball).
- Temporal anticipation is when a performer knows what is going to happen but is unsure of when it will happen.

While temporal anticipation is useful, having *both* temporal and spatial anticipation is much more effective. The fact that many sports performers, particularly in 'open' activities involving rapid changes in actions, rely heavily on anticipation means that as well as using anticipation to their own advantage, they can use the principles behind it to disadvantage their opponents (see PRP above).

Factors affecting anticipation are:

- predictability of stimulus;
- speed of stimulus;
- time stimulus is in view;
- complexity of response;
- practice;
- age.

Factors affecting response time

There are numerous factors that may influence the reaction time of a performer, some of which are discussed below.

Stimulus–response compatibility

The compatibility of a stimulus and response (S–R) is related to how naturally connected the two are. If a certain stimulus occurs, what response does it usually cause? The more natural, or usual, the response, the quicker the reaction time.

The converse obviously applies. For example, in hockey, a player's natural response to a ball played down their left-hand side is to reach over with the stick in the left hand and lay the stick down, taking the ball on the reverse (stimulus–response compatibility). However, if the coach wants a player to move across and take the ball on the open stick in order to be 'strong on the ball' after receiving, this, for most beginners, is S–R incompatibility (unnatural), therefore RT would be increased considerably.

Experienced sailors can reduce their reaction time to almost zero as they move the tiller of the boat in relation to wind changes (S–R compatibility). It appears almost natural.

Predictability of stimulus occurring

The more predictable a stimulus is, the more effective the response can be in terms of time and accuracy. If a performer can predict in advance what is going to happen by being able to pick up on various cues and signals or advance information, then RT can be reduced dramatically. This pre-cueing technique, as it is sometimes called, has the reverse relationship caused by Hick's law regarding choice reactions.

A player's RT can only be reduced, however, if they pick up on the correct cues and predict the correct stimulus.

Previous experience/practice

The more experienced a performer is and the more practice they have had of making choices, and relating the compatibility and probability of certain responses to certain stimuli, the more likely it is that their RT will be faster. The effect is obviously greater where choice RT rather than simple RT is involved. Hence the experienced badminton player, when placing the shuttle in various parts of the court, knows, through a good deal of appropriate practice, that only certain types of shot can be played by their opponent from this position. This will allow them almost to pre-select plans of action (see Motor programmes and control of movement, page 169), that is, to anticipate, thus reducing their reaction times and response times to what appears to be almost instant processing.

Figure 6.12 Experienced defenders can pick up on the appropriate cues/signals and anticipate attackers' movements/actions

Intensity of stimulus

There is evidence to support the view that as intensity of stimulus increases (e.g. larger, brighter rackets or balls), RT decreases, for beginners in particular.

Age

It is generally accepted that while being relatively limited in early childhood, RT improves rapidly through the developing years up to the optimum level, which is thought to be the late teens/early twenties. After this, it levels off, slowing down considerably as old age approaches. Lack of experience on which to base quick and effective decisions has been suggested to explain children's limited RT. Practice and experience will delay the effect of age.

Gender

Research has tended to support the view that males have shorter reaction times, although female reaction times deteriorate less with age. The factors already discussed, however, have much more of an influence than gender.

Arousal

The level of arousal of a performer is seen as a significant influencing factor on their ability to make decisions quickly (response preparation time). As an introduction to the concept, arousal can be viewed as the energy or excitement levels of the individual, generated at the time the performance is taking place. These levels can vary from extremely high, almost agitated behaviour, to the lowest level, sleep. Clearly neither of these extreme states is recommended for the performer in sport, as they do not create the optimum state of mental readiness for effective decisions to be made.

Fatigue

As the performer becomes tired, their levels of concentration often decline. As a result, they may not detect relevant cues and their RT will slow.

Presence of a warning signal

If the performer has the opportunity to be prepared for the expected stimulus, their RT can improve. For example, a sprinter will receive the instructions, 'take your marks' and 'set' before the starting pistol is fired. During a game situation, teammates will often call or make a gesture to indicate where the ball may be placed or be expected to arrive from. Similarly, the use of calls for set moves prepares the player for what may happen in the immediate future.

Strategies to improve response/ reaction time

- Mental rehearsal – going over responses in your mind.
- Concentration/ignoring irrelevant signals.
- Practise reacting to specific stimuli/signals/cues (groove the response).
- Improve physical fitness.
- Anticipate.
- Concentrate on warning signals and early movements.

Exam-style question

Response time is an important factor in performance.

1   Explain the relationship between 'reaction time', 'response time' and 'movement time'.

2   What factors could affect the response time of a performer?

(5 marks)

Feedback

The final part in the information-processing system is feedback. Strictly speaking, feedback is a processing term referring to information coming from within the system rather than information coming from the outside world. Feedback is now generally referred to as all the information that a performer receives as a result of movement (response-produced information).

When a performer is taking part in physical activity in any shape or form, information is fed back into the system either during or after the activity. This information can come from within the performer or from outside, relating to the adequacy of their performance. This information is used both to detect and to correct errors during the activity, and to make changes/improvements the next time the skill is performed.

As well as changing performance, feedback can also be used to reinforce learning and motivate the performer. It has been argued that without feedback, learning cannot occur. The nature of the feedback will alter depending on the performer's stage of learning, but it is vital that all information is accurate, limited to key points and relevant. Feedback in the early stages should be as frequent as possible – reducing as learning progresses in order to reduce the possibility of feedback dependency.

Types and forms of feedback

Intrinsic feedback

Sometimes referred to as internal or inherent feedback, this type of feedback comes from within the performer, from the proprioceptors. When a golfer swings at the ball, they can feel the timing of the arm movement and the hip movement in conjunction with a perfect strike of the ball. This is also referred to as kinaesthetic feedback. The golfer can see and hear their club swing, and hear the ball being struck, which serves to back up the proprioceptive information being received. All this information is inherent to the task. The more experienced and skilled a performer is, the more effective their use of intrinsic feedback will be.

Extrinsic feedback

Sometimes referred to as external or augmented feedback, this type of feedback is information received from outside the performer about the performance; it is given and used to enhance (augment) the already received intrinsic feedback. This is the type of feedback that is generally referred to in teaching and coaching. It can also be received from teammates within the context of a game. Performers usually receive this type of feedback by visual or auditory means; for instance, the coach or teacher tells or shows a performer the reasons why success or failure has occurred.

This form of information is used extensively during the cognitive and associative phases of learning. A less experienced performer will rely on guidance from the coach or teacher concerning their performance, as they have not yet developed their kinaesthetic awareness fully and cannot interpret feedback arising intrinsically.

Figure 6.13 Sir Alex Ferguson provides extrinsic feedback to his players

Extrinsic feedback can be made up of a mixture of several different types and forms:

- continuous;
- terminal;
- knowledge of results;
- knowledge of performance;
- positive;
- negative.

Continuous feedback

Continuous feedback is also referred to as ongoing or concurrent feedback. This type of feedback is received *during* the activity. It is most frequently received as proprioceptive or kinaesthetic information. For example, a tennis player can 'feel' the ball hitting the 'sweet spot' of the racket when playing strokes during a rally.

Terminal feedback

This is feedback received by the performer *after* they have completed the skill or task. It can be given either immediately after the relevant performance or some time later.

Positive feedback

This type of feedback occurs when the performance of a task is correct or successful. It can be used to reinforce learning, increasing the probability of the successful performance being repeated (e.g. a coach or teacher praising a beginner when they catch a ball successfully).

Although positive feedback is thought to facilitate perceived competence and help intrinsic motivation, it is important that a teacher does not give too much positive feedback, thereby distorting a performer's perceptions of their own performance and possibly affecting motivation.

Negative feedback

This type of feedback occurs when the performance of a task is incorrect. For example, a basketball player will receive negative feedback in various forms if they miss a set shot: they see the ball has missed, friends comment, they realise they did not put enough power behind the ball, and the teacher or coach may indicate faults and suggest correction. All this should help to ensure that further shots are more successful.

Knowledge of results and knowledge of performance

Knowledge of results (KR) is an essential feature of skill learning. Without knowing what the results of our actions have been, we will be unable to modify them in order to produce the precise movements needed for the correct performance of a skill. One of the more important roles of a teacher or coach is to provide this type of information. Knowledge of results is usually given verbally (e.g. a netball coach saying 'You missed the net by 10cm', or an athletics coach shouting out lap times during training). This type of feedback about goal or task achievement is thought to be very useful in the early phases of learning, when beginners like to have some measure of their successful performance. An eight-year-old child will see his/her performance in terms of 'I scored a goal today', or 'Our team won all the games', not in terms of the quality of his/her own performance.

Once KR has been given it is usually necessary for the teacher or coach to provide information about why or how the result came about. A hockey coach, when trying to develop passing, may give KR in the form of: 'Your pass was far too wide'. They may support this by adding: 'The reason it was so wide was because your left shoulder was not pointing towards your partner, your feet were not in the right position and your stick did not follow through in the direction the ball was meant to go'. This gives the performer additional (augmented) extrinsic information in order to help them know not only the result of the action (KR), but also why the result was incorrect and how to correct the performance. This type of feedback about the actual movement pattern is more like the feedback given by a teacher and is known as knowledge of performance (KP). Although most of the traditional research has been carried out with regard to KR, due to its ease of measurement, there has been a definite shift in emphasis towards researching KP, particularly with the increased availability of more modern computer and video technology allowing greater mechanical analysis of technique and performance.

Knowledge of results, as used in most psychology or coaching texts, is referred to as: 'Information provided to an individual after the completion of a response that is related to either the outcome of the response or the performance characteristics that produced that outcome' (R. Magill).

Activity 9

For each of the activities listed below, give an example of knowledge of results and knowledge of performance which may be given to the performer:
- high jump;
- basketball shot;
- swimming race.

The use of feedback

Feedback can be used to help with:

- the correction of errors;
- reinforcement;
- motivation.

There are numerous studies to support the importance of feedback (KR) in the learning process. In referring back to Fitts and Posner's phases of learning, feedback can be used to move the performer through the three phases of the learning process.

Once in the autonomous phase, the performer should be less reliant on KR and should, through their knowledge and understanding of the activity, be able to detect their own errors and, in conjunction with kinaesthetic feedback, be able to make corrections to their own performance.

Although skills can be learned without feedback, it is generally accepted that feedback makes the learning process more efficient by improving error correction and developing better performance. If we relate this to the discussion of motor programmes in the next chapter, we will see that if a performer receives additional information, the quality of his or her generalised patterns of movement (schemas which help initiate and control movement) can be effectively enhanced, particularly in the early phases of learning. When considering the use of feedback, the teacher or coach needs to be aware of the following:

- current skill levels of the performer (phase of learning);
- nature of the skill (complexity/organisation/classification) and its transferability.

In relation to the above points, the coach or teacher has to decide on the following aspects of feedback:

- general or specific;
- amount (too much or too little);
- how to present it (visual/verbal);
- frequency (e.g. after every attempt, or a summary after several attempts – the performer must not become dependent on extrinsic feedback);
- time available for practice/processing.

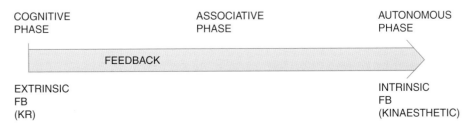

Figure 6.14 How feedback moves the performer through the three-stage model

Although the quantity, distribution and whether it is positive or negative are important considerations, the most crucial aspects of feedback are quality and appropriateness.

KR must not provide too much information, otherwise the performer will not know what to pay attention to or how to use the feedback to help future attempts. Attention must be directed to specific or major errors, particularly with beginners. If major errors are left out, this could lead to the performer assuming them to be correct, strengthening the incorrect S–R bond and making it much more difficult to deal with later. As well as telling the beginner what the problem is, a teacher or coach must provide information on how the performer can correct the error.

Feedback (KR) must be meaningful and relevant to the phase of learning. Beginners might need general information, whereas experienced performers may require more specific details. Sometimes, however, beginners may need much more specific information. For example, a more experienced badminton player would understand the comment, 'Your positioning is not right', and would probably rectify the fault immediately. The same statement made to a beginner would be of little value, as they would need much more specific feedback with regard to the position of the feet, the angle of the upper body, the preparation of the racket prior to the shot, and so on, in order for them to make the necessary corrections. It is important that the feedback given is useful to the performer and not just repetition of what is already obvious to them. Such repetition is called redundant feedback.

Researchers have found that time intervals after the performance have a bearing on how KR should be used. A teacher needs to be aware that once KR has been given, the performer has to have time to assimilate the information and put the KR into action. However, too long a delay could allow the performer to forget what has happened or to lose understanding of the relevance of the KR being given.

Feedback can also be used as reinforcement. Reinforcement, as you already know, increases the probability of certain behaviour being repeated. Using feedback to strengthen the bond between stimulus and response is useful.

Positive feedback has a great role to play in reinforcement. Both KR and KP can be useful in motivating a performer, maintaining interest and effort (direction and intensity). Seeing performance improve (e.g. an athlete improves their personal best or a tennis player increases the accuracy and percentage of successful first serves) should ensure that performers keep practising. It is very helpful if this is carried out in a formal way, with statistical evidence being logged by the teacher or coach. This information can be used both for the evaluation of current performance (error detection) and for future target setting. In this way, feedback can be used as an incentive. Using feedback in conjunction with goal setting has been recognised as being very effective in the learning process.

Activity 10

In pairs, complete ten trials of an aiming skill (e.g. throwing a bean bag into a hoop or making a badminton serve into a marked area) while blindfolded. Each student should attempt the skill under three conditions:

- no feedback;
- limited feedback – yes or no, depending on the accuracy of the attempt;
- detailed feedback – information relating to distance, force, direction, etc.

Record the results and discuss how the nature of feedback influenced performance.

What you need to know

 * The human motor system can be viewed as a processor of information, with sensory information passing through various stages.
 * The performer is involved in gathering data, processing the relevant stimuli to form a decision, which is then executed by the muscular system.

* The process consists of three basic stages:
  * stimulus identification (input);
  * response selection (decision making);
  * response programming (output).
* The effectiveness with which a performer processes various forms of sensory information often affects overall performance.
* Reaction time is an important measure of information-processing speed, and is affected by many factors.
* In order to assess the effectiveness of the decision and completed actions, feedback is obtained from a variety of sources, either internally or externally.
* Feedback provides information about errors to help make corrections and improve performance. It can act as reinforcement for correct actions and help to develop motivation.
* The quality of feedback information is important to ensure that learning is effective.
* Performers at different stages of learning will use various forms of feedback in different ways.

Review questions

1 What is meant by information processing?

2 Draw a simple model of information processing and give practical examples from tennis or badminton for each of the parts.

3 What are receptors? Explain the different types.

4 What happens within the three stages of stimulus identification, response selection and response programming?

5 Draw and label Whiting's model of information processing and explain the terms.

6 What are the various parts of the memory process?

7 Draw a simple model to show your understanding of how the different parts of memory link together.

8 What is the process of selective attention?

9 What is response preparation time better known as?

10 Explain the difference between simple reaction time and choice reaction time.

11 How does Hick's law relate to response preparation time?

12 What other factors affect a performer's speed of reactions?

13 What is anticipation?

14 What are the possible good and bad effects of anticipating?

15 Explain the difference between spatial and temporal anticipation.

16 What does PRP stand for? Explain a situation in a game where it could be used to benefit performance.

17 What is the single-channel hypothesis?

18 What are KR and KP?

19 When using feedback, what does a teacher or coach need to be aware of?

20 In what ways can extrinsic feedback be used to modify performance?

CHAPTER 7

Motor control of skills and its impact on developing effectiveness in physical activity

Learning outcomes

By the end of this chapter you should be able to:

- explain the term 'motor programme';
- outline the relationship between motor programmes and the long-term memory;
- discuss the different forms of motor control, including open-loop control and closed-loop control;
- explain how motor control varies, depending on the skill and ability of the performer;
- evaluate the different types of feedback used to detect and correct errors;
- outline the schema theory and explain the different sources of information used to produce movement;
- discuss strategies to develop strong schema.

CHAPTER INTRODUCTION

In discussing information processing in the last chapter, we mentioned the output stage. This phase of actual movement and control of movement is an important area to understand, as performers and coaches can use this knowledge to develop training programmes to enhance learning and reproduction of skilled movement in a competitive situation. We have referred to the notion of 'plans of action' or 'motor programmes' being selected from the long-term memory. These coded motor programmes are said to pass out by the short-term memory via the body's effector systems, causing movement to occur. There are several theories which attempt to explain how this takes place, involving both conscious and subconscious processes.

Motor programmes and control of movement

The traditional view of a motor programme was that it was a centrally organised, pre-planned set of very specific muscle commands which, when initiated, allowed the entire sequence of movement to be carried out, without reference to additional feedback. The term 'executive motor programme' refers to a sequence of linked movements which are stored in the long-term memory and retrieved when required. This view helped to explain how performers sometimes appear able to carry out very fast actions that have been well learned (particularly closed skills), without really thinking about the action, almost like a computer. In other words, they use very little conscious control. This has obvious links to Fitts and Posner's autonomous stages of learning, which we covered in Chapter 6.

> **Key term**
>
> **Executive motor programme:** A series of sub-routines organised into the correct sequence to perform a movement.

Each executive motor programme has a series of sub-routines which have to be performed in the correct order if the skill is to be completed effectively. Figures 7.1 and 7.2 illustrate two skills and their respective sub-routines.

In relating this notion of automatic movement to information processing, you can appreciate that the limited capacities of the memory process would easily be overloaded, and would take considerable time if every part of every action had to pass via the short-term memory. The notion of a motor programme being decided on and initiated from the short-term memory appears to solve the overload problem, where, in relatively stable situations, movement can be carried out without the need for modification.

This type of control of movement is called open-loop control, without feedback.

> **EXAMINER'S TIP**
>
> Ensure you are able to evaluate the motor programme theory and its limitations.

Activity 1

1. Identify the core skills required in your chosen practical activity (refer to the syllabus).
2. For each core skill, identify the sub-routines and highlight two key points of technique for each one.

Open-loop control

Motor programmes, or pre-learned mastered movements initiated on command, are thought to be developed through practice. A series of movements is built up, starting with very simple ones, until certain actions are stored as complete movements. These complete movements or motor

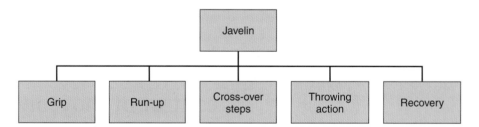

Figure 7.1 Possible sub-routines for a javelin throw

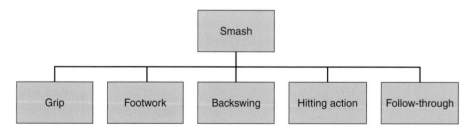

Figure 7.2 Possible sub-routines for a badminton smash shot

programmes can be stored in the long-term memory and retrieved at will; the whole movement to be carried out can then be initiated by one complete command. It is suggested that such skills are built up in a hierarchical or schematic way, as illustrated in Figures 7.3 and 7.4.

Closed-loop control

Within the closed-loop model, the loop is completed by information from the various sensory receptors feeding back information to the central mechanism, as illustrated in Figures 7.5 and 7.6.

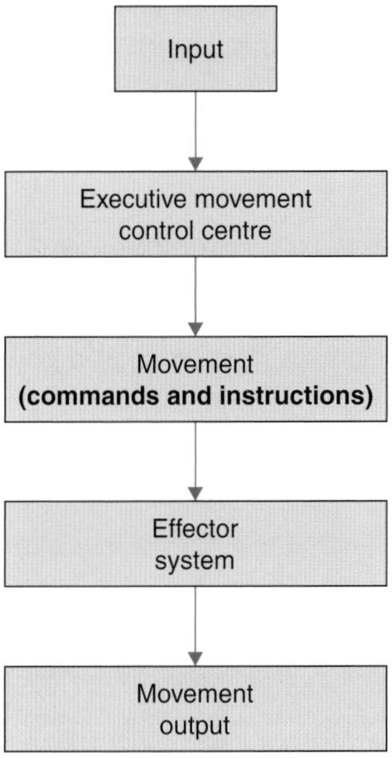

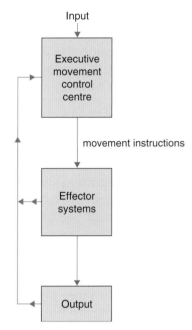

Figure 7.5 Simplified model of closed-loop control

Figure 7.3 Simplified model of open-loop control

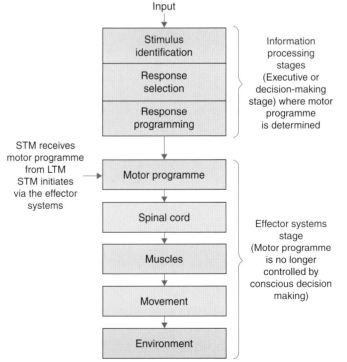

Figure 7.4 Expanded model of open-loop control

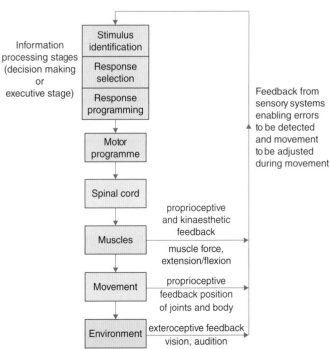

Figure 7.6 Expanded model of closed-loop control

While it is accepted that there are many types of feedback, in this view of feedback control, the feedback is internal (kinaesthetic), allowing the performer to compare what is actually happening during the movement with the point of reference, namely the correct or currently learned and stored motor performance. This evaluation of the movement currently being undertaken means that any errors can be detected and acted on. All feedback goes back through the processing system, which means that the process of detecting and correcting errors is relatively slow.

Research has shown that the closed-loop system of movement control generally works more effectively with movements taking place over longer periods of time (continuous skills such as running) or with skills requiring slower limb movements (e.g. headstand or handstand). Closed-loop models are not thought to be effective for controlling quick, discrete movements; in such cases, open-loop control of movement appears to be a better explanation for what happens.

In practice, while in certain actions one specific mode of control may dominate, the fact is that most sporting activities involve fast, slow, simple and complex movements in a whole variety of coordinated ways. This suggests that performers are continually moving between open-loop and closed-loop control, with all systems of control being involved in controlling the performer's actions.

J.A. Adams suggested that the motor programme was made up of two areas of stored information:

1   Memory trace – used for selecting and initiating movement, operating as an open-loop system of control prior to the perceptual trace. It does not control movement.
2   Perceptual trace – used as the point of reference (memory of past movements) and to determine the extent of movement in progress. Thus the perceptual trace is operating as a closed-loop system of control, making the ongoing adjustment where/when needed.

For example, a trampolinist during a routine will initiate a series of movements using the memory trace. During the sequence, the feedback gained via their kinaesthetic awareness will allow them to adjust their movements (perceptual trace) based on their previous experience. If they are moving away from the centre of the trampoline,

they can make the relevant changes. Similarly, if they are losing height during the routine, they can attempt to gain additional height on the next bounce.

EXAMINER'S TIP

Make sure you can explain the difference between open- and closed-loop theory, as well as outline the role of the memory trace and the perceptual trace.

Exam-style question

Compare and contrast the open and closed loop systems of motor control.

Use sporting examples to support your answer.

(10 marks)

Figure 7.7 A trampolinist will adjust their position based on feedback from their perceptual trace

The quality or strength of all these traces is built up and developed through practice, with the performer using both intrinsic and extrinsic feedback, particularly knowledge of results (KR), which in the early cognitive stages is very often provided by the teacher or coach. Once the perceptual trace, in particular, is strong and well developed, the performer is able to carry out his/her own error detection and correction. (Performer moves from associative phase to autonomous phase and learning.)

Activity 2

For each of the skills listed below, decide if the movements involved are under open-loop or closed-loop control:

- continuous netball chest pass;
- forward roll to balance;
- hockey penalty flick;
- walking along an upturned bench;
- running 200m in 40 seconds, with the aid of a stopwatch to monitor your time;
- side-stepping between a series of cones;
- badminton rally;
- five basketball free throws.

Discuss the results with a partner.

However, there are several criticisms of the motor programme theory:

- It assumes that there is a separate memory trace for each movement pattern, which has to be accommodated and recalled from the long-term memory.
- It also suggests that practice should be accurate and that variance would hinder learning, which recent research has refuted.
- Performers sometimes produce movements that are spontaneous and unusual, for which a memory trace could not be stored.

Exam-style question

1   Explain the term 'schema'.

   (a) Outline the four sources of information used to produce co-ordinated movements.

   (b) Use a practical example to support your answer.

(5 marks)

Schema theory

At the beginning of this chapter we stated that motor programmes were traditionally considered to be a specific set of pre-organised muscle commands that control the full movement. This suggests that specific motor programmes for all possible types of action are stored in the long-term memory, awaiting selection and initiation. If we accept that motor programmes operate via continuously changing closed-loop and open-loop control (with or without the use of feedback), it is the stored motor programme which either directs all movements or is used as the point of reference for a movement to be compared against.

R.A. Schmidt presented his well-known schema theory as a way of dealing with the limitations, as he saw them, of Adams's closed-loop theory. Schmidt proposed that schemas, rather than the memory and perceptual traces suggested by Adams, explained recall of movement patterns. Instead of there being very specific traces for all learned or experienced movement, schemas as Schmidt saw them were 'a rule or set of rules that serve to provide the basis for a decision'.

Key term

Schema: A generalised series of movement patterns which are modified depending on the situation and the environment.

These generalised patterns or rules of movement solved the following dilemmas:

- How do we store possibly thousands, if not millions, of specific programmes of movement?
- How do we initiate and control fast and more complex movements?

In addition, if we can only initiate movement via memory traces developed through practice:

- How do we initiate movement in totally new situations that we have never faced before and have no memory trace of, or programme of movement for?

Schmidt suggested that we learn and control movements by developing generalised patterns of movement around certain types of movement experience (e.g. catching, throwing). A performer does not store all the many specific but different types of catching and throwing; rather they collate various items of information every time they experience either catching or throwing. This helps in building up their knowledge of catching or throwing in general. Performers thus construct schemas which enable them at some future time to successfully carry out a variety of movements.

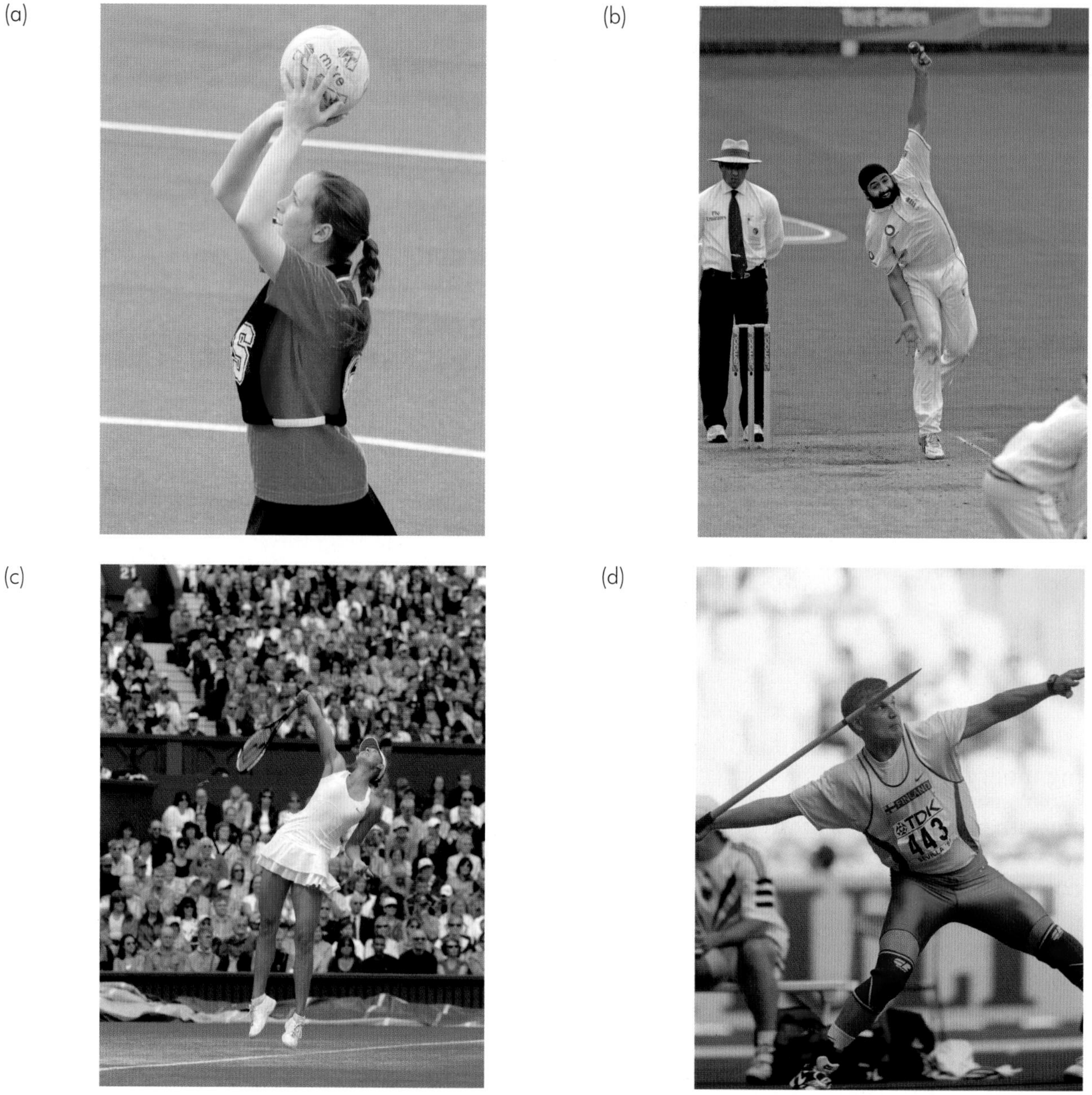

(a)

(b)

(c)

(d)

Figure 7.8 All the throwing actions are based on a similar schema, which is adapted to suit the different skills

A schema for throwing can be adapted:

- returning a cricket ball to the wicketkeeper;
- a long pass in basketball/netball;
- a goalkeeper in football setting up an attack;
- throwing a javelin;
- playing darts.

By collating as much movement information as possible with regard to throwing, we can adapt to new situations because we know the general rules associated with throwing long, short, high, low, and so on. Variety of practice is essential. In order for schemas to be constructed and developed, the performer has to collate information from four areas of the movement (see Table 7.1).

Table 7.1 Recall and recognition schemas

Recall schemas Information is stored about determining and producing the desired movement (similar to memory trace).	1	Initial conditions (where we are)	• Knowledge of environment • Position of body • Position of limbs
	2	Response specification (what we have to do)	• Specific demands of the situation • Direction • Speed • Force
Recognition schemas Information is stored enabling evaluation of movement.	3	Sensory consequences (what movement feels like)	• Information based on sensory feedback • During and after movement • Involves all sensory systems
	4	Response outcomes (what has happened)	• Comparisons are made between actual outcome and intended outcome • KR is important

Whenever a performer takes part in an activity, s/he will collate these four areas of information to form schemas of movement and store them in the long-term memory. The fact that these are abstract rules of response will enable the performer to cope in unfamiliar surroundings. In order to increase the possibility of the performer making the correct decision and being able to carry it out effectively, variety of practice is essential. It is important that the teacher or coach not only ensures repetition, but that practice is organised in order to take into account the various demands that the skill places on the performer in the real-life situation.

Strategies/methods to enable schema to develop

- Varied practice conditions.
- Avoid blocked or massed practice.
- Practice relevant to the game (e.g. opposition).
- Include plenty of feedback – continuous and terminal.
- Realistic practice.
- Tasks should be challenging/gradually more difficult.
- Slow-motion practice.
- Include transferable elements.

What you need to know

* Motor programmes are pre-planned sets of muscular movements, stored in the memory, which can be used without feedback.

* Motor programmes are organised in a hierarchical structure, with sub-routines making up executive programmes.

* Sub-routines, for example:

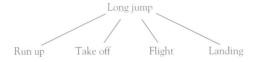

* Sub-routines are short, fixed sequences which, when fully learned, can be run off automatically without conscious control.
* Open-loop explains how we perform fast movements without having to think about them (subconsciously).
* Pre-learned mastery of motor programmes is essential for open-loop control; feedback is not integral in motor control.
* Feedback and kinaesthesis are imperative in closed-loop control.
* Schema are seen as generalised sets of movement patterns stored in the long-term memory, allowing performers to tailor movements to the specific demands of the situation they are faced with.
* Schema are built up through practice and experience.
* Schema theory works on the basis that there are four sources of information which are used and stored in order to modify the programme of movement.
* Variability of practice helps to develop schemas by the performer experiencing different situations.
* Schema theory suggests that every variation of a particular task/skill does not require the learning of a new motor programme.
* The principle of transfer between tasks/skills is supported by schema theory. (See Transfer of learning in Chapter 8.)

Review questions

1 What are motor programmes?

2 What are the sub-routines of a tennis serve?

3 Explain open-loop and closed-loop control of movement.

4 Outline the function of the memory trace and the perceptual trace.

5 Suggest two criticisms of the motor programme theory.

6 What is a schema?

7 Explain the function of recall schemas and recognition schemas.

8 What four sources of information are used to modify schemas?

9 Why is variability of practice important for the development of schemas?

10 What are the main strategies a coach can adopt in order to develop quality schemas?

CHAPTER 8

Learning skills in physical activity

Learning outcomes

By the end of this chapter you should be able to:

- explain the importance of motivation with reference to learning;
- outline the drive reduction theory;
- explain the term 'arousal' and outline its relationship to motivation;
- discuss and evaluate the various theories of arousal, including drive theory, inverted U theory and catastrophe theory;
- suggest different motivational strategies to ensure active participation in physical activity;
- outline the various theories of learning, including operant conditioning, cognitive/insight learning and social/observational learning;
- explain how reinforcement and punishment can influence learning;
- outline Thorndike's laws of learning;
- discuss and evaluate the concept of transfer of learning and its impact on learning skills.

Motivation

Motivation is a key area of sport psychology. It is recognised as an essential feature in both the learning of skills and the development of performance. In addition, it plays an important role in a learner's preference for and selection of activities. Psychologists all accept that motivation is necessary for the effective learning and performance of skills; however, the enormous amount of motivation-related research has been very diverse, with psychologists posing many questions, including:

- What motivates a learner/performer?
- What motivational factors can influence learning achievement and overall quality of performance?

- Is motivation the same for all people in all activities?
- How can we maintain motivation?
- Why do people take part in certain activities and not others?
- Why do people stop participating in sport?

In evaluating the research we find that there are, once again, no simple answers. What becomes obvious is that in order to gain an understanding of this complex and multifunctional concept, we need to consider a wide variety of research. By taking an integrated approach to analysing motivation we will try to bring together the main aspects of various psychological perspectives. 'Motivation' is the global term for a very complex process.

Defining motivation

Answering the question 'What do we mean by motivation?' has been one of the fundamental difficulties faced by psychologists, and explanations differ according to the psychological perspective adopted. The term 'motivate' comes from the Latin for 'move', and motives are seen as a special kind of cause of behaviour which energise, direct and sustain a person's behaviour (Ruben and McNeil 1983).

It has been suggested that human beings have both primary motives (e.g. survival and function) and secondary motives, which are acquired or learned, such as the need for achievement and self-actualisation, which are complex, higher-order cognitive behaviours.

Motivation was historically linked with the concept of homeostasis, that is, maintaining the body's physiological balance. In order for a person's body to function correctly, it requires certain essential elements: food, water, heat and rest (primary needs). If these basic elements are not available or are lacking in any way, the body needs to obtain them. Maslow highlighted the basic needs of a person as being a mixture of the physiological and psychological. If the body has developed a need, it will eventually strive to meet that need – it will be driven psychologically to meet its needs. As well as being psychological, the desire to overcome physiological deprivation implies a motivational state.

- Physiological needs result in psychological drives.
- Drives are described as a tendency to fulfil a need.
- Drives result in behaviour.

Maslow (1954) produced a psychosocial model referring to a human being's hierarchy of needs (see Figure 8.1).

- This is a humanistic viewpoint.
- The primary or basic needs at the bottom of the triangle's hierarchy must be satisfied first. The needs at the top of the hierarchical structure are more difficult to achieve. Food and drink (basic) → acceptance → understanding → self-actualisation.
- Each person will achieve self-actualisation in ways individual to themselves.

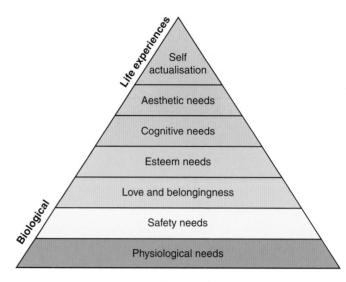

Figure 8.1 IN DEPTH: Maslow's hierarchy of needs

- The strength of various drives varies occasionally, according to the person and the situation. Personal and social needs have been shown to take over from physiological and safety needs.
- The pursuit of needs/goals that are in the future is one of the unique features of human behaviour. Individuals differ in their ability to set and realise such goals.

Motivation has been defined as:

the internal mechanisms and external stimuli which arouse and direct our behaviour. (G.H. Sage 1974)

The direction and intensity of one's effort. (Sage 1977)

A drive to fulfil a need. (D. Gill 1986)

Defining motivation in this generalised way can have certain disadvantages. Learners and performers may misunderstand the term when advised to 'be more motivated', inferring certain character problems associated with themselves. It can also cause potential problems when motivational strategies are employed.

In analysing the definition we can see that it involves four main aspects:

1 Internal mechanisms – motivation is linked to and affected by a person's inner drives.
2 External mechanisms – motivation is linked to and affected by external factors that we can experience within our learning/performing situations.

3 Arouse behaviour – motivation is linked to a person's state of arousal that energises and drives our behaviour. The strength of the energised state will determine the degree of intensity of effort used to achieve the goal-related behaviour.

4 Direct behaviour – motivation in its various forms can affect our goals or selection of activities, as well as our maintenance of behaviour in activities (Richard Gross sees motivation as 'goal-directed purposeful behaviour').

Motivation therefore refers to a general energised state which prepares a person to act or behave in some way. Motives relate to the direction that the behaviour will take or the goal which is set.

Why do performers take part in physical activities?

- The wish/desire/drive to participate in/perform well at a sport.
- Goal-directed behaviour.
- Desire is associated with the expectation that the outcomes will be positive.
- The drive to achieve/will to win.

Types of motivation

A person's behaviour is affected by many different kinds of motives, derived from both internal and external mechanisms.

Intrinsic motivation

The study of intrinsic motivation has been linked to cognitive theories. Intrinsic motivation is used to explain how learners/performers strive inwardly, being self-determined in trying to develop competence or excellence of performance. A person who is intrinsically motivated will want to take part in the activity for *its own sake*, for pure love of the sport. They will focus on the enjoyment and fun of competition, try to develop their skills to the highest possible level (pursuit of excellence), and enjoy the action and excitement of seeking out new challenges and affiliations in doing so. A performer pushing themselves hard in difficult circumstances, and feeling a sense of control and pride at achieving a high level of personal skill, is said to be intrinsically motivated. Intrinsic motivation is greatest when learners/performers feel competent and self-determining in dealing with their environment.

The flow experience Sports performers sometimes experience a situation when the timing of movements and actions appears perfect. They seem unable to do wrong. Everything they try works! It is one of those perfect days. They are said to be experiencing the ultimate intrinsic experience. Csikszentmihalyi (1975) describes this as the 'flow experience'. In his research he identified the common characteristics of the flow experience as:

- a feeling that the performer has the necessary skills to meet the challenge;
- complete absorption in the activity;
- clear goals;
- the merging of action and awareness;
- total concentration on task;
- apparent loss of consciousness;
- an almost subconscious feeling of self-control;
- no extrinsic motivation (goals, rewards, etc.);
- time transformation (appears to speed up);
- effortless movement.

Many researchers in this area have tended to concentrate on analysing the factors which have a negative impact on intrinsic motivation, whereas Csikszentmihalyi (1990, 1999) has focused on what makes a task intrinsically motivating. Such a peak experience, during which performers are able to lose themselves in the highly skilled performance of their sport, has been likened to Maslow's self-actualisation, explored above. Although it cannot be consciously planned for, the development of flow has been linked to the following factors:

- positive mental attitude (confidence, positive thinking);
- being relaxed, controlling anxiety and enjoying optimum arousal;
- focusing on appropriate specific aspects of the current performance;
- physical readiness (training and preparation at the highest level);
- optimum environment and situational conditions (good atmosphere);
- a shared sense of purpose (team games), good interaction;
- balanced emotional state, feeling good and in control of one's body.

By focusing on aspects of their preparation which can help the development of the above factors, elite performers can increase the probability that the flow experience can occur. Psychological preparation is just as important as physiological performance (Jackson et al. 2001).

Obviously, limitations in any of the above factors can result in disrupted flow. For example:

- injury;
- fatigue;
- crowd hostility;
- uncontrollable events;
- worry;
- distractions;
- lack of challenge;
- non-optimal arousal;
- limited cohesion;
- negative self-talk;
- poor officials;
- poor preparation;
- poor performance.

Extrinsic motivation

Extrinsic motivation is related to Sage's external mechanisms. If used appropriately, extrinsic types of motivation (contingencies) can serve a very useful purpose in effectively developing certain required behaviours (learning) or levels of sporting performance. Rewards can expedite learning and achievement, serve to ensure that a good performance is repeated, or form an attraction to persuade a person to take part in certain activities (incentive).

While extrinsic motivation is most obviously seen in terms of tangible or materialistic rewards, it can also be intangible.

When using extrinsic rewards and reinforcements to enhance motivation, a teacher or coach needs to be aware of how often they are used (frequency). Should reward or reinforcement be used at every good or successful attempt or every so many times (ratio)? How quickly after the event should reinforcement be used (interval)? What is the most effective type of reinforcement to use? (See Table 8.1.) The value or quantity of the reward is also important (magnitude). In being aware of the above factors, a teacher or coach clearly needs in-depth knowledge of the likes and dislikes of the people being taught. The use of rewards is therefore closely linked to our earlier discussion on reinforcement of learning (see page 191).

Table 8.1 Tangible and intangible extrinsic motivation

Tangible	Intangible
• Trophies • Medals • Badges • Certificates • Money	• Social reinforcers • Praise from teacher/coach/peers • Smile • Pat on the back • Publicity/national recognition • Winning/glory • Social status • Approval

Research into the use of reinforcement principles has produced the following recommendations when considering extrinsic motivation:

- Positive reinforcement is 80–90 per cent more effective.
- Avoid the use of punishment, except when behaviour is intolerable or unwanted.
- In order to be effective, extrinsic feedback and reinforcement must meet the needs of the recipient (they must be important to or desired by the individual).
- Continuous reinforcement is desirable in the early stages of learning.
- Intermittent reinforcement is more effective with more advanced performers.
- Immediate reinforcement is generally more effective, particularly with beginners.
- Reward appropriate behaviour (cannot reward all behaviour):
  - reward successful approximations, particularly by beginners (shaping) – performance will not always be perfect (trial and error);
  - reward performance – do not just focus on the outcome (i.e. winning);
  - reward effort;
  - reward emotional and social skills.
- Provide knowledge of results (information regarding accuracy and success of movement – see Feedback on page 163).
- The use of punishment should be restricted or avoided, since although it can be effective in eliminating undesirable behaviour, it can also lead to bitterness, resentment, frustration and hostility. It can arouse a performer's fear of failure and thus hinder the learning of skills.

Activity 1

Look at the list of strategies for the use of extrinsic rewards. Try to give practical examples of how a teacher or coach might implement them in real life.

Activity 2

Consider top-level sports performers such as Johnny Wilkinson, Sir Steve Redgrave and Dame Kelly Holmes. In discussion with a partner, try to suggest what motivates them to carry on once they have reached the top.

Combining intrinsic and extrinsic rewards

Both intrinsic and extrinsic motivation play important roles in the development of skilled performance and behavioural change (learning). Extrinsic rewards are used extensively in sporting situations. Most major sports have achievement performance incentives linked to some form of tangible reward system. At first glance it would appear that the additive effect of extrinsic rewards – money, cups and medals – and the high level of intrinsic motivation should result in performers showing a much greater level of overall motivation.

Intrinsic motivation can be affected by extrinsic rewards in two ways. The performer may perceive the reward as an attempt to control or manipulate their behaviour (the fun aspect becomes work). The performer may also perceive the reward as providing information about their level of performance. A reward could be perceived by a performer as increasing the individual importance of a particular achievement. In receiving the reward, that level of achievement is perceived as high. If they do achieve and gain the reward (positive information), this sign of high ability can help intrinsic motivation. If they fail to achieve the reward (negative information), however, they may perceive this as a sign of incompetence or low ability, thus lowering future intrinsic motivation.

If a person perceives extrinsic rewards as controlling their behaviour or providing information that they are competent, then intrinsic motivation will be reduced. To increase intrinsic motivation, the reward should provide information and positive feedback with regard to the performer's level of competence in performance.

Teachers and coaches should therefore try to involve the performer in decision making and planning with regard to their training programmes and performance goals. By becoming involved, the performer will feel a shared responsibility for any success or achievement, thus increasing their intrinsic motivation because they feel in control and competent. The now obvious link between competitive success and increased intrinsic motivation was shown by Weinberg (1978).

As success and failure in competitive situations provide high levels of information with regard to a person's level of competence or incompetence, it is important that a teacher or coach ensures that intrinsic motivation is not lost by a person who experiences defeat. This is done by emphasising performance or task goals and concentrating on more subjective outcomes (e.g. an action performed well). For instance: although you lost the tennis match it was to a better player; your number of successful serves increased and your tactical use of certain ground strokes also improved. By focusing on the subjective evaluation of success or performance outcomes (winning is not everything), teachers, coaches and parents can improve the performer's positive perceptions of themselves (self-image, self-confidence) and thus dramatically increase intrinsic motivation.

In conclusion, intrinsic motivation is highly satisfying because it gives the performer a sense of personal control over the situation in which they are performing. Being intrinsically motivated will ensure that an individual will train and practise enthusiastically, thus hopefully developing their acquisition of skill (learning) and overall performance.

Extrinsic rewards, however, do not inherently undermine intrinsic motivation. It is essential that physical education teachers and coaches use them effectively, in addition to other strategies. They must increase a learner's/performer's perceptions of success in order to develop intrinsic motivation within the overall educational and performance environment.

Successful strategies for the use of rewards to help develop intrinsic motivation should include:

- Manipulation of the environment to provide for successful experience.
- Ensuring that rewards are contingent on performance.

- Emphasising praise (verbal/non verbal).
- Providing variety in learning and practice situations.
- Allowing learners to participate in decision making.
- Setting realistic performance goals based on the learner's ability and present skill levels.

EXAMINER'S TIP

Questions may focus on explaining different types of motivation with suitable practical examples. You should also be able to discuss the advantages and disadvantages of using different types of motivation.

Activity 3

What happens when there are no further badges or trophies to obtain? How might a coach try to ensure that levels of motivation are maintained?

Drive reduction theory

While drive reduction theory is primarily linked to motivation, it has strong links to learning and our understanding of S–R bonding (see the section on Arousal, below). C.L. Hull's (1943) theory suggested that continual repetition on its own may not serve to increase the strength of the S–R bond and thus shape the required performance. The strength of the S–R bond (learned behaviour) is affected by the:

- level of motivation or drive (desire to complete the task);
- intensity of the stimulus/problem;
- level of incentive or reward;
- amount of practice/reinforcements.

Hull believed that learning could only take place if drive reduction (acting as reinforcement) occurred, that is, the performer achieved the task they were driven to attempt, and all behaviour (learned performance) derived from a performer's need to satisfy their drives.

There have been many criticisms of Hull's work, but in relating it to physical education and sport we can see that once the S–R bond is strengthened and performance of the task has become a habit, the performer is no longer driven to keep working (drive reduction). In order to develop skills learning or performance levels further and prevent inhibition or lack of drive, a teacher or coach must set further

goals or more complex tasks to ensure that drive is maintained. Practices must be organised so that the learner is constantly motivated, preventing inhibition from occurring.

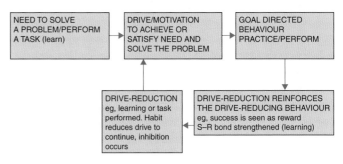

Figure 8.2 Hull's drive reduction theory

It is also important that the teacher or coach ensures that only correct technique or good performance leads to the drive reduction, as it is *this* S–R bond that will be reinforced. Bad technique or habits must not be allowed to achieve drive reduction.

Simplistic summary of drive theory

- We are all motivated or have desires to achieve or solve problems – these are known as drives.
- When faced with learning a new skill, we generally have a drive to achieve competent performance.
- Once we have practised and achieved this skill, our drive naturally reduces as we have accomplished what we wanted to do.
- This reduction in our drive acts as a form of reinforcement and strengthens the S–R bond.
- If we continue simply to do the same thing, inhibition occurs.
- At this point, more/new goals need to be set.

Exam-style question

1 Motivation is a vital factor in learning new skills.

(a) Why is motivation an important factor?

(b) Explain the terms 'intrinsic' and 'extrinsic' motivation.

(5 marks)

Arousal

Any discussion of motivation is closely linked to theories of arousal. In the everyday use of the terms it is not always easy to distinguish between motivation and arousal. They are also closely related to the notions of stress and anxiety. In our earlier consideration of Sage's definition of motivation, we stated that motivation was affected by both intrinsic and extrinsic factors that served to energise and direct behaviour. Arousal is linked to the energised state that drives a person to learn or perform, and is therefore associated with the intensity dimension of motivation. Evidence suggests, however, that arousal is not just an internal state. Arousal is a topic which not only influences elite performance, but can have a considerable effect on a learner at the early stages of development. It is therefore a topic which is relevant to most aspects of sports psychology.

Figure 8.3 Arousal is a physiological state of alertness and anticipation which prepares the body for action

Definition of arousal

Arousal can be defined as being a general mixture of both the physiological and psychological levels of activity that a performer experiences. These levels vary on a continuum, from deep sleep to intense excitement.

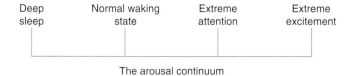

| Deep sleep | Normal waking state | Extreme attention | Extreme excitement |

The arousal continuum

Highly energised states can be caused by an individual or team competing in an important competition. Arousal is not to be seen as good or bad, positive or negative, as it appears to represent the level of energy or effort that a learner/performer develops and applies to any sporting or learning situation. A sports performer can be highly aroused as a result of both winning and losing a competition, or even looking forward to a competition (apprehension or excitement).

Placing the body under any form of physical (physiological) or mental (psychological) stress produces levels of arousal which can affect both information processing and final performance. If activities require a great deal of decision making to be done quickly and accurately, then the effects of arousal are even more marked. Traditionally, arousal has been linked to and measured by its physiological effects.

> **Key term**
>
> **Arousal:** The energised state of readiness of the individual to perform a task, motivating them to direct their behaviour in a particular manner.

Arousal theories

Arousal theories suggest that our bodies need to be in a state of homeostasis (physiological and psychological balance). If the body is deprived or affected (put under stress – perceived or actual) in any way, physiologically or mentally, then arousal levels in the body are increased and we are motivated to behave in such a way as to reduce these levels to the optimum level of arousal. Typical physiological reactions that are associated with increased arousal levels can be measured by heart rate, blood pressure, electronic activity, electromyograph, galvanic skin responses and biomechanical indicators such as adrenaline and epinephrine.

If an athlete is preparing for a big race (highly active), they need to be in a highly alert state (arousal). The body needs to ensure that it can meet all the physiological demands that may be placed on it. Muscles need to be supplied with blood sugars, oxygen, and so on. The sympathetic system of the autonomic nervous system (ANS), that is, the glands, hormonal and endocrine systems, also help to maintain and prepare the body for action. The parasympathetic system of the ANS, on the other hand, will work to restore the body's resources for future use.

Reticular activating system

The reticular activating system (RAS), which is part of the ascending structure of the spinal cord's link to the forebrain, is responsible for maintaining the general level of arousal or alertness within the body. It plays a part in our selective attention processes and serves either to inhibit or to excite incoming sensory information to help our attention processes. The psychologists' interest in arousal has tended to focus on the links between the physiological aroused state and the experience of associated emotions. Just as periods of high intense exercise (e.g. playing football or netball) are associated with all the symptoms of a highly aroused state (e.g. high levels of adrenaline, increased HR, breathing rates), aroused states can be associated with the emotional states of fear, anger, apprehension, tension, worry and anxiety. Some evidence suggests that these emotional states are reciprocal, that is, they affect each other. They are closely linked to the physiological state. For the purposes of this chapter we are mainly interested in the psychological effects of arousal.

The various emotional states mentioned above are easily developed and often experienced, particularly when exploring the unfamiliar (coming across something new or being asked to do something important or perform at a new high level of competition) and in the learning or acquiring of motor skills, as well as the ultimate performance. Research has shown that levels of arousal can affect levels of perception, attention and movement control, all of which are important in the learning and performance of motor skills.

As a learner's/performer's levels of arousal are important, it must be equally significant that they have the appropriate levels of arousal in order to promote effective concentration, attention and decision-making levels to produce optimum performance. Teachers and coaches have been aware for a long time of the need for performers to be mentally prepared and alert; this is commonly referred to as a sports performer being 'psyched up' (readiness to respond). The intensity of arousal levels is often a crucial factor in both competitive sport and learning situations. If arousal gets too high, a learner/performer can become anxious; equally, if it is too low, they may become bored and demotivated. Both states result in a negative effect on learning and performance.

> **Key term**
>
> **Reticular activating system (RAS):** Cluster of brain cells located in the central part of the brainstem, which maintains levels of arousal.

Drive theory

Early research carried out by Hull in 1943, and later modified by J. Spence and K. Spence in 1966, suggests that the relationship between arousal and performance is a linear one. All performance was originally thought to improve directly in proportion to increases in arousal (see Figure 8.4).

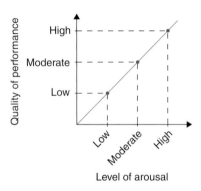

Figure 8.4 Original drive theories' view of the arousal/performance relationship

In other words, the more a sports performer was aroused, the better they would perform. Further research by Spence and Spence adapted this view slightly. This relationship has been expressed in the equation:

$$P = H \times D$$
$$\text{Performance} = \text{habit strength} \times \text{drive}$$

Hull saw drive as being synonymous with arousal. Habit strength was seen as the learned response, or performance behaviour; essentially, it is a theory related to learning – Hull saw the likelihood of learned behaviour (dominant response) occurring as being greater as drive (arousal) levels increased. This theory has very close links with Zajonc's theory of social facilitation. However, learned habitual behaviour may not always be the correct behaviour. The theory goes on to suggest that if the performer is a beginner trying to carry out newly acquired skills, then increased drive (arousal), for whatever reason, may cause the performer to rely on previously learned skills; thus the dominant response may be an incorrect response, so as arousal increases, performance for the beginner will tend to deteriorate.

A good example would be a beginner learning to serve in tennis. They have just been taught correctly how to serve, practised several times, appear to understand and carry out a reasonable serve. However, in a following competitive match, their first serve hits the net, and because of the increased pressure (drive/arousal) to get the second serve in, they subconsciously revert to their previously learned, error-ridden serve, a little tap over the net in order to get the ball in play.

Thus in the early stages of learning, the effects of increased arousal on skill acquisition could lead to the dominant response being an incorrect one. In the latter stages of learning, (autonomous) increased drive (arousal) levels would have a positive effect, as the dominant response would be the well-learned (habitual) and generally correct one. This is often called a grooved skill. The many criticisms of this theory, as a result of further research, together with observations of real-life situations in which even top-class performers with highly developed habitual skill levels have been seen to fail in high-arousal situations, have meant that this approach has generally lost credibility.

> **Key term**
>
> **Dominant response:** The typical behaviour pattern of an individual, which can be skilled or unskilled, in the completion of a task.

EXAMINER'S TIP

Ensure you are able to critically evaluate the strengths and weaknesses of all the arousal theories. You should be able to support your answers with practical examples.

EXAMINER'S TIP

Take care not to confuse 'performance' with 'dominant response' when discussing the drive theory.

The inverted U hypothesis

This explanation of the relationship between arousal and performance originated as a result of work carried out as early as 1908, when the Yerkes and Dodson law first suggested that complex tasks are performed better when one's level of drive (arousal) is low, while simple tasks are performed better when drive/arousal is high. It recognises that there are different degrees of arousal, over- or under-arousal, and that different people can be

affected in different ways, depending on the type of task they are faced with. Most sports performers and coaches can relate to the principles of the inverted U hypothesis, as most of them have experienced performances when both under- and over-arousal have inhibited their performance. They have also experienced times when their preparation has been exactly right, decisions have been made correctly and effectively, and an excellent performance has resulted. This view contends that the relationship between arousal and performance is curvilinear, hence the inverted U shape of the graph (see Figure 8.5). Performance is said to improve up to a certain point of arousal; if arousal continues to increase beyond the optimal state, the performance will begin to decline.

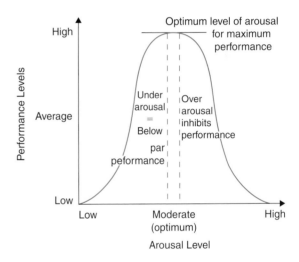

Figure 8.5 The inverted U principle states that increased arousal improves performance only to a certain point, after which further increased levels of arousal will have an adverse effect

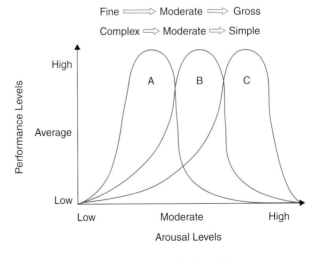

Figure 8.6 The inverted U principle for different tasks: optimum arousal is higher for more simple tasks with more gross motor control

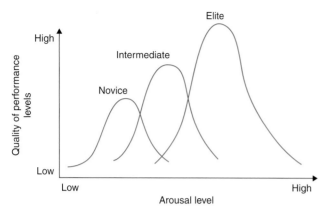

Figure 8.7 The relationship between arousal and the level of expertise or phase of learning

Key term

Inverted U theory: Theory proposing that as arousal levels increase, so does performance, but only up to an optimum point, after which the performance deteriorates.

Activity 4

Using Figure 8.6, try to place the following list of activities on one of the three curves, A, B or C, in relation to the level of arousal you think might be appropriate to carry out the skill effectively:

- free throw in basketball;
- rugby prop;
- gymnastic routine;
- boxing;
- putting in golf;
- tennis;
- archery;
- rifle shooting;
- figure skating;
- shot put;
- powerlifting;
- swimming 100m;
- running a marathon;
- taking a penalty kick in football;
- slip fielder in cricket.

It has been argued, however, that as a general principle, optimum levels of arousal are not the same for all activities or for all performers. The idea that optimum levels of arousal are variable, according to the type and complexity of the task in relation to the individual performer, has meant that the basic principles can be generalised and used by teachers and coaches to explain and predict behaviour in a whole host of situations. Teachers and coaches began to realise that the usual, all-rousing, pre-event pep talk was not necessarily the answer for all performers.

It has been found that motor skills generally need an above-average level of arousal. If the skills or activity involve mainly gross movements and relatively simple skills, using strength, endurance and speed, requiring little decision making, then higher levels of arousal will be more effective. Activities involving very fine, accurate muscle actions, or complex tasks requiring higher levels of perception, decision making, concentration and attention, will be carried out more effectively if the point of optimum arousal is slightly lower.

It is therefore very important that a teacher or coach assesses the appropriate levels of arousal for each task, in order to ensure that the optimum level is achieved. Even within teams, the different requirements of each particular role or position may require different levels of arousal at various times (e.g. batting and bowling in cricket, where loss of concentration and coordination could be disastrous, require different levels of arousal to those of a general fielder). Adjusting arousal levels to suit both task and situation could involve the coach in trying to increase or decrease a performer's arousal levels. Levels of excitement and anxiety caused by high arousal may need to be controlled by various stress management techniques. As you can appreciate, many sports or tasks involve combinations of both fine and gross skills, along with varying levels of information processing linked to complexity. Even within the context of a single game, different players will need different levels of arousal at different times. Past experience, amount of practice and stage of learning will also have an effect on the appropriate choice of level of arousal.

Beginners need different levels of arousal to those of a professional sportsperson. In addition, the level of complexity is relative to the stage of

Figure 8.8 Archery requires fine muscular control and high levels of concentration; as such, optimum levels of arousal would be lower than those of a powerlifter, for example

learning and/or experience. What for an experienced performer is a relatively easy task may be very difficult and involve a great deal of information processing for a beginner. Even at moderate levels of arousal, a beginner may go to pieces and be unable to cope with what is required of them; an even lower level of arousal may be more appropriate in such circumstances.

EXAMINER'S TIP

Learn how to draw and label a graph correctly, especially the axes.

The inability of a performer, particularly a beginner, to process the relevant information effectively has been linked to what has been called perceptual narrowing. These concepts help us to understand that as arousal levels increase, a performer tries to pay more attention to those stimuli, cues and signals which are more likely and relevant in order to help them carry out the task (cue utilisation). They focus their attention (perceptual narrowing). However, a performer's ability to focus their attention is severely hampered if arousal levels continue to increase. Perceptual narrowing continues, which may cause a performer to miss important cues and signals (ineffective cue utilisation), which could have a detrimental effect on performance.

Key terms

Perceptual narrowing: Process carried out by the performer to focus on relevant cues as their arousal levels increase.

This effect is even more noticeable if the cues and signals are not what was expected. Extreme levels of arousal can cause such acute levels of perceptual narrowing that a person is not able to concentrate or make decisions effectively, and can even hinder the smooth control of physical movements. This state of hyper-vigilance is

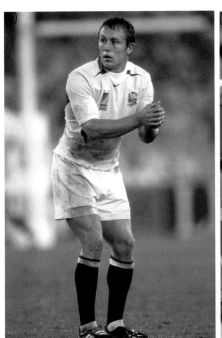

Figure 8.9 Even within the context of a game/competition, different players will need different levels of arousal at different times

commonly known as blind panic. Perceptual narrowing is therefore an important aspect of both learning and performance, where, in a state of high arousal, reactions to expected stimuli can be enhanced and reactions to inappropriate or unexpected cues and signals can be inhibited.

It would be more appropriate, therefore, when dealing with inexperienced performers or beginners in a learning situation, to ensure that levels of arousal are initially very low. Audiences, evaluation and competitive situations are best avoided. Teachers and coaches need to get to know the learner/performer and be aware of the effects that the situation can have on them (interactional perspective).

Activity 5

Consider a game or activity that you take part in regularly. In conjunction with a partner, think of the levels of appropriate arousal you might need at various stages in the game and with certain types of skills.

Activity 6

In discussion with your group, try to recall a specific situation in which you have experienced panic and been unable to concentrate on making the correct decisions. What sort of things triggered these feelings? How did perceptual narrowing affect your cue utilisation?

Catastrophe theory

Several modifications to the inverted U hypothesis have been put forward. One of the more interesting is that suggested by Hardy and Frazey (1987). The catastrophe theory is similar to the inverted U hypothesis in that both argue that if arousal increases it will have a positive effect on performance up to a certain optimal level. Hardy and Frazey suggest, however, that any further increase in

arousal will not result in a gradual fall-off in performance, as seen in the symmetrical shape of the inverted U graph; this shape can be altered by a slight reduction in arousal. Slight reductions of arousal return the performer to the previous optimum level and effective performance. For example, in a game of squash/tennis, a player becomes argumentative and angry over a call, causing his/her game to deteriorate, but calming words from the coach restore a balanced performance. Hardy and Frazey then argue that in highly competitive and important matches, where high physiological arousal combines with high cognitive anxiety, if the same squash player becomes sufficiently upset (over-aroused) for it to have a detrimental effect on his/her game, the deterioration is much more extreme and cannot be arrested merely by calming the player down a little. 'Going over the top' in this situation will have a dramatic effect on the ability to concentrate, make decisions and play shots effectively – in other words, a catastrophe. Recovery from this catastrophe can be very difficult; extreme mental toughness will be required if the player is to work their way gradually back to optimum arousal and peak performance.

Key term

Catastrophe theory: Theory suggesting that an increased level of arousal will have a positive effect on performance and over-arousal may cause deterioration in performance, but the performer may recover their composure and regain optimum level of arousal.

Figure 8.10 The idea of catastrophe theory may explain why sometimes even extremely talented and highly motivated performers may not be able to get back to peak performance levels once they have become over-aroused

Figures 8.11 and 8.12 illustrate the different shape and effect (catastrophe predictions) of arousal on performance:

● At point A, cognitive anxiety (worrying) and physiological arousal (somatic) are high – reaching this threshold creates a catastrophic effect.

● At point B, the performer either continues with their extreme over-arousal, causing performance to decline further to C, or they get to grips with their problem, taking serious steps to calm down and refocus – performance will gradually improve to point D, when arousal levels can return to the optimum levels: performance may once again reach the maximum effective level.

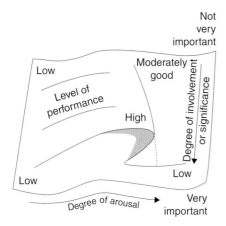

Figure 8.11 A three-dimensional 'catastrophe model' of arousal and performance in sport

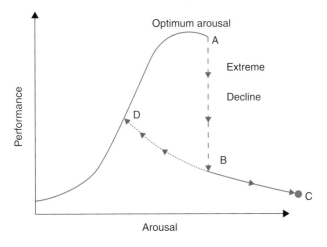

Figure 8.12 Catastrophe theory
Source: Adapted from L. Hardy and J. Frazey (1988) 'A catastrophe for sport psychology', in *Bass Monograph* 1, p.21 (British Association of Sports Science N.C.F., Leeds)

Activity 7

With a partner, discuss high-profile sporting situations which can be applied to the catastrophe theory. Draw and label a graph illustrating two scenarios: one showing the performer recovering, and one in which the performance continues to decline.

Theories of learning

Conditioning theories

In the early twentieth century, behaviourism was thought to provide a scientific basis for the explanation of human behaviour. This approach placed emphasis on the learning environment, where behaviour in response to specific stimuli could be observed and used to make predictions about future behaviour in relation to similar situations or stimuli. The early behaviourist approach was based on what became known as stimulus–response theories, or theories of association, where the outcome, or product, was more important than understanding the process.

Behaviourism has been referred to as a very mechanistic and generalised approach, implying that all learners can have their behaviour shaped or conditioned through regular association (i.e. practice) and manipulation of the learning practice environment by the teacher or coach. The performer learns to associate certain behaviour (response) with certain stimuli from within the environment. Once this connection between a particular stimulus and response occurs, the performer's behaviour becomes habitual, enabling predictions to be made about that person's future responses to the same or similar stimuli. Although dating from before the last century, stimulus (S) and response (R) theories as we know them owe much to the work carried out by Pavlov, Thorndike and Skinner. Although Pavlov (classical or respondent conditioning) and Skinner (operant conditioning) both represent the behaviouristic S–R approach to learning, there are some important distinctions we need to consider.

Operant conditioning (Skinner 1904–1990)

In his later work on instrumental or operant conditioning, Skinner drew heavily on Thorndike's (1874–1949) three laws of learning. He saw the learner as being involved in the learning process. Behaviour was not seen as a reflex or as inevitable, with the learner having no choice or alternative, as is the case in classical conditioning. For Skinner, the learner's behaviour in the present situation was very much a result of the consequences of their previous actions.

The learner associates the consequences of their previous actions with the current situation (stimulus) and responds accordingly, taking into account whether those previous consequences were satisfactory, pleasing and successful, or unsatisfactory, unpleasant and unsuccessful. These consequences would serve either to strengthen the bond between a certain stimulus and response or to weaken it. Skinner suggested that these bonds could be further strengthened or weakened by the use of appropriate reinforcement, thus increasing or decreasing the probability of that behaviour happening again in the future. Both positive and negative reinforcement could be used to increase the probability of a certain behaviour happening again, and punishment could serve to weaken the bond and thus reduce the probability of certain unwanted behaviour or performance reoccurring.

Key terms

Reinforcement: Methods used to strengthen the stimulus–response bond and increase the likelihood of the action being repeated.
Punishment: Methods used to weaken the stimulus–response bond and decrease the likelihood of the action being repeated.

EXAMINER'S TIP

Take care not to confuse negative reinforcement with negative feedback or punishment. Develop an understanding of the role of reinforcement and give practical examples to support your answer.

Activity 8

Design a series of three progressive practices using operant conditioning for a sport of your choice.

Thorndike's laws of learning

Skinner's studies in operant conditioning developed from considerable early research by Thorndike, who, in developing his own research on trial-and-error learning, linked to S–R bond theory, proposed many laws of learning, the most famous of which are outlined below.

Law of readiness In order for learning to be really effective, the performer has to be in the right frame of mind psychologically, as well as being physically prepared and capable of completing the task (i.e. appropriate maturational development, motivation and prerequisite learning).

Law of exercise In order for the bond between the stimulus and response to be strengthened, it is necessary for regular practice to take place under favourable conditions. Repetition of the correct technique is important, sometimes referred to as 'the law of use'. However, Thorndike suggests that failure to practise on a regular basis could also result in 'the law of disuse', when the bond is weakened. Appropriate or favourable conditions could be created by the use of reinforcement.

Law of effect The law of effect is central to understanding the essential differences between classical and operant conditioning. In his experiments to support this law, Thorndike placed a hungry cat in a 'puzzle box', from which it could escape to be fed by 'operating' the correct mechanism. Initially, although highly motivated, the cat struggled to get out, reacting in a very random way. Eventually, through a process of trial and error, when repeatedly placed in the box, the cat reduced its time in the box from 5 minutes to 5 seconds and was fed (pleasurable experience).

Thorndike concluded that:

1 What happens as a result of behaviour will influence that behaviour in the future.
2 Responses that bring satisfaction or pleasure are likely to be repeated.
3 Responses that bring discomfort are not likely to be repeated again.

This is not the same as classical conditioning, where the stimulus always produces the same response, whether it is good or bad. However, Thorndike's basic premise was that behaviour is shaped and maintained by its consequences.

Shaping is the gradual procedure/process for developing difficult/complex behaviour patterns in small stages. For example, if a badminton player receives a return which is only half-court and not too high, s/he will smash. If this proves to be successful, and therefore pleasurable, it will serve to strengthen the connection between the stimulus (half-court return) and the response (smash), thus making it more likely that this behaviour will be repeated the next time the same situation occurs. However, a problem sometimes associated with trial-and-error learning is that a beginner might learn a poor or wrong technique which may be effective in a limited way. This may result in having to relearn at a later date in order to weaken the S–R bond which has been developed.

Skinner went on to suggest that certain additional reinforcement or motivational techniques, such as praise or rewards, could serve to support even further his view of the law of effect.

The consequences of operants for behaviour (i.e. performance) can be:

1 positive reinforcement – strengthens behaviour;
2 negative reinforcement – strengthens behaviour;
3 punishment – weakens behaviour.

The above reinforcements or punishments can come in various guises.

Definition of reinforcement Reinforcement can be defined as any event, action or phenomenon which, by strengthening the S–R bond, increases the probability of a response occurring again. In other words, it is the system or process that is used to shape future behaviour.

Positive reinforcement usually follows when a learner has demonstrated a desirable performance (e.g. the basketball player has developed the correct set shot technique and receives praise from the coach). This will hopefully motivate and encourage the performer to repeat the correct set shot technique and try to improve.

Negative reinforcement also serves to increase the probability of a certain desirable behaviour happening again, but it is by the withdrawal of a possible aversive stimulus (e.g. a teacher or coach constantly shouting at their team from the sideline suddenly stops shouting). The team or players would assume that they were now behaving or performing in the correct way and thus would try to repeat the same actions or skills again.

Make sure that you do not confuse negative reinforcement with negative feedback or punishment.

Activity 9

In discussion with a partner, try to think of other types of positive reinforcements that may increase the probability of a response being repeated.

Definition of punishment Punishment is an event or action, usually an aversive stimulus, used to try to reduce or eliminate undesirable behaviour (e.g. a penalty is given in football for a foul within the penalty area, or a red card is given to a player who repeatedly infringes the rules of the game). Punishment can be effective, but may result in frustration and bitterness, and is seen by many as a negative approach.

Figure 8.13 Punishment is used to eliminate undesirable behaviour; it tells us what not to do, rather than what we should do

When and how to use reinforcers In using reinforcement techniques, a teacher or coach needs to be aware of the effect that different reinforcers may have, and how and when to use them effectively to ensure the appropriate learning and performance of motor skills. Within operant conditioning, once the teacher or coach has decided on the desired level of performance or skill level, they will use their knowledge to employ reinforcers to condition the learner's behaviour in the appropriate way. It may be that the teacher plans lessons in order that success is gained quite easily in the first part of the session. Success itself can act as the reinforcer. As the skills become more demanding, praise for achieving aspects of the desired response may be given. The teacher or coach must ensure that the praise is given soon after the correct behaviour is performed in order that the beginner can link it to their actions (temporal association) and has no doubt what it is for (see Feedback on page 163).

Activity 10

1   In discussion with a partner, and using the table below, make a list of tangible and intangible reinforcers and punishments which could be used with a learner in the associative phase of learning.

Reinforcers		Punishments	
Tangible	**Intangible**	**Tangible**	**Intangible**

2   Complete the same table for a professional sports performer.
3   Discuss the differences between the two tables.

In using reinforcers, a teacher or coach needs to consider the following:

1   How often to use them (too much or too little, partial or complete).
2   Ratio of positive to negative.
3   How soon after response.
4   What type to use.
5   Size and/or value of reinforcer.

All these points will be affected by the teacher's and beginner's interpretation and perception of the reinforcers used.

EXAMINER'S TIP

For each of the theories of learning, make sure you are able to explain the concept, discuss the advantages and disadvantages, and apply them to a practical situation in which they would be best suited to developing a skill or performance.

Cognitive theories

As research of human behaviour and performance developed further, many psychologists began to move away from the traditional behaviouristic approaches. Cognitive theorists saw the individual as being central to the process of learning, not merely reacting in a reflex manner (response) to outside influences (stimulus). Understanding of the total relationship between the many stimuli within the environment at any one time – and indeed their link to previous and future stimuli – was an essential part of cognitive theory.

Relationships between stimuli and certain responses were not learned in isolation, but were part of the learner's awareness of a variety of interrelated variables and experiences. It was argued that this would involve a whole host of cognitive processes, such as use of senses, perception/interpretation, problem solving and being able to relate the present situation to previous similar experiences, thus involving memory.

The main early supporters of this approach, whose views have become synonymous with the cognitive approach, were known as gestaltists. They believed that the whole is greater than the sum of its parts. They argued that in the learning situation, a beginner will continually organise and reorganise mentally, in relation to previous experiences, the various aspects they are faced with in order to solve a problem in the present situation, that is, they would 'figure it out'. The timescale involved, together with the strategies and methods used, were perceived as different for each individual.

This view of learning is known as insight learning: a learner suddenly discovers the relationship between the many stimuli they have been faced with and 'it all comes together' (e.g. a learner suddenly gets the timing of a serve right). Insight learning often results in the performer progressing very quickly after periods of apparently little progress. It is then important that further questions, problems or goals are set in order to motivate the learner to develop their performance further.

The association of S–R by trial-and-error learning (or chance, which is then reinforced when correct, thus gradually strengthening the bond) has no role to play in the cognitive perspective. Learning is not seen as a random process. What is learned within insight learning is therefore not a set of specific conditioned associations, but a real understanding (cognitive) of the relationship between the process and the means of achieving the end result. For instance, if it is explained to a defending hockey player why, when they are the last person in defence, they should not commit themselves, but should jockey their opponent, keeping goal-side, as this will enable other players to get in position to help or put pressure on the attacker, possibly forcing a mistake, the player is more likely to understand when and why to carry out the coach's instructions in future situations, and also to see the relevance of their role.

This, it is argued, is better in the long run than simply being told what to do, or possibly being punished if they do dive in and commit without thinking through their actions. In practice, following the cognitive approach, it would be important that the teacher or coach had an in-depth understanding and knowledge of both the individual learner and the various coaching strategies relevant to the skills being taught. It seems that a variety of experiences are essential for learners to develop insight of the present task or problem using knowledge gained from previous situations.

There is evidence to suggest that insight in the learner can be further developed by the teacher providing helpful hints or cues. This is particularly useful when considering transfers from previously learned activities or skills (see Transfer of learning on page 197). Gestaltists would suggest that a learner experiences the 'whole' skill or activity, learning individually to develop his/her own map of understanding, rather than making part or part-whole, step-to-step associations.

This whole learning approach allows learners to develop their own strategies and routes of understanding alongside general principles, thus enabling the quicker learners to progress at their own rate: this has obvious links to the promoting of motivation and the development of an individual's full potential.

Exam-style question

Skills can be learnt in many ways.

How would a coach use 'operant conditioning' to develop new skills?

(5 marks)

Socialisation

In global terms, socialisation is seen as the lifelong process of transmitting a culture by teaching and learning behaviours appropriate to the accepted norms, values and expectations of a society.

Socialisation, particularly within a sporting setting, is a dynamic process linked to the way in which people are influenced to conform to expected appropriate behaviour and to learn how to adopt a balanced and healthy lifestyle. Socialisation plays an important role in social integration.

General socialisation is heavily influenced by prime socialising agents. These are seen as:

- parents/family;
- teacher/school;
- peers/friendships;
- coach/club;
- media;
- role models.

Although the parents and family are seen as the most important agents of socialisation, all the others can exert a great influence in helping to create role models, real or imagined, that can be imitated. While socialisation can be considered in the global or national context of learning the norms, values and expectations of society, it can also be viewed in the more specific context of how:

- sport can act as an agent of socialisation for society in general;
- performers are socialised into specific sports'/teams' or groups' norms, values and expectations;
- through socialisation, individuals are able to learn the values associated with a healthy lifestyle. Active participation not only encourages positive behaviours and morals, it also promotes a better understanding of the benefits, leading to a positive attitude and regular participation.

Sport as an agent of socialisation

Sport in its widest sense is seen by many as an important aspect of life in most societies, and therefore a fundamental component of the socialisation process experienced by the vast majority of young people. Research in this area, although often criticised, argues that performers, particularly young children, who take part in sport are being taught both physical (motor) and cognitive skills, which will enable them to participate fully and effectively within society as a whole (social learning).

The focus of this research has been on personality, moral behaviour, leadership roles, character building, cooperation, social roles, and so on. It has been claimed that games teach young performers to develop appropriate attitudes and values by providing specific learning experiences. It has been shown, however, that not all learning in these situations is positive. The specific type of experience is important and must be taken into account. The increasing professionalisation of sport can serve to promote the win-at-all-costs attitude, which may lead young performers to imitate deviant behaviour, such as cheating and aggression. It has also been suggested that the traditional values and roles portrayed by sport and performers have heavily influenced gender stereotyping, both within sport (e.g. females as weaker and less suited to sport) and outside. This influence is coming under increasing criticism from within society at present. It is felt that sport and physical education should be doing much more to influence the image of women positively, together with that of other equally under-represented groups in both sport and society in general.

Social learning and observational learning

Social learning

Social learning theory came about as an important alternative explanation to conditioning. It was Bandura who, in the 1960s and 1970s, carried out more extensive research in this area. Although he viewed learning and behaviour as being linked to reinforcements (as had conditioning theories), he viewed the reinforcements as being more closely related to vicarious reinforcement. He considered this vicarious reinforcement as the result of two elements, observation and imitation, particularly when related to the acquisition of social and moral behaviour. In introducing certain cognitive factors which can only be inferred from a person's social behaviour, social learning theorists, and Bandura in particular, emphasise the notion of learning through observation.

We discussed the concept of socialisation through sport above. The social learning perspective has been the traditional theme behind this notion. Learning is seen as taking place within a social setting in the presence of others, with the learner and the socialising agent involved in a two-way (reciprocal) interaction. An individual therefore observes other people's behaviour in various ways, not necessarily through direct interaction. The behaviour is observed, the consequences are assimilated and the behaviour is then copied in the appropriate situation at the appropriate time.

Observational learning

In identifying observational learning, social learning theorists have emphasised a type of learning distinct from conditioning. New behaviour and attitudes are acquired by a performer in a sporting situation through watching and imitating the behaviour of others. The person who is being observed is referred to as the model, and modelling is a term used synonymously with observational learning.

Within physical education and sport, demonstrations are often used by teachers and coaches to give beginners a good technical model to work to. Very often this also serves to help a learner's specific confidence (self-efficacy). The degree of this effect will be enhanced if the person doing the demonstration is of similar ability (teammate) and/or is of high status (professional performer). In addition to showing a current technical model, observational learning, or modelling, can also influence a performer's attitudes and moral behaviour by inhibiting or encouraging certain behaviour/performance.

Teachers and coaches often hope that the consequences of disciplining a certain team member for unacceptable behaviour (e.g. substituting a player for fighting or arguing) will not only have an effect on the specific player, but will also affect the behaviour of other team members who are watching. The other players will internalise the consequences of their teammate's behaviour and are thus warned against copying it.

Modelling is not always carried out at a conscious or intentional level, either by the observer or the model. Very often the model does not intend their behaviour to be copied and is usually unaware that their behaviour is acting as a model for others. The behaviour of top professional sports performers can therefore have either positive or negative repercussions for the behaviour of beginners.

Figure 8.14 Is David Beckham a positive role model for beginners?

Although role models are an important factor within observational learning, they do not always have to be real or in direct contact with the observer. Remote sports stars, cartoon characters or fictional media-related models can prove equally influential. By identifying with the model, the performer will not only replicate existing behaviour, but may also reproduce certain behaviour in novel situations.

People of influence in physical education and sport have to be aware that unacceptable models of behaviour or attitudes are often being presented and may influence the behaviour of others (e.g. gender stereotyping and aggression). Although for

most learners and beginners the model is known directly by the observer and is usually a significant other (e.g. parent, teacher, coach, teammate or professional sportsperson), the degree of the effect or endurance of observational behaviour will depend on several factors.

Bandura's frequently cited Bobo doll experiments, in relation to children learning aggressive behaviour through the observation of others, led him to suggest that imitation is more than just copying a model's behaviour and depends very much on how appropriate, relevant, similar, nurturant, reinforced, powerful and consistent the behaviour is. Further research has shown that the learner not only imitates the behaviour, but also identifies with the role model.

Important characteristics of models

Appropriateness

If the behaviour of the model being observed is perceived by the observer as being appropriate in relation to accepted norms and values, it will increase the probability of the behaviour being imitated. For instance, in our society male aggressive behaviour appears more acceptable than female aggressive behaviour (accepted norm), and therefore young beginners/learners are more likely to copy male aggressive behaviour than female. This has obvious repercussions for male/female stereotyping in western culture.

Relevance

In relation to the young performer's perceptions of the model, how relevant is the behaviour? Young males are more likely to imitate male models of aggression than are girls, as they have in general been socialised into seeing this as part of the accepted male role in society. The behaviour should also be realistic (i.e. a live performance is more likely to have an effect than a video).

Similarity

Children as young as 3 years are already beginning to recognise their 'gender roles', and will identify more readily with similar models.

Nurturant

Whether the model is warm and friendly will have an effect on the likelihood of their behaviour, attitudes and morals being imitated. A teacher presenting an activity in a friendly, unthreatening way is more likely to be taken notice of and is thus nurturing the appropriate behaviour.

Reinforced

If a model's behaviour is reinforced or rewarded in any way, it is more likely to be imitated. Again, this has repercussions for the media, which very often, directly or indirectly, draw attention to certain behaviour, thus reinforcing it in the eyes of the beginner. The imitation of gender-appropriate behaviour is often reinforced by parents (significant others).

Powerful

The more powerful the model, the more significant the effect is perceived to be (i.e. more likely to be copied if highly skilled).

Consistency

The more consistent the model's behaviour is, the more likely it is to be imitated. Research has shown, however, that sometimes a role model's inconsistent behaviour can inadvertently have an effect on young performers' behaviour.

A performer will take into account the above factors and evaluate them in relation to the consequences of the behaviour. These consequences can be viewed in two ways, the second being more crucial than the first:

1 What were the consequences of the model's behaviour?
2 What are the perceived consequences of modelling the same behaviour for the observer (learner/beginner)?

The consequences may either be immediate or appear at a later stage.

If observers can imitate a certain behaviour at a later appropriate stage, they are said to have learned it socially. In physical education and sport, more long-term learning can also occur when young performers begin to think, feel and act as if they were the role model, rather than consciously

copying technical motor skills. Over a longer period, young performers can assimilate the attitudes, values, views, philosophy and levels of motivation demonstrated by significant others (teacher or coach), to ensure that they become a 'model' professional themselves.

Bandura's four-stage process model of observational learning

While social learning theory (and other learning theories) takes into account the effect of reinforcement, Bandura's original model referred to learning without any direct rewards or reinforcement. He argued that beginners/performers learn and behave by observing other performers or events (vicarious experience), not merely from the direct consequences of their own behaviour.

The practical application of Bandura's research to observational learning can be related to the four stages of the modelling process identified in Figure 8.15. This will help teachers and coaches to ensure that learners are focused and maintain their attention, in order to produce a learned, competent performance.

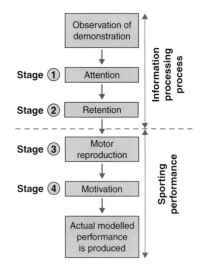

Figure 8.15 Adapted model of Bandura's observational learning process

Stage 1: Attention

In order to ensure that a performer learns through observing, it is very important that they pay careful and specific attention to the model. The level of attention paid to a model will depend on the level of respect that the learner has for the perceived status and attractiveness of the model. A beginner, for instance, is much more likely to take notice of and try to emulate a highly skilled professional or a coach who has significant knowledge of the activity.

Attention is gained by models who are:

- attractive;
- successful;
- powerful;

or by those whose behaviour is:

- functional.

Teachers and coaches must also be aware of the beginner's/learner's stage of learning, in order to ensure that they do not overload them with too much information. A good coach will ensure that a beginner focuses on the main points and that their attention is not distracted in any way from the task. It is important that the demonstration:

- can be seen and heard;
- is accurate;
- focuses attention on specific details and cues;
- maintains the level of motivation.

Stage 2: Retention

In order that modelling is effective, the beginner must be able to retain the skill in their memory and recall it when appropriate. One way of achieving this is to use mental rehearsal. Another way is to ensure that the demonstration/practice is meaningful, relevant or realistic. By using symbolic coding in some form, a coach can help the performer retain the mental image of the skill. Thus retention often involves cognitive skills.

Stage 3: Motor production

While a performer can pay attention and retain a clear picture of what is required of them, in general they will need time to practise the modelled technique if they are to be able to carry out the skill themselves. It is important, therefore, that the model is appropriate to the capability level of the learner/observer: the observer must be able to act out the task. If complex tasks are being developed, the methodology of teaching and practice must allow for general progression and provide opportunity for staged success.

Stage 4: Motivation

If performance of the model is successful, this will provide the motivation for the learner to try to reproduce it at the appropriate time. Without motivation, a learner will not carry out the previous three stages (i.e. pay attention, remember and practise the task).

According to Bandura, the level of motivation is dependent on:

- the level of external reinforcement (praise, appropriate feedback);
- the level of vicarious reinforcement;
- the level of self-reinforcement (sense of pride or achievement);
- the perceived status of the model;
- the perceived importance of the task.

> **EXAMINER'S TIP**
>
> Practise drawing and labelling the model. It may help you to explain how the process works during an examination.

Practical application of Bandura's model

In order to make demonstrations more effective, a teacher or coach should:

- make sure the learner is aware of the importance and relevance of the skill to the final performance;
- refer to a high-status model;
- get someone of similar ability to demonstrate to help self-efficacy;
- make sure the performer can see and hear well;
- show complex skills from various angles and at different speeds;
- highlight the main aspects of technique;
- focus attention on a few points, particularly for beginners and children;
- not allow too long a delay between instruction and demonstration;
- allow time for mental rehearsal;
- not allow too long a delay between demonstration and mental rehearsal;
- repeat the demonstration if necessary;
- reinforce successful performance.

Transfer of learning

Having considered the complexity, organisation and classification of a skill/task, a teacher needs to consider structuring the learning environment in order to take into account the concept of transfer. The instructional approaches used to introduce and teach skills/tasks to performers often depend on the relationship between various skills that have either been taught previously or are going to be taught in the future. The transfer of performance and learning from one situation to another has been an essential element of organisational and instructional approaches for many years.

There is evidence to support the following general points:

1 That different types of transfer possibilities exist.
2 That certain practice conditions can either help or hinder the actual effect or degree of transfer.
3 That the amount and direction of transfer can be affected by many factors.
4 That teachers need to be aware of the principles associated with transfer.
5 That teachers need to be able to apply these principles in order to structure effective teaching or coaching situations.

Types of transfer

The following are types of transfer:

- proactive;
- retroactive;
- positive;
- negative;
- bilateral.

Proactive transfer

When a skill/task presently being learned has an effect on future skills/tasks, this effect is said to be proactive. A teacher ultimately aiming to teach basketball may start off by introducing beginners to throwing, catching, passing, moving and dribbling, thus building up skills to be transferred into the future game situation. Simplified forms of more complex activities are introduced.

Retroactive

When a skill/task presently being learned has an effect on previously learned skills/tasks, this effect is said to be retroactive. This transfer is seen as working backwards in time.

(a) (b)

Figure 8.16 The movement skills required for a springboard diver can be developed on the trampoline

Positive transfer

Positive transfer, as the term suggests, is when skills/tasks that have been learned/experienced help or facilitate the learning of other skills. This can be positive retroactive or positive proactive. Similarities in both skill components and information-processing characteristics will help increase the possibilities of positive transfer. If these similarities are pointed out, particularly to beginners in the associative phase of learning, the effect of transfer can be enhanced further.

It is suggested that transfer possibilities are greater between tasks that have common elements. If the S–R bond expected in one task were the same as earlier learned S–R bonds, the effect of transfer would be greater. For example, a diver wishing to improve their coordination of turning and twisting might take part in trampolining practice in order to develop more control and possibly increase their understanding of rotation and twisting. The components in the practice situation (trampolining) are very similar to the main task and are realistic, thus improving the likelihood of positive transfer occurring.

It is important, therefore, if we accept this basic principle, that a teacher or coach must ensure that practice situations are as realistic as possible. Research on similarities between stimulus and response has shown that maximum positive transfer is produced when the stimulus and response characteristics of the new skill are identical to those of the old skill. Other theories have supported the idea that it is general principles of understanding and movement that are transferred as well as the specific elements of a skill. Thus, when the information-processing requirements (cognitive components) are similar, the effect of transfer is greater.

A player involved in a team game, such as football or hockey, would be able to transfer their spatial awareness, and their tactical understanding of passing, moving and tackling, from one game to another. Having learned to throw a cricket ball, the basic principles of the movement can be transferred to throwing a javelin (see Schema theory on page 173). This view of positive transfer being more likely between activities with similar cognitive elements (information-processing conditions) has been termed transfer-appropriate processing.

Negative transfer

When one skill/task hinders or inhibits the learning or performance of another skill/task, this is known as negative transfer. Sports performers and coaches tend to believe that this happens on a regular basis. Thankfully, the effects of negative transfer are thought to be limited and certainly temporary. It is thought to occur when a performer is required to produce a new response in a well-known situation (familiar stimulus). Stimuli are identical or similar, but the response requirements are different. Initial confusion is thought to be created more as a result of the performer having to readjust their cognitive processes than because of problems associated with the motor control of the movement. The familiar example of tennis having a negative effect on badminton is often quoted, but although the two games have similar aspects (tactics, use of space, court, net, racket, hand–eye coordination, etc.), the wrist and arm action are very different.

When a basketball or hockey coach changes tactics at set plays, any initial negative transfer is thought to be a result of the players having to readjust cognitive processes, rather than an inability to complete the movement required of them. For example, a rugby player has always been taught to fall to the ground when tackled in order to set up a ruck for his teammates. If the coach changes tactics and decides to develop a mauling game, it will be difficult for the player to stay on his feet in the tackle in order to set up a maul.

In order to overcome or limit the effects of negative transfer, teachers and coaches should be aware of areas that may cause initial confusion. Practices need to be planned accordingly, ensuring that the players are aware (direct attention) of possible difficulties they might experience. At the same time, the teacher or coach needs to be aware of possible positive effects and try to ensure that these outweigh the negative possibilities. In addition, the psychological habits of positive attitude, sustained motivation and a conscientious approach to training and practice can also be transferred positively in order to limit any negative effect, as can an understanding of how to deal with new problems.

Bilateral transfer

In our earlier discussion of transfer we considered transfer from one skill/task to another. Bilateral transfer, however, occurs when learning is transferred from limb to limb (e.g. from the right leg to the left leg). When a basketball coach tries to develop their player's weaker dribbling hand by relating it to earlier learned skills with the strong hand, they are using bilateral transfer. This involves the player in transferring both motor proficiency and levels of cognitive involvement. The performer is thought to adjust and transfer the parameters of stored motor programmes linked to one limb action to the other (schema theory). Thus, with the appropriate practice, the levels of learning developed with the performer's stronger or preferred hand or side can be transferred to the weaker hand or side.

Activity 11

Select a skill (e.g. a badminton serve or basketball lay-up) and attempt to execute the skill with your non-dominant hand. Discuss your experiences with a partner and explain how you modified your technique in an attempt to improve.

Strategies a coach/teacher could employ to promote positive transfer

- Ensure that the movement and cognitive requirements of the skills are similar.
- Ensure that the performer understands the principles of transfer.

Exam-style question

Compare and contrast drive theory, inverted U theory and catastrophe theory as explanations for the relationship between arousal and performance of motor skills.

(10 marks)

- Ensure that the performer is involved in the analysis of the skills.
- Ensure that the original skill is well learned before starting the new skill.
- Ensure that the performer practises the skill in a closed situation before trying it in a game.
- Ensure that practice is realistic.
- Ensure a variety of practice once the basics are mastered.
- Ensure that the principles of games are understood (e.g. width in attack, depth in defence).

Links to complexity and organisation

- If a task is complex but low in organisation, transfer is promoted by practising an easy version of the task first, before moving on to a more difficult version.
- If a task is simple but high in organisation, more difficult practices can be introduced.

What you need to know

- * Motivation is seen as energised, goal-directed, purposeful behaviour.
- * Motivation is closely linked to inner drives and arousal.
- * Motivation can affect the direction and intensity of behaviour.
- * Motivation can be intrinsic or extrinsic.
- * Extrinsic motivation is behaviour motivated by external rewards – tangible and intangible – or punishment.
- * Intrinsic motivation develops as a result of internal drives to achieve feelings of personal satisfaction and fulfilment (the flow experience).
- * Rewards should be monitored carefully and linked to giving information regarding a performer's level of competence.
- * Arousal is a physiological state of alertness and anticipation which prepares the body for action.
- * The reticular activating system (RAS) is responsible for maintaining the general level of arousal within the body.

* The concept of arousal is linked very closely to motivation.
* Drive theory states that there is a linear relationship between arousal and performance (the more the better!).
* The inverted U hypothesis suggests that the relationship is curvilinear. Increased arousal improves performance up to a certain point. Increases in arousal beyond this optimum level will have a detrimental effect on performance.
* Levels of optimum arousal will be different according to the complexity and nature of the specific task in relation to the individual's characteristics and the specific situation.
* Over-arousal can create perceptual narrowing.
* Catastrophe theory suggests that in highly competitive situations the deterioration in performance caused by over-arousal is much more extreme than the inverted U theory maintains.
* The key components of the behaviouristic perspective are stimulus (S) and response (R). The S–R theory is based on the concept that learning involves the development of connections or bonds between specific stimuli and responses.
* In operant conditioning, reinforcement is central to shaping behaviour.
* The teacher or coach must try to produce feelings of satisfaction to give strong reinforcements (law of effect).
* Hull's drive theory links motivation to the strengthening of the S–R bond.
* Cognitive theories suggest that performers must be able to understand events. The concept of insight is a major aspect of cognitive theories.
* When the skill/performance (response) achieved relates closely to the desired action (response) the teacher can:
  * give knowledge of results;
  * give praise/positive feedback/positive reinforcement.

  This will strengthen the S–R bond and promote success.
* If the required skill/performance is not produced, the teacher can weaken the bond between the stimulus and the inappropriate response (S–R) by:
  * giving negative feedback;
  * using punishment.
* Most behaviour in sport takes place within a social setting.
* Socialisation is the general continuous process of transmitting a culture to people and teaching them behaviour appropriate to the accepted norms, values and expectations of society.
* As a member of a sports group/team, a performer can be socialised into the 'modelled' norms of that subculture. These may be carried over and influence behaviour outside the sporting situation.
* The family is the most important prime socialising agent. However, teachers, coaches and high-status models and peers can also heavily influence a performer's behaviour.
* Social learning theory advocates that we learn and acquire new behaviours and attitudes, both acceptable and unacceptable, as a result of vicarious reinforcement through observation and imitation.

* The person being observed is the model.
* The effect of observational learning is dependent on the model having certain characteristics.
* Observational learning can take place without intention.
* The effect and level of social learning through observation is increased if the model is of a high status and their behaviour is reinforced.
* Demonstrations are an important aspect of observational learning.
* The process of observational learning involves four stages: attention, retention, motor production and motivation.
* Transfer refers to the influence of one activity/skill on another. There are a variety of types of transfer and transfer can be effective forwards or backwards in time.
* Transfer between tasks that are very similar is greater than transfer between dissimilar skills.
* The relationships between skills/concepts and cognitive processes need to be pointed out and explained to learners in order to increase the probability of positive transfer taking place.
* Teachers should try to minimise the possibility of negative transfer occurring.

Review questions

1 What is a theory of association?

2 Explain the S–R bond.

3 What does reinforcement mean?

4 How do positive and negative reinforcement affect the probability of behaviour occurring?

5 How does punishment affect behaviour?

6 What is the law of effect?

7 Give a practical example to show your understanding of how behaviour is shaped and maintained by its consequences.

8 What does 'insight learning' mean?

9 Why is the cognitive approach to learning thought to be most effective?

10 What do social psychologists mean by 'socialisation'?

11 What part can sport play in the process of socialisation?

12 What are socialising agents?

13 Why is observational learning important to social learning theory?

14 According to Bandura, what are the main characteristics of a model that influence the likelihood of imitation taking place?

15 Explain Bandura's four stages of observational learning.

16 What is meant by the term 'motivation'?

17 How is arousal linked to motivation?

18 Outline the differences between drive theory and the inverted U hypothesis in relation to arousal and performance.

19 What does a curvilinear-shaped graph imply?

20 How does catastrophe theory differ from inverted U theory?

21 In what ways can arousal levels affect learning and performance?

22 Explain the factors that can affect the level of optimum arousal.

23 Explain the different types of extrinsic and intrinsic motivation and provide examples of each.

24 Why is intrinsic motivation thought to be more effective than extrinsic motivation?

25 What factors should a teacher or coach be aware of when using extrinsic rewards?

26 Identify three disadvantages of extrinsic motivation.

27 If a performer is intrinsically motivated, will the introduction of extrinsic rewards enhance motivation? Explain your answer.

28 Explain three ways to develop intrinsic motivation.

29 In what ways can a teacher try to reduce the effect of negative transfer?

30 Give two practical examples of negative transfer.

Introduction

Sport sociology is an approach which attempts to determine the place of physical activity within different cultures. Society is a dynamic concept as it is constantly changing and adapting; sometimes it evolves gradually over centuries, while at other times revolutionary changes are experienced almost overnight. Sport reflects and influences the society of which it is an integral part.

The chapters in this section highlight the impact society has on sport, and vice versa, and the ongoing nature of this process, which continues to affect *your* personal experiences of participating in sporting activities. Imagine a situation where you have no facilities in which to train, no clubs to belong to, and where the system of coaching is so underdeveloped that athletes cannot improve. Imagine living in Victorian times, and think how different your experiences would have been in terms of leisure, recreation, sport and education. For example, by comparing our contemporary experience to the Victorian era, we can see that:

- there is now more equality of opportunity for different social groups [OPE];
- sport has enhanced international communication;
- sport as big business has created questions about ethics and the politics of sport;
- perhaps more importantly, experiencing the human emotions connected to participation in sporting activities is what makes it a valuable subject of study.

Factors affecting sport in society

Several factors can influence and be influenced by the system of sport. These are outlined in the diagram below. The arrows suggest the symbiotic relationship.

Consider each factor and try to extend them into subcategories. For example, education factors might include:

- state and private schools;
- facilities;
- government policies;

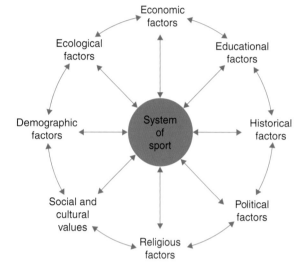

- national curriculum;
- physical education.

It would be useful at this stage to choose one factor that interests you and research what influence it may have had on sport, or vice versa, either in the past or today. This should give you some understanding of the type of issues that will be covered in later chapters. We will study:

- the term 'physical activity', and the benefits of physical activity to the individual and society; special consideration will be given to current issues of increasingly sedentary living, especially in terms of the impact on young people;
- the conceptual understanding of what constitutes physical activity – physical recreation; physical education; outdoor education and recreation; and sport;
- the historical development of physical activities, ethnic sports and the role of the nineteenth-century public schools in their promotion and organisation of sports and games;
- the development of sport, from a dominant amateur status to an increasing professionalisation;
- contemporary sporting issues, such as funding; the administration of sport and sporting policies for participation and excellence; performance-enhancing products; sponsorship and the media; violence; and the impact of the 2012 Olympic Games;
- the role of sport in the United Kingdom, the United States of America and Australia.

CHAPTER 9

The concept of physical activity

Learning outcomes

By the end of this chapter you should be able to understand:

- the terms 'physical activity', 'exercise', 'healthy, balanced lifestyle' and 'lifetime sport';
- the benefits of regular participation in sport;
- the need for regular participation in physical activity, by considering factors such as increasingly sedentary lifestyles, especially among young people;
- the barriers facing young people in their participation in regular physical activity;
- the definitions, characteristics and benefits of:
  - physical recreation and outdoor recreation;
  - physical education and outdoor education;
  - sport, with particular emphasis on the terms 'prowess', 'endeavour', 'sportsmanship', 'gamesmanship' and 'deviancy'.

What is meant by 'physical activity'?

'Physical activity' is an umbrella term encompassing any activity that requires an individual to exert a certain amount of energy, resulting in an increase in their heart rate. Physical activity may include:

- many different activities, from walking, skipping and playing games, to athletic, outdoor and adventurous activities, such as skiing or canoeing;
- participating on a recreational basis and/or performing within a more competitive and organised sporting structure, including adhering to externally enforced rules.

IN CONTEXT

To remain healthy, the current British Heart Foundation recommendation is 60 minutes of exercise per day which results in raising an individual's heart rate.

When an individual raises their heart rate sufficiently, a certain number of times a week, they can be said to be improving their health and potentially reducing their risk of cardiovascular disease.

Figure 9.1 The physical activity continuum

Healthy: The state of being bodily and mentally vigorous and free from disease.
Exercise: To exert one's muscles, especially in order to keep fit and healthy.
Healthy, balanced lifestyle: Where an individual achieves a healthy state or equilibrium, especially in the ratio of time shared between the active and non-active aspects of their life.

Government targets for increasing participation

Recognising the relationship between increased physical activity and improved health, for the individual and society, since the mid 1980s the government has become increasingly involved in developing policies to try to improve activity levels among the population as a whole, but with a specific focus on *young people*. The opportunities the Government create through the provision of facilities and programmes will have a marked impact on all sections of the population, but especially young people [OPE]. Below are some of the targets which have developed:

1 Enhance the take-up of sporting opportunities by children and young people aged 5 to 16 years, to increase the percentage of schoolchildren in England who spend a minimum of two hours per week on high-quality PE and school sport, within and beyond the curriculum, from 25 per cent in 2002 to 75 per cent by 2006, and to 85 per cent by 2008, and to at least 75 per cent in each School Sport Partnership by 2008 (joint target with the Department for Education and Skills).
2 Halt the year-on-year increase in obesity among children under 11 years by 2010, in the context of a broader strategy to tackle obesity in the population as a whole (joint target with the Department for Education and Skills and the Department of Health).
3 By 2008, increase by 3 per cent the number of people who participate in active sports at least 12 times a year, and the number who engage in at least 30 minutes of moderate-intensity sport at least three times a week.

As a class or as an individual, calculate the amount of time you spend in physical activity per week. How does this compare as a percentage to the time you spend on non-active pursuits, such as reading?

Benefits of physical activity for young people

Physical activity has important beneficial effects on the current and future health of children and young people. This message has been highlighted in summaries of relevant evidence in the report of the Chief Medical Officer (2004) and by Biddle, Gorely and Stensel (2004).

The potential benefits are:

- healthy growth and development of the musculoskeletal and cardiorespiratory systems;
- maintenance of health–energy balance (in order to encourage a healthy weight);
- avoidance of risk factors for coronary heart disease, such as high blood pressure and abnormal lipid profile;
- opportunities for social interaction, achievement and mental well-being especially self-esteem;
- general cognitive functioning and academic achievement in school (Sibley and Etnier 2003);
- less likelihood of smoking or using alcohol or illegal drugs (Physical Activity Task Force 2002).

Esteem: To have great respect or high regard for someone or something. Talented athletes who reach the pinnacle of their sport are awarded honour and prestige that raises their social status. Sociologically this can provide a finer analysis than a purely social class differentiation. Such athletes may become role models to younger children. An athlete's own self-esteem is also raised by a sense of achievement.
Opportunity: Individuals experience different opportunities/constraints, such as family background, socio-economic status, leisure time and disposable income.
Provision: Participation by different community groups is influenced by increasing accessibility of facilities, transport, equipment, space and a variety of activities.

Being physically active as a child may also lead to improved health status as an adult. If young people emerge from their school years feeling confident about their physical skills, their bodies and their ability to participate in physical activities, this may result in them being more physically active throughout adulthood. There is currently limited evidence on the tracking of physical activity from childhood to adulthood. However, children who are inactive are very likely to become inactive adults (National Association for Sport and Physical Education 2004).

Other potential benefits for adults of physical activity in childhood are as follows:

- Maintenance of optimal body weight in childhood reduces the risk of obesity in adulthood.

Activity 2

Below is some information on the New Healthy Schools Physical Activity Toolkit and YHeart. Read this and then research some brief information on two of the other projects listed above.

New Healthy Schools Physical Activity Toolkit

The National Healthy Schools Programme (NHSP) is led by the Department of Health (DoH) and the Department for Education and Skills (DfES), and is an important delivery vehicle for cross-government policy for children and young people.

To achieve National Healthy School status, schools have to meet minimum criteria on four specific health themes:

1   personal, social and health education (PSHE);
2   healthy eating;
3   physical activity;
4   emotional health and well-being.

Physical activity has only recently been introduced as one of the four core themes and is a significant development in the programme.

YHeart

Be Active!

It only takes **60 minutes** a day to keep active.

Yes, that's all it takes! You just need to do something physical like **dancing, cycling, swimming** or even **walking your dog!** So long as it makes you slightly out of breath.

YOU could do it as 4 slots of 15 mins each day if time is tight.

Team sports like football, basketball and netball are also great. It just depends what you're into. Or, you can stay in the comfort of your own home, and use an exercise tape or video.

Ready, Steady, GO!

1   Put on your favourite music and dance!
2   Take your dog (or someone else's) for a walk.
3   Don't catch the bus, leave home a bit earlier and have a brisk walk. It's FREE! Think of ALL the money you will save on fares!
4   Borrow an exercise video or tape – work out to your own routine. (Some libraries have them or try the health and fitness section of your nearest record shop, bookshop).
5   Always run up stairs!

Check this out BEFORE you start.

- Set yourself an activity routine.
- Always start and end each session with a few minutes of gentle activity to warm up and cool down.
- The best form of activity is something you enjoy and can fit into your daily routine. This way, once you have started you won't be tempted to find an excuse for not keeping it up!
- Sixty minutes a day will make all the difference.

Source: British Heart Foundation website: www.bhf.org/yheart

- Maximisation of bone development can reduce the later risk of osteoporosis – appropriate activity can lead to increases in bone mineral density of 5–15 per cent.
- Maintenance of childhood aerobic fitness potentially has a beneficial effect on adult risk of cardiovascular disease.

Some of the current projects which are trying to establish the relationship between activity and health, and to encourage greater participation in young people, are listed below:

1 New Healthy Schools Physical Activity Toolkit
2 Schools on the Move
3 TOP Activity
4 Get Moving, Get Active Participation Award
5 Yheart

The 2005/6 School Sport Survey highlighted the important roles which physical education and sport play in school life, suggesting that they:

- help to raise standards;
- improve behaviour and health;
- increase attendance;
- develop social skills.

According to researchers, schools are an appropriate setting for the promotion of physical activity, and other health behaviours, for a number of reasons:

1 Schools provide one of the few opportunities to address the full range of individuals in a population, and a last chance to access a captive audience, at no extra cost.
2 Schools provide a range of opportunities for pupils to engage in physical activity, such as break-time, travel to and from school, physical education lessons and extracurricular clubs.
3 Elements of the traditional school curriculum relate directly to health.
4 Any positive impact that schools have on young people has the potential added benefit of having a lifetime, as well as an immediate effect.

Key term

Lifetime sport: Physical activities which an individual can participate in regardless of age, such as swimming or golf.

There is some debate about the value of the traditional physical education curriculum, in which team games are a central theme. The problem is that many people do not choose to continue with team games into adulthood. There has been a trend in recent years to deliver other activities within schools which may prove more popular as lifetime sports.

The Department of Health (DoH) and the Department for Education and Skills (DfES) believe that the 2012 Olympic Games in London provides the ideal opportunity to increase the level of interest in sport and relate this to the benefits of a healthy lifestyle. Schools will be at the forefront of this ambitious agenda, since it is while they are in school that most children get their first opportunity to try sport and discover their talent and potential. Cross-sectional and longitudinal studies have shown that the rate of academic learning per unit of class time is enhanced in physically active students, so that lack of curricular time is not a valid reason for denying children a daily programme of high-quality physical education. Research is unequivocal on the point that children who are physically active tend to be healthier, happier and better learners than their sedentary peers.

Activity 3

Using the information provided, and the results of your discussions, list the benefits of physical activity under the following headings:
- Physical;
- Cognitive;
- Personal and social;
- Society.

Factors contributing to an increasingly sedentary lifestyle

As a society, we are becoming increasingly concerned about the levels of inactivity among many groups of people, but especially among young people, because of the significant impact this will have on their future physical and mental health – not to mention the cost to society.

Young people are participating less in physical activity today for a number of reasons:

- more variety of leisure activities available, such as watching TV and playing computer games;

- safety risks of young people being away from parental control, so young children play less actively than they used to;
- children do not walk to school as much as they used to;
- curricular and extracurricular time given to physical activity has decreased, as well as some theory work being introduced into PE lessons;
- there is a particular problem among teenage girls, whose participation levels drop dramatically due to social pressures and the perception of sport being unfeminine.

Activity 4

Talk to a group of young people who choose *not* to participate very much in physical activity, and draw up a list of reasons for this.

Possible barriers to regular participation by young people

These include the following:

1 Lack of time – due to school work, part-time work, domestic responsibilities, and so on.
2 Cost – many activities are beyond the reach of a large number of young people, especially those from low socio-economic backgrounds.
3 Media – the image of sport portrayed by the media, such as the coverage of more male-orientated sports, rather than female sport.
4 Discrimination (racism, sexism, and so on) – this may be overt (e.g. a clause in a private members club) or covert (e.g. people's attitudes within a sports club towards a young person from a different socio-economic group or a certain race) [OPE].
5 Environment – young people in rural areas may experience fewer opportunities in terms of provision for different activities (e.g. swimming pools require a sufficient catchment area).
6 Safety constraints – we are becoming a more safety-conscious society in terms of personal risk and concerns about being at risk from other people.
7 Poor self-image/body image – people with a poor self-image or body image are less likely to participate in sport [OPE].
8 Competing leisure interests – young people are able to undertake many different types of recreational activities today, and sport has to compete within this arena.
9 School club links – though the government is trying to improve links, these are traditionally poor in the UK [OPE].
10 Extracurricular activities are dependent on the goodwill of teachers – in some countries, such as France, sport and physical education are compulsory [OPE].
11 Competitiveness – some young people do not enjoy the competitive emphasis of sport.

IN CONTEXT

In the UK, the dramatic drop in active participation in recreational and sporting activities after young people have left school (known as the post-school gap) is the worst in Europe.

We began this chapter by referring to physical activity as an umbrella term for a variety of activities, which people participate in with different motivations; for example, as a:

- recreational activity;
- form of compulsory education;
- sport.

Now we need to discover exactly what we mean by these terms.

Exam-style question

How might a school Physical Education department give children experience of education, physical recreation and sport?

(5 marks)

Recreation, physical recreation, active leisure

The word 'recreation' originates from the Latin word *recreatio*, which means to restore health. Recreation has long been connected with individual relaxation and recuperation, and during the nineteenth century was mostly valued for restoring people's energies for work. Thus, recreation was considered to be of benefit to society as well as the individual. Many theorists (e.g. H. Meyer, C. Brightbill, G. Butler) espouse the idea that recreation must be of 'value', either to the individual or society. This is always a problem area, because it begs the question: whose values are more important? This is particularly significant when considering the provision for recreation by public agencies, such as local authorities, churches, schools, industries, voluntary agencies and government departments. What are the presumptions under which they organise their services?

Over time, however, people have participated in physical recreational activities for many different reasons, such as to socialise, to keep fit or simply for the feel-good factor, as active participation will provide the individual with a sense of well-being and self-fulfilment. J.S. Shivers concentrates on the idea of recreation as an 'experience'. Recreation wholly absorbs the individual at any one moment and helps to provide 'psychological homeostasis', that is, the satisfying of psychological needs and the process of mental rebalancing. Recreation is the harmony and unity experienced between mind and body, which occurs at the *time* of the experience – the *value* is felt later.

Today, the most widely accepted view of recreation is simply activities in which people participate during their leisure time. Recreation can incorporate sedentary activities, such as reading, as well as the physical activities/sports which will be our main focus of study.

> Recreation consists of activities or experiences carried on within leisure, usually chosen voluntarily by the participant – either because of satisfaction, pleasure or creative enrichment derived, or because he perceives certain personal or social gains to be gained from them. It may also be perceived as the process of participation, or as the emotional state derived from the involvement. (R. Kraus 1971)

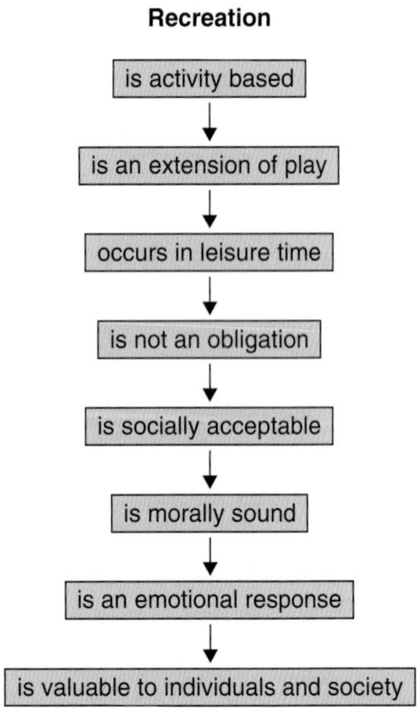

Recreation

is activity based

↓

is an extension of play

↓

occurs in leisure time

↓

is not an obligation

↓

is socially acceptable

↓

is morally sound

↓

is an emotional response

↓

is valuable to individuals and society

Figure 9.2 Values of recreation

Activity 5

In your own words, explain the following phrases used in Kraus's definition of recreation:
- 'carried on within leisure';
- 'chosen voluntarily';
- 'personal and social gains'.

Key terms

Recreation: 'any activity, either individual or collective, which is pursued during one's leisure time' (M. Neumeyer).
Physical recreation: Where the activity requires the individual to expend a reasonable amount of energy, also known as active leisure.
Leisure time: This refers to surplus time – time left over when practical necessities such as work, sleep and other needs (including family and social duties) have been attended to.

Activity 6

Write to your local borough council to discover their aims and policies for recreation provision in your area. This can provide a useful insight into the planning of recreation as a social institution.

EXAMINER'S TIP

An *aim* is what someone is trying to achieve.
A *policy* is how they intend to achieve the aim, that is, what action will be taken.

Activity 7

1 Make a list of activities you participate in during your leisure time.
2 Categorise them into active and non-active.
3 Write down the reasons why you participate in each activity.
4 Compare lists with someone else in your group.

Characteristics of recreation

The characteristics of recreation are as follows:
- freedom and free time;
- self-expression;
- satisfaction and self-fulfilment;
- quality of experience;

- no pressure or obligation to take part;
- range of activities;
- experience and development.

NB for outdoor recreation see page 219.

IN CONTEXT

Recreation planning certainly has its place within our modern and rapidly changing society, but for many people, true recreation is not about having their leisure time organised in the same way that the world of work is organised, as this brings its own constraints.

- Services should be developed so that people can find recreation and fulfil individual needs.
- Access should be available to all citizens.
- Planning for recreation *activities* can be measurable and operable, but planning cannot guarantee a recreation *experience* (a particular incident or feeling).
- Education can be extended to include leisure skills, helping people to realise and achieve their potential. (This will be discussed in more detail below, in the section on Physical education.)

IN CONTEXT

Many people prefer outdoor and adventurous activities, as there is more of a sense of freedom from institutionalised provision. However, planning is still needed by local authorities and other relevant organisations, such as the Association of National Park Authorities, in order to protect the environment from erosion, tourism, and so on.

Activity 8

List the benefits of physical recreation to:
- the individual;
- society.

Figure 9.3 Play, recreation, leisure or sport?

In summary, recreation can be viewed as:

- a personal experience (the value to the individual) [OPE];
- the nature of an activity (e.g. active or non-active) [OPE];
- an institution and structural framework (e.g. provision by a local authority) [OPE].

Activity 9

Beach volleyball (see Figure 9.3) has grown significantly in the last decade. How can it meet the needs of the individual in terms of recreation and sport?

Physical education

What is physical education?

Physical education is an academic discipline (an organised, formal body of knowledge), which has as its primary focus the study of human movement. It may be viewed as a field of knowledge, drawing on the physical and human sciences and philosophy, with its main emphasis on physical activity. As this field of knowledge has broadened, the subject-specific areas have increased. Sub-disciplines have emerged which have diversified the subject and related it to career opportunities. Examples of such sub-disciplines are: sport sociology, biomechanics, sports medicine, exercise physiology, sport philosophy, history of sport, sports psychology and sports management. You will probably recognise some of these from your own AS level physical education course.

Physical education at this level may seem a far cry from what you have experienced during your time at school. At this stage, it is necessary to know what is meant by the term 'physical education', and to appreciate that over the last century a philosophy has developed (and will continue to develop), sometimes changing radically the practice of this subject.

Activity 10

Discuss the following philosophical viewpoints with a partner or as a class:

- All participants, regardless of athletic ability, should have equal amounts of playing time on the school curriculum.
- Physical educators should be role models and practise on the playing fields what they preach in the classroom!
- Physical education is only useful in that it provides a break from academic lessons.
- Physical education should be compulsory.

Physical education is an educational process which aims to enhance total human development and performance, through movement and the experience of a range of physical activities within an educational setting. Total development means acquiring activity-specific skills and knowledge, as well as fostering positive attitudes and values which will be useful in later life. Physical education can help us to achieve a quality of life and a vitality which can be lacking in sedentary lifestyles.

Key term

Sedentary: A tendency to sit about, without taking much exercise.

Activity 11

Consider the key words below and provide an example for each one (e.g. Knowledge: the learning of rules).

- Range of physical activities;
- Movement;
- Activity-specific skills;
- Knowledge;
- Values;
- Educational setting.

Aims and objectives

Physical activity involves doing, thinking and feeling. Children need to know *how* to perform or express themselves; to know *about* physical activities; and to benefit from the enriching experience of knowing how it *feels* to perform.

Already we have given physical education some very difficult challenges. We are assuming that all the outcomes are positive, but this is clearly not the case. Among your peers there will be those who enjoy their physical education experiences, but there will also be some who definitely do not! Before we can hope to achieve the positive benefits, we must clarify the aims, objectives and desired outcomes of the physical education curriculum.

Aims

Physical education aims to:

- develop a range of psycho-motor skills;
- maintain and increase physical mobility and flexibility, stamina and strength;
- develop understanding and appreciation of a range of physical activities;
- develop positive values and attitudes, such as sportsmanship, competition and abiding by the rules;
- help children to acquire self-esteem and confidence through the acquisition of skills, knowledge and values [OPE];
- develop an understanding of the importance of exercise in maintaining a healthy lifestyle.

Objectives

Physical education can affect different areas of development. For example:

- The children will be able to complete a 20-minute run – physical development.
- The children will execute the correct technique for a gymnastic vault – motor development.
- The children will be able to explain the scoring system in badminton – cognitive development.
- The children will display enthusiasm and enjoyment and participate in extracurricular activities – affective or emotional development.

A balanced physical education programme

A balanced programme should attempt to offer a variety of activities selected from each group in

Table 9.1 (below), in order to maximise fully the opportunities to be gained from the different activities. There should be a balance of activities which are:

- team-orientated;
- individual;
- competitive;
- non-competitive movement-based.

Table 9.1 What a child receives from quality physical education

Physical skills	Physical fitness	Knowledge & understanding	Social skills	Attitudes & appreciations
↓	↓	↓	↓	↓
in:	such as:	of:	such as:	such as:
<ul><li>games;</li><li>gymnastics;</li><li>dance;</li><li>swimming;</li><li>track and field;</li><li>outdoor and adventurous activities;</li><li>fitness programme.</li></ul>	<ul><li>functional fitness capacities essential to health and well-being;</li><li>cardiorespiratory efficiency;</li><li>muscular strength;</li><li>muscular endurance;</li><li>flexibility;</li><li>motor ability capacities: speed, balance, agility, coordination and reaction time.</li></ul>	<ul><li>safety;</li><li>physical skills;</li><li>physical fitness;</li><li>body systems;</li><li>learning processes;</li><li>social skills;</li><li>scientific principles of movement;</li><li>environmental concerns;</li><li>rules;</li><li>strategies;</li><li>community recreational opportunities.</li></ul>	<ul><li>fair play;</li><li>cooperation, teamwork and sharing;</li><li>responsibility;</li><li>leadership and citizenship;</li><li>competition;</li><li>communication: listening, speaking, performance and demonstrating;</li><li>operating with rules;</li><li>self-control: work under pressure;</li><li>following directions;</li><li>resourcefulness;</li><li>self-direction;</li><li>consideration of others.</li></ul>	<ul><li>desire to participate in physical activities;</li><li>desire to be physically active;</li><li>interest in health and responsibility for personal care;</li><li>appreciation of fair play operating within the rules;</li><li>respect for team-mates, opponents and officials;</li><li>appreciation of own abilities and the abilities of others;</li><li>appreciation of the relationship between exercise and health;</li><li>appreciation of the quality effort in the work of others;</li><li>feelings of pride and loyalty in the accomplishments of self, school and others;</li><li>interest in a positive self-concept.</li></ul>

Source: The British Journal of Teaching Physical Education, Autumn 2002

Table 9.2 A balanced physical education programme

Games				Movement
Invasion	**Net**	**Striking/field**	**Rebounding**	
football	tennis	cricket	squash	gymnastics
netball	volleyball	rounders		dance
hockey	table tennis	softball		trampolining
rugby				athletics
				swimming

Activity 12

Ask a group of your peers about their experiences of physical education (including the types of activities, and what they enjoyed most or least). You can ask general or more specific questions.

Activity 13

1 Study the aims of physical education and see how you might link these to the activities shown in Table 9.2.

2 Tick the activities which you have experienced during your secondary education. Do you think you received a balanced physical education programme?

3 Conduct a survey of approximately six schools in your local area. Try to find out what they offer their pupils. Can you find parallels or many variations? Does what is on offer reflect the different nature of the schools?

Who chooses the physical education programme?

In the UK there is a decentralised system, by which the teacher and the individual school have the power to produce their own programme, though they are increasingly bound by government guidelines. The national curriculum now sets out which subjects are to be taught at each key stage of a pupil's schooling. Physical education is compulsory from Key Stage 1 (ages 5 to 7) through to Key Stage 4 (up to age 16).

National curriculum The national curriculum attempts to raise standards in education and make schools more accountable for what they teach. Physical education continues to be one of only five subjects which pupils of all abilities must pursue, from their entry to school at age 5, until the end of compulsory schooling at age 16.

Attainment targets and programmes of study have been written for physical education. Children are required to demonstrate the knowledge, skills and understanding involved in areas of various physical activities, including dance, athletics, gymnastics, outdoor and adventurous activities, and swimming. There are four key stages.

Key Stage 1

During key stage 1 pupils build on their natural enthusiasm for movement, using it to explore and learn about their world. They start to work and play with other pupils in pairs and small groups. By watching, listening and experimenting, they develop their skills in movement and coordination, and enjoy expressing and testing themselves in a variety of situations.

Breadth of study
During the key stage, pupils should be taught the knowledge, skills and understanding through dance activities, games activities and gymnastic activities.

Figure 9.4 Key Stage 1 – programme of study

Key Stage 2

During key stage 2 pupils enjoy being active and using their creativity and imagination in physical activity. They learn new skills, find out how to use them in different ways, and link them to make actions, phrases and sequences of movement. They enjoy communicating, collaborating and competing with each other. They develop an understanding of how to succeed in different activities and learn how to evaluate and recognise their own success.

Breadth of study
During the key stage, pupils should be taught the knowledge, skills and understanding through five areas of activity:

a) dance activities
b) games activities
c) gymnastic activities

and two activity areas from:

d) swimming activities and water safety
e) athletic activities
f) outdoor and adventurous activities.

Figure 9.5 Key Stage 2 – programme of study

Key Stage 3

During key stage 3 pupils become more expert in their skills and techniques, and how to apply them in different activities. They start to understand what makes a performance effective and how to apply these principles to their own and others' work. They learn to take the initiative and make decisions for themselves about what to do to improve performance. They start to identify the types of activity they prefer to be involved with, and to take a variety of roles such as leader and official.

Breadth of study
During the key stage, pupils should be taught the knowledge, skills and understanding through four areas of activity. These should include:

a) games activities

and three of the following, at least one of which must be dance or gymnastic activities:

b) dance activities
c) gymnastic activities
d) swimming activities and water safety
e) athletic activities
f) outdoor and adventurous activities.

Figure 9.6 Key Stage 3 – programme of study

Key Stage 4

During key stage 4 pupils tackle complex and demanding activities applying their knowledge of skills, techniques and effective performance. They decide whether to get involved in physical activity that is mainly focused on competing or performing, promoting health and well-being, or developing personal fitness. They also decide on roles that suit them best including performer, coach, choreographer, leader and official. The view they have of their skilfulness and physical competence gives them the confidence to get involved in exercise and activity out of school and in later life.

Breadth of study
During the key stage, pupils should be taught the knowledge, skills and understanding through two of the six activity areas.

Figure 9.7 Key Stage 4 – programme of study

Activity 14

1   Summarise the general requirements for each key stage of the national curriculum.
2   What factors may a teacher have to take into account when devising a syllabus?

The importance of physical education

Physical education develops pupils' physical competence and confidence, and their ability to use these to perform in a range of activities. It promotes physical skilfulness, physical development and a knowledge of the body in action. Physical education provides opportunities for students to be creative, competitive and to face up to different challenges, as individuals and in groups and teams. It promotes positive attitudes towards active and healthy lifestyles.

Students learn how to think in different ways, to suit a wide variety of creative, competitive and challenging activities. They learn how to plan, perform and evaluate actions, ideas and performances, to improve their quality and effectiveness. Through this process, pupils discover their aptitudes, abilities and preferences, and make choices about how to become involved in lifelong physical activity.

The DfES also conducted a survey in the 1990s, which showed that many schools are still not devoting two hours a week to physical education, as recommended.

Activity 15

Suggest reasons why one-third of secondary schools in the UK do not manage to provide the recommended two hours of physical education per week.

Physical education as preparation for leisure

As young people approach the end of their compulsory years of schooling, it is necessary to foster an awareness of the opportunities available in the community. As a result of the philosophy of educating children for their leisure time, schools began to offer options in the later years of schooling, where a wider variety of activities could be experienced, sometimes using community facilities. This was made possible by smaller groups, guided by additional non-specialist staff. Students should be informed about and put in contact with local clubs and sports centres.

This is an area of weakness in the UK, as there are traditionally poor links between schools and community sport, as a result of trying to maintain a distance between sport and physical education.

Developments in school sport

The term 'sport' refers to the 'physical activities with established rules engaged in by individuals attempting to outperform their competitors' (Wuest and Bucher 1991). Sport provides different opportunities for physical activity while at school. Its main focus is on improving performance standards, rather than the educational process, and it takes place mainly outside the formal curriculum. It is usually viewed as an opportunity for children to extend their interest or ability in physical activities.

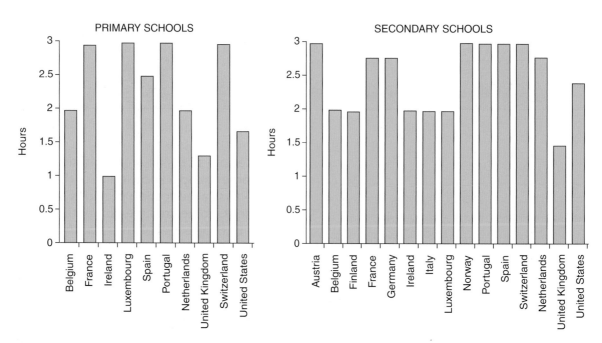

Figure 9.8 The amount of time devoted to PE in schools in the UK compared to the rest of Europe and the USA
Source: European Union of Physical Education Associations

Figure 9.9 School sport encourages teamwork

Table 9.3 Advantages and disadvantages of competitive sport

Advantages	Disadvantages
Children have a natural competitive instinct, and as they are more motivated to practise, enjoyment of sport increases	Continued feelings of failure can cause stress and anxiety
Can raise self-esteem and help children learn how to cope with failure and success	The need to win can encourage unsporting behaviour

The changes which have taken place in society and education since the mid 1980s (e.g. extracurricular opportunities) have affected school sport, with a reduction in emphasis on the sporting elite, which sometimes required a disproportionate amount of resources for a small number of children. Extracurricular clubs, open to all, became more acceptable. However, extracurricular activities were affected by some of the following factors:

1 The teachers' strikes in the early 1980s – the contractual hours and lack of monetary incentives tended to diminish teachers' goodwill, and clubs were disbanded.
2 Financial cuts were felt in terms of transport.
3 The local management of schools allowed schools to supplement their funds by selling off school fields.
4 The increasing amount of leisure and employment opportunities for children meant they were less attracted to competing for their school team.
5 The anticompetitive lobby became more vocal – they espoused the theory that competition in sport was not good for children's development.

Through its Department for Children, Schools and Families, the government has put forward a number of initiatives to increase the range and amount of school sport available to young people aged 5–16 years:

- By 2008, they hope to engage 75 per cent of children in each school partnership in two hours of high-quality PE and school sport per week, within and beyond the curriculum.
- By 2010 the ambition is to offer all children at least four hours of sport, made up of at least two hours of high-quality PE within the curriculum, and at least an additional two to three hours out of school, delivered by a range of school, community and club providers.

Some of the initiatives in operation are set out below:

1 Club Links – This programme links schools with local sports clubs and is being delivered through the national governing bodies of 22 sports.
2 Competition Managers – The government's Department for Culture, Media and Sport is appointing Competition Managers to develop a programme of inter-school competitions in a number of pilot areas. The Department aims to have a Competition Manager in all School Sport Partnerships by 2010.
3 Step into Sport – This is a joint initiative with the Department for Children, Schools and Families, and is one of the eight strands in the national School Sports Strategy. Step into Sport provides sports leadership and volunteering opportunities for young people aged 14–19 years.
4 Sport kitemarks for schools – Following consultation on proposals to introduce changes to sport kitemarks, two key changes have been agreed:
    1 Kitemarks will reward delivery of the national PE, School Sports and Club Links strategy. They will therefore only be open to schools which are in a School Sport Partnership.
    2 Kitemarks will be awarded annually, and this will happen automatically through the

national school sport survey, so there will be no need to complete a separate application form.

A high-quality physical education for all children is central to the Government's new PE School Sport and Club Links Strategy (PESSCL).

Physical education or sport?

This is an ongoing debate, which resurfaced in the 1995 document *Sport: Raising the Game*, with the government's decision to give competitive sport a higher status. The terms 'physical education' and 'sport' are complex. There is an overlap between them, but the central focus of each one is different. The aim of physical education is to educate the individual, while sport has other purposes, such as achieving excellence, fitness and earning an income. A good physical education programme can be the foundation on which extracurricular opportunities can be extended and enhanced. However, physical education teachers should not necessarily feel pressured into allowing a 'sport' ethos to creep into the curriculum.

Sport education

'Sport education' is a term used to describe a pupil-centred rather than teacher-centred approach. Children are encouraged to be continually involved in the learning process. This gives every child an opportunity to have some form of success within school physical education, even if they are not particularly physically gifted. Children are given responsibility for organising aspects of lessons, such as equipment management, practice drills and working constructively in teams to include each member. Inclusion of all children is therefore a key factor.

Outdoor and adventurous activities

Outdoor and adventurous activities take place in the natural environment, including situations which are dangerous and challenging, suggesting conquest of natural obstacles or terrain. Examples of such activities are rock climbing, skiing and skydiving. New activities continue to develop, mostly as a result of technological advances, such as jet-skiing and windsurfing.

It is possible to participate in these activities through a recreational and/or an educational approach:

- Outdoor education: participation in outdoor and adventurous activities in the natural environment, developing educational values. For example, a school may offer orienteering within the school grounds, or arrange a visit to a national park or other area where adventurous activities may be undertaken.
- Outdoor recreation: participation in outdoor and adventurous activities within the natural environment in an individual's free time.

When individuals participate in a *recreational* capacity there are no rules as such, no winners or losers and therefore no officials. There is usually a code of etiquette, however, concerning safety and the conservation of the natural environment.

Activity 16

1 List as many activities as you can which take place in the natural environments of water, mountains, air and countryside.

2 Where people do not have easy access to these areas, how could you adapt the urban environment for them to learn the basic skills of some of these sports?

Recently, many of these activities have become *sports*, involving scoring systems and officials, for example, white-water slalom races and speed climbing. These activities can place the individual in situations which are dangerous and challenging, and which induce exhilaration, fear and excitement. They can be competitive, but more often the competition is against the elements or the human body rather than against another person. When an individual is facing the elements, the main challenge they face is differentiating between real and perceived risk.

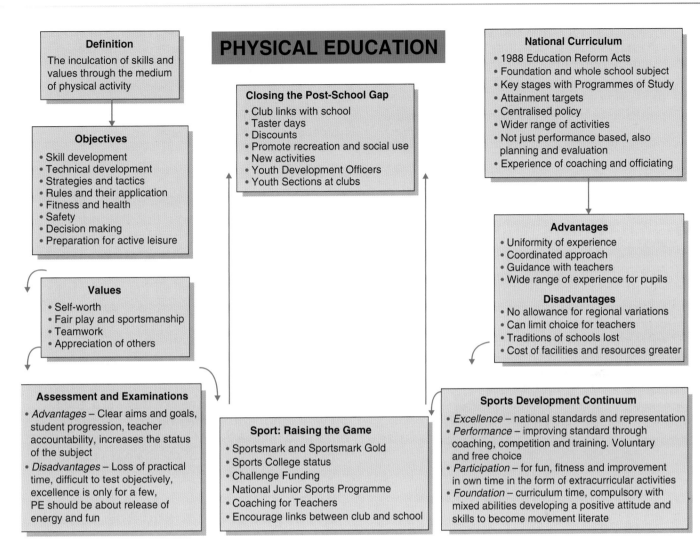

Figure 9.10 Physical education

Risk: The possibility of incurring injury or loss; being exposed to danger or a hazard. Outdoor and adventurous activities pose situations of real and perceived risk.

Real risk: Risk from the natural environment, such as a rock fall. Leaders need to be aware of the potential risks when planning routes and so on.

Perceived risk: This is where the sense of adventure comes from, and leaders need to be aware of this. If the perceived risk is too great for the ability level of the performer, however, feelings of anxiety could become overwhelming.

The personal qualities required for and enhanced by these activities include:

- self-reliance;
- decision-making skills;
- leadership;
- the ability to trust others;
- trustworthiness.

Such activities are not usually done alone, and the ability to work with others to overcome obstacles is often important.

Growth of outdoor and adventurous activities

There has been considerable growth in both traditional (e.g. canoeing, rock climbing, abseiling, climbing) and 'new' (e.g. jet-skiing, snowboarding, mountain biking) adventure sports. The reasons for this growth can be explained by:

- increasingly sedentary lifestyles, which make some people seek more active and exciting leisure time;

- increased leisure time and standards of living, which make these activities more accessible;
- the development of new and exciting sports technology;
- the appreciation of the natural environment, particularly as a release from urban pressures.

According to Mortlock, there are four broad stages of adventure:

- Play – little challenge in developing skills/boredom could set in.
- Adventure – more challenging environment/skills developed under safe conditions.
- Frontier adventure – the individual is placed in more difficult terrain where well-learned skills can be put to the test/challenge/conquest.
- Misadventure – where things go wrong, either due to lack of preparation or due to more extreme terrain and climatic conditions.

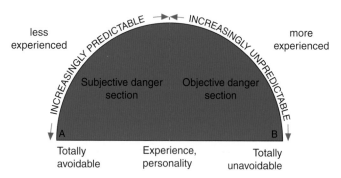

Figure 9.11 Mortlock diagram
Source: C. Mortlock (1984) *The Adventure Alternative*, Cicerone Press

Note: Beginners will work at the left end of the base line AB. Experienced climbers will work from the right end of the base line.

Activity 17

1 If you were a leader of a mixed ability group, which stages of adventure would you aim to achieve for your group, and which factors would you aim to avoid?

2 Plan an activity which could come under the outdoor education umbrella. Note the pitfalls which could arise.

Danger

Danger is the state of being vulnerable to injury. In the sporting arena this risk is heightened in outdoor and adventurous activities. Two types of danger are outlined by Mortlock. Subjective danger is that which is under the control of the individual, such as the choice of safe and appropriate equipment, and the choice of route. There is no such control over objective danger, however, such as an avalanche.

Risk assessment

Fears about liability are preventing people from teaching and learning about risk. Outdoor activities *are* dangerous. The freedom to face, assess and manage the risk is what attracts people to these sports. Society has become increasingly averse to facing risk and all efforts are made to protect children from dangerous situations. Is this really a healthy attitude? Every time we cross the road we make a risk assessment.

'Risk assessment' is becoming a familiar term to anyone involved in leading other people. There is a danger that precautions like this will actually prevent schools from offering experiences of outdoor activities. Sport is not above the law and the changing attitudes of society have had an impact in this area, as elsewhere.

Outdoor education and the school curriculum

There are strong reasons why outdoor education should be included in the school curriculum: namely, the benefit to the personal and social education of children, through experiential learning. Other subjects could also utilise and benefit from outdoor education, which has useful cross-curricular implications.

The national curriculum does not require that outdoor education is taught, though schools can arrange for it to be included. The skills which can be experienced and learned directly are an intrinsic element of Key Stages 3 and 4 of the adventurous activity option in physical education.

In an already constricted timetable, few schools have the commitment to the subject to support and sustain outdoor education:

- The Education Reform Act 1988 increased the problems schools experienced in offering these activities.

- The fundamental changes to the way in which schools are funded have also seriously affected the opportunities for teachers to gain valuable in-service training in order to achieve the appropriate qualifications.
- Local education authorities may no longer have access to sufficient funds to provide for this training.
- The law regarding charging pupils for out-of-school activities may cause schools to limit or abandon such activities, as voluntary contributions may not be sufficient. This could mean that only the wealthier schools are able to participate, so these activities would retain their elite image.
- The increasing concern over safety issues presents another problem for schools.

Figure 9.12 Outdoor activities should be available to everyone

Tourism and environmental safeguards

Outdoor pursuits are growth sports, but there are also some problems which need to be addressed. The UK lags far behind many other countries in its provision of outdoor activities, and many outdoor education residential centres have been threatened with closure.

The areas in which these activities often take place are country parks, nature reserves, green belt areas, areas of outstanding natural beauty and national parks. Conflicts can emerge between the sport participants, landowners and the environment. The UK is a relatively small island, with high-density population. Problems caused by the growth in tourism and outdoor activities will be felt here more keenly than in much larger countries such as the USA and France, which have lower population density.

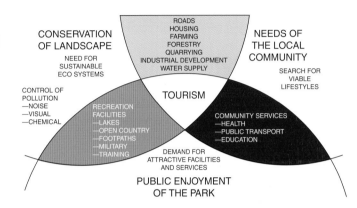

Figure 9.13 Causes of conflict in a national park

Some of the problems caused are:

- erosion of land and river banks;
- pollution caused by motor sports;
- the increase in the number of vehicles disturbing wildlife and local residents.

The most radical solution would be to ban the activities, but it might be more viable to plan for these activities in order to minimise the damage inflicted on the environment. The agencies concerned need to liaise with each other to produce effective strategies. These agencies include the home country sports council, the CCPR, the governing bodies of the individual sports, local authorities, the Countryside Commission and the Association of National Park Authorities.

IN CONTEXT

The Outward Bound Trust began to pioneer outdoor activities in the 1940s. It has five centres in Britain, including Aberdovey in Wales, Ullswater in the Lake District and Loch Eil in Scotland. It is now a worldwide organisation. Outward Bound works in partnership with the Duke of Edinburgh's Award Scheme. Its main aim is to promote personal development training for young people, placing them in challenging situations, such as physical expeditions, skills courses and the city challenge (an urban alternative). The challenging and often rugged activities include living in the wilderness, mountain climbing, canoeing, skiing and touring on bicycles.

Exam-style question

The following activities are examples of outdoor education activities:

Abseiling   Orienteering   Canoeing   Hill Walking

What can young people gain from outdoor education and why do our children not have the opportunity to experience regular or varied outdoor education?

(5 marks)

What is sport?

We know that Sport England refers to numerous activities as sport; we have sports clubs; hunting is called a sport; and a person can be referred to as 'a good sport'. In general, we use the term loosely in normal conversation, but when we are relating important sociological concepts to sport (such as discrimination, funding and the relationship of sport to physical education), it is necessary to be specific about what we mean by the term.

Classification of sporting activities

When we examined the nature of physical education – in particular the need for children to experience a balanced physical education programme – we referred to activities such as games and movement. These, in turn, could be classified into further categories; the Council of Europe and the Sports Council have identified four main categories of sporting activity:

1 Conditioning activities – These are activities which are designed primarily to improve the physical and mental condition of the performer. Examples of such activities would be aerobics and circuit and weight training.

2 Competitive games and sports – The main aim of competitive participation is to find out who is the best given equal circumstances. Games can be classified under:
   1 invasion – where opponents invade each other's territory;
   2 net – where opponents are separated by a net;
   3 striking and fielding – where teams take it in turns to field or bat;
   4 target – where accuracy at a target is crucial, as in archery;
   5 fighting – where opponents are in combat, as in boxing.

3 Athletic – This category includes races, field athletics and weightlifting. The athlete who wins the 100m is the person who reaches the tape first. All race events, whatever the form of locomotion, are decided in this way: the high jumper clears the bar; the thrower achieves the furthest distance. In terms of outdoor and adventurous pursuits, activities such as skiing are athletic.

4 Aesthetic or gymnastic movement – These activities rely on the repetition of a movement pattern. Technical expertise (technique) and artistic interpretation are the two main factors which are assessed. The body is used as an art form, with appearance and individuality forming important elements. The 'performance' is assessed. In activities such as ice skating, where the winners are chosen by judges, there can be more questionable outcomes than in competition sports. This type of assessment is called qualitative or subjective assessment.

A definition of sport would be useful here, in order to examine the key elements. Sport can be defined as:

> institutionalised competitive activities that involve vigorous physical exertion or the use of relatively complex physical skills by individuals whose participation is motivated by a combination of intrinsic and extrinsic factors. (Coakley 1993)

What do we mean by some of these terms?

Institutionalised means:

- a standardised set of behaviour recurs in different situations;
- rules are standardised;
- officials regulate the activity;
- rationalised activities involve strategies, training schedules and technological advances;
- skills are learned formally.

Physical activities have the following characteristics:

- skills, prowess, exertion;
- balance, coordination;
- accuracy;
- strength, endurance.

The extent of the physical nature of the activity may vary and can lead us to question whether an activity such as darts, for example, is a sport. Darts is referred to as a sport via the media, but the fact

Activity 18

1   Rearrange the activities listed below under the following categories: Adventure, Conditioning dance and Sport:

- trampolining;
- skiing;
- rugby;
- weight training;
- white-water rafting;
- judo;
- basketball;
- ballet;
- circuit training;
- jet-skiing;
- swim racing;
- netball.
- hockey;
- tap-dancing;
- t'ai chi;
- lacrosse;
- aerobics;
- rhythmic gymnastics;

2   We have already shown how the Games category can be further subdivided. Give the following game activities a subclass and consider similar games that could be allocated to each subdivision:

- basketball;
- golf;
- boxing;
- rounders;
- tennis.

that it does not require much physical exertion can place it lower down on the sport continuum, even though it meets other criteria for inclusion as a sport. Any activity which does not demonstrate all the characteristics listed above would be seen to have less status as a sport.

> ### Key terms
>
> **Physical endeavour:** When the body is working very hard and expending a considerable amount of energy.
> **Physical prowess:** Outstanding or superior physical skill.

Motivation for participation in sport

Motivation can be intrinsic or extrinsic. Intrinsic motivation involves:

- self-satisfaction;
- fun;
- enjoyment;
- own choice;
- 'play spirit'.

Extrinsic motivation involves:

- money;
- medals;
- fame;
- obligation;
- praise.

Most people will combine both types of motivation in the approaches they adopt towards sport participation. The golfer Colin Montgomerie says:

> I used to get tense about the money angle of it, the financial situation you found yourself in when suddenly you had to putt for a prize the size of someone's salary. Now it's not the financial side, it's trying to beat my peers. I don't need to be paid. Don't tell the sponsors that. But when I finish a tournament and I've beaten my peers, I don't need to be paid. The feeling I have is terrific, of success and freedom, if you like. That's what I do it for. (*The Daily Telegraph*, 16 October 1999)

Huizinga identified the following characteristics of sport:

- dexterity – involves an element of skill;
- strategy – aspect of planning or tactic;
- chance – sporting outcomes are usually unpredictable, based on luck, injury, weather, etc.;
- exultation – the 'feel good' factor/intrinsic elements of fun and enjoyment.

Activity 19

Think of a couple of activities you participate in regularly, but possibly at different levels and with different attitudes. List the reasons why you participate in each of these.

Two friends who kick a football around in the street are involved in an informal, social occasion. Physical exertion is present and skills are developing, but the people are involved in recreation rather than sport. If they challenge two other friends to a competition, this has moved to a situation called a contest or match. It is competitive, but still under informal conditions. Only when they follow formalised rules and confront each other under standardised conditions can their situation be called sport.

Merely playing a recognised physical activity is not enough to allow us to call it sport. The situation under which it operates also needs to be considered.

Activity 20

Using a variety of equipment, devise a game within a group.

1   What characterised the development of this game?
2   What would you have to do to change it into a PE lesson?
3   What would you have to do to turn this game into an Olympic activity?

Sportsmanship

Figure 9.14 A report on issues in tennis was conducted in 2003

EXAMINER'S TIP

Though you may not be examined directly on the historical development of sport, it is worth remembering that sport in the present day is a culmination of many centuries. To truly understand the values and judgements we make about sport today, we need to be able to analyse it in the context of the past.

Sportsmanship and fair play are values we still accept today and we expect our athletes to act as role models. These values emerged during the nineteenth century within the elite public schools and the code of amateurism.

IN CONTEXT

There are two fundamental dimensions to the issue of ethics in sport:

● the way in which sport is run;

● what happens on the field of play.

UK Sport's Sporting Conduct initiative is concerned primarily with the latter.

UK Sport carried out a series of spectator surveys on fair play issues at high-profile events in football, cricket, golf, rugby union, rugby league and tennis.

The current phase of the initiative involves in-depth discussions with players, coaches and officials about the values and norms of their sports. Working closely with the Centre for Ethics, Equity & Sport at the University of Gloucestershire, the research team ran a series of discussion groups with tennis coaches in 2006, and are continuing a longer-term involvement with first-class cricketers and umpires.

IN CONTEXT

At the highest levels of football in the UK, it is expected that when a player is injured, the other side will kick the ball out of play in order that the injured player can be attended to.

Is sportsmanship still relevant today?

Table 8.1 Tangible and intangible extrinsic motivation

Still relevant	No longer relevant
• We still teach respect for people in young children. • Fair play awards at the highest levels of competition. • The Olympic oath taken by all Olympic athletes. • Athletes who display this type of behaviour are portrayed positively by the media. • UK Sport's Sporting Conduct initiative.	• Gamesmanship, and even cheating, is considered necessary and even acceptable. • Increase in sport-related prosecutions. • Increase in drug taking in many sports (even golf is reported to have instances of doping on the professional circuit).

Activity 21

Give reasons to account for *why* sportsmanship may have declined.

The benefits of sport

Sport can:

- act as an emotional release;
- offer individuals an opportunity to express their individuality;
- help in the socialisation of people (i.e. encourage a collective spirit and persuade people to turn away from social unrest);
- provide people with values which are viewed positively by society, such as fair play and sportsmanship;
- help people achieve success when other avenues of achievement are not available to them;
- help highlight issues which can be changed;
- help achieve health and fitness;
- have economic benefits to individuals (income) and national economies;
- create a challenge and provide enjoyment.

Key term

Sportsmanship: A moral approach towards participation in sport whereby the performer abides by the unwritten rules of the sport, such as fair play.
Gamesmanship: A cunning act of bending the rules, without actually breaking them, in order to gain an advantage.
Deviance: Any behaviour that goes against society's norms and values.

IN CONTEXT

A tennis player who bends down to tie their shoelaces prior to an opponent serving, in order to interrupt their flow, would be demonstrating gamesmanship.

An athlete resorting to performance-enhancing drugs in order to win would be guilty of deviancy.

EXAMINER'S TIP

Gamesmanship is behaviour that cannot be penalised by an official.

Problematic areas

- Sport can help to retain and reinforce discrimination.
- Too much emphasis can be placed on winning, and financial rewards intensify this.
- Gamesmanship has become more acceptable in the modern-day sports world.
- Competition, if not handled well, can be damaging to an individual.
- Excessive behaviour, such as deviancy, can be encouraged through sport.
- Spectator sport can begin to outweigh active participation.
- Media coverage can dominate sport, and the type of coverage can determine the wealth of a sport.

Exam-style question

Discuss factors that can affect young people's participation in physical recreation and sport and why should every effort be made to increase activity levels amongst young people?

(10 marks)

Activity 22

Draw up two lists: one of gamesmanship behaviour and one of deviant behaviour, within a variety of sports.

Activity 23

Using an A3 sheet of paper, list as many key words as you can under 'recreation', 'leisure', 'physical education', 'outdoor recreation' and 'sport'.

EXAMINER'S TIP

When asked to 'list', remember that the first answers given will be taken relevant to the mark allocation.

Activity 24

Trace the symbol **OPE** throughout Chapters 9 to 11 in order to fully appreciate the integration of these three terms throughout the specification.

What you need to know

* Physical activity is an umbrella term for a variety of energetic pursuits, from games to athletic, gymnastic and outdoor and adventurous activities.
* You can participate in physical activities either recreationally or on a more formalised and structured level.
* Regular participation in physical activities provides benefits to the individual and to society.
* The benefits of regular participation to the individual occur on a physiological level, such as improved cardiovascular endurance; on a psychological level, as in releasing aggressive tendencies; and on an emotional level, such as making an individual feel a worthwhile person with a sense of achievement.
* Many factors are responsible for people adopting a more sedentary lifestyle, such as the growth in electronic games.
* Young people in particular are at risk from future health problems. The government needs to develop policies to try to counteract the problem, but first needs to understand some of the barriers facing young people in terms of their participation levels.
* The recommended level of physical activity necessary to induce health benefits is currently considered to be at least an hour a day. However, there is no consensus on the amount of physical activity children need and much further research is required.
* Physical recreation involves participation opportunities for all members of the community in their leisure time and of their own free will. It operates on a relaxed and more informal level. Opportunities can be provided by social agencies, such as a local authority, and must have a positive effect on an individual's life.
* Outdoor recreation is the participation in outdoor and adventurous activities in the natural environment in an individual's free time (e.g. a skiing trip with friends).

* Physical education is the instilling of knowledge, skills and values through the medium of physical activity in an educational setting.
* Outdoor education is participation in outdoor and adventurous activities in the natural environment within an educational setting (e.g. a school ski trip).
* Sport is the most formalised of all the concepts. It is institutionalised and competitive, and requires a more highly developed level of skill.
* The values and attitudes we attribute to sporting activities have developed over a number of centuries.
* The level of self-esteem generated within individuals is very often determind by the quality of the provision and opportunities made available within their environment [OPE].

Review questions

1 What is meant by the term 'physical activity?'

2 Name six benefits of regular exercise to the individual. Include physical, psychological and social benefits.

3 What are the current recommendations for maintaining a healthy lifestyle?

4 What are some of the problems associated with research in terms of physical activity levels for children?

5 Why is the government concerned about levels of inactivity in young people?

6 What are the barriers facing young people in relation to increasing the amount of physical activity they do?

7 What word does the term 'recreation' derive from and what does it mean?

8 What is the implication of the words 'activity' and 'experience' when applied to the term 'recreation'?

9 What are the key terms that characterise physical education?

10 Name five aims of physical education.

11 What is the main difference between outdoor education and outdoor recreation?

12 What constraints determine the level of outdoor education while at school in the UK?

13 What are some of the benefits and problems associated with participating in sporting activities?

14 What are the four main classifications of sporting activities?

15 What is the difference between sportsmanship and gamesmanship?

CHAPTER 10

Sport and culture

Learning outcomes

By the end of this chapter you should be able to:

1 United Kingdom:
   - show knowledge of the characteristics of ethnic sports and understand the reasons why some (e.g. the Haxey Hood, Ashbourne Football, cheese rolling and the Highland Games) have survived;
   - explain the role of nineteenth-century English public schools in organising and promoting games;
   - explain the changes that have occurred within the sporting culture of the UK, especially in terms of the move from an amateur to a professional approach;

2 United States of America:
   - describe the characteristics of the USA;
   - explain the nature of sport in the USA;
   - analyse the game of American football;

3 Australia:
   - describe the characteristics of Australia;
   - explain the nature of sport in Australia;
   - analyse the game of Australian Rules football.

CHAPTER INTRODUCTION

This chapter explores the effect of different cultures on the development of sport and physical activities. Physical activities, or games, are cultural institutions which are determined by the culture in operation in a particular country, but they may also influence how that culture operates. Discovering the meanings and significance of games in various cultures, along with their function in relation to cultural values and related social structures, is an interesting project.

Culture denotes the way of life of a society, encompassing the language, customs and dress, as well as the symbols and artefacts which people develop. These are passed down through the generations, with whatever modifications any single generation chooses to make. Some cultures evolve gradually, while others can be revolutionary, changing almost overnight. Individuals are socialised into learning the cultural values of their society, and institutions and social structures are established to achieve specific aims for that culture.

Does sport reflect culture?

When we take part in a game or sport, we subject ourselves to special rules and behaviour, which may reflect opinions and values held in other areas of life. Four main factors can determine which values are dominant within a culture:

1   the natural environment which 'houses' the culture;
2   the level of technology;
3   the dynamics of the social structures;
4   the education system.

IN DEPTH: Sport as religion

In many early cultures, physical and sporting activities could not be seen as separate from religion. Over the centuries, sport gradually became more secular, as society increasingly lost its traditional forms of worship. Today, many people argue that modern-day sport acts as a new form of religion, or quasi-religion (see Table 10.1).

Economic systems

Before we look at specific cultural aspects of the UK, the USA and Australia, it would be useful to gain a general understanding of how modern societies can vary simply in terms of their economic systems. Very often, the economic system operating in a particular country can tell us much about the values of that society.

The term 'economic system' stems from the control of material resources and is often dependent on political ideologies. There are several forms, including:

- Market economy – which allows market forces to determine the allocation of resources. Factors of production are determined by supply and demand. This type of system allows freedom of choice and can allocate resources efficiently, leading to economic growth. However, it leads to inequality of income, and those with the most money usually hold the most power. It is also open to monopolies, which can lead to exploitation (e.g. the USA).
- Socialism – a system that involves collective ownership of the means of production and a major role for the state in the provision of services. In its extreme form of communism it

dominated the centrally planned economies of Eastern Europe until 1989. China, North Korea and Cuba are still mainly governed in this way.

- Mixed economy – one that combines a market economy with some centrally planned or state-run enterprises. It is a way for governments to regulate the workings of the market through legislation (e.g. the UK).
- Transitional economy – this occurs in countries which have previously had centrally planned economies and are now allowing market forces to operate at least in some parts of the economy. Many East European countries are in transition.

Some would argue that the focus on maximising profits has led to the development of the 'good life', while others would claim that the single scale of success, namely monetary values, can alienate many within a population.

United Kingdom

Surviving ethnic sports

Looking at the origins of sports and pastimes, it is clear that they were initially *functional* (e.g. for military and hunting purposes). When societies became able to focus less on survival, many activities took on a recreational dimension, such as children's play, and the feasts and festivals which often had religious associations, either pagan or Christian (see Figure 10.1). Our main focus here will be from the Victorian era to the present day, but it is useful to have an understanding of previous eras.

Festivals were held in honour of events that were important in people's daily lives, such as the change of season, the harvest, and the summer and winter solstices. As pagan customs were taken over by the Church they were given new religious meanings. 'Holy days' were put aside for feasting, which is how the word 'holiday' originated. Many towns and villages had their own special festivals

Figure 10.1 Functional and recreational origins of sport

Table 10.1 Sport as religion

Sport (a) as religion (b)	Difference between sport (a) and religion (b)	Sport and religion as cultural practices
Both have buildings for communal gatherings: (a) stadiums (b) churches	(a) Profane and material (b) Sacred and supernatural	Created by people as a means to live among others – both are 'social constructs'
Both have procedures and dramas for improvement: (a) skills, timeouts (b) prayer books, retreats	(a) Focus on material issues in pursuit of pleasure, fame, etc. (b) Transcend material life to spiritual level	To make life satisfying and meaningful
Both have organisations and hierarchies: (a) IOC/athletic directors/coaches (b) CofE/bishops and priests	(a) Grounded in rules/relationships (b) Grounded in faith	Both have males in controlling and powerful positions
Both have festivals and special values as a result of cultural occasions: (a) Super Bowl (b) Easter Sunday	(a) Competitive (b) Non-competitive	
Both have ritual events before, during and after major events: (a) initiations, anthems, half-time talk (b) baptisms, hymns, sermons	(a) Spirit of self-achievement and advancement at expense of others (b) Spirit of service and love for others (a) Rituals are instrumental and goal-orientated (b) Rituals are expressive and process-orientated	Both are open to change (e.g. the acceptance of women footballers and women priests)
Both have heroes and legends: (a) halls of fame (b) saints	(a) Clear-cut and crude (b) Mystical and pure	
Both are used to enhance other values in society		
Both evoke strong emotions and are meaningful in people's lives		
Both emphasise asceticism: discipline, self-denial; repetition; development of character; 'no pain, no gain'		Both have separate sections and cults which may have evolved by being marginalised by the main cultural ideology

Source: Adapted from J. Coakley (1998) *Sport in Society,* McGraw-Hill

and saints' days. Wakes, which were pagan in origin, were annual religious occasions giving thanks for the harvest. Festivals and feasts went hand in hand with religious events. They were social occasions celebrated on a grand scale, with drinking, debauchery, blood sports and tests of manliness in numerous physical events.

Easter is the most important feast of the Christian Church, and it fixed the dates of the holy days connected to it – Lent, Shrove Tuesday and Ash Wednesday. Shrove Tuesday is the last day before the fasting of Lent, and was a time for feasting and fun. Recreations took place within a wide social pattern, and activities included mob football, wrestling, animal baiting, skittles and bowls.

Activities like mob football continued to develop, allowing for conjugal and territorial conflicts to be sorted out in an enjoyable manner. They were often disorderly and violent, allowing energies to be vented. Many activities remained at the local level, played with a few simple rules (or none at all), and were passed down through the generations by word of mouth. This was known as popular recreation.

> ### Key term
>
> **Popular recreation:** Recreational activities which were popular before the onset of the Industrial Revolution. They were rural in nature, requiring little in the form of equipment and facilities.

Forms of popular recreation were:

- occasional, often annual events, due to limited time and energy;
- simple in nature, passed down orally through the generations;
- affected by prohibitions if considered unnecessary to society by the ruling class;
- outlets for leisure pursuits, which took place during feasts and festivals;
- mainly local in nature, due to lack of mobility and frequent wars.

The Haxey Hood

The Haxey Hood is a kind of rugby game, where a leather tube is slowly walked by a large unorganised rugby scrum to one of four pubs,

Figure 10.2 The Haxey Hood

where it remains until the following year's game. The official story is that in the fourteenth century, Lady de Mowbray was out riding towards Westwoodside, on the hill that separates it from Haxey. As she went over the hill, her silk riding hood was blown away by the wind. Thirteen farm workers chased the hood all over the field. So amused was she by this act of chivalry and the resulting chase, that she donated 13 acres of land on condition that the chase for the hood would be re-enacted each year. This re-enactment over the centuries has become known as the Haxey Hood.

Today, at 12 noon on the day of Epiphany (6 January), work in the parish comes to a standstill and people start to make their way to Haxey village to take part in the traditional ritual. At approximately 12.30 p.m., the officials start a tour of the alehouses involved, receiving free drinks from the landlord at each one as a token of good luck, each of them hoping the Hood will find its way to their pub.

Ashbourne's Royal Shrovetide Football

The Haxey Hood has similarities to other village combats, such as Ashbourne's Royal Shrovetide Football, a match which has occurred annually on Shrove Tuesday and Ash Wednesday, in the town of Ashbourne in Derbyshire, since at least the twelfth century. One of the most popular origin theories suggests the macabre notion that the 'ball' was originally a severed head, tossed into the waiting crowd following an execution. The game is played over two days, starting each day at 2 p.m. and lasting until 10 p.m. If the goal is scored ('goaled') before 5 p.m., a new ball is released and play restarts from the town centre; otherwise play ends for the day. Despite the name, the ball is rarely kicked, though it is legal to kick, carry or throw it. Instead, it generally moves through the town in a series of 'hugs', like a giant scrum in rugby, made up of dozens, if not hundreds of people.

The two teams that play the game are known as the Up'Ards and the Down'Ards. Up'Ards are traditionally those town members born north of Henmore Brook, which runs through the town, and Down'Ards are those born south of the river. There are two goal posts, 3 miles apart, one at Sturston Mill (where the Up'Ards attempt to score), the other at Clifton Mill (where the Down'Ards try to score). Although the Mills have long since been demolished, part of their millstones still stand on the banks of the river at each location, once serving as the scoring posts. In 1996 the scoring posts were replaced by smaller millstones mounted on purpose-built stone structures, which require the

players to actually be in the river in order to goal a ball – this was seen as more challenging!

The actual process of goaling a ball requires a player to hit it against the millstone three successive times. The game is played through the town, with no limit on player numbers or playing area. Shops in the town are boarded up during the game, and people are encouraged to park their cars away from the main streets.

Gloucestershire Cheese Rolling and Wake

The annual Gloucestershire Cheese Rolling and Wake has been taking place for hundreds of years. At the top of the hill are the remains of a fort used by the ancient Britons; the Romans are known to have inhabited the area too, so the tradition might be Roman in origin. Documentary evidence shows that cheese rolling on Cooper's Hill was already an established tradition in the early 1800s. It could have evolved from early fertility rites and hopes of a successful harvest, or to safeguard the commoners' rights of the inhabitants of the hill. Local residents are determined that the tradition will never die. It is now a well-established tourist attraction, though health and safety concerns could threaten its survival in the twenty-first century. The landowners of Cooper's Hill have become increasingly concerned about public liability, a view which might not be helped by exaggerated reports of injuries. During the cheese rolling, fit, mostly young men and women throw themselves down a very steep hill in pursuit of a rolling cheese. The winner takes the cheese – along with a lot of bumps, scratches and bruises.

Highland Games

The first Highland Games in Scotland were held more than a thousand years ago, prompted by clan chiefs and kings. Events covered a variety of sporting, martial and religious purposes. The clan chiefs used the games to recruit people: race winners made good messengers at a time when there were no proper roads; the strongest men were employed as bodyguards; and the pick of the dancers and pipers were chosen to entertain.

Men of the villages and parishes gathered annually on what was, for many, their only holiday, to test their strength and ability against each other using the tools of their trades. Hence

Figure 10.3 Ashbourne's Royal Shrovetide Football

Figure 10.4 Gloucestershire Cheese Rolling and Wake

throwing hammers, putting rounded stones, heaving weights and tossing tree trunks (popularly known as tossing the caber) became the order of the day. Highland dancing and bagpipe playing competitions also featured.

Similar meetings developed in the north of England, known as the Lakeland Games, but it is the Highland Games which have survived, maintaining their original glory and status among the local community and acquiring international renown as a major tourist attraction.

It was the English aristocracy who fell in love with the Scottishness of the Highland Games. The most famous is the Braemar Royal Highland Gathering, which was promoted to its royal status in 1866 for a visit by Queen Victoria. The gathering was intended to provide reasonable employment for a band of semi-professional athletes.

The gathering is held on the first Saturday in September, which became the customary date in order to accommodate (mostly aristocratic) parties coming north for the grouse shooting season. There were some changes to the games after the Second World War, the biggest coming in 1952, when the amateur and women's events were introduced for the first time. Increasingly, it has become the practice of 'exiles' to make a point of going home at this time of year, if at all possible. The gathering has become an expression of nationalism. Today, meetings provide a greater

variety of events than ever before, with traditional Highland dancing and piping providing a contrast with the athletic efforts on the track and in the heavy events, which remain as popular as ever.

Cultural traditions which have survived the rapid changes of the modern world generally have certain factors in common:

Figure 10.5 Highland Games

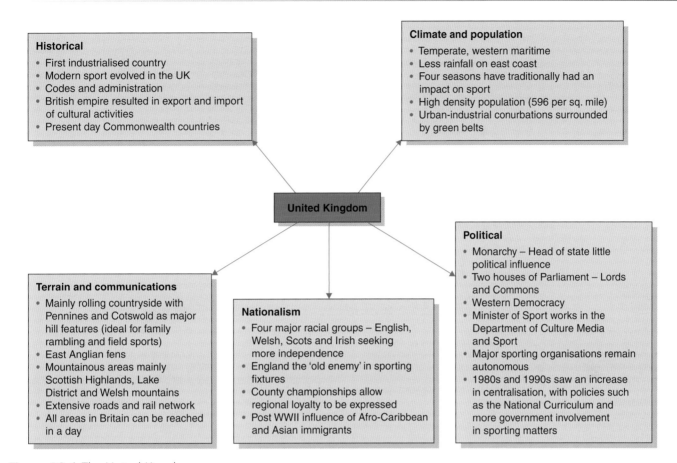

Historical
- First industrialised country
- Modern sport evolved in the UK
- Codes and administration
- British empire resulted in export and import of cultural activities
- Present day Commonwealth countries

Climate and population
- Temperate, western maritime
- Less rainfall on east coast
- Four seasons have traditionally had an impact on sport
- High density population (596 per sq. mile)
- Urban-industrial conurbations surrounded by green belts

United Kingdom

Political
- Monarchy – Head of state little political influence
- Two houses of Parliament – Lords and Commons
- Western Democracy
- Minister of Sport works in the Department of Culture Media and Sport
- Major sporting organisations remain autonomous
- 1980s and 1990s saw an increase in centralisation, with policies such as the National Curriculum and more government involvement in sporting matters

Terrain and communications
- Mainly rolling countryside with Pennines and Cotswold as major hill features (ideal for family rambling and field sports)
- East Anglian fens
- Mountainous areas mainly Scottish Highlands, Lake District and Welsh mountains
- Extensive roads and rail network
- All areas in Britain can be reached in a day

Nationalism
- Four major racial groups – English, Welsh, Scots and Irish seeking more independence
- England the 'old enemy' in sporting fixtures
- County championships allow regional loyalty to be expressed
- Post WWII influence of Afro-Caribbean and Asian immigrants

Figure 10.6 The United Kingdom

- They tend to be in isolated geographical areas which are less prone to outside influences and where changes take much longer to occur.
- They tend to be rurally and agriculturally based, reflected in the strength-based events and activities which may once have had a utilitarian purpose.
- The connection to an area gives it a cultural identity and bolsters local pride. This could be deemed tourism, even in previous centuries, as the events would attract people from other areas.
- Local competitions began as communities gathered together for recreational purposes.
- They often require simple, unsophisticated facilities and equipment.

Exam-style question

Many ethnic sports still occur in the UK today. Give an example of a surviving ethnic sport other than the Highland Games. Identify characteristics of ethnic sports and give reasons for their survival.

(5 marks)

Victorian Britain

Victoria became queen in 1837. Her reign was a period of dramatic social change, which is reflected in the development of games and sport during the nineteenth century.

The United Kingdom became the birthplace of modern sport, with many sports becoming rationalised, that is, rule-bound, with codes of behaviour or etiquette. The middle and upper classes, through their public schools, were to be one of the most influential social factors in this development.

Nineteenth-century public schools

The sons of the gentry were educated at large, prestigious, fee-paying boarding schools. There were originally nine elite institutions, called 'Barbarian' schools because they maintained the gentry tradition: Eton, Harrow, Rugby, Shrewsbury, Charterhouse, Westminster, Winchester, St Paul's and Merchant Taylor's.

The emergence of the middle classes resulted in them building their own proprietary colleges,

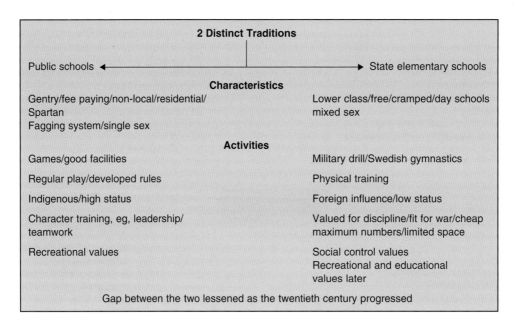

Figure 10.7 Public school traditions

based on the elite schools. Examples of these 'Philistine' schools are Cheltenham College, Marlborough and Clifton.

Technical/formal development of activities

The development of sport in public schools radically changed previous concepts of sport. The boys brought to their schools their experiences of games like cricket and mob football, and country pursuits such as fishing and coursing. Before the formalisation of team games, the boys would leave the school grounds and participate in rowdy behaviour, which often involved poaching, fighting, trespassing, drinking alcohol and generally bringing the school's reputation into disrepute, causing conflict with local landowners and gamekeepers.

However, at this stage they began the process of organising their own activities and devising new ways of playing games. These were often associated with individual architectural features of the different schools, such as cloisters for fives, and the Eton wall game. The latter is an old form of football, and survives to this day. It developed from a long red brick wall which separates the school playing fields from the Slough road. Ten players per side work the small ball along a narrow strip, 4 to 5 yards wide and 118 yards long. The players are assigned a playing position and specialised role according to their physique. The wall was built in 1717, but the game only became popular in the nineteenth century.

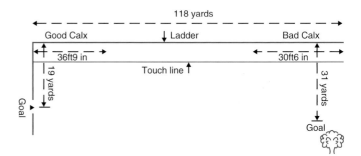

Figure 10.8 The Eton wall game

Activity 1

Can you think of reasons why a game peculiar to this school should continue to be played?

Thomas Arnold, the head of Rugby School, encouraged the boys to develop activities which could be played on the school grounds and which would also highlight the more moral features of teamwork, such as self-discipline, loyalty and courage – character-building qualities suitable for the prospective leaders of society.

Cricket was already a fairly well-established game in society and, as such, it was considered suitable for the boys. Mob football, on the other hand, was played by the lower classes in society and was not so acceptable, until the boys devised a more organised format. The game of rugby supposedly began at Rugby School, when William Webb Ellis picked up the ball during a game of football and ran with it.

Table 10.2 Cricket, football and society

Cricket	Football
Earliest established game in English society, accepted by boys' families	Still a 'mob' game in the nineteenth century
Differing positional roles made it acceptable for both social classes to play	Played by the lower classes in society
Reflected the ideals of athleticism: teamwork/honour/etiquette; team before individual	Not popular with the gentry until boys devised rules within the schools
	'Contact' nature of the game meant that the social classes would play separately for a long time

The boys were in charge of organising the games, and senior bands of boys (prefects) would be in control, forming games committees (e.g. the Harrow Philathletic Club). The masters actively discouraged some activities (poaching and gambling), while others were allowed to exist on an informal recreational basis among the boys (fives and fighting). They actively encouraged the boys to organise team games.

Initially, inter-school fixtures were not feasible as no two schools had the same rules. However, by the mid nineteenth century, headmasters and staff had started to organise sports. Games were seen as a medium for achieving educational aims with a moral social sense; they could also help to combat idleness and were viewed as a form of social control. Boys who excelled in games were admired by the other pupils, becoming the 'games elite'.

The technical development of games encompassed the following:

- boys brought local variations to the schools from their villages;
- played regularly in free time;
- developed individual school rules/skills/boundaries, etc.;
- played competitively (house matches);
- self-government meant boys organised activities initially;
- later, codified rules allowed inter-school fixtures;
- development of games elite.

Athleticism

The cult of athleticism stressed the physical and social benefits of sports:

- The physical benefits were seen to counteract the effects of sedentary lifestyles, and sport was viewed as therapeutic, invigorating and cathartic. It was also seen as a break from work.
- Sport would take place within a competitive situation, which would help the boys learn how to cope with both winning and losing, in a dignified manner. It helped to develop leadership qualities, and being captain was considered an office of high status.

The house system was fundamental to the competitive sport events, in which the manner of the performance was considered more important than the result.

Athleticism also adhered to middle-class values of respectability and order, values such as sportsmanship, leadership and abiding by rules. The middle classes were to become the organisers and administrators of society, particularly highlighted in their role within the governing bodies of sports clubs.

It was the public schools which instituted the idea of the sports day, which operated as a public relations exercise for the old boys, parents and governors of the school. School funds could benefit from generous donations and valuable publicity could be gained.

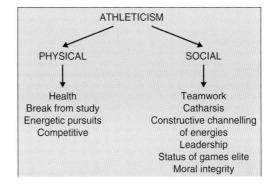

Figure 10.9 The benefits of athleticism

Activity 2

'The public schools were the first centres of excellence for sport and resembled modern-day sports schools.' Discuss.

Athleticism: Physical endeavour with moral integrity.

EXAMINER'S TIP

Make sure you understand the difference between the terms 'technical' and 'moral'.

The moral development of games encompassed:

- teamwork and group loyalty;
- playing to the written and unwritten rules of the sport;
- fair play and sportsmanship;
- courage and bravery;
- character building and leadership skills.

IN CONTEXT

Thomas Arnold became headmaster of Rugby School in 1828. He directed a crusade against 'personal sin', including bullying, lying, swearing, cheating and running wild. Pupils were to remain on the school grounds; he forbade shooting and beagling, as these activities encouraged poaching; and fights were to occur only within his presence, as well as being supervised by the prefects who enforced his authority.

Arnold is known for his contribution to muscular Christianity, but he valued games only for what they could contribute towards the social control of the boys. The development of athleticism followed the cooperation of the boys in maintaining discipline and achieving Arnold's reforms.

The novel *Tom Brown's Schooldays* by Thomas Hughes was published in 1860, and highlighted the Victorian ideal of the physical side of the Christian gentleman.

Activity 3

Read the extract from *Tom Brown's Schooldays* and answer the questions which follow:

1 Comment on the level of technical development of the physical activity described.

2 Explain the different social relationships being identified.

3 Discuss the values being reinforced as part of a character-building process.

'Huzza, there's going to be a fight between Slogger Williams and Tom Brown!'

The news ran like wildfire about, and many boys who were on their way to tea at their several houses turned back, and sought the back of the chapel, where the fights come off.

'Just run and tell East to come and back me,' said Tom to a small School-house boy, who was off like a rocket to Harrowell's, just stopping for a moment to poke his head into the School-house hall, where the lower boys were already at tea, and sing out, 'Fight! Tom Brown and Slogger Williams.'

In another minute East and Martin tear through the quadrangle, carrying a sponge, and arrive at the scene of action just as the combatants are beginning to strip.

Tom felt he had got his work cut out for him, as he stripped off his jacket, waistcoat, and braces. East tied his handkerchief round his waist, and rolled up his shirt-sleeves for him: 'Now, old boy, don't you open your mouth to say a word, or try to help yourself a bit,—we'll do all that; you keep all your breath and strength for the Slogger.' Martin meanwhile folded the clothes, and put them under the chapel rails; and now Tom, with East to handle him, and Martin to give him a knee, steps out on the turf, and is ready for all that may come: and here is the Slogger too, all stripped, and thirsting for the fray.

It doesn't look a fair match at first glance: Williams is nearly two inches taller, and probably a long year older than his opponent, and he is very strongly made about the arms and shoulders,—'peels well,' as the little knot of big fifth-form boys, the amateurs, say; who stand outside the ring of little boys, looking complacently on, but taking no active part in the proceedings. But down below he is not so good by any means; no spring from the loins, and feeblish, not to say shipwrecky about the knees. Tom, on the contrary, though not half so strong in the arms, is good all over, straight, hard, and springy, from neck to ankle, better perhaps in his legs than anywhere. Besides, you can see by the clear white of his eye, and fresh bright look of his skin, that he is in tip-top training, able to do all he knows; while the Slogger looks rather sodden, as if he didn't take much exercise and ate too much tuck. The time-keeper is chosen, a large ring made, and the two stand up opposite one another for a moment, giving us time just to make our little observations. The combatants, however, sit there quietly, tended by their seconds, while their adherents wrangle in the middle. East can't help shouting challenges to two or three of the other side, though he never leaves Tom for a moment, and plies the sponges as fast as ever.

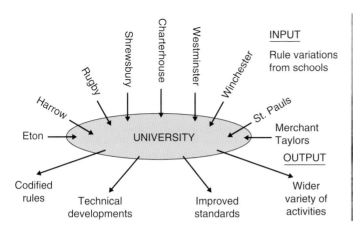

Figure 10.10 The input and output of the universities

Figure 10.11 The early days of rugby: 'Will he do it?' by George Elgar Hicks

Athleticism spread nationally and worldwide via the following means:

- old boys'/girls' network;
- universities codified rules, developed activities technically, improved and devised new ways of playing;
- sports clubs and governing bodies became significant administrative features;
- officers in army and navy influential with troops;
- clergy influenced parishioners;
- teachers went back into schools;
- employers encouraged games in their workforce;
- the British Empire enabled the spread of these developments around the world.

Exam-style questions

Late nineteenth-century public schools are associated with a passion for all sport, and team games in particular. Explain how these schools and their ex-pupils influenced the emergence of national sport.

(5 marks)

Professionalism and amateurism

Key term

Amateurism: Participating in sport for the love of the game, rather than for financial gain.

The concept of amateurism was thought to reflect the ancient Olympian spirit, placing the ideals of fair play and team spirit high above any material objectives. In the 1850s Dr Penny Brookes founded the Much Wenlock Olympic Games and formed a

National Olympic Association. He had a pure sense of amateurism, and encouraged the citizens of Much Wenlock in Shropshire to delight in the challenge of sport with no thought for reward. The first Games were held in 1850, and included events such as football, cricket, quoits, a blindfold wheelbarrow race, and chasing a pig through the town. It had all the trappings of a rustic festival, and perhaps reinvented the Cotswold Games, first started in 1612 in Chipping Camden. By 1870 the events included track and field athletics, such as the pentathlon and tilting at the ring (a version of the jousting tournament).

The public school influence established its own definition of amateurism, which superseded the Much Wenlock version. Much of the public school version of athleticism was Olympian in outlook, combining physical endeavour with moral integrity, where the struggle was fought for the honour of the house or school. Baron Pierre de Coubertin visited both Much Wenlock and Rugby School in 1890, in the years preceding the foundation of the modern Olympic Games. In England there were two distinct phases of amateurism:

1   Originally, amateurs were gentlemen of the middle and upper classes who played sports in the spirit of fair competition.
2   There was a shift in the definition of an amateur, from a straightforward social distinction, to a monetary one. Originally, earning money from amateur sport was not perceived as a problem.

Fair play was the bedrock on which amateurism was based. It was important to adhere to the rules of the game, but it was expected that a player would discipline himself rather than wait for a referee's decision. A situation was recorded that the football club the Corinthians, founded in 1882, would withdraw their goalkeeper on the awarding of a penalty to the opposing side, on the principle that they should accept the consequences of a foul.

There were advantages and disadvantages to the amateur code. It promoted restraint in victory and graciousness in defeat; the acceptance of rules and consequent respect for decisions. However, it excluded the working classes, which was a moral argument for its abolition. In 1894 the Rugby Football Union and the Northern Union split, due to the refusal of the authorities to allow northern players to have enough leisure time to compete on the same basis as players in the south. Employers could not accept 'broken-time payments' (compensation for loss of wages), and thus excluded manual workers who needed time to train and travel for sport. Similar conflicts occurred in rowing and cricket.

Table 10.3 sets out the development of these two concepts, and looks at the effect they have had on certain sports.

Table 10.3 Amateurism and professionalism

Amateurism	Professionalism

● Evolved in nineteenth-century England.
● Code brought in by upper class.
It is an ideal based on participating in sport for the love of the game, rather than for monetary gain, with participation deemed to be more important than winning.
● The gentleman amateur was a social class distinction of the amateur code.
The gentleman amateur was drawn only from the upper classes and was regarded as having qualities of refinement associated with a good family – a man who was courteous, cultured and well educated. Although they might have participated in some activities with their lower-class professional counterparts, there was no shame should they lose, as they were not being paid and were not involved in serious training.
● Amateurism encompassed the belief in fair play and abiding by the spirit as well as the rules of the game.
● Originally it had a monetary as well as a social class distinction in its efforts to exclude the lower class.
● The Corinthians were the epitome of amateurism.
The Corinthians were true to St Paul's letter to the Corinthians, which stated that 'not everyone can win but those that do should do so according to the rules and spirit of the time'. The Corinthians were drawn from the elite of Victorian society and followed this code during games.
● The meanings behind amateurism are arbitrary and socially determined; hence they change over a period of time.
	● Earning money from sport is a very old concept, going back to ancient civilisations such as the Roman Empire.
	● Professional sport is an avenue of upward and downward social mobility.
	Professionalism means engaging in a sporting activity for financial gain or as a means of livelihood; training is synonymous with improving standards and specialising in an activity.
	● The gladiator was an early form of a professional sportsman.
	Gladiators are trained to fight in arenas to provide entertainment. This began as a concept in ancient Greece/Rome, but is now used to denote professional sport. The similarities between a gladiator and a professional footballer are that both athletes:
	  ● *are involved in a physical contact sport, relying on physical strength and speed;*
	  ● *have a strong likelihood of injury, resulting in an early end to a career;*
	  ● *are treated as expendable – the 'hire and fire' policy;*
	  ● *are bought and sold through transfer deals and treated as commodities;*
	  ● *are paid by results;*
	  ● *have little control, as they are 'owned' by a coach/manager;*
	  ● *have high media status and are treated as heroes.*
	● Certain social factors are necessary for professional sport to flourish. Consider the following similarities between ancient Rome and industrial England in the nineteenth century:

- Sports have undergone major changes in their amateur/professional status.
  - **Rowing** was originally open to amateurs and professionals, but the gentleman amateurs disliked being beaten by their social inferiors. This resulted in a strict amateur definition, instigated by the Amateur Rowing Association, called the 'manual labour clause':
  The formal exclusion of manual workers by the Amateur Rowing Association in 1882 excluded anyone who was by trade 'a mechanic, artisan or labourer', but it was abolished in 1890. It was a device to retain a social distinction in sport, as the gentry amateurs did not wish to be beaten by lower-class professionals; nor could they socialise with them after the sporting event.
  - **Rugby football** developed in nineteenth-century English public schools, and was based on amateurism. The working class in the northern industrial towns adopted the game, but they needed to be paid to play, or at least to receive compensation for loss of earnings while playing.
  Broken-time payments were made to compensate working-class players for loss of earnings while playing sports such as soccer and rugby football. This tended to lead to professionalism in some sports and was looked down on by the gentleman amateurs.
  In rugby this was to lead to the north–south split in 1896 – southern amateurs/northern professionals. By 1996 even the Union game had moved over to professionalism, as a result of player pressure.
  - In **cricket**, the amateurs and professionals could play together under the auspices of 'gentlemen vs players'. The gentlemen were the amateurs and the players were the professionals.
- The revival of the modern Olympic Games in 1896 was based on the amateur code, as Coubertin had been impressed with the values associated with athleticism in nineteenth-century British public schools.

  - *mass of a population living in close proximity;*
  - *large section of population with disposable income and leisure time;*
  - *need for excitement;*
  - *commercialism.*
  This ties into the bread and circuses theory, which suggests that the masses can be kept relatively content through sporting activities. A cynical viewpoint might suggest that this can be used by governments to alleviate social problems, by channelling people's energies in a socially acceptable form.
- Professionalism was evident in a variety of sports in the nineteenth century:
  - **Pedestrianism** was an early form of race walking. In the eighteenth and nineteenth centuries, with only horse racing and boxing as rivals, pedestrianism was very popular and was associated with a lot of gambling, with men being measured against time, distance and other walkers. Captain Barclay was a famous walker who, in 1809, walked 1,000 miles in 1,000 consecutive hours.
  - The term **pedestrian** was also used to refer to a lower-class individual who competed in sporting activities for money, particularly rowing, foot races and cricket. It was the forerunner to the term 'professional'.
  - In **prizefighting**, individuals were taught to defend themselves in gladiatorial schools in 'sword and buckle' contests. It was patronised by the wealthy and powerful, who wagered huge sums on the outcome of contests, though they would never have been combatants themselves. The activity employed virtually a professional core of men, fighting in regular circuits, mostly concentrated around London. Rules were fairly loosely enforced and death was not uncommon. When the sport was outlawed, contests were organised on private land, away from the magistrates. Notable figures were Broughton, Mendoza and Tom Cribb.
  - **Athletics** developed under amateur rules in public schools, but in society a professional circuit was very popular. As with many professional sports in the nineteenth century, there were problems with bribery, corruption and fixing of events.

Continued

Table 10.3 *Continued*

Amateurism	Professionalism

• During the twentieth century other terms emerged to describe performers who received some form of payment, including **shamateur**, which describes an amateur who receives under-the-table payments (trust funds were set up to try to combat this problem), and **stamateur**, which describes state-sponsored amateurs and was common in Eastern bloc countries.
• Amateurs can now officially receive financial aid from sponsorship, trust funds and organisations such as Sport Aid and the National Lottery.
	• Public schools employed professional watermen to coach the **rowing** teams when the prestige of winning became ever more important.
	• In professional sport in nineteenth-century England, the role of the different social classes was as follows:
	  • lower class – performers;
	  • middle class – agents, promoters, managers;
	  • upper class – patrons.
	• The inclusion of sports such as tennis and basketball in the Olympic Games in the twentieth century highlights the problems encountered by the modern-day sports world in trying to adhere to the pure ideal of amateurism.

EXAMINER'S TIP

Make sure you do not confuse the term 'amateur' with a low level of performance. Remember, you can represent your country at the top of your sport and technically be an amateur.

Mass participation involves the majority of a population engaging in sporting and recreational activities for the purposes of keeping fit, socialising, and so on. Many students confuse this with amateurism. In many of these instances, people may not be conforming to a pure form of sport, but rather a more recreational approach (see Chapter 9 for more information on the concepts of physical activity).

When achieving sporting excellence becomes the main focus of an athlete, it could be deemed that they adopt a professional approach to sport, whether or not they receive direct payment from that sport. A professional approach can be described in the following terms:

• time and commitment to training (often full-time);
• perfection of recognised skills and techniques;
• high quality coaching, often on a one-to-one basis;
• need for sophisticated facilities and equipment;
• adhering to externally enforced rules and regulations, usually from a governing body;

• strict penalties for infringement of rules;
• winning is taken very seriously;
• extrinsic rewards are a main feature, whether these are medals, fame or money;
• standards of sport performance increase;
• support services of sports science and sports medicine are combined with coaching methodology.

Amateur sports have become squeezed by the pressures of the modern world, especially in terms of the need for money (in very large quantities), to enable the sport to achieve international success. Money either comes from government funding, commercial sponsorship, gate receipts, TV rights or donations. (The relationship between commercialisation, sport and the media is discussed in greater detail in Chapter 12.) It is important to recognise here that successful, entertaining sports tend to attract the most spectators, and TV coverage is particularly significant in this respect. It is also undisputed that when athletes train full-time, the standards of the sport are raised considerably. Therefore, traditional amateur athletes who train full-time (and therefore do not work) require forms of funding. In a sport such as rugby union, where there was also a professional game (rugby league), it was inevitable that players would begin to drift over to the game which would also pay them a substantial income. The pressure on rugby union to turn professional meant that this was only a matter of time.

Sports which have remained amateur struggle to fund athletes and competitions, as they are more reliant on sponsorship or government funding.

United States of America

In the early twenty-first century, the USA is one of the strongest world powers. As a nation, it might be described as:

- pluralist – different ethnic groups are autonomous but interdependent, and have equal power;
- egalitarian – a belief that mankind should have the opportunity for equality (politically, socially and economically).

The dominant sporting ethos in the USA is that of professional sport, reflecting the capitalist drive of American society. Competition became accepted as early as the 1870s as a basic principle in sound economics, and therefore part of the great American enterprise. Competition has become a prime value in education, politics and the military.

> **Key term**
>
> **Capitalism:** This is an economic system based on free trade and private ownership of the means of production, property and capital, according to individual choice.

In modern competitive societies:

- games were valued for the character traits they were thought to foster;
- cooperation was valued, but individual achievements were highly rewarded;
- there was a sharp division of labour and intense specialisation.

The traditional pioneering background of the USA has led to a favouring of physical strength and the ability to 'play the game'. Americans also value cooperation, which is reflected in their desire to form voluntary associations. Many of the pioneers sought companionship in collective effort, and it is through team sports that Americans combined their desire for individualism within a collective endeavour.

> **Activity 4**
>
> Explain how professional sport reflects a capitalist system.

> **Key term**
>
> **Frontier:** This refers to the limit of knowledge of a particular field. Sport is often called 'the last frontier', as we still do not know the limitations of human achievement in sport. It is an emotive term for Americans as it also links to the history of settlement in the country, as each frontier moved from east to west. Qualities required to push back any frontier, be it geographical or sporting in nature, are bravery, courage, strength and determination.

> **Activity 5**
>
> Imagine the trek west to settle in uninhabited areas of wilderness, with a hostile indigenous population to overcome.
>
> 1. What personal qualities would be most likely to prove successful in such circumstances?
> 2. Can you relate any of these qualities to success in sport?

An interesting point to note is that during the nineteenth century, America inherited many team games from the UK, yet these developed along different lines. The Americans rationalised and systemised sports at a time when the British were trying to resist this trend.

Development and structure of government

Following the War of Independence in 1776, the American colonies achieved their objective of freedom from Britain in 1781. They wished to detach themselves from the elitist, closed, British social class system, which excluded the majority of people from opportunities of self-improvement, on the grounds that they were not of the preferred social status.

A new government with a federal constitution was founded, effectively creating a republic. A federal constitution is where the powers of government are divided between the national and the state or provincial governments. This was an important concept: the people had just broken away from a distant system of power over which they had little control, and they did not want to replace it with another, so they sought to restrict the powers of the new national government via the constitution of the United States, which serves as the supreme law of the land. These characteristics were to extend to sport as well as politics.

Key terms

American dream: The new, competitive, capitalist economy aimed to provide people who had determination, talent and drive with the opportunity to be successful. In theory, individuals can achieve upward social mobility regardless of social class. This is popularly known as rags to riches in the land of opportunity. In sport, this can be achieved from Little League to professional and Olympic sport. Sporting terms reflect this need to achieve:

- Win at all costs.
- Nice guys finish last.
- Lombardian ethic (see below).

Isolation:

- New World trying to produce a new identity/escape from older culture.
- A variety of emigrants in a pluralist culture no longer dominated by Britain.
- An attempt to be separate and different.
- Professional sport, rather than nineteenth-century, English, class-based amateurism.
- Winning at all costs, rather than the process of participation being important.
- Reflects the technological changes of the new era.

The USA:

- is a democracy with a representative government, which means the people elect leaders to represent them;
- is a republic, where the chief of state is also elected by the people, unlike a monarch who inherits the title;
- has a constitutional government, operating under a set of laws and principles outlined in the Constitution;
- has a federal system, with a sharing of power between the national, state and municipal governments.

Activity 6

Consider the impact of the factors in Figure 10.12 on the system of sport in the USA.

Sport in the USA

By the 1920s these cultural links had become clearly defined, with the growth of spectator sports cleverly marketed in order to raise money and create profits. This occurred at both professional and intercollegiate levels, and national organisations, such as the National Collegiate Athletic Association (NCAA), were established to control rapid growth.

IN DEPTH: Concepts of American sport

There are three main sporting concepts operating in the United States.

1. The dominant concept is the Lombardian ethic, which is based on the Protestant work ethic of self-discipline, clean living and mental alertness. The popular image of this ethic is taken from the saying of the coach, Vince Lombardi: 'Winning isn't the most important thing; it's the only thing.' This emphasises the competitive, achievement-orientated, reward-based type of sport behaviour.

2. The counter-culture is an attempt by some sections of American society to change the emphasis in sport to one where the process is what is important and the outcome does not matter. It comes from the American sportswriter Grantland Rice's slogan: 'It's not whether you won or lost but how you played the game.' This tends to take an anticompetitive viewpoint. The New Games Foundation aims to change the way people play by reducing the amount of equipment and skill, and replacing them with informal situations, emphasising group effort rather than group reward.

3. The middle line is the radical ethic, which is perhaps the nearest to the British stance, where the outcome is important, but so too is the process. The quest for excellence can be strived for and achieved, but not at the expense of other values.

EXAMINER'S TIP

Make sure you understand the Lombardian ethic and how it is integral to professional sport.

Sport and entertainment

There are four major popular sports in the USA: football, baseball, basketball and ice hockey. These sports have become a business, and athletes are marketed as well-known assets who can help to

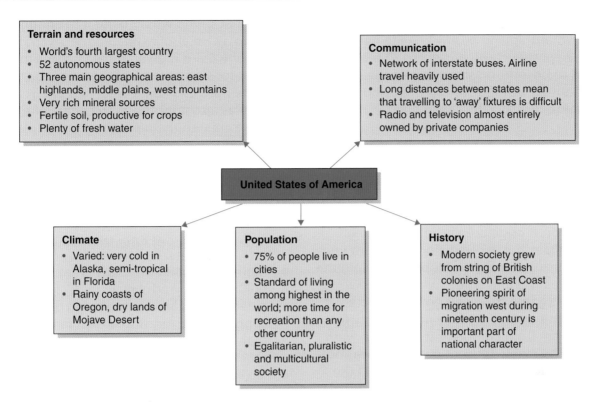

Terrain and resources
- World's fourth largest country
- 52 autonomous states
- Three main geographical areas: east highlands, middle plains, west mountains
- Very rich mineral sources
- Fertile soil, productive for crops
- Plenty of fresh water

Communication
- Network of interstate buses. Airline travel heavily used
- Long distances between states mean that travelling to 'away' fixtures is difficult
- Radio and television almost entirely owned by private companies

United States of America

Climate
- Varied: very cold in Alaska, semi-tropical in Florida
- Rainy coasts of Oregon, dry lands of Mojave Desert

Population
- 75% of people live in cities
- Standard of living among highest in the world; more time for recreation than any other country
- Egalitarian, pluralistic and multicultural society

History
- Modern society grew from string of British colonies on East Coast
- Pioneering spirit of migration west during nineteenth century is important part of national character

Figure 10.12 The United States of America

Figure 10.13 Map of the United States of America

generate funds and advertise products with their skill, showmanship and positive health images. The sports are packaged and presented to the public, and tend to be loud, brash and energetic – productions on a grand scale. Is this a show rather than a game, display rather than play?

American football

American football might be described as technological, territorial, physically violent and intimidating, a team effort and the epitome of specialisation. It originated from the game of rugby in Britain, but evolved along different lines within its new culture. It developed further in the elite colleges and universities and became a more middle-class game. Its development reflected America's attempts to create a new identity for itself, separate from Europe, and the game was influenced by many different cultures. It was not constrained by the amateur traditions, and the 'win' ethic emerged alongside professionalism.

The pro draft is a feature of the game where college teams have been used as 'farm teams' by the professional sides, also ensuring a certain equitable distribution of college players. The status of American football was reflected in the Thanksgiving Day tradition as a 'holiday granted by the State and the nation to see a game of football' (*New York Herald*, 1893). The original contest was between the two big sides – Yale and Harvard – but soon spread across the country.

Walter Camp was a prominent figure in the development of the game and instigated rules such as a scrimmage, whereby the team in original possession would snap (centre) the ball back to a quarterback, who would hand it to another back in logical play. He also instigated the 5-yard rule, where one team is given three chances to make 5 yards or lose possession of the ball. The chalk lines that emerged as a result created a 'gridiron' effect, which was also adopted as the name of the game. This rule created the need for exacting plays and the introduction of players running interference for the ball carrier. Strategies and tactics to win have become highly specialised, with game and coaching analysis, and instant replays to check the accuracy of officials' decisions.

The characteristics of American football are:

- high scoring and fast play;
- skilful and powerful play;
- creates entertainment through the media and sponsors, and tends to attract families rather than having single-sex traditions, as with soccer in the UK;
- facilities are extensive and of a high standard, for both players and spectators;
- teams operate as businesses controlled by owners, and are heavily marketed with their accompanying merchandise;
- origins as a white, male, middle-class game;
- games are very competitive and draws do not feature;
- professional ethos of the Lombardian ethic, with material rewards for success, reflects the capitalist system;
- because of the size of the USA, there is no tradition of home and away fans as in the UK, and the crowds are therefore less partisan;
- well-integrated children's leagues;
- route through to the elite via the college system, which also feeds the professional game.

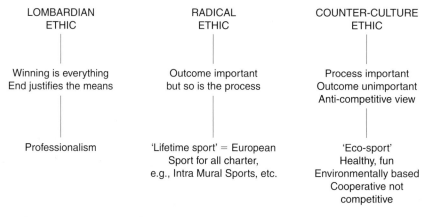

LOMBARDIAN ETHIC	RADICAL ETHIC	COUNTER-CULTURE ETHIC
Winning is everything End justifies the means	Outcome important but so is the process	Process important Outcome unimportant Anti-competitive view
Professionalism	'Lifetime sport' = European Sport for all charter, e.g., Intra Mural Sports, etc.	'Eco-sport' Healthy, fun Environmentally based Cooperative not competitive

Figure 10.14 Concepts of American sport

Figure 10.15 Does American football epitomise the US character?

Violence in sports can result in chaotic brawls, both by athletes and spectators. These may involve the use of a wide range of implements or whatever else may be found on hand. In sports that are inherently violent, violence sometimes goes beyond what is permitted by the rules.

Competitive sports may involve aggressive tactics, but actual violence is considered to fall outside the boundaries of good sportsmanship. Contact sports such as American football involve certain levels of physical violence, but include restrictions and penalties for excessive and dangerous acts of force. Violence in sports may include threats, or physical harm and may be carried out by athletes, coaches, fans, spectators, or the parents of young athletes.

Causes

Some athletes may be genetically predisposed to violence or (particularly in male athlete cases) have unusually high testosterone levels. Animal behaviour **ethology** studies may also lend a clue, as athletes may resort to violence to establish territory.

The sporting arena has also been used as a platform for countries to settle their disputes in front of the world's media.

Athletes sometimes resort to violence in hopes of injuring and intimidating opponents. Such incidents may be part of a strategy developed by coaches or players.

In both the stands and the streets, fans may resort to violence to express loyalty to a team, to release frustration with a team's performance, or to intimidate opponents. Violence may also be related to nationalism or as an outlet for underlying social tensions. It is often alcohol-related.

Ritual violence: High school, college, and even professional sports teams often include initiation ceremonies known as *hazing*, as a rite of passage. A 1999 study by Alfred University and the National Collegiate Athletic Association (NCAA) found that approximately four out of five college US athletes (250,000 per year) experienced hazing. Half were required to take part in alcohol-related initiations, while two-thirds were subjected to humiliation rituals.

Although the nature of American football is very physical and aggressive in comparison to soccer in the UK, there are fewer disturbances by spectators. Some of the possible reasons for this may be:

- The size of the country makes it more difficult for home and away clashes, reducing the amount of intense head-to-head clashes with fans
- The origins of the game are middle class, in the institutions of higher education rather than in the working-class system as in the UK
- The legal consumption age of alcohol is higher in the USA
- The traditional family appeal of the game is in stark contrast to the more male and macho appeal in the UK.

Activity 7

Contrast football in the UK with its counterpart in the USA and suggest some cultural and historical differences which have resulted in two very different games. Why is there less violence among American supporters?

Exam-style question

Discuss sport and commercialism with reference to the 'American Dream' and Aussie Rules football.

(10 marks)

Despite their small numbers, Aborigines have produced some of Australia's most famous sporting champions. Names such as Catherine Freeman, Evonne Goolagong-Cawley, Lionel Rose, Arthur Beetson and the Ella brothers have become legends.

Whether it be in league hockey, tennis or even squash there have been great contributions made by either Aborigines or Torres Strait Islanders. And it's not only their successes that make their contributions to sport significant, but also how they were able to make those successes under the conditions and opportunities that were available to them. For every Aborigine who makes it to the top, there are thousands who could have made it but never had the opportunity. Many Aborigines have had to compete on uneven playing fields without a sporting chance, having to overcome the hurdles of racism and poverty.

Australia

Colonialism

The British Empire was the largest in history and for a time was *the* global power. At its peak, it was often said that 'the sun never sets on the British Empire' because the sun was always shining on at least one of its numerous colonies or subject nations.

As a result, its legacy is widespread in sports and education, among other things.

Before the British settlement of Australia, the tribal populations, such as the Aborigines, would have had their own recreational pastimes. They lived in nomadic tribes, creating and maintaining their own territory in which they had freedom to hunt and fish.

Many sports were linked to their subsistence lifestyle. Traditional physical activities would have a functional base; they would also have had strong religious and ritual meanings. With the exception of tournaments, rules were few, easy to understand and often temporary; officials were not needed; winners were rarely honoured as this was not the main purpose of participation.

- Through play and friendly contests males maintained fitness and military prowess.
- Tournaments were inter-tribal. They followed rules of fair play and were used to settle personal scores or tribal disagreements.
- Sport was used to strengthen internal relationships and social intercourse.

The Aborigine population has been decimated by military action, disease and exile into remote areas. Colonisation also led to the loss of land

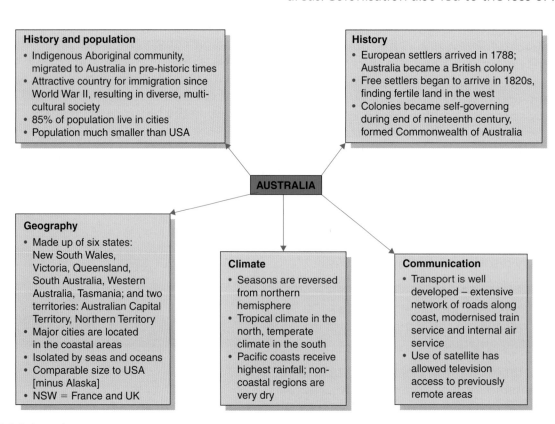

History and population
- Indigenous Aboriginal community, migrated to Australia in pre-historic times
- Attractive country for immigration since World War II, resulting in diverse, multi-cultural society
- 85% of population live in cities
- Population much smaller than USA

History
- European settlers arrived in 1788; Australia became a British colony
- Free settlers began to arrive in 1820s, finding fertile land in the west
- Colonies became self-governing during end of nineteenth century, formed Commonwealth of Australia

AUSTRALIA

Geography
- Made up of six states: New South Wales, Victoria, Queensland, South Australia, Western Australia, Tasmania; and two territories: Australian Capital Territory, Northern Territory
- Major cities are located in the coastal areas
- Isolated by seas and oceans
- Comparable size to USA [minus Alaska]
- NSW = France and UK

Climate
- Seasons are reversed from northern hemisphere
- Tropical climate in the north, temperate climate in the south
- Pacific coasts receive highest rainfall; non-coastal regions are very dry

Communication
- Transport is well developed – extensive network of roads along coast, modernised train service and internal air service
- Use of satellite has allowed television access to previously remote areas

Figure 10.16 Australia

Aussie Sport is a national sporting initiative committed to the development of young people through sport. The Australian Sports Commission (ASC) and the state departments of sport and education work closely together to foster positive community relationships, to ensure a coordinated approach to junior sport in their area.

Aussie Sport is about:

- supporting quality teaching and coaching;
- promoting and developing quality sport for young people;
- making sport more accessible, easier to play and more enjoyable;
- developing essential sporting skills in young people;
- fostering greater community involvement in junior sport;
- introducing modified versions of major games (e.g. Kanga Cricket for children, developed by the Australian Cricket Board);
- using the skills of coaches as well as teachers.

rights, recognised and compensated for in the Native Title Act 1994. Even more recently (2008) an official apology has been given to the Aborigines.

The personnel who were sent abroad to impose British culture and values were the 'old boys' of English public schools. Their obsession for their team games had an enormous impact on the traditional activities of the native people. In Australian schools, reserves and missions the main games became cricket, rugby and netball.

During the five decades following World War II (1939-1945), most of the territories of the Empire became independent. Many went on to join the Commonwealth of Nations, a free association of independent states.

Aboriginal culture has seen a revival within a more liberal society: for example, Aborigines have been included in the Australian Sports Commission (ASC), founding the 'Aboriginal Sport and Recreation Programme'. National competitions exclusive to Aborigines have been organised.

Figure 10.17 Map of Australia

The effects of colonisation and post-colonial developments include:

- discrimination
- loss of old ways of playing
- schools acted as a vehicle for fostering British sporting pastimes
- ancient religions and rituals replaced by Christianity
- tribal hierarchical structures replaced by British systems of government and legislation.

Government

Australia is a member of the Commonwealth of Nations. The federal government is located in Canberra and conducts the national affairs. Similar to the USA, the Australian states each have their own parliament and governor. It is a society based on democracy, with each citizen entitled to vote once they reach the age of 18. Legislative authority is held by the federal parliament, and political power rests with the prime minister, who heads the government.

Australia has a multi-tiered system of government: a Commonwealth government; eight state and territory governments; and a large number of local or municipal governments. The Queen, through her representative, the Governor General, is still head of state. The political system follows the British Westminster system of bicameral parliamentary democracy.

Similar to the situation in the USA, the national television networks are beginning to show features on school sport, from school initiatives to information on individual students and sports events. This is a way of encouraging a community interest in school sport.

Talent identification

Attempts to screen for talented sportspeople have tended to focus on athletes who are already in the system, and who have shown a commitment to their particular activity. The Australians have tried to take this one step further, by looking for potential talent in those not currently participating.

Sport-specific profiles have been established (that is, the requirements for a particular sport from both a physiological and a psychological viewpoint), and

testing has moved into schools, to try to match each child to the sport they have been deemed most suited to. The teachers within the school environment carry out the initial tests, covering physical measurements and psychological assessments, on young people aged 14–16 years. The top 10 per cent then progress to phase two, with more sport-specific testing taking place in laboratories.

These children become part of a squad within the talent development programme. The state and the individual sporting associations are responsible for the funding, and variations occur depending on the resources of facilities and coaching. Children who do not make the grade are encouraged to join local clubs to develop their talents.

In order to reduce the duplication of testing for a variety of different sports, each with its own interests at heart, the federal government has released funds for the development of elite athletes, under the Olympic Athlete Programme. The talent search is carried out by a national coordinator and eight state coordinators. These then liaise with the sport-specific agencies, academies and school/recreation departments. Perhaps it was no coincidence that this followed the awarding of the Olympic Games to Sydney in 2000. The sports most suited to this type of testing, and most likely to achieve 'quick' results, are reflected in those chosen for the search. These are: athletics, canoeing, cycling, rowing, swimming, triathlon, water polo and weightlifting.

The response has been very encouraging. In 1995, 40 per cent of all schools eligible to take part did so. At phase one, 100,000 children took part; at phase two, 10,000 children; and at phase three, 1,000 children. The aim of the programme was to improve international standards of performance, but there were positive developments for individuals who were tested and introduced to the sports they were most suited to, and it encouraged a national interest in the Sydney Olympics.

Types of sport

The English colonial influence is evident in the sporting traditions of the Australians, both in the type of games, such as cricket and rugby, and in the attitudes of how you play the game (dress codes, etc.). There is a strong middle-class influence on and participation in sport. There is not such a working-class tradition as in the UK.

Figure 10.18 Steve Waugh, one of Australia's highest-scoring batsmen

- One of the first recorded cricket games was between two teams from the HMS *Calcutta* in 1803. Today, Australian cricket attracts thousands of spectators. Competition against England (the Ashes) incites nationalist fervour.
- The Australian tennis teams are renowned and have won several Davis Cup competitions.
- Horse racing is an Australian passion (e.g. Melbourne Cup).
- Swimming is popular, perhaps inevitably so, as a result of the country's climate and coastline. The 'Australian crawl' was introduced at the turn of the twentieth century.

It is also interesting to note the recent tendency for the UK to emulate the Australian system for sport, for example, basing the UK Sport Institute (UKSI) on the Australian model.

> **Key term**
>
> **Colonial:** The policy and practice of a power in extending control over weaker peoples or areas.

Government involvement in sport

The Report of the Australian Sports Institute Study Group in 1975 concluded that Australians 'spend an enormous amount of time and money on sport – thinking, talking, reading and writing about it, saving and spending for it and above all, loving it'.

Organisation of Australian sport

The Australian system evolved from a community-based club structure, catering mainly for mass participation in sport. The advantage of this was that individuals could participate to their own level of ability. The disadvantage was a concentration on amateurism and volunteers. (Australia was even slower to accept professionalism in participation and sport management than the UK, from where it had inherited the amateur ethos.) The result was increased government involvement and funding in the 1980s, recognising the need for a more professional approach.

A controversial but successful catalyst came about with the attempts of media giant Kerry Packer, who started to commercialise and professionalise cricket in 1977, establishing a professional World Series of Cricket.

Until the 1980s, youth sport had a different emphasis. The focus for youth sport tended to be more specific – developing elite performance. The disadvantage of this was a high drop-out rate among adolescents. The result was more programmes in the 1980s and 1990s to stimulate 'sport for all' policies.

Clubs and associations were uncoordinated and fragmented up to the 1980s. The disadvantage of this was that individual needs were catered for, rather than promoting an integrated approach for federal funding.

> **Activity 8**
>
> Explain the social and cultural influences that have resulted in sport having such a high profile in Australian society.

Current organisation

Figure 10.19 represents the current state of the organisation of Australian sport. From top to bottom, it is clear that the government gives both elite support and funding support in general. The Australian Institute of Sport (AIS) and the ASC supply the national sporting organisations with funds and services. State organisations fulfil a similar role at state level. Local government is mostly involved in supporting the regional and local sport organisations with services and facilities.

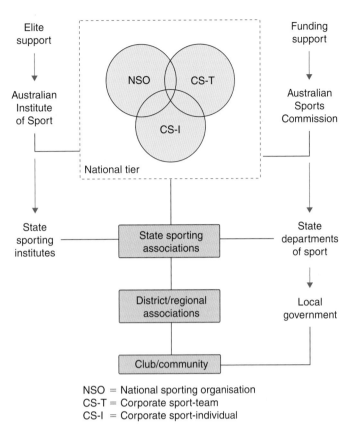

Figure 10.19 The Australian sport system
Source: Westerbeck 1995

NSO = National sporting organisation
CS-T = Corporate sport-team
CS-I = Corporate sport-individual

Government involvement therefore occurs at three levels: local, state and national.

Private sport management companies

Private sport management companies (e.g. IMG International Management Group) emerged to:

- secure sponsorships;
- advise on marketing strategies;
- manage sport teams/personalities;
- negotiate television rights and endorsement contracts.

Their growing influence is very evident in golf, with the Australian Open, the Australian Masters and the Greg Norman Classic. This ensures ongoing professionalism, but has been blamed for focusing on commercial rather than sporting interests.

Australian Rules football

This game dates back to 1858, when two men, Harrison and Wills, decided to design a purely Australian game. The game which emerged showed signs of influences from cricket (oval pitch), Gaelic football (played by Irish troops) and the English game of rugby. Cricket pitches were used and were controlled by the cricket clubs. The Melbourne club is the oldest, founded in 1858. This game also helped to keep cricketers fit in the winter months. Even today, the size of the playing area is not a set distance, but has minimum and maximum dimensions. The reason for this game not being successful internationally is the size of the pitch; it is difficult for already established pitches to be converted. The areas in Australia where the game flourishes are reported to have extensive facilities.

Characteristics of Australian Rules football are outlined below:

- Premier matches form a series.
- Professionals play for their state rather than the home state of their club.
  - *Advantage*: poorer states can use players who have moved to bigger clubs.
  - *Disadvantage*: calculated at player's residence since age 15 rather than birth.
- There is a draft system similar to that in the USA.
- Heroes have not achieved national status due to the regional nature of the game.

The expansion strategy the league adopted in the late 1980s has paid big dividends to the broad AFL, including its teams, players and fans. The fact that demand for seats at the final outstrips supply is a sign of its success.

The report that shaped Australian Rules – 'Establishing the basis of future success' (1985) – drew from a combination of management and business expertise. At the time the situation was parochial, supported by a 'tribal' band of followers and was financially vulnerable.

The dominant six teams (Carlton, Hawthorn, Richmond, North Melbourne, Essendon and Collingwood) had secured 95 per cent of the grand final places in the previous 20 years, and half of the 14 clubs were effectively bankrupt. Net assets of the entire league were barely Aus$5million, and TV rights were being picked up by Channel Seven for a meagre Aus$850,000 a year.

Ground attendances were dominated by 'tribals', that is, committed fans who attended most of their club games all season. A smaller section attended games which were high-profile clashes.

Table 10.4 Average attendance (1987 & present day)

		Ave. Attendance per game	Total attendance
1987	14 clubs	19,369	3 million
Present day	16 clubs	36,793	6.5 million

This latter section regarded Australian Rules as one of a range of potential leisure pursuits, and were more open to innovations like night football and inter-state franchises. Potentially, they offered a wider audience than the tribals. The report recommended that the VFL retain the tribals and engage more spectators by expanding the VFL into the other states, and by competitively and financially equalising the teams and the competition through an American-style annual player draft, salary caps and revenue sharing.

Broadcast media revenue rose quickly to about Aus$5.5 million after the commission took over and put the rights to tender. Revenues have soared since to Aus$100million+ as the new five-year contract with the Seven and Ten networks (and through them, Foxtel).

The Australian Football League — the body that runs the Aussie Rules Competition —has a single broadcasting contract that earns it well over Aus$20million per year from television channels that broadcast the sport. This is in stark contrast to the 120 other sporting bodies in Australia – out of 130 – that get virtually nothing through TV broadcasts.

The commission agreed that since the AFL came into being in 1990, there has been more of a challenge balancing the interests of the traditional tribals and potential new spectators looking for more excitement.

The expansion of the codes catchment and revenue has combined with higher media rights payments and sponsor revenue to boost AFL revenue from just under Aus$90 million in 1997 to about Aus$270 million currently.

About Aus$120 million of that flows through the 16 clubs and through them to player payments, which have risen from an average Aus$22,000 in 1987 to Aus$220,000. A portion is also allocated by way of special payments of up to Aus$5million a year to financially weaker clubs (for example, Melbourne's, Western Bulldogs and the Kangaroos) to ensure their survival.

Another slice of the revenue pie supports AFL development programmes, and the financially stronger AFL is both directly and indirectly underpinning the re-development of club facilities and game venues.

Some of the benefits of commercialisation are well known:

- The AFL will be able to keep prices down
- Extensive media coverage will boost the game at grass-roots level leading to future generations of players and spectators
- Facilities can be upgraded
- More exciting competitions can be staged.

However, can too much too many harm a sport?

Activity 9

Compare the structural variations in Australian Rules football and American football. Consider the key elements of set pieces, restarts, tackles, violence and punishment, and the nature of each sport, such as scoring and pitch. Give cultural reasons for the differences you have identified.

Commercialisation is threatening to destroy the original nature of the sport. It is becoming more a spectacle engineered by public relations and mass consumption experts, who wish to market the game for the consumer-oriented society. The more local nature of the game is changing as these become city or even state conglomerations.

Status

Sport has a high status in Australia. The reasons for this include:

- Health and fitness are traditionally important in the settlement of a country in harsh conditions. This is similar to the frontier spirit of the USA.
- Australia was a 'new' nation and wished to advertise itself by promoting a positive image.

- It has built itself on egalitarian/equal opportunities principles, again similar to those of the USA, and set itself apart from the traditionally more class-driven UK. This created more equal access to sporting opportunities.
- The media has played a large part in generating a health-conscious and sporting nation.
- The education system has always placed a high priority on physical education in schools, and many policies and campaigns have emphasised this point.
- The Government has made sport a priority with the explicit intention of being a top nation in international competitions. As such it has centralised and funded elite level sport. The resulting success at international level has been proof of its policies and has generated a 'feel good' factor and sense of nationalism.
- The Australian Institute of Sport now acts as a model for other nations. The founders of the English Institute of Sport paid many visits to Australia to learn from their vast experience in this field.

EXAMINER'S TIP

If you are asked to compare or contrast different cultures, it is important that you state each one clearly, rather than assuming that by mentioning one, the examiner will know that you understand the other. The examiner must be able to see a direct comparison in order to link the two.

Activity 10

Provide a definition and brief example of the following terms:

- decentralised/centralised;
- democracy/egalitarian;
- pluralist/assimilation/ethnic groups;
- dominant culture/subculture;
- legislative;
- nationalism;
- functional/utilitarian/recreational;
- autonomous/state-controlled;
- capitalist/socialist;
- republic/federal.

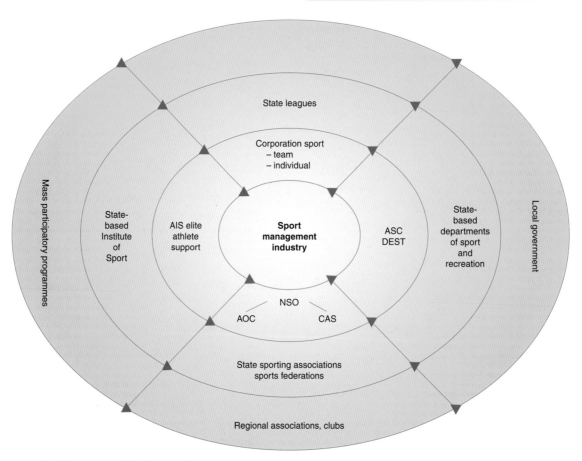

Figure 10.20 The four pyramids of Australian sport

What you need to know

United Kingdom:

* The traditions of recreational and sporting activities go back many centuries.
* The United Kingdom was the birthplace of modern sport.
* Sports were rationalised and codified, mainly in the nineteenth century.
* The social class system was to prove influential in the manner and values that sports developed.
* Amateurism and professionalism became monetary as well as social class distinctions.
* Amateurism used to be the dominant sporting value in nineteenth-century England.
* Today, amateurism has become squeezed by professionalism, having to bow to the commercial pressures of the modern-day sports world.
* The middle classes became the moral force in society and instigated the administration and bureaucracy that was to epitomise modern sport.
* The UK originally housed the headquarters of the national and international governing bodies of sport.
* The USA and Australia were both to receive a legacy of British culture in sport, though they adapted these activities to suit their own developing cultures.

United States of America:

* There is a decentralised system – each state operates its own administration.
* There are exclusive private clubs, but these are different from UK sports clubs.
* Careers in sport tend to take the route of collegiate sport as a feeder for the professional leagues, as well as maintaining amateur eligibility.
* Collegiate sport is run on commercial lines, with control exerted by cartels.
* The dominant sports reflect the capitalist culture from which they evolved.
* The government tries not to become too involved, but has produced much legislation in particular areas.
* Children's sports programmes tend to stress the dominant sporting values of adults, and there is a tendency for an overemphasis on winning.

Australia:

* As in the USA, a variety of scenery and climate allows for wide variations in sports, though with fewer opportunities for winter sports.
* Australia has felt the influence of the British sports scene and has maintained links with the UK for a longer period of time than the USA.
* Australia has similar government administrations to those of the USA.
* Mass participation and the pursuit of excellence are important objectives, though the latter has recently attracted more world attention.
* The original characteristics of sports have been adapted within the more isolated continent and now have their own unique character.
* Sport and physical education are given time on the timetable, and outside sports coaches are used within the school setting.

Review questions

United Kingdom:

1 List four characteristics of popular and rationalised recreation.

2 Briefly outline the popular recreational activities of Haxey Hood and Ashbourne Football.

3 Suggest reasons to account for the survival of activities such as the Highland Games.

4 What were the characteristics of nineteenth-century public schools and state schools?

5 Describe the process of technical development of activities in public schools.

6 Define the term 'athleticism' and discuss its influence on society.

7 What influence did the universities bring to bear in the development of sports?

8 Why was athleticism acceptable to the middle classes?

9 What is meant by the term 'self-government' in relation to the organisation of games in nineteenth-century public schools? Provide examples of how this system operated.

10 Explain the influence of the various social classes on the development of football.

11 In what way was the development of cricket different to that of football?

United States of America:

1 What does the term 'federal' mean?

2 What are the three concepts of American sports? Briefly outline what is meant by each one.

3 What are the common characteristics of American football?

4 How do capitalism and professional sport complement each other?

Australia:

1 What European influences are evident in Australian Rules football?

2 Why has the Australian government placed so much emphasis on achieving excellence in sport?

3 What problems have American football and Aussie Rules football faced in trying to be successful in other cultures?

4 Explain the relationship between the UK, USA and Australia in terms of:

- historical and political aspects

- sporting aspects.

11 Participation to excellence: Relevant organisations and their policies

Learning outcomes

By the end of this chapter you should understand the following:

- participation to excellence:
  - the sports development pyramid;
  - terms such as 'opportunity', 'provision' and 'esteem' [OPE];
  - the role of leading sport organisations and their policies for participation and excellence;
- sport organisations:
  - Department for Culture, Media and Sport (DCMS);
  - local authorities;
  - UK Sport;
  - UKSI (and devolved National Institutes of Sport);
  - Sport England and other home country organisations;
  - national governing bodies;
- funding of physical activity – public, private, voluntary and the National Lottery;
- factors influencing the participation levels of groups such as women, the elderly, ethnic minorities, the young and people with disabilities.

CHAPTER INTRODUCTION

This chapter explores the role that sport assumes in the political and social arena. It examines the organisation, administration and policymaking process of sport, helping you to reflect on major sporting and social issues. The importance with which the government in power views sport makes a huge difference to the opportunities available, from the grass roots of sport to sporting excellence.

Before we study the provision for sport at varying levels of participation, we are going to look at a summary of participation trends outlined by the DCMS, which will highlight the significance of this chapter.

Participation

A summary of participation trends

- The quality and quantity of participation in sport and physical activity in the UK is lower than it could be, and levels have not changed significantly over recent years:
    - for sport: only 46 per cent of the population participate in sport more than 12 times a year, compared to 70 per cent in Sweden and almost 80 per cent in Finland;
    - for physical activity: only 32 per cent of adults in England take 30 minutes of moderate exercise five times a week, compared to 57 per cent of Australians and 70 per cent of Finns.
- Young white males are most likely to take part in sport and physical activity, and the most disadvantaged groups are least likely to do so. Participation falls dramatically after leaving school, and continues to drop with age. But the more active you are in sport and physical activity at a young age, the more likely you are to continue to participate throughout your life.
- The UK's performance in international sport is better than we might think. UK Sport's index of success places us third in the world. However, we are not as successful in the sports we care most about as a nation.
- The UK successfully hosts major sporting events each year (such as Wimbledon and the London Marathon), with little government involvement. Problems have arisen with the so-called 'mega events' (Olympics, FIFA World Cup, UEFA European Championships, World Athletics Championships and Commonwealth Games), which require significant infrastructure investment. Historically, there has been poor investment appraisal, management and coordination for some of these events.
- Total government and lottery expenditure on sport and physical activity in England is estimated to be roughly £2.2 billion per year. A significant proportion of this is distributed via local authorities. The funding of sport and physical activity is fragmented, and some strands of funding may not be sustainable, as money from the National Lottery and TV rights is decreasing and local government budgets are being squeezed. In contrast, there is major public investment planned for school sports facilities.
- Broadly speaking, sport and physical activity are delivered through four sectors:
    1. local government (e.g. your local council);
    2. education (schools, FE and HE);
    3. voluntary sector (clubs and national governing bodies of sport);
    4. private sector (e.g. privately owned golf clubs). The role of the health sector in physical activity is also important. However, government's interaction with these sectors is through a complex set of organisations, with overlapping responsibilities and unclear accountability. The situation is further complicated at the international level, because some sports compete as United Kingdom/Great Britain, some as home countries, and some as both.

Participation pyramid

As part of our study we need to investigate the various levels of participation in sporting activities. This will range from:

- the broad base of the pyramid, where the main emphasis is on participation; to the
- apex of the pyramid, where the focus is on the standard of performance.

For ease of study, society will be categorised into distinct groups based on age, disability, gender, socio-economics, culture and race, and we will consider each one in relation to the opportunities for sporting participation provided.

Figure 11.1 Sports development continuum model

The need for a more coordinated and fair approach to the provision of sporting activities addresses two main areas:

1 sports development: enabling people to learn basic sports skills, with the possibility of reaching a standard of sporting excellence;
2 sports equity: redressing the balance of inequalities in sport, that is, equality of access for everyone, regardless of race, age, gender or level of ability.

Sport England has a sport development continuum:

● Foundation – learning basic movement skills, knowledge and understanding; developing a positive attitude to physical activity.
● Participation – exercising one's leisure option for a variety of reasons – health, fitness, social.
● Performance – improving standards through coaching, competition and training.
● Excellence – reaching national and publicly recognised standards of performance.

Sport England is required to widen the base of the participation pyramid by ensuring equality of opportunity through the provision of facilities and sporting programmes in order that people from all sections of society are able to feel the benefit from participating in a variety of activities. Many of the organisations and policies are outlined below

> ### Key term
>
> **Participation:** The active involvement of people in recreational and sporting activities.

The organisation of sport in the UK

The organisation of sport and physical education has a dynamic aspect, so it is important (and more interesting!) if you try to keep up to date with changes as they occur. The web addresses for some of the major organisations are provided below (these are correct at the time of writing).

The main focus of this section is to appreciate that opportunities for participation and excellence should not be the result of luck or coincidence, but the culmination of specific aims and policies of organisations with a remit to develop sport at these levels. The opportunities people have to initiate and

further develop their interest in sporting activities are dependent on many factors, including:

● provision within their country/community;
● personal factors, such as race, gender, age and socio-economics.

We need to understand how sport and politics interact. It will be useful to begin with a definition of politics:

> the science and art of government; dealing with the form, organisation and administration of a state or part of one, and of the regulation of its relations with other states… Political [means] belonging to or pertaining to the state, its government and policy. (Oxford English Dictionary)

We will look at some of the key words that make up this definition and consider their possible meaning in relation to sport.

> ### EXAMINER'S TIP
>
> You may not be examined directly on the aspect of sport and politics, but it can help you to understand and appreciate in more depth the issues we will discuss during this section of the book.

Administration

The administration of sport can be seen as developing from the community. For example, a local sports club forms the base of the pyramid, with its regional, national and international counterparts above. The international governing bodies of sport (the International Olympic Committee, the Commonwealth Games Federation and the European sports bodies) are political bodies and their dealings must reflect the political climate in which they operate. They are concerned with:

● governing sport;
● making decisions;
● creating and distributing finances and resources.

IN DEPTH: Relations with other states

The relationships between states with regard to sport began as soon as worldwide travel and unified rules of competition developed. Sport can have a positive and a negative influence within and between societies.

Positive	Negative
• International goodwill • Promotes cultural empathy and understanding between nations • Athletes are seen as ambassadors of their country • The Olympic Charter sets out the view that sport promotes world peace by improving international understanding and respect • The sense of belonging to a country encourages patriotism and nationalism	• Patriotism and nationalism are more powerful when conflict is prevalent • Reinforces conflict • Results in winners and losers: winners can be viewed as superior and powerful, whereas losers are inferior and powerless • Success is attributed to countries as much as to the athletes themselves • Other nations can be seen as 'the enemy'

Policy

Policy suggests decision making based on the ideology (set of ideas) or philosophy of those in power. This is relevant from local to international situations. Numerous indicators can be used to determine the importance a government places on sport:

- the expenditure for sport;
- the position or status of sports ministers within a government;
- the type and amount of sport legislation produced.

Politics reflects the power systems within a culture – who has the power and how do they use it? Sport and physical activities have sometimes been used by various governments, individuals and administrators for political reasons.

The commercial world plays an extremely important role in sports decision making, at local, national and international levels. The cost of staging sports events such as the Olympic Games, for example, is extraordinarily high:

- The construction of stadiums requires capital which often only governments can raise.
- The running of events increasingly involves those who pay international television fees.
- Revenue for major events requires huge commitment from governments.

IN DEPTH: Political uses of sport

Social factors

Sport can be used to introduce or reinforce social harmony. Government inquiries into inner-city riots usually refer to the need to provide better sporting facilities. This can be taken to have various meanings:

- Boredom creates dysfunctional activity. By providing the highest standard of sporting facilities and educating people to use them constructively in their leisure time, we can help to improve people's quality and enjoyment of life, giving them less reason to become involved in antisocial activities.
- The 'bread and circuses' theory – this is more controversial, and claims that sport can be used to divert the attention and energy of the masses away from the problems of the political and social system in which they live.

Figure 11.2 Does sport divert people's attention away from political and social problems?

IN CONTEXT

In the film *Gladiator*, the emperor stages a festival of games to keep the population happy and has bread thrown to the crowds to make him popular.

Sport as 'character-building'

Sport would also seem to have socialising qualities, which can be used as a political tool. For example, involvement in team games helps develop the ability to work in a team, as well as qualities of cooperation, leadership, obeying rules and respecting authority; team games have always been popular with governments when they emphasise the value of a population participating in sporting activities.

Propaganda

Sport can be used as political propaganda. For example, in the 1930s, the Nazi youth groups aimed to indoctrinate young people in the values of Nazi Germany.

Defence and work

Sport has also been used to raise the fitness level of populations in order to better prepare them for defending their country, make them more productive in the workplace and decrease health costs.

So we can see that there are various reasons why national governments become involved in sport. Figure 11.3 summarises these points.

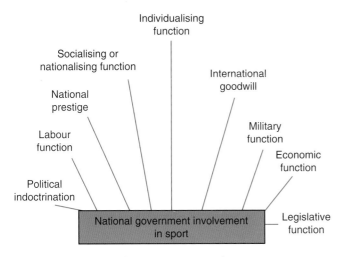

Figure 11.3 National government involvement in sport

Activity 1

1   Choose four functions of sport from Figure 11.3. Explain in detail how each one operates.
2   Consider the stance of the Department for Culture, Media and Sport. Which of these functions is the British government most concerned with?

Sport and government in the UK

We have been suggesting that sport cannot be seen as an activity which only has relevance to those who practise it; it also serves various functions of a society. In the current climate, the government policies for participation and excellence in sport have become crucial to all the other sports organisations, such as Sport England and UK Sport. It is therefore necessary at this stage to determine exactly why the national government would become more involved in sports policy.

Government policies

In recent years, both Conservative and Labour governments in the UK have sought increasingly to assume more control over physical education and sport. Why should the government wish to spend money on sport and leisure? The stance taken is that sport can make a valuable contribution to delivering the four key outcomes of:

1   lower long-term unemployment;
2   less crime;
3   better health;
4   better qualifications.

It can also develop:

● individual pride;
● community spirit to enable communities to run regeneration programmes themselves;
● neighbourhood regeneration.

Key terms

Function: The special activity, purpose or role of an organisation or person. An example of the function of a school would be to educate young people.
Funding: Income that is generated, internally or externally, and expenditure incurred to meet the function of the organisation.

The role of central government

Minister for Sport In the 1960s, the creation of the post of Minister for Sport provided a focus for the coordination and formulation of policy:

● Sport was located firmly within a wider cultural and leisure brief.
● Sport now had a voice at Cabinet level.

Executive summary

Findings

Arts and sport, cultural and recreational activity, can contribute to neighbourhood renewal and make a real difference to health, crime, unemployment and education in deprived communities.

1. This is because they:
    a appeal directly to individuals' interests and develop their potential and self-confidence
    b relate to community identity and encourage collective effort
    c help build positive links with the wider community
    d are associated with rapidly growing industries.
2. Barriers to be overcome are:
    a projects being tailored to programme/policy criteria, rather than to community needs
    b short-term perspectives
    c promoting arts/sport in communities being seen as peripheral, both to culture/leisure organisations and in regeneration programmes
    d lack of hard information on the regeneration impact of arts/sport
    e poor links between arts/sport bodies and major 'players', including schools.
3. Principles which help to exploit the potential of arts/sport in regenerating communities are:
    a valuing diversity
    b embedding local control
    c supporting local commitment
    d promoting equitable partnerships
    e defining common objectives in relation to actual needs
    f working flexibly with charge
    g securing sustainability
    h pursuing quality across the spectrum: and
    i connecting with the mainstream of art and sport activities.
4. Social exclusion issues arise with various groups irrespective of their geographic location. This is particularly the case with ethnic minority groups and disabled people where special and systematic arrangements need to be made:
    a to invest in people and capacity within these groups and to build an information base against which future progress can be measured
    b to cater specifically for their needs in general regeneration programmes and culture/leisure policies
    c to engage directly with people within these groups, and actively to value and recognise diversity
    d to develop, monitor and deliver action plans to promote their access and involvement and to meet their needs.

Figure 11.4 Executive summary – policy action team 10
Source: Department for Culture, Media and Sport

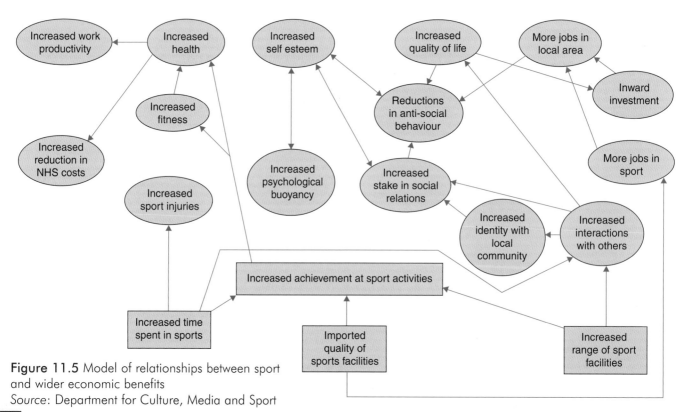

Figure 11.5 Model of relationships between sport and wider economic benefits
Source: Department for Culture, Media and Sport

However, the department also had responsibility for the arts, broadcasting, films, tourism and heritage. In addition, it was responsible for the funding of national galleries and museums, and sport had to compete in this arena.

Certain limitations of the role of the Minister for Sport can be identified:

- The role of the minister is to advise and consult, not to direct.
- S/he coordinates sport rather than controls it.
- S/he now comes under the DCMS, which also has competing responsibilities.

However, these limitations should not be overstated, for the minister can exert considerable influence on policy, when required. This would mainly depend on:

- the prominence of sporting issues to the government;
- the quality, ambition and style of the minister in office.

Make sure you know who the current Minister for Sport is and try to keep track of any initiatives, opinions or events with which s/he becomes involved.

Table 11.1 The benefits of sport

Nature of benefit	Experienced by excluded	Strength of evidence	Nature of evidence			
			Lab/experimental	National/large survey	Case study	Meta analysis/study review
National Identity	−	+				
Prestige	++	+			*	
Reduced health Costs	− −	+ +		*	*	*
Trade		+ +		*		
Communal Community/ family coherence	− −				*	*
Lower law and order costs (especially for youth)	− − −	+			*	*
Job creation	+ / −	+			*	*
Environmental (created/ renewed)						
Personal Physical health (heart, lungs, joints, bones, muscles)						
Better mental health (coping, depression)	− − −	+ + + +	*	*	*	*
Better self-esteem/ image/ competence	+ / −	+ +	*		*	*
Socialisation/ integration/ tolerance	+ + +	+ + +	*		*	*
General quality of life	+ +	+ +	*		*	*

Source: Department for Culture, Media and Sport

Note: The strength of positive and negative experience in column 2 and of evidence in column 3 is shown by the number of + and − signs. * indicates where the particular form of evidence is available.

Department for Culture, Media and Sport (DCMS)

www.culture.gov.uk

Following restructuring, this department assumed control of sport, becoming the central government department responsible for government policy on areas including the arts, sport and recreation, the National Lottery, libraries, museums and galleries, broadcasting and films. Sport therefore has to compete alongside these other areas.

In 1999 a radical new structure to strengthen the role of UK Sport was introduced. A 'Sports Cabinet' was set up under the chairmanship of the

Secretary of State for Culture, Media and Sport, to work alongside UK Sport and bring together ministers with responsibility for sport in the four home countries (England, Northern Ireland, Scotland and Wales).

Game Plan: A strategy for delivering government sport and physical activity objectives (December 2002)

Game Plan provides a broad context and research evidence for sports policy. It covers broad issues:

- Grass-roots participation could be improved.
- International success is better than perceived.
- The hosting of mega events has not always been successful.
- There are problems of funding in sport.
- There are complex structures responsible for delivering sport policy.

In less than a decade, numerous government policies for sport highlight government's belief in the importance sport is beginning to have in the UK. The following organisations must try to address many of these issues. In some cases their responsibilities overlap.

Sport England

www.sportengland.org

Policies for participation	Policies for excellence
• Sport: Raising the Game (1995) • A Sporting Future for All (2000) • Game Plan (2002) • Best Value through Sport • Step into Sport: Leadership and Volunteering	• Sport: Raising the Game • A Sporting Future for All • Game Plan • Best Value through Sport • Step into Sport: Leadership and Volunteering • PE School Sport and Club Links Strategy (PESSCL)

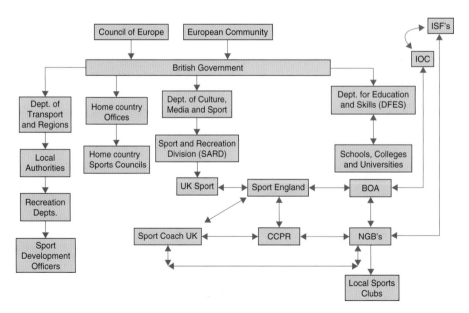

Figure 11.6 Organisation of sport in the UK

Sport England began its role in January 1997 and is accountable to Parliament through the Secretary of State for Culture, Media and Sport, who operates under the DCMS. Sport England also operates ten regional offices in England, providing partnerships across public and private sectors.

Objectives

The objectives of Sport England are to lead the development of sport in England by influencing and serving the public. Its aims are:

- start – get people to participate;
- stay – retain people once they have started;
- succeed – achieve higher levels of performance.

Members of the Council are appointed by the Secretary of State for Culture, Media and Sport. Their responsibilities include:

- approving all policy matters and operational and corporate plans for Sport England;
- bringing independent judgement to issues such as strategy and resources;
- ensuring all financial matters are regulated and operate efficiently.

A series of advisory panels guide Sport England in the following areas:

- lottery;
- local authorities;
- women and sport;
- disability;
- racial equality;
- government body investment.

Funding

The work of Sport England is jointly funded by:

- the Exchequer, for maintaining England's sports infrastructure;
- the National Lottery via the Sport England Lottery Fund, which is earmarked for the development of sport in England;
- sport as part of the overall social inclusion policy and neighbourhood regeneration work.

(Details of policies can be found on pages 277–282.)

Policies for participation	Policies for elite/ excellence
<ul><li>Active programme</li><li>Sportsmark/ Activemark</li><li>National Junior Sports</li><li>Sport Action Zones</li><li>Step into Sport</li></ul>	<ul><li>World-class programme</li><li>Academies Scheme</li><li>Sportsearch Programme (TOP)</li></ul>

The Sports Council for Wales

www.sport-council-wales.org.uk

The Sports Council for Wales is the national organisation responsible for developing and promoting sport and active lifestyles. It is the main adviser on sporting matters to the Welsh Assembly Government and is responsible for distributing funds from the National Lottery to sport in Wales.

The Council fully subscribes to the Welsh Assembly Government's vision for a physically active and sporting nation, as outlined in its strategy document *Climbing Higher*. Its main focus is to increase the frequency of participation by persuading those who are currently sedentary to become more active; and to encourage people, young and old, to develop a portfolio of activities through which to achieve healthy levels of activity.

The themes of the Council's work are:

- Active young people;
- Active communities – developing people and places;
- Developing performance and excellence.

In early 2005, the Minister for Culture, Welsh Language and Sport published the Assembly Government's sport and physical activity strategy, Climbing Higher. To support *Climbing Higher*, the Sports Council for Wales has published a *Framework for the Development of Sport and Physical Activity*. This document will underpin the minister's vision and set out how the Sports Council for Wales will work to deliver his aspirations, working even more closely with government and other partners to develop innovative and evidence-based approaches to building an active Wales.

The *Framework* commits the Sports Council for Wales to a shift from grants management to sports development, through the marketing of physical activity, advocacy for sport and innovation in programme development, in particular, supporting people through training and supporting organisations, with development and evaluation of good practice.

sportscotland

www.sportscotland.org.uk

This is the national agency for sport in Scotland. Its mission is to encourage everyone in Scotland to discover and develop their own sporting experience, helping to increase participation and improve performances in Scottish sport.

sportscotland operates three national centres: Glenmore Lodge, Inverclyde and Cumbrae. These centres provide quality, affordable and residential sporting facilities and services for the development of people in sport. They also act as the parent company of the Scottish Institute of Sport (SIS), which prepares Scotland's best athletes to perform on the world stage by providing performance-planning expertise and individually tailored programmes for Scottish governing bodies and athletes.

sportscotland sets out its vision as follows:

We passionately believe in the benefits of sport, from the enjoyment and sense of achievement that participation brings, to the shared pride that national success generates.

We are committed to the development of safe sport for all people in Scotland.

Three principles underpin all of our work:

1 Developing a sporting infrastructure
2 Creating effective sporting pathways
3 Embedding ethics and equity throughout sport

1 Developing a sporting infrastructure

The development of Scottish sport is dependent on an infrastructure of people, organisations and facilities. This infrastructure has to be maintained, grown and sustained in the long term.

2 Creating effective sporting pathways

Sporting pathways are all about creating opportunities for people to participate in sport at any level and at any stage in life.

3 Embedding ethics and equity throughout sport

We are committed to ethical and equitable sport, tackling discrimination, promoting equality of opportunity and ensuring safe and fair participation and performance.

Sport Northern Ireland

www.sportni.net

As a lead facilitator in the development of sport, Sport NI will work with partners to:

- Increase and sustain committed participation, especially amongst young people;
- Raise the standards of sporting excellence and promote the good reputation and efficient administration of sport;
- Sport NI's aims will be achieved by developing the competencies of its staff who are dedicated to optimising the use of its resources.

Its main partners include:

- district councils;
- education and library boards;
- governing bodies of sport;
- government departments and statutory agencies;
- voluntary clubs and organisations;
- the education sector;
- the commercial sector.

Sport Northern Ireland is also responsible for distributing Lottery Sports Fund awards. It is part of a broad sport network and has a close relationship with its equivalent organisations in England, Scotland and Wales, as well as the UK Sports Council, which has responsibility for UK-wide sport.

Activity 2

What are the similarities and differences between the aims of the different home country sports councils?

UK Sport

www.uksport.gov.uk

Established in 1997 by Royal Charter as part of the restructuring programmes, UK Sport took responsibility for issues that need to be dealt with at a UK level. UK Sport's mission is to help UK athletes become world-class performers. It is to take on a role above that of the home country sport councils on issues that require strategic planning, administration, coordination or representation for the benefit of the UK as a whole. It is funded through Exchequer and lottery funding. In 1999–2000 it received approximately £12 million and £20.5 million from these sources respectively, to fund sporting projects of UK significance. The figure rose to £25 million of National Lottery money in 2003.

UK Sport has a remit to:

- encourage and develop higher standards of sporting excellence in the UK;
- identify sporting policies that should have a UK-wide application;
- identify areas of unnecessary duplication to avoid administrative waste;
- develop and deliver appropriate grant programmes in conjunction with the governing bodies and home country sport councils;
- oversee policy on sport science, sports medicine, drug control, coaching and other

areas where there is a need for a consistent, UK-wide policy;
- coordinate policy for bringing major international events to the UK;
- represent the UK internationally and increase the influence of the UK at an international level.

It performs these aims through four key directorates:

1 Performance Development – provides advice to UK governing bodies on their planning processes; allocates Exchequer funding; advises on applications for awards from the Lottery Sports Fund.
2 UK Sports Institute – Central Services is based in London, with regional network centres. The Olympic sports are mainly catered for and it is primarily for potential and elite athletes, including athletes with disabilities. The main support services of sport science, sports medicine, lifestyle management services, information services and a range of facilities help to create an environment where world-class athletes are more likely to develop.
3 International Relations and Major Events – the globalisation of sport, and the cultural, social

IN CONTEXT

Figure 11.7 Chris Hoy benefits from Lottery funding

Since 1997, UK Sport has operated world-class programmes designed to support our leading Olympic and Paralympic athletes in their mission to win medals at the world's biggest sporting events. With only limited funding available, money has always been directed at those sports and individuals that can demonstrate that they have the capability to deliver medal-winning performances when it matters.

With the benefit of lessons learned over the Sydney and Athens Olympiads, this approach has been developed into one of 'No Compromise', which means that the best athletes ultimately benefit from the resources they need if they are to realise their medal ambitions.

Funding is targeted at athletes via their sport's governing body, through the World-Class Pathway programmes. Podium and Development level athletes will be surrounded by a performance programme that includes coaching, training and competition support, medical and scientific services and access to the best facilities the UK has to offer.

In addition, recognising that succeeding in the majority of Olympic and Paralympic sports effectively means a full-time commitment on behalf of athletes, UK Sport makes a contribution towards living and sporting costs via a means-tested Athlete Personal Award.

The schemes are funded by a mix of Government Exchequer and National Lottery money.

Source: UK Sport's website: www.uksport.gov.uk

and economic benefits accrued by events such as the Olympic Games and the World Cup, make it imperative for the UK to be in a strong position, at the centre of international decision making. There is a need to promote and enhance the position and reputation of the UK sports system internationally. It links with organisations such as the European Union and the British Council to develop initiatives in places like South Africa.

4 Ethics and Anti-doping – the directorate is responsible for the coordination of an effective testing programme and a comprehensive education programme. Its quality work was recognised in 1997 by the awarding of a certification of management, the first organisation in the world to receive one.

This trend towards coordinating policies for sporting excellence began in the 1980s. The formation of the National Coaching Foundation, now Sport Coach UK, was an integral part of this movement.

United Kingdom Sports Institute

The aim of the United Kingdom Sports Institute is to provide elite British sportspeople with the practical and professional support needed to compete on the world stage. Each home country has its own institute.

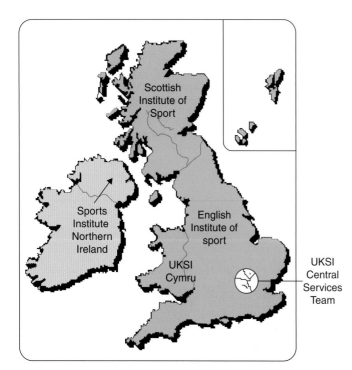

Figure 11.8 The United Kingdom Sports Institute

> **IN CONTEXT**
>
> The English Institute of Sport (EIS) is a nationwide network of world-class support services, designed to foster the talents of our elite athletes. Services are offered from nine regional multi-sport hub sites and an evolving network of satellite centres. High-performance training venues provide the platform for success.
>
> The strategy and ethos of the EIS is set by its national team, with services delivered by a coordinated network of regional teams which feature complementary skills and experience. The range of services supplied by the EIS spans sports science and sports medicine. Support includes applied physiology, biomechanics, medical consultation, medical screening, nutritional advice, performance analysis, psychology, podiatry, strength and conditioning coaching, sports massage and sports vision. The Performance Lifestyle programme provides supplementary career and education advice.
>
> The quality of the delivery is assured by the close relationship the EIS is developing with national governing bodies, performance directors, coaches and the athletes themselves. Almost 2,000 competitors are currently in the EIS system.

Youth Sports Trust

The Youth Sports Trust is a registered charity, set up in 1994 to improve sporting provision for young people in the UK. Its mission is to develop and implement a linked series of quality sports programmes, known under the umbrella term, the National Junior Sports Programme. The Trust also works alongside the DfES to support maintained secondary schools that are applying for Specialist Sports College status. The organisation is becoming increasingly influential in the coordination and provision of sport, both in schools and in the local community.

Policies for participation
● National Junior Sports Programme
● Step into Sport
● School Sports Coordinators
● Sports Colleges

Local authorities

We have already mentioned the burden on local authorities to provide leisure facilities in their area. This is decreed under mainly permissive legislation, such as the Physical Training and

Recreation Act 1937 and the Local Government Miscellaneous Act 1976, which stated that a local authority 'may provide…such recreational facilities as it thinks fit'.

Activity 3

Why should a local authority spend large sums of money on sport when it is a permissive duty rather than a mandatory one?

Leisure, by the year 2000, had become mainly the responsibility of one specialist department. Excluding educational provision, authorities' net expenditure on revenue support for sport exceeds £500 million a year in England and Wales.

Pressures on local authorities

Local authorities operate within certain restrictions: sport and physical recreation have to compete with nine other departments: the arts and cultural provision; libraries; entertainment and catering services; museums; heritage and conservation; tourism; youth and community services; adult education; and selective social services.

The term 'leisure' encompasses a wide range of activities, like sport and physical recreation, education, tourism, social and cultural. This is illustrated in Table 11.2.

As legislation is mainly permissive (i.e. not compulsory), it is not surprising that wide variations in provision and expenditure can be found between local authorities.

Positive aspects

Positive features emerge, nonetheless:

- Financial expenditure has remained reasonably steady.
- Leisure is a popular demand by local residents.

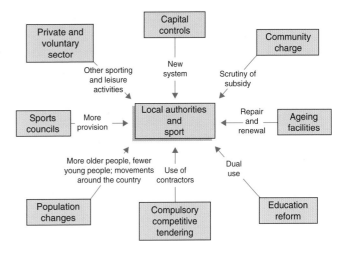

Figure 11.9 Pressures on local authority sports policy

- Leisure is increasingly valued for its own benefits, and not just as a means of meeting other policy objectives, such as reducing vandalism or improving the nation's health.
- From the 1990s, leisure was also perceived to be of economic benefit to a local area, particularly in its ability to attract tourism.

IN CONTEXT

The role of a sport development officer covers the following areas:

- **research;**
- **marketing;**
- **negotiating;**
- **planning;**
- **communication;**
- **organisation and evaluating.**

Best value

Many local authorities place sport as a central feature in their work on:

- healthy living;
- regeneration;
- social inclusion and other key objectives.

Table 11.2 Various leisure activities

Sport	Education	Tourism	Social	Cultural
Sports centres	Libraries	Museums	Youth clubs	Theatres
Playing fields	Swimming pools	Conservation	Community centres	Art galleries
Ski slopes		Country parks		

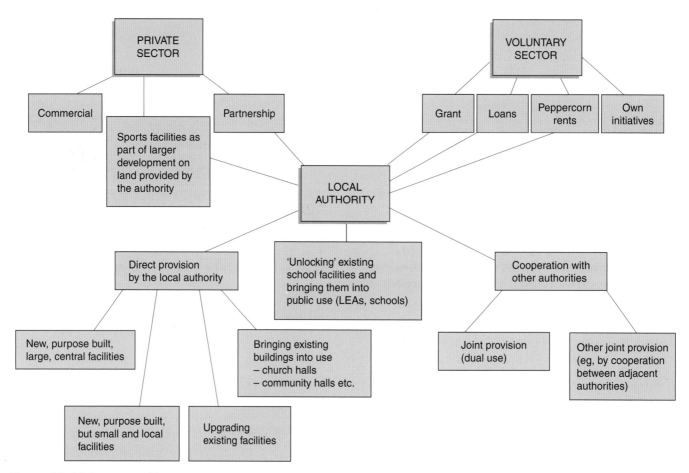

Figure 11.10 Provision of leisure services

The document *The Value of Sport* responds to the challenge 'Why invest in sport?', and demonstrates that sport can make a difference to people's lives and to the communities in which they live. It emphasises that for every pound spent on sport there are multiple returns in improved health, reduced crime, economic regeneration and improved employment opportunities.

As well as providing opportunities for participation, local authorities also need to provide opportunities for excellence. With the successful bid for the London Olympic Games in 2012, the county of Essex, through its Action Plan for Essex, hopes to capitalise on the social and economic legacy of the Olympic Games.

IN CONTEXT

The Weald Country Park in Essex will host the mountain biking event in the 2012 Games. Essex County Council has established a new post with responsibility in Essex for the London 2012 Games, in order to provide leadership and coordination to this work.

EXAMINER'S TIP

You will not be examined directly on specific local authorities, but you should be aware of the complexity of a local authority's contribution to sport participation.

Local provision for leisure

Provision for physical recreation in any local area comes from three main sources:

- private;
- public;
- voluntary.

Activity 4

What are the objectives of each sector: private, public and voluntary?

Governing bodies of sport

History

With the increasing popularity of sport during the late nineteenth century, it became necessary for individuals and clubs taking part to agree on a common set of rules or laws. In most areas, this led directly to the formation within each sport of a governing body, with the task of agreeing rules for the sport so that all clubs and individuals could compete on equal terms.

The people responsible for establishing the governing bodies were mainly the educated middle and upper classes, and there is still a tendency for sport administration in the UK to be the domain of the middle classes.

Structure

It is difficult to generalise across all the governing bodies, as some are extremely wealthy (e.g. the Football Association), while others are still heavily reliant on grants. However, there are some common characteristics:

- executive boards and officers;
- elected by clubs through local, regional and county representatives;
- many have separate organisations in the four home nations (England, Scotland, Wales, Northern Ireland);
- many still have separate organisations for men and women.

Activity 5

With reference to the financing and management of sports provision for the general public, briefly explain what is meant by:
1   the private sector;
2   the public sector.

There are approximately 300 governing bodies in the UK. Many are unpaid volunteers, though this situation has been improved somewhat by the appointment of paid administrators (largely dependent on the size and scale of the individual governing body). Figure 11.11 shows the

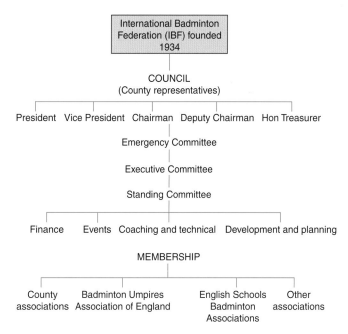

Figure 11.11 Organisation and administration of the Badminton Association

Private sector	Public sector	Voluntary sector
• Privately owned/registered companies • Trading on normal profit and loss/self-financed • Membership entrance fees • Managed by owners/their employees • Must operate and survive in open market/make a profit/compete	• Business operations run by local authority departments • Trading on set prices/charges, etc. • According to a pre-set budget • May involve subsidies as a matter of policy/Council tax or equivalent • Managed by local authority employees	• Business operations owned by 'members' • Possibly on trust/charity basis • Trading on normal profit and loss/break even • Managed through a members' committee • May employ staff • Financed by membership fees/fund-raising/sponsorship

hierarchical structure of the Badminton Association, an example of a governing body.

These organisations proudly retain their independence from political control and each other. They become a more collective voice when represented to Sport England by the CCPR. Their main functions are to:

- establish rules and regulations (in accordance with the International Sports Federation);
- organise competitions;
- develop coaching awards and leadership schemes;
- select teams for country or UK at international events;
- liaise with relevant organisations, such as the CCPR, Sports Council, local clubs, British Olympic Association and the International Sports Federation.

Recent changes for governing bodies

Examples of some changes are as follows:

- The growth of new sports, setting a challenge to the older, traditional sports.
- The decline in extracurricular school sport and a dependence on the governing bodies to try to fill this gap.
- Blurring of the definitions of amateur and professional sport.
- The need to compete internationally with countries which have developed systematic forms of training has made the governing bodies develop the coaching and structuring of competitions, as well as devoting more money to the training of their elite sportspeople.

Activity 6

Research in your class the development of a particular governing body. Choose from different categories (e.g. traditional, professional, a new growth sport, or a sport which has recently experienced rapid change).

Governing bodies have a variety of finance sources: drawn from member clubs, associations and individual members, or receiving grants in aid from Sport England. The 1990s and 2000s have seen the dominance of television sports coverage, and consequently sponsorship has affected many sports.

Governing bodies have had to meet this challenge and market themselves in the modern world if they wish to take advantage of these opportunities. Sports like snooker, badminton, squash and athletics have moved into the arena of big business. Commercial sponsorship is now a desirable form of income.

Activity 7

Research your local centre (e.g. a sports centre, a country park, a water-based recreational facility). Note the following points carefully, being as thorough as possible:
1 its provision of a variety of activities;
2 its costing system;
3 access for people with disabilities;
4 opportunities for the Sports Council's target groups;
5 ease of access for the local catchment area;
6 opening hours;
7 social areas;
8 club use;
9 competition use of the centre.

Following your findings, write a report which concentrates on the positive as well as the negative, with any recommendations.

Most governing bodies, particularly if they are in receipt of lottery funding, are required to draw up policies for increasing participation in their sport, and also to develop talent to the highest levels. The example used on page 273 is taken from the Lawn Tennis Association (LTA).

Figure 11.12 and Table 11.3 provide examples of sports club administration and organisation.

Activity 8

Write a list of the possible aims and objectives of a leisure centre manager.

EXAMINER'S TIP

Make sure you know which organisations could be examined directly.

Lawn Tennis Association Blueprint for British tennis

'An effective performance pathway is essential if we are going to succeed in our drive to get more men and women in the top 100. From Ariel Mini Tennis upwards, the pathway helps coaches identify whether young players are on the path to winning.'

The true measure of success will always be the number of players in the top 100.

The Blueprint for British tennis sets out the vision, direction and proposed outline plans for the future of the sport in this country.

Focus will be on:

1 Getting the best coaches working with the best talent in the best facilities
2 Providing the best technical and sports science support and advice in the most accessible way, to the right people when they need it
3 Establishing a straightforward, high-quality competitive framework that gives juniors the stimulus they need to get on – and stay on – the winning pathway.

Developments in British Tennis

● A new Tennis Leadership Team in place
● The development of a clear business cycle for tennis
● The Men's and Women's games now firmly on an equal footing at the High Performance Level
● Player funding now transparent
● The Talent Identification, Performance and Sports Science teams in place
● The work in Technical Support and Sports Science/Medicine is balanced between delivery in the field and in making the National Tennis Centre (NTC) the development and research hub of British Tennis
● The National Tennis Centre is a superb facility … links with Sports Science, and the catering team, wide variation of court surfaces, gymnasia, superb training and accommodation facilities.

The field network of High Performance Centres (19) and Satellite Clubs (168) has been set up and funding targeted more effectively, although tennis still remains expensive for parents.

The County structure has been overhauled: County & Club team of NTC support Tennis Operations Managers, Tennis Development Managers, Tennis Development Officers and the five Facility Project Managers.

The Tennis Foundation is responsible for a sustainable inclusive tennis delivery across all local authority tennis facilities for all age groups; this includes parks, leisure centres and indoor facilities located on local authority land and the whole of the education sector (schools and universities/colleges) and disability development and performance. The Tennis Foundation will make tennis more accessible and also help to attract and retain more people in the game and generally help boost overall participation in our sport. The National Competition Framework and Junior Competition Plan aim to rapidly increase the number of regularly competing juniors.

Funding of physical activity

Funding for sport in the UK is a mixture of government, private and commercial incentives. These may include:

● government;
● National Lottery (www.lottery.culture.gov.uk);
● voluntary sector;
● governing bodies;
● SportsAid (previously Sport Aid Foundation) (www.sportsaid.org.uk).
● sponsorship.

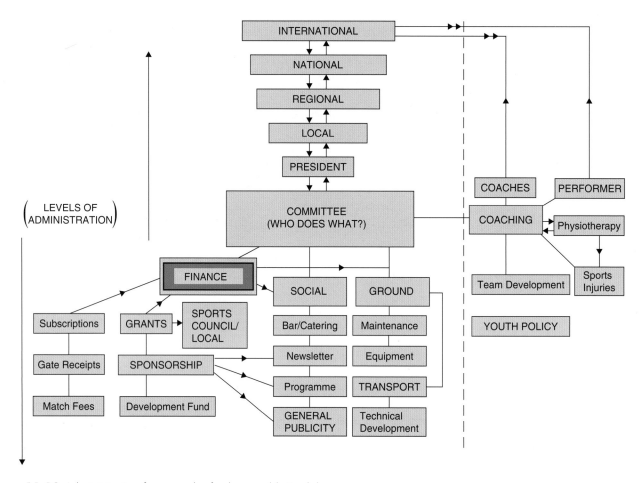

Figure 11.12 Administrative framework of a large athletic club

Central government

The Exchequer funds sport, via the DCMS. Funds are allocated to Sport England and UK Sport for fostering, supporting and encouraging the development of sport and physical recreation. They in turn provide grants to governing bodies in sport.

The DCMS is developing new funding agreements; for example:

- UK Sport is the proposed distributor of the lottery funding to ensure equal treatment of all UK athletes. Sport England is responsible for the distribution in England of sport's share of the lottery funding.
- In 1999/2000, Sport England received £4.5 million and UK Sport received £12.6 million in Exchequer funding from the DCMS to assist their work.
- Children's Play received central funding.

- The Football Licensing Authority has been reconstituted as a Sports Ground Safety authority.

Local government

Local authorities spend nearly £900 million per annum on sport and active recreation in England. It is a heavy burden for an already overstretched budget.

The voluntary sector

This is the area in which most sporting activity occurs. Individuals come together to form clubs and associations which are run to benefit the participants. They are generally self-financing. Annual subscriptions and match fees provide the bulk of the revenue and indicate the grass-roots development of sport in the UK.

Governing bodies

Governing bodies receive their income from grants from the home countries' sport councils, sponsorship, affiliation fees, donations, insurance, commission and royalties, marketing, interest receivable and profit on sale of investments.

Expenditure goes on elite squads, matches, publications, salaries and personal expenses, international affiliation fees, promotions, press and publicity, development officers, and so on.

Wide variations exist, depending on the size and type of governing body. For example, in a female club sponsorship may be harder to find; and commercial markets are not readily available to all professional organisations.

SportsAid

The Sports Aid Foundation, now SportsAid, was set up in 1976, to enable top amateur athletes (at both junior and senior levels) to train with privileges similar to those enjoyed by state-sponsored athletes abroad. It is another self-financing organisation which draws funds from commercial, industrial and private sponsors and from fund-raising projects. Outstanding competitors generally receive the money. They receive grants according to their personal needs, the cost of their preparation, training and competition, and they are usually recommended by their governing body. Since 1976, over £5 million has been given to more than 5,000 competitors. Grants are awarded through the foundation's charitable trust to talented athletes who are in education, on low income or have disabilities.

SportsAid has three main objectives:

- to further the education of young people through the medium of sport;
- to encourage those with social or physical disadvantages to improve their lives through sport;
- to enable those living in poverty to take advantage of the opportunities offered by sport.

A typical national grant is £500 per year. A regional grant is usually £150–£250 per year. To qualify for a national SportsAid grant you must be:

- aged 12–18 years (special cases may be made);
- in genuine financial need and therefore not in receipt of a National Lottery World Class Performance grant;
- a member of a national squad.

(a)

Funding (in £ millions) allocations				
	1998–1999	1999–2000	2000–2001	2001–2002
ESC (of which Sportsmatch)	36.5 3.2	37.9 3.4	38.0 3.4	 3.4
UKSC	11.6	12.6	12.6	12.6
Children's Play	0.4	0.5	0.5	0.5
FLA	0.9	0.9	0.9	0.9

(b)

	1997–1998	1998–1999	1999–2000
Sports	**50,144**	**49,434**	**51,923**
of which:	out turn	provision	plans
English Sports Council of which: Sportsmatch	36,925 3,200	36,489 3,200	37,873 3,373
United Kingdom Sports Council	11,824	11,600	12,600
Children's Play	400	400	500
Football Licensing Authority	896	896	900
British Chess Federation	49	49	50
Other sports support	50		

Figure 11.13 Funding allocations 1999–2002

In December 1999, SportsAid was asked to play a vital role in the development of young British sport talent by partnering Sport England in the World Class Start Programme. The costs were met by a combination of lottery money and funds raised by SportsAid's ten new regional charities. Governing bodies received the lottery's contribution – approximately £10 million – so that they could employ coaches, stage training camps and provide essential support for potential world-class performers. The contribution of SportsAid was to offer direct financial assistance to the athletes and their families.

IN CONTEXT

Those who have benefited from SportsAid's help over the last 30 years are too numerous to mention, but they include Sir Steve Redgrave, Sir Matthew Pinsent, Dame Kelly Holmes, Dame Tanni Grey-Thompson, Amir Khan, Jonathan Edwards, Darren Campbell and Roger Black.

Lottery money has given British sport a fantastic boost, but it can't do everything. That's why the work of SportsAid is so important. If you are young, ambitious and just beginning to experience success, SportsAid is where you go for help. (Sir Steve Redgrave, five-time Olympic gold medallist)

Activity 9

The National Lottery has had a considerable moral, economic and social impact. What do you consider to be the advantages and disadvantages of the good causes scheme, and what suggestions would you make for change?

The National Lottery

In 1994 the Sport England Lottery Fund was launched with a broad policy strategy. It achieved many successes, including the Priority Areas Initiative; funding for 1,000 community projects in the first year; promise of funding for the new national stadium; and funding for talented young stars.

The Lottery Sports Fund has earmarked £20.5 million a year for UK Sport to administer to our top UK medal hopes, through the World Class Performance Programme, and to help attract and stage major sporting events in the UK. Sport now benefits by around £300 million per year from the lottery.

- World Class Events Programme
  Aim: To stage major international events, such as the Olympics, Paralympics, World, European and Commonwealth Games, in the UK.

(a)

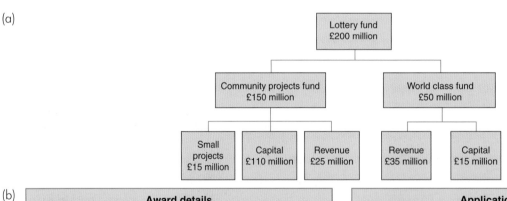

(b)

Award details	
Months and awards	53
Projects founded to date	2,936
Total awarded to date	£934,179,807
Total project cost to date	£1,634,854,001
Average projects funded per month	55
Average amount awarded per month	£30,846,302
Number of countries covered	All
Number of sports covered	61

Application details	
Total applications to date	7,073
Total amount requested to date	£3,603,486,322
Total project cost to date	£5,555,048,103
Average applications per month	133
Average amount requested per month	£67,990,308
Number of countries covered	All
Number of sports covered	78

Figure 11.14 Distribution of lottery funds

Funds: £3 million per year, providing 35 per cent of the cost of bidding and staging events.

- **World Class Start Programme**
  Aim: To help governing bodies identify and develop young talent by providing qualified support staff.
  Funds: £10 million per year.
- **World Class Potential Programme**
  Aim: To help governing bodies develop potential medal winners by setting up training and competition programmes.
  Funds: £15 million per year.
- **World Class Performance Programme**
  Aim: To support our elite athletes.
  Funds: Since 1997, grants totalling over £64.6 million have been committed to over 30 sports in the programme, and 2,100 athletes have received support.

Activity 10

Discuss whether athletes in receipt of National Lottery funding should be accountable for their results.

Sponsorship

The private sector contributes approximately £400 million per year to sport, involving more than 2,000 British companies assisting schemes from national excellence programmes to local grass-roots schemes. (Sponsorship and its links with the media will be discussed in the next chapter.)

Sporting policies for participation and excellence

Activemark

Activemark is an award scheme for primary schools that recognises good practice within physical education provision. The Activemark and Activemark Gold awards schemes recognise and reward primary, middle and special schools that provide young children with the opportunity of receiving the benefits of physical activity. It has been developed in partnership with the British Heart Foundation (BHF) and has the theme: 'Get Active, Stay Active'. To achieve an award the school needs to:

- offer a broad and balanced physical education programme;
- provide an environment that encourages physical activities;
- teach children the importance of staying active for life;
- provide enhanced curricular provision through some additional opportunities for physical activity;
- have an effective inclusion policy for pupils with disabilities.

Activemark Gold recognises all the above plus:

- realistic, in-depth physical education and physical activity development plans;
- a commitment to providing a range of additional, high-quality opportunities for physical activity.

A team of assessors appointed by Sport England reviews the schools against these rigorous criteria.

Kitemarks will reward delivery of the national PE, School Sports and Club Links strategy in future. They will therefore only be open to schools that are in a School Sport Partnership.

Active Sports Programme

This scheme, coordinated by Sport England, is based on four policy headings:

1 Active schools – forms the foundation.
2 Active communities – looks at breaking down the barriers to participation and considers equity issues.
3 Active sports – links participation to excellence, such as participation in the Millennium Youth Games.
4 World Class England – operates four programmes: World Class Start, World Class Potential, World Class Performance and World Class Events.

They are meant to act as building blocks and are not necessarily linear. They also complement the sports councils' participation pyramid of foundation, participation, performance and excellence. The majority of the funding comes from the National Lottery and the regional set-up is strengthened via local authorities. There is a framework around all experiences available to potential participants, such as the National Junior Sports Programme, Sportsmark and Coaching for Teachers.

Sports Leaders UK Leadership Awards

There are four different awards, catering for different age groups and needs:

- JSLA – The Junior Sports Leader Award is for 14–16 year olds and is taught mainly in schools within the national curriculum for physical education. The award develops a young person's skills in organising activities, planning, communicating and motivating.
- CSLA – For those over 16 years old, the popular Community Sports Leader award is taught in schools, colleges, youth clubs, prisons, and sports and leisure nationwide.
- HSLA – The Higher Sports Leader Award builds on the skills gained through the CSLA to equip people to lead specific community groups, such as older people, people with disabilities and primary school children. The award includes units in event management, first aid, sports development and obtaining a coaching award.
- BELA – The Basic Expedition Leader Award is for those interested in the outdoors, and builds the ability to organise safe expeditions and overnight camps.

Sport Action Zones

Sport Action Zones (SAZs) are a response by Sport England to address the issue of sporting deprivation in the most socially and economically deprived areas of the country. Participation levels in these areas are considerably below the national average.

Sport is believed to be valuable in contributing to the lives of people in these areas, as well as helping in the regeneration of the communities. Sport is acting in association with many other agencies, across health, education, lifelong learning initiatives, and so on. At the time of writing, 12 such zones have been created, evenly spread around the country, including inner cities and rural areas. Sport England, in association with other partners, helps to fund the zones for an initial five-year period.

Examples of the kind of work the zones are carrying out include:

- working with young people involved in antisocial behaviour;
- working with community health services to support people in poor health;
- providing education, training and support for community sport workers in other sectors who might use sport to meet their objectives;
- setting up local clubs where none exists;
- making local sport centres more accessible;
- engaging with local community groups, especially ethnic minority groups.

Sportsmark

The Sportsmark scheme was introduced in the government report *Sport: Raising the Game* in 1995. It recognises and rewards the schools that provide the best physical education and sports provision to their pupils and the local community. The additional Gold Award is presented to those offering exceptional provision. To obtain the award, various criteria have to be achieved.

ACE UK (Athlete Career & Education Programme)

This programme is modelled on the Australian Institute of Sport (AIS). It provides a tailored service that encourages athletes to take control of all aspects of their lives. ACE UK enables them to identify their personal strengths and weaknesses, and supports them to integrate career, education and sporting demands in order to ensure all-round success in their lives. Sports performers who are part of the World Class Programme, are BOA Gold Passport holders or have left these schemes during the past 12 months are eligible to benefit from the programme.

Sporting Ambassadors programme

This programme gives sports heroes and heroines (approximately 200 at present in a wide range of sports) the chance to motivate and inspire young people to participate in sport. They communicate through primary, secondary and special schools, and youth and sport clubs, emphasising the benefits of physical activity and a healthy lifestyle.

The ambassadors:

- visit the different venues;
- present cups, certificates and badges, and show their own achievements;
- speak at school assemblies and to small groups about their experiences as elite performers;
- coach groups of young people.

Sports colleges

Sports colleges are part of the specialist schools programme run by the DfES. They will have an important role in helping to deliver the government's Plan for Sport:

They will become important hub sites for school and community sport, providing high-quality opportunities for all young people in their neighbourhood. (Richard Caborn, Minister for Sport)

School sport coordinators

By 2006, there were 3,200 school sport coordinators, working across families of schools with 18,000 primary link teachers.

The partnership around a sports college starts with an average of four schools, ultimately growing to eight schools. Each partnership receives a grant of up to £270,000 a year. This pays for the full-time partnership development manager.

A primary link teacher (PLT) is located within each of the primary/specialist schools in the partnership, with a remit to improve PE and school sport at the primary school. They have 12 days a year to spend on their work as link teachers.

The school sport coordinator (SSCo) is based around families of schools, with a team comprising a partnership development manager and a PLT. Their role is to enhance opportunities for young people to experience different sports, access high-quality coaching and engage in competition. They are released for two days a week.

The partnership development manager (PDM) is usually located within a sports college, and manages the development of the partnership and the links with other PE and sport organisations.

The overall aim of the partnership is to ensure that children spend a minimum of two hours a week on high-quality PE and school sport. Six strategic objectives have been set:

1   Strategic planning – develop and implement a PE/sport strategy.
2   Primary liaison – develop links, particularly between Key Stages 2 and 3.
3   Out of school hours – provide enhanced opportunities for all pupils.
4   School to community – increase participation in community sport.

5   Coaching and leadership – provide opportunities in leadership, coaching and officiating for senior pupils, teachers and other adults.
6   Raising standards – raise standards of pupil achievement.

Academies

Academies are a new type of school. The school leadership needs to draw on the skills of sponsors and other supporters in order to develop educational strategies to raise standards and contribute to diversity in areas of disadvantage.

They are all-ability schools, established by sponsors from business, faith or voluntary groups, working in innovative partnerships with government and education. Running costs are met in full by the DfES. Local education authorities are expected to consider the scope for such establishments in areas of disadvantage. They offer a broad and balanced education, specialising in one or more subject areas.

Sports schools

There is a small selection of specialist sports schools in the UK, but again there is no centralised approach. Some examples are Millfield, Kelly College, Reeds School and Lilleshall. The advantages of such institutions are the combination of top-quality coaching, education, accommodation, medical science, a pool of similar talent, an organised competition structure and links with professional clubs. However, there are some disadvantages. They form a private network of schools which results in an exclusive system, inevitably drawing from a limited pool of talent. Young people may have to experience residential, institutionalised life away from home, and the physical and psychological demands are high.

PE School Sport and Club Links Strategy (PESSCL)

A high-quality physical education for all children is at the heart of the government's new strategy and brings together a number of existing programmes. PESSCL is to be delivered by the DfES and the DCMS through various programmes (see below). Linked delivery on coaching will also support the strategy, and local authorities need to come together to ensure the effective delivery of these programmes. Over the last few years the government has invested £459 million to transform PE and school sport.

Gifted and talented

It is part of the government's wider strategy to improve gifted and talented education. It aims to improve the range and quality of teaching, coaching and learning for talented sportspeople, in order to raise their aspirations and improve their performance, motivation and self-esteem. It also aims to encourage young talent to join sports clubs, and to strengthen the relationship between schools and national governing bodies (NGBs). Up to 10 per cent of pupils in primary and secondary schools will be supported. It will include the introduction of talent development camps for pupils in years 6 and 7. Nationally, the programme will include:

- a web-based resource for teachers, coaches and parents;
- a national support network for talented young athletes with disabilities;
- NGB-organised national performance camps for elite young athletes;
- a national faculty of gifted and talented trainers to provide continuing professional development;
- extracurriculum provision for academically able 11–16 year olds in PE and sports studies;
- a school-based profiling and tracking system.

Step into Sport

Sport relies on 1.5 million volunteer officials, coaches, administrators and managers. Step into Sport is aiming to build on this trend and extend grass-roots interest in this area into a more coordinated strategic approach by NGBs, county sports partnerships and clubs. It should ensure that clubs are ready to receive, develop and deploy a steady supply of volunteers.

Between 2002 and 2004, Step into Sport was delivered in almost 200 school sport coordinator partnerships across all 45 county sport partnership areas, by a consortium of the Youth Sports Trust (via the Top Link programme – see National Junior Sports Programme, below), the British Sports Trust (via Sports Leader Awards) and Sport England, each with their own responsibilities.

This is a new initiative funded by the DCMS and the Home Office Active Communities Unit, which brings together the British Sports Trust and Sport England to encourage young people to become more involved with sport in their local communities. The aim is to provide a structured pathway to attract over 48,000 young people, aged 14–19 years, into voluntary sports coaching. The network of partnerships will be focused mainly around the government's Sport and Education Action Zones.

National Junior Sports Programme

The National Junior Sports Programme was launched in February 1996 by the Sports Council, working alongside the Youth Sports Trust. Its aim is to encourage young children from the age of four to become involved in sport. It will provide kit, coaching and places to play, and the more talented performers can be identified from a wider base. It is a rolling programme and many teachers are trained. The advantage is that it can fit neatly into the current physical education system. There are five main elements:

- Top Play (4–9 year olds);
- Top Sport (7–11 year olds);
- Champion Coach;
- Top Club (11 years+);
- Top Link.

There have been growing calls for more 'inclusive' physical education programmes. These programmes need to cater for the diversity of students, their needs and the schools they attend. It is possible that the government focus on competitive team sports, since the publication of *Sport: Raising the Game*, may not have been successful, as studies suggest these are not the sporting activities which attract this age group (Coalter 1999). Sustaining a broader choice at school is likely to support lifelong participation.

In the New Opportunities Fund, lottery fund money will be available for schemes that encourage the value of sport as character building and diversion, such as summer play schemes and after-school clubs.

The National Junior Sports Programme is intended to support the national curriculum as an additional resource for teachers.

Coaching for Teachers is a joint initiative, funded by Sport England and coordinated by SportsCoachUK, with support from the British Association of Advisers and Lecturers in Physical Education (BAALPE) and the Physical Education Association (PEA), to involve teachers in extracurricular activities.

School Club Links

The overall aim is to increase the proportion of children guided into clubs from SSCo partnerships. The primary focus is on seven major sports (tennis, cricket, rugby union, football, athletics, gymnastics and swimming). The reasons for their selection included:

- the capacity of the NGB;
- they are central to the national curriculum;
- their ability to help lead other sports;
- popular with both sexes;
- multi skills;
- mix of individual and team sports;
- focus of government initiatives and investment.

The key organisations working together are the DCMS, Sport England, the Youth Sports Trust and the relevant governing bodies.

Let's consider how one governing body, the Football Association, is meeting the aims of the School Club Links Programme

World Class Programme

- The World Class Programme provides funding for training, coaching, and so on.

- Performers are selected and recommended by their governing bodies.
- The governing bodies are required to draw up development plans and need to meet the targets they set if they are to maintain the same level of funding.
- For the performer to receive a personal award, they must meet rigorous requirements of training, competing and uphold the ethical standards outlined by the national governing body.
- The money comes from the lottery and the Exchequer.

The examples given on page 283 relate to a World Class Potential performer in badminton (2002).

The World Class Programme

This was established to help national governing bodies develop a comprehensive system through which talented individuals can be identified to achieve success consistently in important international competitions, such as the Olympics and Paralympics.

Table 11.3 The FA School Club Links Programme

Opportunities	Description
FA Charter Standard Schools Programme	Involves primary, middle, secondary and special schools, independent and state. Requires as part of the criteria for all schools to form a partnership, with a local charter standard club for boys and girls
FA Charter Standard Development Club	Requires clubs which have met the development criteria (minimum of five teams) to create a partnership with a local school or schools as part of their football development plan
FA Charter Standard Community Clubs	Requires clubs (minimum ten teams, male and female) to form school club links and appoint a voluntary schools liaison officer
FA TOP Sport Football Community Programme	Targets young people aged 7–11 who are less likely to be participating in football for their school due to more limited opportunities and helps them move on to Charter Standard Club
Active Sports Girls Football Programme	The Active Sports programme is a fundamental part of the FA's strategy for the development of girls' football. The framework includes a school club link scheme for 10–16 year olds called Kick Start
FA Soccability Community Programme	This is an educational programme designed as part of the FA TOP Sport Football Programme to assist young people with disabilities to participate in football

Sportsearch programme

How it works	Benefits
Complete ten physical tests and a number of fitness tests	Helps young people to discover what sports they are good at
Results entered into a PC	Links them to local sports clubs
Young person answers series of questions about preferences	Creates a database of clubs, and links to other sport agencies
Programme provides a ranked selection of sports	Coordinates the technology and investments of National Grid for Learning (NGfL)
Programme gives appropriate contacts to pursue the sport	Forges cross-curricular links with numeracy, literacy and IT
System advises young people on fitness, allows them to access a national database, take part in surveys, competitions and past research projects	Develops research projects with and for young people

World Class Start	Potential for future success
World Class Potential	Medal within 8 years
World Class Performance	Medal within 3 years
World Class Events	
World Class Coaching Programme	

World Class Start

This programme will help identify and nurture a specific number of potential performers with the necessary characteristics to achieve future world-class success. Consortia of local authorities and other providers will be helped to put in place coaching schemes and support programmes to give children the best possible sporting start.

World Class Potential

This programme will assist the development of talented performers to win medals in future (next ten years) international competitions.

World Class Performance

This programme supports the training programmes of elite performers who can win medals in the next six years.

Partnership funding is expected to cover 10 per cent of costs. Funding overall is £50 million per year.

- World Class Start – £10 million p.a. Sport England Lottery Fund
- World Class Potential – £15 million p.a. Sport England Lottery Fund
- World Class Performance – £25 million p.a. UK & Sport England Lottery Fund

It is also hoped that £1 million per year will be raised by SportsAid for individuals in the World Class Programme.

Equal opportunities?

In the last section we looked at the different organisations involved in sport and physical activities. We now need to ask the following questions:

- Who are these organisations working for?
- Which groups are they targeting in their aims to increase participation?
- How and why are they trying to develop sporting excellence?

	Weekly training commitment	**Structured cell training**
Level 1	4–6 hours	2 hours weekly
Level 2	9–12 hours	4 hours weekly
Level 3	11–14 hours	4 hours weekly
Level 4	12–20 hours	Up to 20 hours weekly JPC/HPC (junior performance cells/high-performance centres)
Level 5	18–24 hours	Central training/up to 20 hours weekly

- What's the role of opportunity, provision and esteem for the various social groups in their quest for sporting participation and/or sporting excellence.

We will concentrate on various social groups and the policies developed to increase their levels of physical activity, and try to establish some of the reasons for low participation. We will also study the meaning of excellence in sport and the opportunities available to different social groups.

Many of the qualities assigned to sport are well recognised – opportunity for self-knowledge, personal achievement, good health, enjoyment, skill acquisition, social interaction, responsibility, development of confidence, and so on. We should therefore be concerned that certain sections of the population are missing out on the chance to benefit from such an enriching experience.

It is important to understand the sociological basis for inequality in sport. This is not intended to be a thorough sociological review, but a tool to help us achieve a greater understanding of the issue.

All men are equal

In the descriptive sense, this is patently untrue: human beings do not possess the same amount of physical, mental or moral qualities. In the prescriptive sense, however, people ought to treat one another with equal respect, dignity and consideration.

Stratification of society

Society can be divided into layers, just like rocks (i.e. rock strata). The divisions are based on biological, economic and social criteria, such as age, gender, race and social class. The dominant group in society, which controls the major social institutions like the media, law, education and politics, can exercise control over the more subordinate groups. This

dominant group need not be the majority – think of previous minority white rule in South Africa. Using this classification, the dominant group in the UK could be described as white, male and middle class; the subordinate groups would be women, ethnic minorities, people with disabilities and those belonging to the working class.

Discrimination can occur when opportunities available to the dominant group are not available to all social groups.

Key term

Discrimination: To make a distinction, to give unfair treatment especially because of prejudice. It occurs when a prejudicial attitude is acted on. Discrimination can be overt (e.g. laws which form part of the structure of a society, like the former political system of apartheid, or a membership clause for a private sports club). This can be officially wiped out by changing the law, but covert (hidden or less obvious) discrimination (e.g. people's attitudes and beliefs) can be very hard to dislodge.

When subordinate groups in society are discriminated against, their opportunities are limited, including opportunities of social mobility (the pattern of movement from one social class to a higher or lower one). This can also be affected by whether the social system is closed (an extreme example is the Hindu caste system in India) or open (a true egalitarian democracy).

Sport and stratification

Sport is often described by sociologists as a microcosm of society: it reflects in miniature all facets of society. This includes the institutionalised divisions and inequalities which characterise our society. Sporting institutions are equally controlled by the dominant group in society, and stratification in sport is inevitable when winning is highly valued. It is highlighted even more when monetary rewards are available.

Sport is often cited as an avenue for social mobility:

- physical skills and abilities – professional sports requires little formal education;
- sport may create progression through the education system (e.g. athletic scholarships);
- occupational sponsorship may lead to future jobs;
- sport can encourage values such as leadership and teamwork skills, which may help in the wider world of employment.

Although 'sport for all' campaigns are no longer a direct function of Sport England, the groups who are targeted by such initiatives are still under-represented in sport participation. More recently, their participation has been addressed at government level, under the DCMS, using the term 'social exclusion groups'.

Social exclusion

Aspects of exclusion are:

- ethnicity;
- gender;
- disability;
- youth;
- age;
- sexuality;
- poverty;
- in rural areas/cities.

Defining exclusion

The Social Exclusion Unit's definition of social exclusion is:

> a shorthand label for what can happen when individuals or areas suffer a combination of linked problems such as unemployment, poor skills, low incomes, poor housing, high crime environments, bad health and family breakdown.

So what role can sport play in this situation? Many studies have been carried out and moves are under way for improving the perception of recreation. When considering this area you will need to address the following:

- Descriptive – explain and give examples of how discrimination occurs for the identified groups in society.
- Reformative – suggest solutions to the identified problems.

Table 11.5 shows a summary of the nature and strengths of the benefits of sport, and also the experiences of the excluded groups without direct action by the state or voluntary organisations.

Constraints and exclusion in sport

These can be broken down into three main categories:

- environmental/structural constraints (economic, physical and social factors);
- personal constraints (internal and psychological);
- attitudes of society and provider systems (policies and managers' practices can act as barriers or enablers).

Combinations of aspects of exclusion can be said to lead to double deprivation, for example, being elderly and from an ethnic minority. If exclusion is prolonged in youth it can have lasting effects in terms of playing recreationally, socialising and competing to achieve.

Sports equity

Overcoming discrimination:	Can be achieved through:
<ul><li>Recognising your own prejudice</li><li>Understanding the difficulty</li><li>Talking to people</li><li>Receiving support from others</li><li>Thinking of alternatives</li><li>Going on a training course</li><li>Using a policy/ guidelines</li></ul>	<ul><li>Sharing common values</li><li>Promoting equality through sport</li><li>Working in partnership</li><li>Endorsing the law</li><li>Challenging discrimination</li></ul>

Race

'Race' refers to the physical characteristics of an individual, while 'ethnicity' is belonging to a particular group (e.g. religious, lifestyle). Racism is a set of beliefs or ideas based on the assumption that races have distinctive cultural characteristics

Table 11.4 Constraints and exclusion in sport and leisure

Constraint/	Children	Youth		Poor/unemployed	Women	Older people	Ethnic minority	People with disabilities/learning difficulties
		Young people	Young delinquents					
Poor physical/social environment	+	+	++	++	+	+	++	+
Poor facilities/community capacity	+	+	++	++	+	+	+	++
Poor support network	+	+	++	++	+	+	+	++
Poor transport	++	++	++	++	++	++	+	++
Managers' policies and attitudes	+	+	++	++	+	+	++	++
Labelling by society	+	+	+++	+	+	+	++	++
Lack of time structure	+	+	++	++		+		+
Lack of income	+	+	+++	+++	+	++	+	++
Lack of skills/ personal and social capital	+	+	+++	+++	+	+	++	++
Fears of safety	++	++	++	++	+++	++++	++	++
Powerlessness	++	++	+++	++	++	++	++++	++
Poor self-/ body image	+	+	++	++	+	+	++	++

Source: Department for Culture, Media and Sport

Note: The number of + signs shows the severity of particular constraints for particular groups.

determined by hereditary factors, and that this endows some races with an intrinsic superiority.

The media promote the popular idea of sport enabling many individuals to 'climb the social ladder', as well as highlighting racism in sport and the lack of equal opportunities.

Sport England and governing bodies have sought to encourage non-discriminatory attitudes to combat racism and to open up organisations to equal opportunities.

Examples of racism in sport

1 Stacking – Refers to the disproportionate concentration of ethnic minorities in certain positions in a sports team, which tends to be based on the stereotype that they are more valuable for their physical skills than for their decision making and communication qualities. In American football there has been a tendency to place ethnic players in running back and wide receiver positions. In baseball, until fairly recently, they have tended to be in outfield positions.
2 Centrality theory (Grusky 1963) – This restricts ethnic players from more central positions which are based on coordinative tasks and require more interaction and decision making. Significantly, coaches who make these decisions are generally white. Sociological studies have revealed the self-perpetuating coaching subculture which exists in American sport (Coakley 1994). When existing coaches need to sponsor a new coach, they are likely to select one with similar ideas to their own.
3 Channelling – Ethnic minorities may be pushed into certain sports, and even certain positions within a team, based on assumptions.

Attempts to overcome racism in sport

'Let's stamp racism out of football' This was a large-scale, national campaign, which began in 1993/94. It was intended to cut racial harassment out of football in the UK. It was supported by the Commission for Racial Equality (CRE) and the Professional Footballers Association (PFA), along with supporters' groups, the FA, the Football Trust, and the Premier and Endsleigh Leagues. In 1994/95, over 10 per cent of clubs took specific action.

The antiracism campaigns were initiated by fans themselves originally, culminating in the national campaign (now called Kick it Out), which has received support from various Ministers for Sport. The focus has now shifted to studying to what extent racism exists at the institutional level.

A recent study by Malcolm and Last at the Centre for Research into Sport and Society at the University of Leicester suggested that at first it would appear that at the elite level there are few barriers for players to overcome. Compared to the number who claim to be of Afro-Caribbean origin on the General Household survey (1 per cent), they seem to be well represented, particularly at the Premiership level (17.5 per cent in 1995/96).

Positional play Over a ten-year period, Malcolm and Last's research found that 50 per cent of black players played in forward positions. These can be glamorous positions, involving high goal scoring and impressive transfer fees. Average black players in the Premier League commanded transfer fees of £1 million more than white players.

However, the main difference occurs in the career paths taken by black footballers. Few break their way into management positions, for example as directors or FA committee members. It is also notable that few Asian players have broken through into the professional ranks.

Race and education

There has been a tendency for teachers to act on a stereotype, labelling children from ethnic minority groups and developing certain expectations of them. This can be self-perpetuating, as children may internalise these misconceptions and regard the sport side of educational life as the only successful route for them.

Sports Participation and Ethnicity in England 1999/2000 The survey was part of Sport England's commitment to better understand the extent and causes of inequity in sporting opportunities for certain groups in the population, and identify ways to overcome them. The findings have particular relevance to the Active Communities programme, which aims to extend sporting opportunities for all.

The findings were:

- For ethnic minority groups, the overall participation rate in sport was 40 per cent, compared to a 46 per cent national average.

- Only the Black Other group (60 per cent) had participation rates higher than the population as a whole. Black Caribbean, Chinese, Pakistani and Bangladeshi were lower than the national average. These figures were similar for women from the same groups. However, the gap between men's and women's participation was found to be greater among ethnic minority groups than in the population as a whole.

The reasons given for constraining factors in participation were similar to those in the population as a whole, for example, 'work/study demands, home and family responsibilities, lack of money, laziness', but some also quoted negative experiences in sport due to ethnicity. These instances were higher for the Black Other men and less relevant for the Chinese section of the population.

Defining ethnicity is fraught with problems, as it is almost impossible to identify a whole group and presume they will have similar experiences. This is particularly so where religion, culture, values, language, generation, age, gender, length of residency in a country and nationality all play a part in creating considerable diversity of experiences, expectations, way of life and behaviours. However, for the purposes of a national quantitative survey it is required that people be classified into 'broad ethnic groups'. The groups people could choose from were:

- White;
- Black Caribbean;
- Black African;
- Black Other;
- Indian;
- Pakistani;
- Bangladeshi;
- Chinese;
- None of these (17 per cent) became 'Other'.

Participation was defined as 'having taken part in sport or physical activities on at least one occasion in the previous four weeks, excluding walking'. It does not include refereeing or coaching.

An important result of the survey is the complexity of the whole issue. There is considerable variation in the levels of participation between different ethnic groups, between men and women and between different sports. The results also challenge the stereotypical view which suggests that low levels of participation in sport by certain groups are more a reflection of culture and choice than other constraints such as provision, affordability and access.

Gender

Gender means the biological aspect of a person, either male or female. Gender roles refer to what different societies and cultures attribute as appropriate behaviour for that sex.

We learn our expected role through a process called socialisation, which simply means the learning of cultural values (which is equally applicable to table manners!). We learn first through primary socialisation (mainly from our close family group at an early age), and then through secondary socialisation from the wider world of institutions. What emerges are the terms 'masculinity' and 'femininity', in relation to gender roles.

Gender role models are first asserted in children's play, and early in primary schools there are clear differences in the preferences of girls for less structured activities. Later come matters of self-image and body image, with sportswomen often being portrayed by the media as either muscle-bound superwomen or sleek and fit in a way that seems far beyond the reach of normal women.

Historical factors regarding the role of women cannot be discounted either:

- Sport was always seen as a male preserve. Males developed and controlled most of the modern-day sports.
- Men, as the dominant group in society, denied or limited opportunities for women in relation to the types of sports they could participate in.
- The role of women was stereotypically seen as being the housewife or mother.
- The types of activities women were encouraged to participate in were those considered appropriate to their role and therefore socially acceptable.
- Middle- and upper-class ladies in the nineteenth century began to play sports such as golf, tennis, horse riding, archery, and so on. These activities were not particularly physically demanding and did not involve physical contact or aggression.
- Activities that females could play socially with males were also highly valued, such as croquet followed by lawn tennis.

- Working-class women had the least leisure opportunities of all.

In the present day, opportunities for women have increased in terms of:

- greater independence;
- more disposable income;
- personal transport;
- availability of more sports, clubs and competitions;
- more media coverage;
- more women in positions of responsibility in sports organisations.

The overriding image of female participation in sport is still the emphasis placed on health, fitness and the stereotypical feminine figure.

Sexism in sport

Sexism is the belief that one sex is inferior to the other, and is most often directed towards women. It is sometimes based on the idea that women are not best suited to roles which carry prestige and influence. Traditionally, women have been denied the same legal, political, economic and social rights enjoyed by men.

It is important not to underestimate the long-lasting effect of attitudes which are handed down through the generations. Sexism against women operates in sport in numerous ways:

The Sex Discrimination Act 1975

This act made sex discrimination unlawful in employment, training, education and the provision of goods, facilities and services; that is, it set down in law that a female should be treated in the same way as a male in similar circumstances.

Competitive sport is excluded by Section 44 of the Act. Separate competitions for men and women are allowed where 'the physical strength, stamina or physique puts her at a disadvantage to the average man'. Problems have occurred where female referees and PE teachers have been denied promotion on the grounds of being a woman, and some successful appeals have been made.

Private sports clubs can legally operate discriminatory policies, under Sections 29 and 34. After an appeal in 1987, the EC recommended that all clubs which are not genuinely private must remove any barriers which discriminate against men or women.

Women and professional sport

Professional sport still tends to favour men, even in activities such as pool, where physical strength differences could be questioned.

Only women who are very dedicated and committed move through from participation to a level of excellence. Myths and negative stereotypes still abound, and the media give much less coverage to women's sport:

- Surveys have shown that national newspapers give less than 6 per cent of total sport space to women's sport.
- There are more sport competitions for men.
- Financial constraints affect women more than men, as they attract less sponsorship to help with training, equipment, travelling and general fees.

Female power in sports organisations and higher levels of administration has not matched the rise in female sport participation.

- Few women reach the top levels of coaching: in 1992 there were only 8 female coaches at the Olympics, compared with 92 male coaches.
- Mixed governing bodies, such as swimming, badminton, tennis, riding and cycling, all show a poor ratio of female decision makers in proportion to the number of female participants.

The problem has increased with a more professional and bureaucratic environment, and perhaps reflects the inappropriateness of the male model of sport, women's lack of access to political systems and the poor recruitment mechanisms operating in these institutions.

However, improvements are occurring slowly. The first woman Vice President of the IOC was appointed in 1997.

Female football in the UK is now a professional sport. The Football Association set up a full-time professional league of women's teams in 2000. Millions of pounds were spent and women players can train full-time. Women's football has been confirmed as the UK's fastest-growing sport. In 1993 there were 500 clubs; this figure had risen to 6,200 clubs by 2005. England ladies have a full-time coach and 1,000 players attend 30 regional centres of excellence.

An interesting competition took place in 2003, when Annika Sorenstam became the first female golfer to take on the men in professional competition in 58 years:

> I'm not putting the guys to the test here, or men against women. I would like to emphasise that. I don't want to get into any political things. I don't have anything to do with that. It's not any goal. I don't want to put the guys on the defensive.

Although it caused a storm of protest from certain quarters, the event went ahead. Annika did not make the cut, but she was certainly not outplayed and gave everyone something to think about.

The Women's Sports Foundation (WSF) This is a voluntary organisation which promotes the interests of women and girls in sport and recreation. There is a network of regional groups and a wide range of activities and events are organised. Their regular publication is *Women in Sport* Magazine.

Female participation in recent years In 1996, the General Household Survey (GHS) reported that men were more likely to participate in a sport or physical activity than women: 87 per cent of men, compared with 77 per cent of women, had taken part in at least one activity during the previous 12 months.

Football is the number one sport for girls and women. There are now 61,000 women competing in clubs affiliated to the Football Association, and there has also been an increase in the number of girls' football teams which are developing within schools. There are 40,000 more under-14 girls playing at school than there were in the mid 1990s.

One problem holding back the amount of girls taking up the sport, however, is the lack of career prospects. There are still only around 19 England-based professional players. The FA has put in place a series of initiatives to increase opportunities for women in football:

- In 1997 it launched its Talent Development Plan for Women's Football.
- Establishment of 42 Centres of Excellence – to develop 10–16 year olds.
- 19 Women's Football Academies – 16 years plus.
- In 2001 the National Women's Player Development Centre was launched at Loughborough University – for the most promising.

Kay (1994) confirmed that women are constrained in their leisure time by the needs of housekeeping and caring for dependants, and by lower car ownership than men. These effects are stronger for women in the lower socio-economic groups. Women's participation in indoor sport has grown, mainly due to the fitness boom and aerobic classes, but participation is still in decline in terms of outdoor sports. In addition to time and transport constraints, fear of attack in urban parks and the countryside have been cited as problems faced by women.

Table 11.6 sets out some of the reasons why women have less time for sport than men.

Girls and physical education policies

Physical education policies, through the government initiatives in the national curriculum, can still appear to show preferences for competitive team games, sex-differentiated programmes and traditional teaching methods that may alienate many girls.

NIKE and the Youth Sports Trust are cooperating in a scheme that aims to support the delivery of physical education and sport to girls aged 11–14 years, in secondary schools.

Windhoek Call for Action 1998

From Brighton to Windhoek: Facing the Challenge is a document produced by the UK Sports Council and the International Working Group on Women and Sport. The publication charts the progress made from 1994 to 1998 in developing a sporting culture that enables and values the full involvement of women in every aspect of sport. It provides an international overview of strategies and action plans adopted by women and sports in various countries. It considers the challenge that lies ahead and the implementation of the Windhoek Call for Action.

What women can do

- Develop a positive attitude to a healthy lifestyle; find out what is available locally and encourage a friend to go with them; be determined!
- Having developed an interest, join a club to gain access to coaching and facilities; lobby a governing body, local authority and the media to increase availability and opportunity of coaching, facilities, competition and coverage.

Table 11.5 How the hours of the week are spent for the average male and female

	Full-time working male	Full-time working female
Work and travel to work	47.2	42.3
Household chores, essential cooking and shopping	12.0	24.5
Other non-discretionary activities (other shopping, caring for children personal hygiene)	13.9	18.6
Free time	45.9	33.6

Source: The Henley Centre 1991

Note: This table assumes seven hours of sleep per night.

- Attend courses to improve career prospects; apply for senior positions; become a coach or administrator; gain relevant qualifications.
- Be aware that family responsibilities can coexist with other aspirations.

What organisations can do

- Ensure equality of opportunity to acquire sports skills.
- Adopt policies on child care, transport, access, pricing and programming of facilities.
- Recognise that women do not form an homogeneous group. Women who have disabilities, are members of an ethnic minority, have heavy domestic responsibilities, have busy working lives or are school leavers will all require some specific action directed at them.
- Positive images of women should be widely seen in a variety of sport promotional material, not only the traditionally female sports. This will help provide much-needed role models for young girls.
- Redress inequalities in competition, coaching and financial assistance, and improve the talent identification process.
- Review recruitment practices, establish appropriate training and allow flexible working hours.
- Publicise the achievements of women's contributions to sport.

IN CONTEXT

The Wimbledon Championships introduced equal earnings for men and women in 2007. The Championships declared a percentage increase in the women's prize pot that outstrips the men's, but the tournament chairman defended the earnings contrast, saying, 'We work off the market situation... This is nothing to do with women's rights, it is to do with the marketplace.' He went on to say:

Women tend to win easily in the early rounds, so they are able to play in the doubles. Some of the early round matches last up to three sets, whereas even Sampras could have a first-round five-setter. Seven different people have won the last seven Grand Slam singles titles and that shows how the competitiveness at the top level of the women's game has grown. We also recognise that the top women take away more money from Wimbledon than the men. Last year Venus Williams took away eight per cent more than Pete Sampras, because she won the doubles, in which Sampras did not take part.

Activity 11

Discuss the reasons for and against female tennis players receiving equivalent prize money to their male counterparts.

Sport and people with disabilities

According to the Labour Force Survey 2004, there are 6.5 million adults with disabilities in Britain – 11.1 per cent of the population. Approximately 5 million have a disability severe enough to limit everyday activities, and 1 million have a learning disability. Of these 6.5 million, 69 per cent are over the age of 60, with 5 per cent under 30 years of age.

Disability sport

This is a term used to suggest a more positive approach towards the participation in sport of people with disabilities. It covers people with a physical, sensory or mental impairment. The term 'disability' is used when impairment adversely affects performance. Other terms used are handicapped sports, sports for the disabled, adapted sport, wheelchair sport and deaf sport.

Many people experience discrimination which effectively excludes them from active social participation. Yet sport can help to integrate people with disabilities into the rest of society and improve their quality of life. DePauw and Gavron (1995) described the barriers as similar to those for women, including a lack of organised programmes, informal early experiences, role models and access, along with other economic, physiological and social factors. Reasons for lower participation are:

- Safety concerns/traditionally considered dangerous.
- Stereotypes – generally society has lower expectations.
- Psychologically, people with disabilities may have less confidence and self-esteem.
- Lack of specialist coaches or leaders who are knowledgeable (e.g. teachers, coaches, leisure managers).
- Lack of access to specialist facilities such as ramps and hoists.
- Discrimination – verbal or institutionalised.
- Fewer opportunities to join clubs or enter competitions.
- Lack of mobility or transport.
- Possibly lower income.
- Lack of media coverage and role models, and therefore a lack of information.

The main barrier to the participation of people with disabilities in the activities of their choice is as much a matter of social attitudes and environmental barriers as their medical condition.

In the UK, the special needs of athletes with disabilities are catered for by six national disability sports organisations:

1 The British Amputee Sports Association;
2 The UK Sports Association for People with Mental Handicap;
3 Cerebral Palsy Sport;
4 The British Les Autres Sports Association;
5 Disability Sport England (formerly the British Sports Association for the Disabled) – probably the most important sports organisation in the UK for people with disabilities;
6 The British Paralympic Association.

The English Federation of Disability Sport (EFDS) acts as the main supporting and coordinating body for the development of sport for all people with disabilities. This is part of a recently restructured disability sport network. In turn, the EFDS has the support and direct involvement of all the major disability sport organisations, and will promote a corporate approach at national and regional level to determine priorities and the implementation of programmes.

Competitive sports have either been designed specifically for people with disabilities, such as goalball, boccia and polybat for the visually impaired, or they have been modified, such as volleyball and wheelchair basketball/tennis.

Current trends tend to focus on the sport rather than on the disability, to allow closer involvement with mainstream sport which previously has not catered for the needs of athletes with disabilities. Increasing participation should provide role models for people with disabilities. It is very important that all these organisations, both mainstream and special needs, cooperate and pool their resources in joint programmes of work; the creation of one umbrella federation might help the situation.

Integration into mainstream sport does not have to mean participating at the same time as everyone else. It is more significant that facilities, competitions, training and coaching should be equally available to people with disabilities as to able-bodied people. However, there is a choice of either participating separately (segregation) to able-bodied people, or participating with the able-bodied (integration). As with many issues, there are advantages and disadvantages to each of these.

Inclusiveness

Developing an inclusive approach to all aspects of school life, including physical activity, can act as a route into inclusion in the wider community. Goalball is a game developed for people with disabilities, but which can be played by everyone.

Advantages and disadvantages of segregated sport

Advantages	Disadvantages
• Security and feeling of safety being among people with similar needs. • Competition may appear fairer when competing against people with similar abilities. • Appropriate modifications can be used. • Specialist staff can focus on the needs of disabled individuals. • Reaching levels of excellence may be more viable.	• Can reinforce the sense of being different to main society – sport may be the one chance they have to socialise within wider society. • Use of facilities at different times. • Does not raise public awareness of the capabilities of people with disabilities. • Can be overprotective.

Goalball:

- A three-a-side game.
- Aim is to score a goal by rolling the ball along the floor into your opponent's goal.
- Developed for visually impaired people.
- Features which enable visually impaired people to play:
  - The ball has a bell inside.
  - The playing court has tactile markings.
  - All players wear eyeshades to ensure that everyone is equal when it comes to visual perception.
- Goalball is currently played in 87 countries.
- It is a Paralympic sport, and has European and World Championships.
- British Blind Sport (BBS) is the organisation responsible for the sport in the UK.
- Approximately 15 clubs and school teams in the UK.
- The BBS organises 10 one-day tournaments a year, termly national schools competitions, national championships and the British Goalball Cup.
- There are at present no award schemes or coaching courses for goalball.

Source: Tutor File Higher Sports Leaders Award British Sports Trust

Activity 12

1   Research the sport of polybat or boccia.
2   What modifications have been made to tennis and basketball for wheelchair athletes?

Improving opportunities

Disability Sport England

www.euroyellowpages.com/dse/dispengl.html

This organisation was formally known as the British Sports Association for the Disabled, which was founded in 1961 by Sir Ludwig Guttman, a neurosurgeon who worked at Stoke Mandeville hospital.

Disability Sport England is about:

- promoting the benefits of sport and making it accessible to everyone, regardless of ability;
- helping talented athletes reach the highest levels, such as the Paralympic Games.

Liaison with the sports councils will mean a more coordinated approach towards laying the foundations for developing young people, talent development, coaching, national governing bodies, local authorities, membership services and management administration.

The aims of Disability Sport England are:

- To provide opportunities for people with disabilities to participate in sport.
- To promote the benefits of sport and physical recreation for people with disabilities.
- To support organisations in providing sporting opportunities for people with disabilities.
- To educate and make people aware of the sporting abilities of people with disabilities.
- To enhance the image, awareness and understanding of disability sport.
- To encourage people with disabilities to play an active role in the development of their sport.

Activity 13

Visit your local leisure facility and note down the positive and negative aspects in relation to people with disabilities using that facility.

Sport England Sport England has supported the development of national bodies for disability sport and the appointment of specialised regional and local development officers. The organisation has implemented various projects aimed at improving sporting opportunities for people with disabilities:

1 The campaign 'Every Body Active' was set up following research which highlighted several major problems encountered by people with disabilities; in particular a lack of awareness among mainstream leisure providers and PE teachers as to the special needs of this group.
2 The 'Pro-motion' campaign established in 1990 is now a national programme, intending to increase awareness, training, liaison and resources.

The Sports Council's policy document *Sport and People with Disabilities* was published in 1993, and is a national statement of intent for which it will be accountable.

Local authorities Local authorities play a crucial role at local level because of their leisure departments. The planning and architects departments are also important when trying to build functional and imaginative facilities. When facility tenders are reviewed and renewed, the needs of people with disabilities must be considered.

Excellence and disability sport

Excellence in sport performance has grown substantially, in both the number of competitions and the variety of activities. The Paralympics (so called because it runs parallel to the Olympics) and the World Championships are notable examples.

As knowledge about training, coaching and the input of sport science increases, the performance levels of athletes with disabilities will undoubtedly improve.

IN CONTEXT

As part of the Essex legacy of the 2012 London Games, a statement of equity and inclusion affirms that: 'The high profile that will be given to disabled people at the Paralympic Games offers an unparalleled opportunity to raise awareness of disability issues and to ensure that disabled sports people are offered the same opportunities as their able-bodied colleagues'.

Classification

This is an attempt to group sports competitors to enable fair competition. It was initially used for sport by gender, where separate competitions developed for men and women, and by weight in sports such as boxing. It is now used to include individuals with disabilities.

Two types of classification are employed:

● Medical classification: this developed in the 1940s and was dominant into the 1990s. It was based on the level of spinal cord lesion. It was designed to enable individuals with similar severity of impairment to compete against one another. It was used for wheelchair athletes and amputees. Many other disability sport federations adopted this system, resulting in a multiple classification system.
● Functional classification: an integrated classification system that places emphasis on sport performance by disability groupings rather than by specific disability. This has enabled disability sport to move on from its original rehabilitation base to elite competitive sport. Wheelchair basketball was the first Paralympic sport to experiment with this system. This system demands that athletes be evaluated on what they can and cannot do in a particular sport.

Facilities

Facilities are gradually improving for users with disabilities, partly under the Safety at Sports Grounds Act 1975, and also through a growing desire to provide access. The programming of activities and the attitudes of staff are also important considerations.

Outdoor facilities are increasing provision, for example, those run by the Calvert Trust and Scope. Several important sports centres exist, such as the

Ludwig Guttman Sports Centre at Stoke Mandeville and the Midland Sports Centre for the Disabled in Coventry.

EXAMINER'S TIP

When mentioning facilities and coaching in relation to disability sport, make sure you are specific and mention accessible facilities or specialist coaching.

Future trends

Competitive sport opportunities have increased due to a number of factors:

1 More focus in society on equal opportunities through legislation such as the Disability Discrimination Act.
2 Increasing number of modified or adapted activities, as well as the development of sports specifically designed for people with disabilities, such as goalball.
3 The increase in expectations within society and among disabled people themselves.
4 More specialist staff.
5 Increase in organisations that focus specifically on disability sport, such as Disability Sport England and specialist governing bodies.
6 A growth in clubs and consequent competitions, culminating in the Paralympic Games.
7 Increasing media coverage and the emergence of certain role models.
8 Increase in technology, such as prosthetics and wheelchairs.

In summary, we can conclude that:

- Societal attitudes are changing towards wider participation and competition by athletes.
- The original purpose of rehabilitation through sport has given way to sport for sport's sake.
- The Olympic sport movement will continue to shape the future direction of disability sport.
- Classification, drug testing, advances in technology, and improved training and coaching, techniques and sports medicine will further influence disability sport.

Sport for people aged 50 and over

This age group is increasingly affluent as personal pensions improved during the twentieth century

Sport for all	Elite level
<ul><li>Increasing numbers of individuals with disabilities will participate at all levels in the sport pyramid.</li><li>Equity issues will continue to be addressed for groups who suffer the lowest levels of participation, particularly females and low income groups.</li><li>Public awareness and acceptance of disability sport will increase.</li></ul>	<ul><li>Structured competitive programmes will operate at local, regional, national and international levels.</li><li>Coordination between sport organisations concerned with disability sport and those that are more sport-specific.</li><li>Athletes with disabilities will continue to specialise in sport events, with classification and competitions becoming sport-specific. This will result in improved standards of performance.</li><li>People with disabilities will participate more as coaches and officials, especially as current athletes retire from competition.</li></ul>

Source: Adapted from K. DePauw and S. Gavron (1995) *Disability and Sport,* Human Kinetics

and people may have more disposable income. They are also generally more active and healthy than ever before, and an increase in physical activity can help to prevent the inevitable onset of ageing. Approximately three slightly strenuous exercise sessions per week, each lasting 20 minutes, are recommended. Medical advice may need to be sought, particularly if the person has not participated in physical activity for some time. The important checks are cardiovascular, respiratory and orthopaedic.

In 2001 there were 89,000 men in their nineties in the UK, and 324,000 women. However, there are barriers to physical activity for older people:

Perception of self (how we see ourselves)	Time barriers (or excuses?)
<ul><li>I'm too fat.</li><li>My health is not good enough.</li><li>I'm too old.</li><li>I'm not the sporty type.</li><li>I'm too shy or embarrassed.</li></ul>	<ul><li>I'm too busy with work.</li><li>I have grandchildren to look after.</li><li>I have an elderly relative to look after.</li></ul>

The social benefits of sport are also stressed, because this can be a time of dramatic change for many people. Some may be widowed; some may retire or be made redundant, and family obligations may change. Active lifestyles can help people overcome great social change. Thus, this group of people comprises a potentially rich market for sport.

Since the Sports Council's campaign '50+ All to Play For' in 1983, more activities have been promoted for this age group. Here are some of the most popular ones:

- Indoors – keep fit; aerobics; dance; carpet and short mat bowls; table tennis.
- Outdoors – walking/rambling; cycling; jogging; archery; canoeing; golf; tennis; swimming; cricket; hockey; bowls.

Many other more adventurous activities are also enjoyed by this age group.

Competitive days need not be over, and many sports have veteran and 50+ sections. Other ways of getting involved are as a sports leader, such as a coach, referee or club official. Organisations which should be involved in developing this kind of activity are: local authority departments responsible for sport and recreation; sports centres and swimming pools; adult education classes; the national and regional sports councils; and the governing bodies of sport.

Benefits of physical activity for older people

Social benefits Physical activity promotes a more positive and active image of older people by:

- increased contribution to society by older people;
- enhanced social integration, formation of new friendships and the widening of social networks;
- role maintenance and new role acquisition;
- maintenance of caring skills.

Health benefits There are many health benefits, even when physical activity is taken up in later life. Some of these are:

- prevention and management of chronic heart disease and stroke;
- prevention and management of type 2 diabetes;
- management of weight and obesity;
- prevention of osteoporosis;
- reduction of accidental falls;
- prevention of (colon) cancer;
- improvement in length and depth of sleep.

Psychological benefits The psychological benefits of physical activity include:

- reduction in stress and anxiety and improvement in overall psychological well-being;
- reduction in depression;
- improvements in cognitive function, self-esteem and self-worth;
- improvements in perception of health;
- a reduction of loneliness and isolation;
- enhanced feeling of worth to society.

Sport for young people

First of all we must recognise that not all young people share common lifestyles: they may have different socio-economic backgrounds, parental attitudes, social experiences, and so on. Youth is often seen as a transition from school and childhood to work and adulthood. Individuals who struggle with this transition often become isolated from the main community and 'drop out'; some may become deviant and when considered in larger numbers can form an underclass. This group will experience exclusion from society. Sport participation is mostly a result of early positive experiences in physical education curricula and recreational activities.

As early as 1960, the Wolfenden Report was concerned that the provision of sport in the UK was poorer than in other European states, leading to the post school gap, which results in a drop in participation on leaving school.

Some constraining factors are:

- the concentration in clubs on the talented youngsters;
- the tradition of single sport clubs in the UK, compared to more multi-sport clubs in Europe.

Physical activities are promoted by a wide range of individuals and agencies, such as:

- the education system, in particular the physical education programme;
- sports clubs and governing bodies;
- play workers;
- the youth service;
- local authorities.

It is necessary for these agencies to coordinate their efforts. For example, national governing bodies and schools associations need to plan programmes jointly which will support a common youth sport policy.

In previous years, the Sports Council targeted the age band 13–24 years. However, recent research (General Household Survey) suggested that low participation was not the problem, but that young people do not play as many sports as children. However, young females still participate less than their male counterparts. On leaving school, more casual sports are enjoyed, alongside adventure sports and health-related activities.

Obesity and young children

The British Heart Foundation report *Couch Kids – the growing epidemic*, published in 2000, says that:

Tackling overweight and obesity must start in childhood for two reasons:
- because it is much easier to prevent becoming overweight than to correct it;
- because it is easier to adopt healthy eating patterns when children are young.

The report contains some alarming statistics:

- Nearly 70 per cent of 2–12 year olds eat biscuits, sweets or chocolate at least once a day, while less than 20 per cent eat fruit and vegetables more than once a day.
- More than a third of children are not meeting the recommended activity guidelines – generally agreed to be at least one hour's moderate-intensity activity each day.

- The time traditionally spent on active play is being spent on sedentary activities such as watching television or playing computer games. More than a quarter of 11–16 year olds watch TV for more than four hours each day.
- Active transport to and from school has decreased. Car journeys to school have doubled in the last 20 years. Just 1 per cent of children cycle to school.

Sport England launched its Sportsmark Award and Activemark to encourage schools to help children adopt more positive attitudes towards physical activity.

Youth and delinquency

A large body of literature has developed worldwide on this issue, suggesting increasing concern at governmental levels. The general consensus appears to be that sport:

- increases self-esteem, mood and perception of competence and mastery, especially through outdoor recreation;
- reduces self-destructive behaviour (smoking, drug use, substance abuse, suicidal tendencies);
- improves socialisation both with peer group and with adults;
- improves scholastic attendance and performance.

Schemes Several schemes run to help this particular group, but usually they are not long enough and participation is voluntary, suggesting that more hardened offenders will not benefit. An experience of a few days to a few weeks may be of benefit in the short term, but if the individual returns to the same physical and social deprivation, the old values and behaviour patterns will re-emerge. Sport, therefore, may form part of the solution, rather than offering a complete answer.

IN CONTEXT

Young people were a crucial element in London winning the 2012 Games bid. The Games, and volunteering in particular, offer great opportunities to develop citizenship and leadership among young people.

Excellence

We have looked at categories of people within society, and particularly at the participation base of the sports pyramid. Now it is time to discover how some people manage to extend beyond the recreational and performance end of the sports continuum, moving onwards to sporting excellence.

What does 'excellence' mean?

Excellence can be defined as a special ability beyond the norm, to which many aspire but few go on to achieve. There are some problems with using words like this. For example, we often talk about personal excellence, but this may not be according to national or international standards. The athletes who broke records half a century ago were excellent for their era, even though today their times or distances would not measure up. A performer could have excellent technique but not achieve the highest scores in top competition.

For our purposes, excellence means the superior, elite athletes at both amateur and professional level, able-bodied and disabled, who reach the pinnacle of performance in their chosen sport. Excellence usually suggests a specialism of one activity, and is judged by international and world standards.

The 'sport for all' base (i.e. the provision of sport for the masses and the elite) is a compatible system – the wider the base of the pyramid, the greater the apex.

Numerous strategies have been developed for various sections of the community, not only to encourage participation, but also to enable talented and committed people to strive for excellence. Historically, the UK has not had a nationally organised plan for identifying talent, and it has mostly been an ad hoc approach, with luck playing a large part. The support system for the development of excellence is mainly located outside schools.

Why pursue excellence in sport?

- Sport represents a challenge in people's lifestyles, which have become increasingly sedentary and controlled.
- Many people are curious about their own and the human species' potential; sport is sometimes called the last frontier, as our limitations are not yet known.
- Sport can provide an alternative employment path, with the added attraction of high social status if high-level success is achieved.
- It gives individuals high self-esteem, and a feeling of worth and quality in their lives.

Social advantages of pursuing excellence These include the following:

- Sporting success can boost national pride and morale (governments are usually keen to be connected with this).
- Sport often results in a reduction in antisocial behaviour.
- The role models of sport attract a large spectator audience.
- There are economic benefits.
- The excellence end of the continuum feeds the base of sport for all.

Disadvantages of excellence

The disadvantages of pursuing excellence include the following:

- It is elitist – it can only serve the interests of a few.
- Costly resources are required for a minority of sports participants.
- Overspecialisation and obsession with a physical activity can occur, which may have damaging physiological and psychological effects.
- The moral value of sport can be lost due to the 'win at all costs' attitude, which is made worse when the stakes become higher.

Figure 11.15 National strategy for achieving excellence

Since the mid 1980s, there has been increasing pressure from all sections of British sport for the administrators to concentrate more resources on the pursuit of excellence. A national strategy for achieving excellence has begun to take root (see Figure 11.15). The key to achieving a nationally coherent programme lies in linking together all the complex jigsaw pieces which currently operate in isolation. The support services of sport science, sports medicine, lifestyle counselling and information technology must also be integrated to produce an effective multidisciplinary approach. The days of the coach being the sole provider of support to the athlete are almost gone – particularly at the highest levels of performance. The coach–athlete relationship is still a crucial element, but other people who hold specialist knowledge also play their part in the development of the athlete. Consistency from all the support team is paramount. The value of sport science is unquestioned, but it must work alongside coaching expertise.

Talent identification

Talent identification can be defined as the process by which children are encouraged to participate in the sports at which they are most likely to succeed, based on testing certain parameters as the first step in progressing from beginner to international athlete. Talent identification follows this as the next phase in the achievement of sporting success.

The UK has tended to rely on a number of uncoordinated factors, such as being spotted by a sport scout, having the opportunity to belong to a club that specialises in a particular sport, or coming from a supportive and higher economic social background. Other countries, such as the former USSR and East Germany, had a much more proactive approach even early in the twentieth century. Today, Australia is leading the way.

The DCMS proposed in its Game Plan for Sport (2002) that it would encourage the delivery of future talent development programmes according to the Long-Term Athlete Development Model (LTAD) developed by Balyi (1998). The model is based on five main principles:

- train and perform well long-term rather than winning;
- train rather than over-compete;
- broad generic skills before specialisation;

- flexible talent development model to account for variation between sports;
- athlete-centred and involvement of parents – better integration of key partners.

Talent identification and consequent development of athletes to the elite stage requires a complexity of factors to come together. The athletes themselves require certain physical, psychological and social advantages:

Physical	Superior health and fitness; body composition for particular sport; trained energy systems; high pain threshold.
Psychological	High competitiveness; high urge to achieve; persistence; dedication; mental toughness.
Social	Access to high-quality facilities and coaching; reliable and sufficient funding; family support; coordinated sport policies; appropriate levels of local, regional and national competition.

Exam-style questions

1   Elite performers need enormous support in order to achieve their potential and to achieve sporting excellence.

   (a) What can schools do to help talented young people achieve their sporting potential?

   (5 marks)

   (b) What does the organisation UK Sport do to increase sporting excellence?

   (3 marks)

   (c) How does public sector funding help to increase participation in physical recreation in the UK?

   (3 marks)

2   Describe each level of the performance pyramid and how do National Governing Bodies support performers at the top of the performance pyramid?

   (10 marks)

A survey by the former English Sports Council (ESC) (1998) showed that 38 per cent of elite performers from 14 sports were from the professional and managerial social groups, compared to 19 per cent of the population as a whole. Only 10 per cent were from the semi- and unskilled groups, compared to 25 per cent of the population as a whole. The conclusion drawn by the ESC was:

that the opportunity to realise sporting potential is significantly influenced by an individual's social background. So, for example, a precociously talented youngster born in an affluent family with sport-loving parents, one of whom has achieved high levels of sporting success, and attending an independent private school, has a 'first class' ticket to the sporting podium.

What you need to know

* The broader the base of sport participation, the greater the talent pool from which to draw in order to increase the chances of sporting excellence.
* Unequal access to the 'sport for all' ideal will negatively affect the sports pyramid.
* Sport initiatives must take careful note of the complex nature of the various groups they seek to help.
* A nationally coordinated approach towards excellence needs to be further developed if Britain is to compete on equal terms with other nations.
* Sports policy is characterised by a high degree of fragmentation between central government departments. There is heavy reliance on local government to provide facilities and opportunities for sport and recreation.
* In local authorities, there is a decentralised approach towards the organisation of sport and recreation, reflecting the political system in the UK. There is a slender thread of cohesion through the organisations, but there are also areas of overlap and conflict.
* As with much of the administration of sport in the UK, it is a mixture of tradition and compromise.
* There has been a steady expansion in the internationalisation of sport, and this has brought challenges for the national governing bodies to adjust their rules and take note of the international sporting calendar.
* The pattern of funding for sport in the UK is dominated by sponsorship. Government grants (local and central) and funds from the governing bodies and private individuals make the next share. Relatively small but important market niches are funded by SportsAid and the BOA.
* British sports bodies must cast off their traditional amateur, elitist approach to join the modern, professional sports world, if the UK is to allow its athletes the same opportunities as those enjoyed in rival countries.
* The type of political and economic system is crucial in determining the nature of state intervention.

Review questions

1 Draw the sport participation pyramid or sport development continuum and briefly explain each stage.

2 Describe the function of the following organisations:
   1 Department for Culture, Media and Sport;
   2 UKSport;
   3 Sport England.

3 What is the role of the Minister for Sport and who holds this position currently in the UK?

4 Why were governing bodies for sport initially established? What are the main functions of governing bodies?

5 What changes have governing bodies had to undertake in modern times?

6 What does the term 'permissive' mean in relation to the provision of leisure by local authorities?

7 Name six forms of finance for sport in the UK.

8 What do the terms 'private', 'voluntary' and 'public' mean in relation to provision for leisure?

9 What are the nine reasons given for explaining national government involvement in sport? Choose two and explain these in more detail.

10 What advantages are there to sport being free from political control?

11 Name four ways in which sport and politics have become entwined in the UK.

12 How can sport policies help the government's overall aim of neighbourhood regeneration?

13 What is meant by the term 'policy'?

14 List ten wider economic benefits which can result from sport.

15 Copy and complete the following table.

16 What is meant by the 'dominant group' in society and how can this group affect sporting opportunities?

17 How can sport be an avenue of social mobility?

18 What does the term 'stacking' refer to in sporting situations?

19 Suggest four strategies which organisations can implement in order to improve the participation of women in sporting and recreational activities.

20 Why is the 50+ age group suitable for sports organisations to target in order to increase their levels of participation in sporting and recreational activities?

21 What does the term 'social exclusion' mean and what measures can be taken to address the issues?

22 What is the significance of the emergence of the term 'disability sport'?

23 What is the significance of the term 'inclusiveness' when referring to disability and sporting participation?

24 What needs to be considered when using the term 'excellence in sport'?

25 Which organisations in particular are concerned with developing excellence in the UK?

26 What advantages and disadvantages are there in the pursuit of excellence?

27 What is 'talent identification' and what strategies are currently in place to develop it in the UK?

28 What physical, psychological and social factors are required for the development of an elite athlete?

29 What is meant by the terms 'opportunity', 'provision' and 'esteem'?

30 How can elite athletes be used to inspire and motivate young people to participate and continue in sport?

31 What is meant by sports science and what contributions can it make to the development of excellence in sport?

32 What do the terms 'commitment', 'resources' and 'expertise' mean in relation to excellence in sport?

Organisation	Major sport policy	Characteristics of policy
Department for Culture, Media and Sport		
Sport England		
UK Sport		
National governing body		
Youth Sports Trust		
British Olympic Association		
International Olympic Committee		

CHAPTER 12

Contemporary sporting issues

Learning outcomes

By the end of this chapter you should be familiar with:

- sponsorship and the media, their individual roles, their relationship to each other and to sport (the golden triangle), and their impact, especially in encouraging wider participation in sport within society;
- performance-enhancing products:
  - drugs – reasons for use, consequences and possible solutions;
  - modern technological products;
- violence in sport:
  - among players and spectators;
  - causes and solutions;
- the Olympic Games:
  - background in the nineteenth century;
  - commercialisation;
  - British Olympic Association;
  - International Olympic Committee;
  - 2012 – opportunities and implications, especially for society and young people;
  - as a political vehicle under government control.

This chapter explores many of the issues that people discuss in their everyday life; those that are reported in the media; those that arouse our passions and force us to develop personal opinions. The information in this chapter should help you to participate in discussions about sport in an informed manner.

Sponsorship

Key term

Sponsorship: This is the provision of funds or other forms of support to an individual or event, in return for a commercial return. It is of mutual benefit to both parties.

Sponsorship is now an intrinsic aspect of sports funding. Through the medium of television, business sponsors of sport can create the images they want, allow identification with sports stars, and introduce 'new' populations to the game and to their products.

What is sponsorship?

Sponsorship is one of the means by which a company can bring itself or its products to the attention of consumers, presenting them in a favourable light. Advertising is the most frequently used marketing tool and speaks to the consumer in a direct way. It announces the availability of a product and creates an image for a brand. It can also provide information on product quality, characteristics, price and performance.

Sponsorship seeks to enhance these messages by association with an event, club or team which shares similar image qualities and values with the brand. This association can be very powerful because it is perceived as an endorsement of the brand by an independent third party. Consumers are aware of the costs of sponsorship, but the message conveyed is more subtle than that from more overtly paid-for advertisements.

Sponsorship is a commercial agreement between a company and a sport to enter into a joint venture to promote their mutual interests. In return for a financial contribution, a sports organisation will allow the use of its name in a variety of commercial activities. Some of the most obvious are:

- display of the brand name on kit, banners around the venue, advertisements in programmes and on other merchandise;
- use of the club, event, team or individual in advertisements and other promotions undertaken by the brand;
- personal endorsement of the sponsor's products by teams or individuals, by use of the products, kit or equipment;
- production of joint websites or developing close links between separate websites.

Examples include Vodafone's sponsorship of Manchester United, Tiger Woods' endorsement of Nike products and Guinness's sponsorship of the Rugby World Cup.

Aspects of sponsorship

A sponsorship agency is an agency which specialises in advising on or organising sponsored events and programmes, and which may be employed by either a sponsor or a sports body. It acts as a broker, bringing together the sponsor and the sports body to create or organise an event or programme which is mutually beneficial to both parties. Examples of sponsorship agencies are West Nally and Mark McCormack International Management Organisation.

An individual athlete may also have an agent who promotes the competitor in order to gain financial benefits for them both. The marketing of athletes or events is an integrated and professionally planned promotion.

Ambush or guerrilla marketing is a term used when one brand pays to become an official sponsor of an event and another competing brand attempts to connect itself with the event without paying the sponsorship fee, and, more importantly, without breaking any laws. They attract consumers at the expense of competitors, undermining the event's integrity and its ability to attract sponsors in the future. The cases that attract most press coverage are the 'big' players with plenty of resources, such as Nike, Reebok and Coca-Cola. One notable exception was provided at the 2002 Winter Olympics in Salt Lake City. Anheuser-Busch paid more than US$50 million for the right to use the word 'Olympic' and the five rings logo. Schirf Brewery, a very small, local company, came up with the clever (and legal) idea of marking its delivery trucks with the slogan: 'Wasutch Beers. The Unofficial Beer. 2002 Winter Games'. Without using the magic word 'Olympic' or the logo of the five rings, the company successfully connected itself to the Games.

The danger to major events like the Olympics and the World Cup is that they rely heavily on corporate sponsorship. These commercial partners need to be assured of sole rights; if they feel their money is not being well spent, they will withdraw their support. Events can ill afford to lose this revenue.

Most sponsorship is paid for in cash, but sponsorship in kind can be useful and effective too. Instead of money, the sponsor might provide equipment, services or management expertise as all or part of its fee for the rights to a sporting activity. Companies may also provide money to sporting organisations in other ways:

- Charitable donations – No commercial return is expected, but companies may use donations to cultivate an image as a good corporate citizen.
- Corporate patronage – A halfway house between donations and sponsorship, patronage generally provides only some recognition of a company's activity, within a relatively small, though influential, group. It is more common in the arts than in sport.
- Corporate hospitality – The opportunity to meet customers and contacts in informal,

enjoyable circumstances to pursue business objectives. This often forms part of a sponsorship package.

- Public/community relations – Sponsorship of sport can be used to meet objectives on a company's social or political agenda. The aim is not to sell products, but to improve a company's image as an employer, corporate citizen or contributor to the economy.

Advantages of sponsoring sport

Sponsors look to sport to add value to the brand proposition. In almost all sectors of all markets there is intense competition among companies and brands. Often there is little to choose from in terms of quality, content or price. In order to make a brand stand out from the crowd, a sponsor will use sport to create a unique position in the mind of the consumer.

At the highest levels, sport involves gold medals, world records, championship cups and global awareness. A leading worldwide brand such as Coca-Cola wants to associate itself with such excellence, and so has chosen to sponsor the Olympics and the football World Cup. But in order to personalise and localise its image and activities, Coca-Cola also supports grass-roots sport to reinforce its global message.

Smaller companies can also benefit from improved awareness, image and sales through sponsorship at a local or regional level. The principles are the same; the only difference is the scale. Companies use sports sponsorship for a variety of reasons, and to attract sponsorship it is important to understand which objective a company is addressing:

- Brand/corporate awareness – Seeks to put a name in front of consumers to provide favourable recognition when those consumers are exposed to other, specific marketing messages.
- Brand/corporate image – Attempts to create a personality and style which distinguishes a product from others in the market and allows for premium pricing, for example.
- Customer relations – Sports sponsorship can open dialogue between companies, establishing the sponsor as a global player, worthy of recognition and suitable to do

business with. Sponsorship can also provide appropriate means of hospitality in order to meet and do business with clients.

- Employee relations – Sports sponsorship can encourage company pride and loyalty, helping to attract and retain staff.
- Community relations – Sponsorship can show that a company cares about its community and is prepared to invest in its future and the welfare of its citizens.

Disadvantages of sponsoring sport

- There has been uneven development across sports, as sponsors tend to come forward when there are already large audiences. Due to their ability to attract media coverage, elite sports are promoted at the expense of minority sports, with the diversion of financial sponsorship causing a decline in the latter.
- Sponsors of sporting events are careful not to be associated with sensitive political issues.
- Some sports have been adapted to suit TV coverage. In cricket, the one-day game has developed to increase the pace, which has placed priority on certain skills. The tobacco company, Rothmans, encouraged attacking and batting skills and defensive bowling, and paid more in sponsorship when the ball was driven to the boundary – which meant that their adverts appeared more frequently.
- Sponsors sometimes withdraw when their objectives are not achieved or when there is no perceived gain.
- Contradictory messages can arise when a product being advertised is considered dangerous to people's health. Tobacco companies were banned from general advertising on British television in 1965. Tobacco companies therefore used sport as a cheap way of advertising their product. The main sporting beneficiaries of tobacco sponsorship have been motor racing, tennis, cricket, golf, show jumping and snooker. However, the Sports Council does not accept tobacco sponsorship and does not make its Sport Sponsorship Advisory Service available to the industry. In the past, tobacco has contributed 10 per cent of total sponsorship, and the government is not able to compensate for this amount. This poses the question: is tobacco bad for health but good for sport?

Bernie Ecclestone's personal empire shows how power in sport can be concentrated. In June 2000 the Fédération Internationale de l'Automobile (FIA), Formula One's governing body, sold the commercial rights to Ecclestone for a 110-year period! For $360 million, Ecclestone was awarded sole rights to negotiate fees from promoters of Grand Prix races, and 'sole authority' to sell television rights worldwide for a sport whose 17 races each year pull in an aggregate TV audience of around 5 billion.

Though sponsorship has provided much needed capital for sport, the bedrock of funding in the UK is still a combination of public funding and the massive voluntary and unpaid commitment of sports enthusiasts.

Any discussion of sport and sponsorship will inevitably include the word 'media' and the relationship between them. This has been termed the 'golden triangle'.

The media

The media includes newspapers, radio and television broadcasting, and the Internet, by which information is conveyed to the general public. The media is based on three main principles:

1 provision of information about events and people;
2 interpretation of events;
3 entertainment.

If the media is privately owned, profit will be an overriding concern. Thus everything is carefully selected and emphasised to create drama and entertainment, which, if successful, will keep the broadcast sponsors happy.

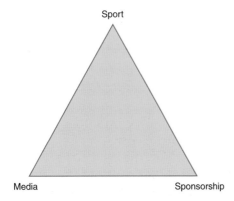

Figure 12.1 The relationship between sport, sponsorship and the media

Newspapers

Today there are two major types of newspapers:

1 The tabloids, such as *The Sun* or the *Mirror*, tend to have a large section devoted to sport, but focus on particular types of sport – mainly those which have broad appeal and are male-dominated.
2 The broadsheets, such as *The Guardian* or *The Times*, tend to cover and analyse sport in more depth; they offer slightly more variety of sport, but there is still a predominance of male sport.

Activity 1

Collect some examples of how sport is reported in different types of newspapers. Analyse the detail given and the style of reporting.

Radio

Radio started to report live events in the 1920s, giving the broadcast an immediacy (this was strengthened by the advent of television broadcasting). In the UK, the BBC traditionally broadcasts sporting events without the advertisers' influence, whereas in the USA they schedule events to maximise advertisers' demands.

Television

Television has the advantage of being able to broadcast instantaneous sporting action to a large audience, relatively cheaply. This low cost compares favourably with drama and light entertainment, and with the high ratings achieved it is not surprising that sport features so heavily in television schedules, particularly at weekends.

The relationship between sports and the media has become symbiotic. In the early twenty-first century, media commentators claimed that BSkyB (part of Rupert Murdoch's News International) would lose 60 per cent of its subscribers if it were to lose its Premier League rights. A bidding war saw the rights for 2001–2004 sold for over US$500 million a year, with BSkyB outbidding its rivals once again.

Television has helped to bring lesser-known or rarely watched sports to the foreground; and it has helped participants to attain superstar status, consequently raising the performers' earnings. This has sometimes put athletes under great pressure to make more performance appearances than is good for their physical and mental health.

However, television reporting can overdramatise problems within the sports world, and deals made between sporting bodies and the media can favour certain sports, such as the alliance between Adidas and FIFA.

The effect of the media

Some sports have changed to make them more attractive for media coverage. Television can also influence participation rates in a sport – positively or negatively.

- When Channel 4 was first established, it boosted the viewing and participating figures for volleyball and table tennis, and provided significant coverage of the Indian team game kabaddi, as it sought new markets in order to compete with other channels.
- Rights to the football World Cup (2002–2006) were sold for US$2 billion, shared between Kirch/Taurus and Sporis/ISL.
- Volleyball became a regular sports feature between 1980 and 1984, with the number of affiliated players rising by 70 per cent. Conversely, when table tennis stopped receiving television coverage, the number of participating players dropped by a third. The governing bodies in both cases were convinced that the changed rates of participation were not coincidences. If women's sports received more coverage, would we see the rise in female participants that so many organisations are trying to achieve?

The increasing concentration of power and money in the hands of a limited number of conglomerates (especially when combined with club ownership and merchandising interests) has led to a growing sense of unease in a number of instances. A notable case saw BSkyB attempt to buy control of Manchester United in 1998, but the UK Monopolies and Mergers Commission blocked the bid. The argument made was that it would further divide the clubs on a financial basis.

Sports commentators

The media reports on what happens in sport (as in other events) and, as such, is objective. However, as readers, viewers or listeners, we must take into account the values and beliefs of those who commentate on the events. Commentators are the mediators who describe and analyse the action for the viewer, listener or reader at home. They can become celebrities in their own right and are sometimes associated with just one sport; for example, Murray Walker (motor racing), John Motson (football), the late Dan Maskell (tennis at Wimbledon) and Harry Carpenter (boxing). The style of presentation has become closely related to the culture of the mass audience. Events are hyped up, with commentators discussing the likely outcome hours (and sometimes days) before the event takes place, advising their audience how to interpret the situation.

Influence of technology

The increase in technology has enabled an effective combination of detailed coverage with fast-action tension. The use of zoom lenses has meant less reliance on fixed-angle shots, and makes possible close-ups of players, catching facial and verbal expressions which spectators at live events could not hope to capture. It is possible to fit cameras in a racing car, under water, and in a goal, providing the television viewer with a privileged position. Action replays and freeze-frames enable detailed analysis to take place. Interactive technology allows viewers at home to make individual choices, such as following their favourite performer.

Communication satellites enable live transmission around the world, which has had a growing impact on viewing audiences. Television rights can now be granted to companies who do not transmit to many homes, with the UK Broadcasting Act of 1990 declaring that all rights to broadcast sport can be sold to the highest bidder.

Media coverage and social values

- Television coverage concentrates on the conduct of participants and spectators, and is generally sympathetic to officials. Different sports receive different emphasis of coverage.

For example, tennis players who behave badly are often described as 'brats', which has a very middle-class tone, whereas in football, the language used might be 'thugs', possibly showing more intolerance of perceived working-class behaviour.

- Gender inequalities in sport can be reflected by the media. Men figure more as participants and as media sport professionals; women tend to comment on women's sports, if at all, although there have been challenges to this situation recently, with Sue Barker at the BBC, for example. Non-contact sports for women, such as tennis, gymnastics and track athletics, receive more positive media coverage. The massive inequality in coverage tends to reaffirm the stereotype that sport is for men, and women have little to comment on.

- The media can help to generate a sense of nationalism, particularly since the development of international coverage of events where the symbols of nationalism are displayed for all to see – rituals, flags, ceremonies, parades, uniforms and anthems – making them highly emotive events.

- In the UK, sportspeople from ethnic minorities can become powerful role models for young people, and their representation can promote equality of opportunity. However, the media can also promote the stereotype that black people can excel in sport and physical activity, but not in other areas of life. Similarly to women, people from ethnic minorities are not prominent in positions of power in the media, such as commentators, directors, writers, producers or photographers.

Who controls sport?

Traditionally, this control was undeniably held by the gentlemanly elders of western society, as a result of personal contacts rather than competence or democracy. They were not prepared for the predatory world of commercial exploitation that was to emerge in the twentieth century.

In the modern era, the power over the organisation of sport and its revenue lies in just a few hands, via a monopolistic ruling body or a small group of individuals or companies. Although some sports stars can wield a certain amount of leverage due to their high wages and crowd-pulling potential, the majority of professionals have to do as they are told. They are bought, sold and transferred as commodities.

Ruling bodies in sport have all lost out to businesses such as Rupert Murdoch's News International, Mark McCormack's International Marketing Group, Ted Turner's Time Warner (owner of Home Box Office), Nike and the Kirch Group.

The Fox, Sky and Star TV networks give Rupert Murdoch unique power in broadcasting. Contracts include NFL and Major League baseball in the USA, Premier League football in the UK, and the cricket World Cup. Murdoch's companies have been extending sports coverage via the Internet too – predicted to be the key medium for future sports fans.

Golf and tennis are among the few major sports which have a relatively democratic form of government, in that the players decide how things should be run and make their own decisions over where and when they will play and which sponsorship deals to take.

The media and young people

The media is often cited as having a huge influence on young people. It is not surprising, therefore, that this influence can have both negative and positive effects. One of the positive effects is that it can inform and educate, and hopefully can be used to increase participation levels among young people. The media conveys a number of different sport themes to young people, including the following:

- *Success theme* – Qualities shown are: competitive, aggressive, domination of others, obedience to authority. Should success also be portrayed as empathy, support, cooperation and equality? Elite sport is shown, while lower levels of participation are rarely broadcast on British TV.

- *Masculinity and femininity themes* – Male sport is shown far more than female sport, although coverage of female sport has increased. Women's sport tends to be shown when it is considered a special feature, whereas male sport is reported regularly. Images presented to young people are that sport is mainly for boys and men. Women's sports magazines tend to focus on activities more consistent with traditional notions of femininity – those emphasising grace, balance and aesthetics, or those focused on producing a 'feminine shape'.

The impact of the media on the sport-related behaviour of young people

Is the media likely to encourage sport participation or turn young people into couch potatoes?

- When children watch and are inspired by a particular sport and its athletes, this can lead them to participate in that sport, by joining clubs and so on. However, when success does not come quickly, many children and parents fall by the wayside.
- The media can introduce young people to sports they might otherwise never have known existed, such as archery and rock climbing.
- Many avid spectators of sport never actually try the activity themselves, and as television coverage of sport has increased, so too has inactivity and obesity.

Despite the last point above, the safest conclusion to draw is that the media have no *net* effect one way or another on active participation in sports and other physical activities (Irlinger 1994). There is a belief that television means that certain people do not attend live sport events, yet research has also shown that people who watch games on television are more likely to attend live events (Zhang et al. 1997).

Does watching sport on television reduce the creativity of young people to be inventive and active? These days, young people enjoy the opportunity to play video sport games, where they can choose their teams and have a truly interactive experience. If children are participating in adult-controlled sport, they often have to follow the instructions of a coach – does this restrict their creativity?

Deviance in sport

The rewards that accrue from being successful in sport are numerous, from medals to money and fame. It is no wonder that athletes since ancient times have used any means at their disposal to try to improve their performance.

Athletes are encouraged to behave in ways that would not be allowed in other areas of life. This can pose special problems for sport. 'On the field' deviance includes 'violations of norms that occur while preparing or participating in sports events' (Coakley 1993). This can be caused by the pressure of media coverage or commercialism, or the pressure to win. Similar behaviour outside of the sporting situation could result in arrest and prosecution.

We will now look specifically at the following issues:

- aggression in sport by athletes;
- spectator violence, in particular football hooliganism;
- drug taking by athletes.

Aggression in sport

Aggression includes any behaviour which *intends* physical or psychological harm to another person. This distinguishes it from other terms used in sport situations, such as assertive, rough and competitive. Intimidation is the threatened intent to harm, using verbal or physical means. Sports vary in their nature, so the extent to which aggression can be expressed also varies. Activities involving physical contact are more easily open to shows of aggression than activities where players are separated from each other. However, a game like netball, which, according to the rules, is a non-contact sport, can often involve aggression.

Theories that sport helps to cause aggression are based on the following:

- participating in or watching sport leads to frustration, which leads to violence;
- sportspeople learn to think of violence as a means to achieve success;
- the dominance of 'male' behaviour in sport leads people to believe that men are naturally superior to women because they have greater strength and more violent tendencies.

People care about the result of sporting action, and victory can be used to reflect superiority in other aspects of life. Frustration can lead to the emotional response of anger, which, in the sporting arena, can be expressed as a violent response. The cause of frustration could be an official's decision during a game or environmental conditions. Frustration can be stimulated when athletes use equipment which is associated with violence.

Aggression is likely to be prevalent when spectators identify strongly with one particular side and are likely to feel anger quite easily when opportunities for aggression and frustration are present. Contact sports are therefore most likely to lead to violence on the pitch, and this is compounded when large rewards are available for winning, and when the expectations of coaches and fans are high. Tolerance of rule violations seems to increase as the level of competition increases. An extreme case is ice hockey, where 'enforcers' are employed to act as hit men, yet these are players who do not necessarily feel anger or frustration associated with the game; they intimidate and carry out violent acts because that is their primary task in the game.

As female participation in contact sports has increased, it has become apparent that they also use violence as a strategy, but research (though limited as yet) generally concludes that they are not as violent as men. Sport has long been a male preserve, and mistakes made during a game often result in sexist comments such as 'playing like a girl'. Thus, some sportsmen feel the need to prove their masculinity beyond doubt by using violent means; this implies that aggressive behaviour can be the result of social conditioning, and is not merely a natural masculine trait.

Spectator violence

A number of general approaches to deviance can be applied to the specific form of deviant behaviour which is termed 'football hooliganism'. Football hooligans have been defined by the Sports Council as 'those people who were dealt with by the police for offences occurring in connection with attendance at football matches'. A dictionary definition of a hooligan is a 'disorderly and noisy young person who behaves in a violent and destructive way'.

A distinction needs to be made between supporters, fans and hooligans. Supporters and fans manage their emotions effectively. Guttman (1986) concluded that spectating at sports events did not result in an increase in violent behaviour. Hooligans, on the other hand, go to matches to engage in aggressive and violent behaviour, before, during and/or after the game. Considering the number of sports events and the amount of

people who are regular spectators, it is clear we are dealing with a minority of people, albeit a media-attracting minority.

Sociological approaches to hooliganism

Early theories of hooliganism concentrated on social class, and tried to explain the behaviour of hooligans in terms of their social status. However, this is no longer a useful way of describing people, as class distinctions are not clear-cut in modern society. Furthermore, while early theories were based on the premise that most football hooligans were uneducated, less well-off members of society, recent studies have discovered that a large number of people who cause trouble at football matches are highly educated professional people, who often need to keep their identities as football supporters separate from their working lives. It is difficult to find any single factor to explain deviancy as it applies to football hooliganism; a synthesis of approaches is required.

Hooliganism at football matches has been exaggerated and distorted, and should be seen in a wider socio-economic and historical context. The media has a tendency to sensationalise the news and to amplify the problem being reported. Football has had a long, fluctuating history of crowd disorder, and Pearson (1983) suggests that such problems date back to mob football in the seventeenth and eighteenth centuries.

- Marsh (1978) argued that aggravation at football matches is effectively a 'highly distinctive, and often ceremonial system for resolving conflict'; that is, it is a ritual action. Behaviour is structured and ordered rather than chaotic; the fighting itself has rules, and much of it is not serious.
- Taylor (1971) argues that football is now a passive spectator sport rather than a participatory one. The increasing professionalism, control by wealthy directors and the change from grounds to stadiums, have taken away any sense of control or participation from the spectators, and football hooliganism could be seen as an attempt to resist these changes.
- Arousal seeking and risk taking appear to be compensatory acts. This idea links with Elias and Dunning's theory (1970), suggesting through the title of their work, 'The quest for excitement

in unexciting societies', that in industrialised societies there are fewer opportunities for people to express themselves freely.

- Brown (1991) believes that some hooligans become addicted to the activity, just like gamblers and alcoholics. Increasing stimulation is needed to generate high arousal because of psychological deprivation. People who have not had enough opportunity to experience a wide range of rewarding experiences can be forced to use narrower strategies to deal with life's problems.

Practical factors which contribute to hooliganism

There are a number of important factors which can contribute to the *level* of violence at sports events:

- Violence shown by the players seems to transmit itself to the spectators.
- Pre-event hype can increase the level of violence, so the media and organisers should take some responsibility for the way they promote the event.
- Controversial officials' decisions can sometimes cause an increase in violence, particularly if this occurs at a crucial stage. The need for competent officials is essential.
- The supporter group dynamics (i.e. the size and structure of the group, their social and cultural backgrounds, the importance associated with the event and the historical relationships of those attending).
- The authorities' strategies for controlling the event.
- The amount of alcohol consumed before the event.

In Britain, the short distance between sporting locations has enabled the establishment of a tradition of away fans travelling to every game. The two sets of fans openly display their allegiance through the symbols of colours, flags, scarves, songs, and so on. This is not possible in larger countries where supporters have further distances to travel.

Dealing with hooliganism

Hooliganism initially took place in football grounds. These were easily accessible, spectators were not segregated and matches occurred at regular intervals. Trouble generally erupted when goals were scored. However, when the authorities began to use strategies like fenced pens with close police scrutiny, the violent activity began to move away from the grounds.

The Taylor Report following the Hillsborough disaster led to measures such as abolishing the football terraces. By the 1994–95 season, all Premier League and First Division clubs had to upgrade their stadiums to all-seater facilities. This led many people to complain of the lack of atmosphere, as they felt that the excitement generated by large crowds had been eradicated.

Video monitoring has been installed at most grounds, so that police can monitor crowd movement closely. Freeze-frames can highlight particular troublemakers. Information is stored on computer at the National Criminal Intelligence Service and allows for police liaison throughout the UK and Europe.

Perimeter fencing was not successful in preventing violence, and neither was the identity card scheme. However, the level of hooliganism has decreased in the last few years. Some have complained that the police measures reduced much of the fun element and increased the risk element too much.

The relationship between sport and aggression has been covered in some detail here. It is a complex social phenomenon which requires a synthesis of perspectives. Frustration combined with anger, opportunities and stimulus cues lead to aggression.

Solutions

To address the issue of violence in sport will require a concerted effort from all sections of society, working together to eradicate or reduce this fundamental problem. This will involve:

- sports performers
- officials
- clubs and organisations
- spectators
- media
- commercial bodies such as business sponsors.

Table 12.1 Effects of various drugs

Types of drugs used	Reasons for use	Side effects	Which sports
Anabolic steroids: artificially produced male hormones (e.g. nandrolone, testosterone)	• Promote muscle growth • Increase lean body weight • Ability to train harder with less fatigue • Repair body after stress • Increased aggression	• Liver damage • Heart disease • Acne • Excessive aggression For females: • Male features • Irregular periods	Power and explosive events (e.g. weightlifting, athletics, swimming)
Narcotic analgesics: painkillers (e.g. morphine, methadone)	• Reduce amount of pain • Mask injury • Increase pain limit	• Highly addictive • Increase initial injury • Breathing problems • Nausea and vomiting	All sports
Stimulants: stimulate body mentally and physically (e.g. amphetamine, ephedrine)	• Reduce tiredness • Increase alertness • Increase competitiveness • Increase aggression	• Rise in blood pressure • Rise in body temperature • Increased heartbeat • Loss of appetite • Addiction • Death	• Cycling • Boxing
Beta blockers: can be used medically (e.g. antenolol, propanolol)	• Steady nerves • Stop trembling	• Low blood pressure • Slow heart rate • Tiredness	• Shooting • Archery • Snooker • Diving
Diuretics: remove fluid from body (e.g. triameterine, bendrofluazide)	• Lose weight quickly • Increase rate of passing urine	• Dehydration • Faintness • Dizziness • Muscle cramps	• Horse racing (jockeys) • Boxing
Peptide hormones: naturally occurring (e.g. erythropoietin) /HCG analogues synthetic (e.g. EPO)	• Stimulate growth of naturally occurring steroids • Build muscle • Mend tissue • Increase oxygen transport	• Muscle wasting • Abnormal growth of hands and feet • EPO – increases red cells in blood • Clotting • Stroke	Similar to steroids
Blood doping: injection of blood to increase number of blood cells	Body more energy to work	• Allergic reactions • Hepatitis or AIDS • Overload circulatory system • Blood clots	• Running • Cycling • Marathons • Skiing

Possible solutions include:

- Players should display sportsmanship on the field; avoid inciting the crowd, e.g. by making gestures; act as role models; respect officials' decisions.
- Before and after games, players and club officials should not make inflammatory statements which could incite trouble.
- Responsible media reporting.
- Players/clubs/community should openly condemn acts of violence.
- Tighter security, including CCTV and controlled ticket sales.
- Heavier punishments and bans for offenders.
- Family enclosures.
- Segregating fans.
- Clubs forming links with the community.
- Community help working with the police to reduce trouble.
- Supporter education, like the fan coaching schemes in Germany, to raise awareness of the implications of/punishments for racism and hooliganism.
- Control of alcohol.

Drugs in sport

The history of drug abuse is as old as sport itself. Athletes in ancient Greece and Rome took substances to improve their performance. However, drug use in modern sport has become regular and systematised. Research shows that it is more than a peripheral problem, and operates at both amateur and professional levels, among male and female athletes, and across a wide variety of sports. Factors which led to an increase in the use of drugs include:

- advances in biology and medicine;
- the use of drugs in the Second World War;
- the development and availability of testosterone, steroids and growth hormones in the 1950s.

Weight trainers, in particular, demonstrated the possible results of using drugs, and other athletes who recognised their potential capitalised on this. Drugs allow athletes to control their bodies, enabling them to alter their bodily functions, although this can result in a *loss* of power in certain circumstances.

Since the mid 1980s, drug taking has become a very common part of top-class sport, in spite of the efforts of various national and international doping committees, and the establishment of the International Olympic Committee Medical Commission in 1967. Those who supply sportspeople with drugs are constantly trying to keep one step ahead of those working to keep sport free of drugs. One of the problematic areas is defining an illegal drug, and the effects that drugs can have on the performer and performance: what is artificial, natural, foreign, fair or abnormal?

The organisations responsible for each sport generally have to take control of the testing for drugs in their sport. This will occur at both national and international levels.

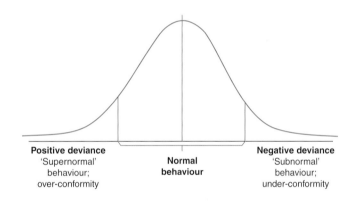

Figure 12.2 *A normal distribution approach to understanding deviance*
Source: J. Coakley (1993) *Sport in Society*, Mosby

Which drugs are used?

The International Amateur Federation Rule 144 on doping states that:

- doping is forbidden;
- doping is the use by or distribution to an athlete of certain substances which could have the effect of improving artificially the athlete's physical and/or mental condition, and so augmenting their athletic performance.

It lists over 80 individual drugs, classified under stimulants, narcotic analgesics and anabolic steroids, and states that chemically or pharmacologically related drugs are also forbidden. 'Ergogenic aids' refer to any substance that improves performance.

Why?

Athletes use drugs for various reasons including:

- for physical benefits, depending on the type of drug used, e.g. steroids to increase aggression and muscle bulk, diuretics reduce weight;
- to enable them to train harder and become the best
- the substantial rewards of fame and money, worth the perceived risks
- high expectations from coaches, spectators, peers and the media
- increasing accessibility
- usage has become 'institutionalised', with coaches and governing bodies either encouraging or turning a blind eye to it
- the perception that 'if you don't take it, you won't make it'.

Solutions

It is difficult to address the problem of drugs because:

- it is difficult to test for them, and masking agents and new drugs are developed;
- some drugs are also used for medical reasons;
- some governing bodies, coaches, countries and competitors support the practice
- widespread testing is expensive and has legal implications
- it is difficult to get access to athletes during training.

Possible strategies include:

- banning drug users from competition for life;
- promoting sportsmanship; education about moral and health aspects;
- random/stricter testing, with unrestricted access to athletes;
- investment in better testing techniques and in differentiating between medical need and performance enhancement;
- promoting positive role models and negatively portraying known drug users;
- national governing bodies may not always be the best people to be in charge of detecting and punishing athletes who take drugs;
- worldwide cooperation between countries and sports organisations so that rules are not complex or different.

Modern technological products

The human body seems to be able to reach ever higher levels of performance. What is helping athletes to improve so dramatically? Technology is undoubtedly the major influence, whether it is in the equipment and facilities, or sports science which assists with coaching and training methods. Athletes' performance is now measured in minute detail (e.g. timing in a 100m race), and technology such as Hawk-Eye can help officials in their decisions.

Equipment for sportspeople

New materials have contributed to amazing advances in sports. For example, Lycra in running suits, super-light, strong metals in bikes and tennis racquets, high-tech shoes and the use of fibre glass in cricket bats. Millions are spent every year developing better equipment for sportspeople. Some improvements are made for safety reasons. Better mats had to be developed in the 1950s as pole-vaulters cleared greater heights. These mats were used in the high jump as well, contributing to a change in the style of jumping, where athletes could safely jump head-first – the Fosbury flop technique used today.

Computers, advances in nutrition, weight-training machines, new playing surfaces, and many more technological advances have moved sport to a new level of play. A quick look around at the facilities available for Olympic athletes provides a striking example of what is now available.

New technology can bring about conflict between manufacturers and governing bodies, as manufacturers want to sell more and gain brand prestige through innovation, while regulations or adaptations of regulations seek to preserve the character of the game. Calloway Golf had its most successful golf club banned as it hit the ball too far, with the governing body reasoning that it did not want to change the courses or the nature of the game, and subsequently regulating against such equipment. Another example was the decision taken by the International Tennis Federation, after the ball size was changed to slow down play at Wimbledon. The manufacturer paid a substantial figure for this, but it received criticism from ex-player and commentator John McEnroe, and the manufacturer was later informed by the Federation that the ball was being phased out.

Assistance for officials

Cameras have assisted umpires and referees in making tough decisions. The photo finish was first used for track events at the 1932 Olympics. This eliminated any doubt as to the winner in crucially close events.

At Sport and Technology: The Conference 2007, Kevin Roberts, Editorial Director of SportBusiness International, commented that 'technology is available, technology is used in sports to reinforce or disprove the views of the human officials; however, without referees or umpires, there is no sport.'

Rugby

Stuart Cummings of the Rugby Football League believes that technology has had a positive influence on the game. The sport has been viewed as one of the 'pioneers' in applying technology. Cummings outlined that when the video referee was introduced in 1996, the sport was the first invasion game to do this. The move brought scepticism from people who thought it would highlight errors, but as Cummings comments:

> During my time as a referee, refereeing at an international level, I always enjoyed the game better from my point of view when the video referee was in place. I always felt confident in my own decisions and that the video screen would prove me right. Technology is great to have and it's important that we are seen to have the right outcomes.

Cummings went on to refer to the four-way open microphone system (two touch judges, one on-field referee and one video referee), which can have problems, citing an instance in Cardiff in 2007, when the video referee came and gave a call

in live play, but it generally works well, for example for offside judgements, which has cleaned up an area of the pitch for the referee. 'I don't personally see it as conflicting, I see the referee using technology to enhance his decision making.'

Instant replay, introduced in the 1980s, has also affected how sports are played – when decisions get tough, it acts as an impartial referee.

Cricket

Many have questioned whether cricket needs technology for one of the most complex decisions that takes place, the LBW (leg before wicket). Cricket embraces technology, and the sport's governing body has spent a great deal of money trying to find the best technology to use, especially at the highest level. It is generally believed that certain conditions concerning technology should be met:

1 The game is played and officiated by humans, therefore technology should not take away any of the theatre of the game.
2 Technology must not change the way the game is played; for example, if Hawk-Eye were to be introduced, five-day test matches would become three-day matches.
3 Technology needs to have a high percentage of accuracy (98–99 per cent).

Four international trials have been carried out to date: in 2002 in the Champions Trophy in Sri Lanka (umpire able to consult with television officials); in 2004 in England (a stump microphone and earpieces for umpires); in 2005 in the Super Series in Australia (umpire could consult television officials regarding any decision); and a trial in England, coming to an end at the time of writing (2007) (players have the opportunity to appeal a decision). In summary, the trials concluded that in some aspects the sport is not ready to embrace the technology. Technical problems were evident (e.g. time delays); and the most interesting result from the recent trial in England is that players did not actually want this technology (being able to appeal).

For line decisions, the technology is excellent, providing there are enough cameras; for thin edges it is not available; for clean catches it does not help; and for LBW decisions, while some aspects are based on fact, the prediction is an opinion.

Football

Interestingly, a lot of decisions are not as simple as yes or no; they are often open to interpretation. Technology used in football, as determined by the International Football Association Board (IFAB), only allows the use of goal-line technology, as 100 per cent accuracy is required. At the Sport and Technology Conference in 2007, Martin Bland (a representative of ProZone Sports, an organisation which provides data and information to assist referees) cited the example of Hawk-Eye in football, which has recently been tested (at Reading FC) and proved to be very accurate, boasting shots at 300 frames per second, three cameras around the goal and a three-second decision turnaround.

ProZone is another piece of technology, which tracks players and referees, not interfering with the decision making because the information is fed back post-match. Bland pointed out that 'it is based on training and developing excellence'.

Technology used in professional football is minimal. Communications systems are used, but the fourth official cannot give a decision; they are responsible for monitoring the technical area, as established by IFAB regulation.

Technology for engaging audiences

The crowd at Wimbledon embraced Hawk-Eye when it was introduced, suggesting that this is a good example of adding to the fans' experience. Similar examples are the yellow first and 10 line in American football, and K-Zone, which charts pitches in baseball. There is a player-tracking system in use in the USA which uses virtual/visual recognition rather than chips (a players' association issue in the USA), and a company called PVI is working on a 360-degree camera array (SpinCam – composed of 100 cameras) to break down play.

Sponsorship through technology

New technologies have brought about a proliferation of means by which to reach and interact with an audience. This creates the potential for a new approach to sponsorship rights, carving up sponsorship opportunities into distinct, platform-based rights, or selling bundles of rights in a comprehensive sponsorship package.

The traditional objectives for sports sponsorship continue to hold true: for sponsors, to enhance brand profile, equity and value; and for rights holders, to generate revenue. However, the traditional model of event sponsorship contracts, including priority rights to acquire broadcast sponsorship and commercial airtime around television coverage of an event, may not be the best way to achieve these objectives in the future.

The technology and consumption trends described above are having two key impacts on the traditional sports sponsorship model:

1   The fragmentation of media – people are spending more time online, watching clips on mobiles and choosing from a hundred TV channels – means that the traditional 'interruption' model of TV advertising is being undermined. This also offers faster and easier global dissemination.
2   With fragmentation comes the need to engage with people. Successful marketing campaigns illustrate this trend – they engage with users to enhance their experience, rather than just bombarding them with branding and hoping it sinks in.

These trends are arguably making sponsorship an increasingly more attractive and valuable marketing medium, and we are already witnessing the interesting consequences for sports sponsorship contracts.

The Flora London Marathon is the largest annual fundraising event in the world, raising over £41.5 million for deserving causes in 2006. As part of the pre-race registration procedure, each of the 35,000 runners now receives their own electronic identification chip. This small silicon chip, with its passive transponder, is attached to the runner's shoelaces and emits a signal each time the runner passes over the 'reader mats', strategically placed at 5km intervals. The chips give an accurate time and position on the progress of all entrants, and the marathon's official results are based on the elapsed time of each runner between crossing the mats at the start and finish lines. The signals emitted by the chip are managed by an integrated, computerised system, designed and developed over seven years by Marathon IT, the London Marathon's independent information technology services provider. The processed data, including analytical graphics, is also used to feed

BBC TV Sport, for immediate on-screen display to millions of viewers worldwide. The same information is routed to the marathon's command post and press centre, where it is disseminated to the world's sports media.

What do the fans think?

The Orange Technology in Football Survey, carried out by the Football Fans Census, spoke to 3,072 soccer fans on the subject of technology between 15 and 22 March 2006. The survey was conducted online and supporters of 215 teams were represented, including all clubs in the Premiership, Football League and Scottish Premier League, with 39 per cent of respondents holding season tickets. The survey respondents were predominantly male (85 per cent), reflecting the male bias among football supporters in the UK and globally.

With England's 1966 FIFA World Cup triumph famously decided by a crucial goal-line decision that is still being debated 40 years on, the Orange survey has revealed that more than three-quarters of football fans would like to see more technology brought into the game to avoid such issues in the future. Sir Geoff Hurst's second goal in that World Cup final was allowed to stand, even though it was unclear whether the whole of the ball had crossed the line.

The survey results revealed that 82 per cent of soccer fans felt that new technology, such as goal-line cameras, TV match officials and smart officials, would considerably improve their enjoyment of the game. With inconclusive goal-line decisions still prevalent in the game today (including the controversy in the 2006 Champions League semi-final between Chelsea and Liverpool), 57 per cent of fans surveyed were adamant that goal-line technology was the most important technological

advancement that was needed in soccer. Chelsea and England player Frank Lampard commented:

> Obviously everyone remembers the famous Sir Geoff Hurst goal from 1966, which luckily went in our favour and helped us win the World Cup! But of course it's still no easier today to work out if a ball has crossed the line, as was shown in our game against Liverpool last year in the Champions League.

Fans are also positive about introducing some of the technological advancements brought into rugby in recent years. Indeed, 68 per cent would welcome soccer adopting the TV match officials that are used successfully in Six Nations Rugby, while 64 per cent admitted that referees' comments being heard by the viewer or listener is something that would improve their enjoyment of the game.

Darrell McLennan Fordyce, head of sports and games at Orange, commented: 'Technology in football is now a huge national debate, and the results from this survey show that fans want it to have a more prominent role in deciding disputed decisions. Orange is a keen supporter of any technological advancements that help to enhance the great game.'

According to the survey results, 30 per cent of soccer fans were interested in having access to player performance data (such as which players are doing the most running, passing, and so on, during a match) on their mobile phones. The appetite for this data is strongly influenced by age: teenagers – the demographic most familiar with mobile technology – are generally positive about the idea; other age groups are generally negative, increasingly so as they get older.

Radio frequency identification (RFID)

The 2006 FIFA World Cup saw the large-scale use of RFID technology in tickets for the first time, with all 2.9 million tickets embedded with an RFID tag. World Cup organisers expected the use of RFID to provide greater security at entry gates and deter the counterfeiting of tickets which has plagued past events.

The technology offers a high degree of security, with organisers claiming that the tickets would not contain personal data, but a number that identifies each ticket holder. However, ticket purchasers had to submit various personal details on the ticket registration forms, which then appeared on the ticket, and the RFID tag had the potential to make the ticket holder visible to tracking devices beyond the turnstile. The level of data being captured and the potential for tracking people raised concerns in some quarters that this is a step towards a Big Brother society or a football ID card scheme.

Overall, however, 59 per cent of fans felt that the improved security and ticketing arrangements outweighed the concerns about personal liberty. However, for a sizeable minority (41 per cent), the concerns the technology raises about personal liberty were significant.

IN CONTEXT

Hawk-Eye's principal application has been to enhance television production by using tracking data to resolve controversial decisions, help explain the game and get the viewer closer to the action. Since 2003, Hawk-Eye has been used at almost all major cricket and tennis events worldwide.

Figure 12.3 Pistorius has been put through his paces under lab conditions and found to have contravened IAAF rules on technical aids when running against able-bodies athletes.

Technology and the athlete

In 2007, Oscar Pistorius agreed to work with athletics authorities to try to discover if his artificial legs give him an unfair advantage when running against able-bodied runners. The Paralympic champion had both legs amputated below the knee as a child and now runs on carbon fibre blades. The International Amateur Athletics Federation (IAFF) paid for research to look at what, if any, advantage Pistorius might have as a result of using these blades. The findings of the research reported that Pistorius uses 25% *less* energy than an able-bodied runner to run at the same speed, and the IAAF ruled that he therefore contravened rules on technical aids. Pistorius is appealing against this decision.

Sport analysis

The use of videotaping in training has helped athletes to improve greatly. Being able to watch themselves perform, athletes now know exactly what they are doing right and wrong. Watching their own performance improve can also provide motivation to carry on working harder.

Figure 12.4 Motion capture aids sport performance, allowing detailed analysis by scientists, coaches and performers

Motion capture is ideal for a wide range of sports applications in research, rehabilitation, physical education and practice. Physical limitations and movement optimisation are of great interest to athletes, coaches, researchers and doctors. Motion capture allows us to learn more about injury mechanisms and prevention. It can also be used to improve a player's technique, for better results in various sports applications.

Sports technology as a career

The sports technology university programme is intended for students wishing to pursue a career in the sports-related industry, with an emphasis on technology, involving the design and development of sports equipment and products, and technological developments in the improvement and measurement of sporting performance. The programme recognises the growth of technology in the sports industries, and the need for technologists to support the development of new equipment and products, as well as improving existing products and methods of measuring performance.

A topic on golf operations within the programme reflects the sophisticated nature of golf as a sport, and provides students with the skills and abilities to operate in a commercial sporting environment. They may be interested in managing golf operations, and/or enhancing golf performance, using technology to maximise the potential of amateurs and professionals alike.

One university offering such a programme has its own sports centre and an extensive sports arena nearby. A new sports biomechanics laboratory has been opened, and facilities include hi-tech 3D motion analysis systems and force platform equipment.

Activity 2

Outline the advantages and disadvantages of technology to:

- the performer;
- the sport;
- the spectator.

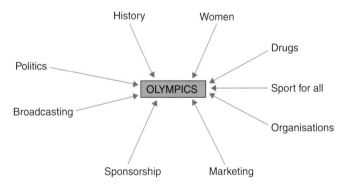

Figure 12.5 What is involved in the Olympic Games?

Modern Olympic Games

Baron Pierre de Coubertin established the modern Olympic Games in 1896, following a visit to England, where he was impressed with the amateur code of public school team games and of athleticism. He also became aware in 1890 of the

Table 12.2 Games comparison 1896/1996

	Athens	**Atlanta**
Days	5	17
Sports	9	26
Events	32	271
Countries	13	200
Athletes	311	10,500
Tickets available	60,000	11 million

Much Wenlock Olympic Games held in Shropshire. He was worried about the poor physical health of his own people and their lack of national pride. He revived the ancient Olympic Games of Greece based on these ideals, hoping to regenerate a sense of French nationalism, along with a romantic view of furthering international understanding.

Coubertin convened a conference in Paris in 1894 to determine the nature of the competition he envisaged:

- eligibility standards of participation;
- an administrative body (the International Olympic Committee – IOC) to oversee the running of the event;
- the first Games to be awarded to Athens for 1896.

Subsequent Games are shown in Table 12.3.

Table 12.3 Modern Olympic Games

Summer Olympic Games	**Winter Olympic Games**
1896 Athens (Greece)	
1900 Paris (France)	
1904 St Louis (USA)	
1908 London (Great Britain)	
1912 Stockholm (Sweden)	
1916 Berlin (not celebrated)	
1920 Antwerp (Belgium)	
1924 Paris (France)	**1924** Chamonix (France)
1928 Amsterdam (Holland)	**1928** St Moritz (Switzerland)
1932 Los Angeles (USA)	**1932** Lake Placid (USA)
1936 Berlin (Germany)	**1936** Garmisch-Partenkirchen (Germany)
1940 Tokyo/Helsinki (not celebrated)	**1940** (not celebrated)
1944 London (not celebrated)	**1944** (not celebrated)
1948 London (Great Britain)	**1948** St Moritz (Switzerland)
1952 Helsinki (Finland)	**1952** Oslo (Norway)
1956 Melbourne (Australia)	**1956** Cortina D'Ampezzo (Italy)
1960 Rome (Italy)	**1960** Squaw Valley (USA)
1964 Tokyo (Japan)	**1964** Innsbruck (Austria)
1968 Mexico City (Mexico)	**1968** Grenoble (France)
1972 Munich (Germany)	**1972** Sapporo (Japan)
1976 Montreal (Canada)	**1976** Innsbruck (Austria)

Continued

Table 12.3 *Continued*

Summer Olympic Games	Winter Olympic Games
1980 Moscow (Soviet Union)	**1980** Lake Placid (USA)
1984 Los Angeles (USA)	**1984** Sarajevo (Yugoslavia)
1988 Seoul (Korea)	**1988** Calgary (Canada)
1992 Barcelona (Spain)	**1992** Albertville (France)
1996 Atlanta (USA)	**1994** Lillehammer (Norway)
2000 Sydney (Australia)	**1998** Nagano (Japan)
2004 Athens (Greece)	**2002** Salt Lake City (USA)
2008 Beijing (China)	**2006** Turin (Italy)
2010 London (Great Britain)	**2010** Vancouver (Canada)
	2014 Sochi (Russian Federation)

Symbols of the Olympic Games

Flag

By 1914, the symbol of the IOC had emerged – the famous five interconnecting rings, all in different colours, displayed on a white background. The rings represent the five continents involved in the Olympic Games – Europe, Asia, Oceania, Africa and the Americas.

Motto

The Olympic motto is *Citius, altius, fortius*, which means 'swifter, higher, stronger'. The following message also appears on the scoreboard at every Olympic Games:

> The most important thing in the Olympic Games is not to win but to take part, just as the most important thing in life is not the triumph but the struggle. The essential thing is not to have conquered but to have fought well.

Goals

The six goals of the Olympic movement are based on Coubertin's original motivations that the Games were to enhance human development, and can be referred to as 'Olympism':

> A philosophy of life, exalting and combining in a balanced whole the quality of body, will and mind.

Blending sport, culture and education, Olympism seeks to create a way of life based on the joy found in effort, the educational value of good example and respect for the universal fundamental ethical principles.

The six goals can be summarised as follows:

- personal excellence;
- sport as education;
- cultural exchange;
- mass participation;
- fair play;
- international understanding.

Olympic flame

This has its traditions in the flame of the ancient Games, which was lit at the altar of Zeus. The tradition of the torch relay from Olympia to the host city began in Berlin in 1936.

Olympic oath

The competitors vow:

> In the name of all the competitors I promise that we shall take part in these Olympic Games respecting and abiding by the rules which govern them in the true spirit of sportsmanship.

Peace

Pigeons or doves were used as a symbol of peace at the first Games in 1896.

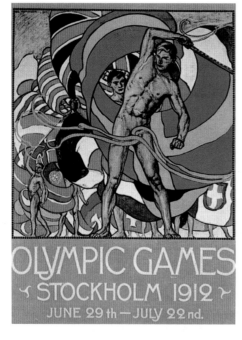

Figure 12.6 Collection of early Olympic programmes, 1912–1964

Olympic Charter

This charter contains the principles, rules and by-laws adopted by the IOC. It governs the organisation and operation of the Olympic movement and lays down the conditions to be observed during the Games. The main purpose is to:

- contribute to building a peaceful and better world;
- educate youth through sport;
- enter into sport without discrimination;
- observe the Olympic spirit of friendship, solidarity and fair play.

Political pressures

The Games have been affected by wider political situations and are often remembered as much for the political events surrounding them as for the athletic feats. One of the key reasons for this is that each set of Games provides a focus for the country hosting the event. Their political systems are given prominent media coverage and it has sometimes been the case that governments have used this to promote their political message.

At the 1936 Olympics in Berlin, Adolf Hitler used the opportunity to promote the values of the Third Reich on the world stage. The German authorities offered considerable support to the athletes, who were to show the superiority of the Aryan race. Jesse Owens, a black American, upset this plan when he won four gold medals, which were withheld by Hitler. As a consequence of war and propaganda, the Games would not be held again until 1948.

Equally, when opponents to the government of the host country wish to make a political protest, they have a prime opportunity to do so, with the eyes of the world watching them. The 1968 Games in Mexico witnessed two black Americans being sent home as a result of their 'black power' salute. This was a protest about discrimination in the

United States. Tommie Smith said, 'If I win I am an American not a Black American. But if I did something bad they would say "Negro".'

The result of political opposition often takes the form of a boycott, when countries refuse to participate in order to deliver a political message – usually a rejection of a political regime. The 1956 Olympics, which were held in Melbourne, Australia, saw the withdrawal of China due to the entry of Taiwan, an enemy of communism. It was not until 1984 that both countries competed at the same time. The Soviet Union boycott of the 1984 Games in Los Angeles had a huge effect on the event. The reasons for the boycott were complex, but involved the following:

- a reaction to the American boycott of the Moscow Olympics in 1980;
- fear of defection of their own athletes to the West;

Activity 3

Read the following extract from George Orwell's 'The Sporting Spirit', taken from *Shooting an Elephant,* which gives a personal account of what he considers to be the link between sport and politics, and answer the questions below.

> I am always amazed when I hear people saying that sport creates goodwill between the nations and that if only the common peoples of the world could meet one another at football or cricket, they would have no inclination to meet on the battlefield.
>
> Nearly all the sports practised nowadays are competitive. You play to win and the game has little meaning unless you do your utmost to win. On the village green, where you pick up sides and no feeling of local patriotism is involved, it is possible to play simply for the fun and exercise, but as soon as the question of prestige arises, as soon as you feel that you or some larger unit will be disgraced if you lose, the more savage instincts are aroused. Anyone who has played even in a school football match knows this. At the international level, sport is quite frankly mimic warfare. But the significant thing is not the behaviour of the players but the attitude of the spectators, of the nations who work themselves into furies over these absurd contests and seriously believe at any rate for short periods – that running, jumping and kicking a ball are tests of national virtue.
>
> As soon as strong feelings of rivalry are aroused, the notion of playing the game according to the rules always vanishes. People want to see one side on top and the other side humiliated, and they forget that victory gained through cheating or through the intervention of the crowd is meaningless. Even when the spectators don't intervene physically, they try to influence the game by cheering their own side and rattling opposing players with boos and insults. Serious sport has nothing to do with fair play. It is bound up with hatred, jealousy, beastfulness, disregard of all the rules and sadistic pleasure in witnessing violence; in other words it is war minus the shooting.

1 What is the author's opinion of competition?
2 How does the author make a distinction between two types of physical activity?
3 What elements of conflict, cohesion and expectancy are given in the passage?
4 What vocabulary does the author use to reinforce the view that modern sport is merely 'mimic warfare'?

Table 12.4 Olympics and politics

Year	Venue	Political activity and affected countries
1936	Berlin	Germany used Games for Nazi propaganda Hitler's Aryan race theory discredited – Jesse Owens, a black athlete, won four gold medals
1956	Melbourne	Soviet Union invaded Hungary; Spain and Holland withdrew in protest China withdrew because of Taiwan's inclusion Egypt and Lebanon did not compete because they were fighting for the Suez Canal
1964	Tokyo	South Africa's invitation cancelled in 1963 Indonesia and North Korea not allowed to compete because they had taken part in an international tournament considered unsatisfactory by the IOC
1968	Mexico City	South Africa's invitation withdrawn because of threatened boycott by other countries, over apartheid 2,001 Mexicans killed and many more injured by army during demonstration against use of government money for the Games (widespread poverty in the country) Black American athletes gave clenched fist salute, against treatment of Black Americans in the USA
1972	Munich	Rhodesia's invitation withdrawn because of apartheid – other countries threatened to boycott if Rhodesia competed Israeli athletes and officials assassinated by Palestinian terrorists
1976	Montreal	30 nations in total did not attend African nations boycotted Games because New Zealand rugby team had toured South Africa French Canadians were angered that the Queen was to perform the opening ceremony Taiwan withdrew Several competitors banned for using anabolic steroids Two Romanians and one Soviet athlete asked for political asylum in Canada
1980	Moscow	Soviet Union had invaded Afghanistan and because of the Soviets' record on human rights and their refusal to withdraw troops, 52 nations boycotted the Games, led by the USA
1984	Los Angeles	Soviet Union withdrew, along with many Eastern European countries, Cuba and others; some felt this was in retaliation for 1980, but official reason given was over 'concern for the safety of their teams' It was felt that the organisers had violated the Olympic Charter
1992	Barcelona	South Africa returned to Olympic competition after the abolition of apartheid Germany competed as one nation Soviet Union had ceased to exist and the individual countries competed in their own right
2000	Sydney	Controversy over IOC bribery and corruption led to changes in the bidding procedures

- the ability of the men's track and field team;
- the ideological problem of being part of successful, capitalist Games.

Activity 4

Table 12.4 charts some of the political situations that have surrounded some of the Olympic Games. Select one of those listed and research what happened in more detail.

The British Olympic Association

www.olympics.org.uk

The International Olympic Committee (IOC) requires that each country organise a National Olympic Committee (NOC). These bodies (approximately 200) are responsible for the well-being of their athletes and for upholding the fundamental principles of Olympism at a national level. Each committee provides training centres and funding to ensure their athletes are able to compete under conditions comparable to those of athletes from other nations. Only an NOC is able to select and send teams and competitors to participate at the Olympic Games. They also supervise the preliminary selection of potential city bids.

The British Olympic Association (BOA) is the NOC for the UK.

Function

The function of the BOA is to:

- encourage interest in the Olympic Games through undertakings such as liaison with schools;
- foster the ideals of the Olympic movement;
- organise and coordinate British participation – the BOA needs to organise the participation of 500 athletes and officials, including all travel arrangements, equipment and horses;
- assist the governing bodies of sport in preparation for their competitions;
- advise on public relations with the press (a relatively recent function);
- provide a forum for consultation among governing bodies;
- organise an Olympic Day in the UK;
- raise funds through the British Olympic

Appeal, mainly from private sources, business sponsors and the general public.

You have probably already noted the absence of a government grant. This is the tradition and uniqueness of the BOA: to be independent of government. Most NOCs receive government funding. Preparations for the 2004 Olympic Games in Athens began early in order to raise the required £6 million.

The BOA has developed a new marketing strategy for its national sponsors through the creation of the British Olympic Gold Club. This Club includes total exclusivity to use the BOA logo in a particular product category in the lead up to and during the Olympic Games. There is a variety of corporate hospitality opportunities, appearances by Olympic medallists, licensing opportunities and regular sponsor workshops.

Since 1988, the BOA has also had to adapt to changes (as have the other organisations already mentioned), and since 1992 it has added the following to its list of duties:

- advice on training, nutrition and sports psychology for Olympic coaches;
- medical and careers advice for athletes;
- sponsoring medical research into fitness and athletic injuries.

The British Olympic Medical Centre at Northwick Park has been restructured, and athletes now have access to all the medical support they require for an Olympic Games. A sport-specific strategy was developed to help athletes cope with the problems of jet lag, acclimatisation and dehydration. The BOA is committed to giving Britain's sporting talent the best chance of achieving international success at the highest level, as illustrated by the superb warm weather training facility that has been set up and is run by the Orlando Regional Health system, using the Disney Wide World of Sport facilities.

Team GB

Team GB represents the whole Olympic team – past, present and future. This is to provide a more positive and familiar association for the public, as BOA is mainly an administrative body. The aim is to heighten awareness of all athletes and of the Olympic movement in the UK.

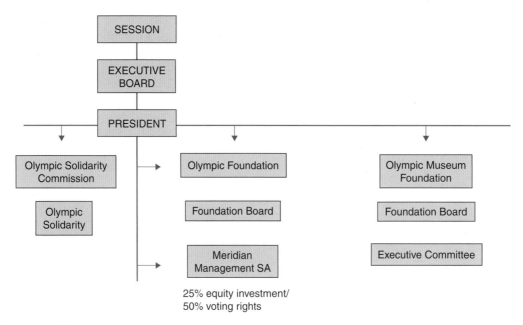

Figure 12.7 *Structure of the International Olympic Committee*

International Olympic Committee

www.olympic.org/ioc

The IOC is the umbrella organisation of the Olympic Movement, whose primary responsibility is the regular staging of the summer and winter Games.

The Executive Board is headed by the IOC President, and also has four Vice Presidents and six additional members. All the members of the Executive Board are elected by the Session, by secret ballot, by a majority vote.

The role of the Executive Board is to:

- observe the Olympic Charter;
- administer the IOC;
- attend to all internal affairs of the organisation;
- manage the finances;
- inform the Session of any rule changes or by-laws;
- recommend suitable persons for election to the IOC;
- establish agendas for the Session;
- appoint the Director General and Secretary General.

Commercial pressures

Today, sport organisations allied with national governments mount elaborate plans to win the approval of the IOC to host the Olympic Games. They do this for a variety of reasons:

- civic and national pride;
- political gain;
- economic benefits.

City bids

The selection of the host city is vitally important, as the success of the Games can often be dependent on the site chosen. Each candidate city must demonstrate to the IOC that its bid to stage the greatest multidisciplinary event in the world has the support of its people and its political authorities. Many factors may play a part, and these are not necessarily purely financial or technical.

A manual for bidding cities was made available for the 2000 bid. It contained evaluation criteria which the candidate cities have to fulfil. The Evaluation Commission is responsible for preparing a complete evaluation report after visiting each city. The procedure now has two phases, owing to the large number of bids:

- Phase I – Selection of the finalists on the basis of the Evaluation Commission report.
- Phase II – Members of the IOC are given the opportunity to visit the finalist cities before voting.

Voting takes place by secret ballot. Each member is allowed to vote for only one city. After each round, if no one city has an absolute majority, the city with the fewest votes is eliminated. Successive rounds are held until one city achieves a majority.

Following allegations of misconduct during the Salt Lake City bid for the Winter Olympics in 2002, suggestions for a selection college were put in place for Turin 2006. This selection college would choose two finalist cities from among the six finalists. The selection of the host city took place immediately afterwards, on the same day. The IOC president was unable to vote for the host city on this occasion.

There are some drawbacks to hosting the Olympics:

- Cost – some cities have faced enormous debts for many years afterwards. The projected costs for the London Games seem to be spiralling since the original estimate and much of the money will not actually come from the government but from the lottery and commercial sponsorship, which is unpredictable.
- The money could be spent on more worthy causes such as health and education; using lottery money takes it from other 'good causes' and many charities may miss out.
- The predicted economic boost from the Games, because of an increase in tourism, may be limited, as sport fans tend to be focussed on the event itself rather than generating money for more general tourist attractions.
- Security – the host city lays itself open to terrorism as it provides a world stage where various groups could maximise the publicity for their cause.
- The facilities tend to be concentrated in one area, making them accessible to only a fraction of the population, with elite athletes likely to make most use of them.

Olympic marketing

Marketing has become an increasingly important issue for all of us within the Olympic Movement. The revenues derived from television, sponsorship and general fundraising help to provide the movement with its financial independence. However, in developing these programmes we must always remember that it is sport that must control its destiny, not commercial interests. Every act of support for the Olympic Movement promotes peace, friendship and solidarity throughout the world. (Juan Antonio Samaranch, IOC President 1980–2001)

It has always been up to the Organising Committee of the Olympic Games (OCOG) to raise the necessary funds. In 1896 this occurred via ticket sales, commemorative medals, programme advertising and private donations. Today it is achieved mainly through the sale of TV rights, sponsorship, licensing, ticket sales, coins and stamps. An estimated US$3.5 billion is believed to have been generated for the Olympic quadrennium 1997–2000.

The IOC retains 7–10 per cent of revenues, with the remainder going to the Organising Committees, the International Sport Federations (ISF) and National Olympic Committees (NOC). Included in these are the International Paralympic Committee and the Paralympic Organising Committee.

Objectives of Olympic marketing

Under the presidency of Samaranch, the IOC established the following objectives via a strategic marketing plan implemented by the IOC's marketing department:

- to ensure the financial stability of the Games;
- to promote continuity of marketing across each Olympic Games;
- to provide equity of revenue distribution between the OCOGs, the NOCs and the International Federations, and provide support for the emerging nations;
- to provide free air transmission across the world;
- to protect the Olympic ideals by safeguarding against unnecessary commercialisation;
- to attract the support of marketing partners to promote Olympism and Olympic ideals.

Sponsorship of the Olympic Games

IN CONTEXT

The International Olympic Committee (IOC) has expanded its investments to include 200 nations, and has made the Olympic Games one of the biggest media events in the world. Sponsorship for the Games operates on a global basis. The Olympic Programme (TOP) involves approximately 44 companies, including Coca-Cola, Adidas and Kodak (Adidas actually brought the idea to the IOC). Sponsorship is vital, as the staging of the event is enormously expensive – a fact that was well recognised after the 1976 Games in Montreal almost went bankrupt. Taxpayers were unwilling to shoulder the burden of cost, while television companies were willing to pay large sums to transmit. Without international coverage (167 countries), the sponsors would not be willing to invest so much, and events might not be able to take place.

The Los Angeles Games marked a turning point, whereby the IOC began to modernise its marketing policies through The Olympic Programme (TOP). However, some problems were apparent. The revenue gained from the 1984 Games came almost exclusively from television rights to the United States, which could cause the IOC to be vulnerable. In addition, sponsors who sold the worldwide rights found that some individual NOCs required them to be bought separately. This led to Levi handing back the rights. Samaranch wished to find alternative sources of funding and have more authority in television negotiations.

TOP allowed exclusive rights to a few selected international companies, paying more than the previous 300 companies had done. In turn, they benefited from linking their products with the Olympic themes of excellence, participation and fair play. It was to prove a valuable symbiotic relationship. Olympic revenue increased dramatically, while dependence on US television rights was reduced.

The Olympic Programme had five phases:

- TOP I: 1985–1988;
- TOP II: 1989–1992;
- TOP III: 1993–1996;
- TOP IV: 1997–2000;
- TOP V: 2001–2004.

The Olympic Games remain, with the Wimbledon Tennis Championships, the only major sporting event without stadium advertising. Many would feel this justifies the claim that commercialism is being controlled. However, it is clearly a marketing judgement as well, since permitting stadium advertising would cause a drop in revenue from both television and sponsors, as there would be a loss of exclusivity.

In 1984, the following sums were paid for the right to use the Olympic rings in advertising and promotion outside the arena:

- Coca-Cola: $30 million;
- Visa International and Mars: $22 million each;
- Eastman Kodak: $21 million.

It costs two or three times as much for such companies to promote themselves through advertising, staff incentive schemes, hospitality programmes, and so on. However, many feel they

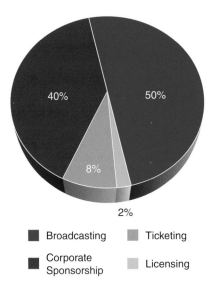

Figure 12.8a Where does the money come from?

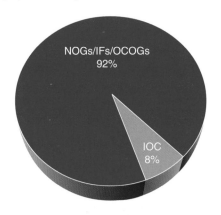

Figure 12.8b Where does the money go to?
Source: International Olympic Committee

| Coco-Cola | John Hancock | Kodak | McDonald's | Panasonic |
| SAMSUNG | Schlumberger | Sports Illustrated | Swatch | VISA | Xerox |

Figure 12.9 The top partners for the Athens 2004 Olympic Games

simply cannot afford not to be involved with the most prestigious sporting event in the world. Market research has also shown that consumers show a decided preference for products displaying the Olympic symbol. It is held in equal esteem with such humanitarian brands as the Red Cross and UNICEF.

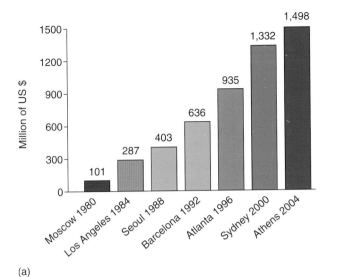

(a)

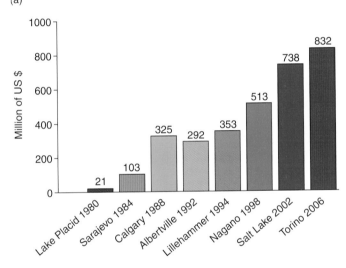

(b)

Figure 12.10 Olympic broadcast revenue charts (a) Olympic Games (b) Olympic Winter Games

The ethics of commercialism are always being addressed, but it is doubtful if ethics would override serious marketing objectives. The one benefit of commercialisation is the opportunity for the Olympic Solidarity fund (see below) to assist underfunded NOCs.

Licensing to sell memorabilia existed even at the time of the 1896 Games. However, it was not until the Lillehammer Winter Games in 1994 that more quality-controlled products were developed.

Broadcasting

The influence of television developed as the twentieth century advanced. Major sporting events could not continue to exist in their current

format without it. It was in Tokyo that the first satellite relay of the Games took place, incorporating stereo sound from all venues. It was the inability of the IOC to attract enough advertising for both the Summer and Winter Games that resulted in the decision in 1986 to hold the two Games alternately every two years. The hope was to improve marketing prospects.

The fundamental IOC policy is outlined in the Olympic Charter, to ensure maximum presentation of the Games to the widest possible global audience, free of charge. TV rights are therefore sold only to companies who can broadcast coverage throughout their respective countries or territories. This policy is set for the 2008 Games. TV rights continue to account for just under 45 per cent of Olympic revenue.

Olympic Solidarity

Established in 1961, Olympic Solidarity is the body responsible for managing and administering the share of the television rights of the Olympic Games that is allocated to the NOCs. This was made possible following the Los Angeles Games in 1984, when the Olympic Solidarity budgets were established on a quadrennial plan, allowing fixed annual assistance to the NOCs. Since the first cycle there has been an increase of 430 per cent.

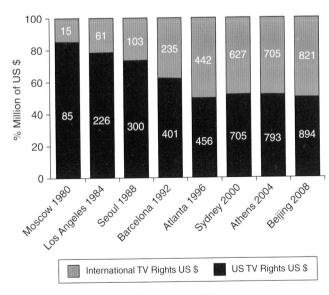

Figure 12.11 Olympic TV rights (US$)

The basic ideas on which it is based are those of generosity, understanding and international cooperation, cultural exchanges, the development of sport and its educational aspects, and the promotion of a society concerned with human dignity and peace. Specific programmes exist for the most disadvantaged NOCs.

The specific aim of Olympic Solidarity is 'to organise aid to NOCs recognised by the IOC, in particular those which have the greatest need of it. This aid takes the form of programmes elaborated jointly by the IOC and the NOCs, with the technical assistance of the IFs if necessary'.

Future of the Olympic Games

Balance is needed to ensure the future of the Olympic movement:

- Commerce must be balanced by philanthropy.
- There must be pageantry to help uphold the traditions.
- Every effort must be made to get most of the world's great male and female athletes to the Olympic stadiums.
- The size of the Games needs to be controlled.
- The wealth they generate needs to be distributed back into the Games and towards worthy initiatives.
- Cultural differences must be recognised.
- There must be an emphasis on belief in the philosophy of 'Olympism' – that there is joy, and educational and ethical value in sporting effort.

London Olympic Games 2012

On 6 July 2005 the International Olympic Committee announced that London was to host the 2012 Olympic and Paralympic Games. The Games will bring more than 28 days of sporting activities to London in the summer of 2012, and aims to provide a lasting legacy for future generations.

It is hoped that the Games will help London's long-term plans for economic growth and social regeneration. Creation of the Olympic Park will involve restoring large tracts of land in east London, with new green spaces and revived wetlands. The Olympic Village is envisaged as a desirable and socially diverse new residential area, providing 3,600 new homes in a community transformed by the Games. The Games will create opportunities for businesses too, creating

thousands of new jobs in diverse sectors, including construction, hospitality, media and environmental services.

Great sporting facilities, including swimming pools, a velodrome and hockey facilities will allow community use following the event, and it is hoped that the Games will inspire a new generation to greater sporting activity and achievement, and help to foster a healthy and active nation. Though the Games will be held in London, other regions are also hoping to benefit.

The Mayor of London's vision is for London to become an exemplary, sustainable world city, based on the three balanced and interlocking elements of:

1 strong and diverse economic growth;
2 social inclusivity to allow all Londoners to share in London's future success;
3 fundamental improvements in environmental management and use of resources.

> ### Key term
>
> **Sustainable development:** This is about ensuring a better quality of life for everyone, now and for generations to come. A widely used international definition is 'development which meets the needs of the present without compromising the ability of future generations to meet their own needs' (*The Brundtland Report*, 1987).

The 2012 Olympic Games and transport

London plans to be a connected and convenient host city for the Olympic and Paralympic Games, with:

- 80 per cent of athletes within 20 minutes of their events;
- five airports, including Heathrow – the best-connected airport in the world;
- 10 railway lines, capable of carrying 240,000 people to the Olympic Park every hour;
- 240km of dedicated Olympic lanes on the road network.

London is used to coping with large numbers of people on the move: 20 million journeys are made on London's transport system every day. The good news for Londoners is that massive improvements will be made to the transport system, making it more efficient and reliable.

IN CONTEXT

The action plan developed for Essex is divided into two main sections:

1 Cross-cutting themes;

2 Action areas.

Table 12.5 Action plan for Essex

Cross-cutting themes	Action areas
• Young people • Equity/inclusion • Sustainability • Friendships and cooperation • Inspiration/aspiration • Entrepreneurship and innovation • Image of Essex	• Supporting volunteers • Preparation and training camps • Increasing physical activity and sports participation levels • Cycling development • Improving sports performance • Culture and festivals • Tourism • Ports of entry, transport and logistics • Winning 2012 Games related and other public sector supply contracts • Business displacement • Learning and development • Weald Country Park • Thames Gateway, south Essex

The 2012 Olympic Games and health

It is hoped that the presence of all the world's top athletes in diverse sporting events – from cross-country running to curling – will inspire a new generation of sports enthusiasts, and potential British Olympic and Paralympic champions.

The Games will provide more resources to make it easier to get healthy in London. Some of the sporting facilities built for the Olympic and Paralympic Games will be maintained after the event for elite sports and community use – including the Olympic Stadium, the Aquatics Centre, the Velopark, the Hockey Centre and the Indoor Sport Centre.

These facilities will provide much-needed opportunities for competitive and recreational sport for Londoners, especially those in growing communities across the Thames Gateway area of east London. They will also improve London's chances to host other international sporting events in the future.

IN CONTEXT

The Mayor of London has launched a Kids Swim Free scheme, which allows children to use public swimming pools in the school holidays, free of charge. Chairman of London 2012, Sebastian Coe, said that the scheme could uncover Olympians of the future.

The 2012 Olympic Games and security

Some people are worried that hosting the Olympic Games could make the city a target for terrorism. London is well prepared for an emergency, and the prospect of such a high-profile sports event will fuel even more work and resources to make the city more secure, now, during the Games and long after.

The UK – and London especially – has unparalleled experience and expertise in proactive multi-agency policing. The Metropolitan Police Service (MPS) is one of the largest police forces in the world and has earned an international reputation for excellence in policing and securing major public events. The MPS was involved in the seven-nation Olympic Security Advisory Group for the 2004 Olympic and Paralympic Games in Athens, so has expert knowledge of making a city a secure and welcoming place for this international sporting event.

What you need to know

* The basic structure of sports has remained the same, but commercialisation has been influential.
* Mass audiences sometimes demand drama and excitement rather than aesthetic appreciation.
* Control of sport needs to be balanced between the owners and the athletes.
* Amateur sports are becoming pressurised by the need to generate more money.
* The relationship between sport and aggression is a complex social phenomenon which requires a synthesis of perspectives.
* Frustration combined with anger, opportunities and stimulus cues lead to aggression.
* Sport, sponsorship and the media are all interdependent for their success and popularity.
* The media can transform sport into a crucial part of people's lives. Without media coverage, sport would have a much lower profile.
* The concept of masculinity tied up with sporting success, achieved through violent means, could have consequences outside of the sport setting.
* Violence among spectators can be determined by the event, the crowd dynamics and other social factors.
* Drug-taking has increased due to greater rewards and accessibility. Athletes generally make their own decisions and cannot be seen wholly as victims of a power system.
* Testing has not developed sufficiently to counteract the use of drugs.
* Technology occurs in the form of:
  * equipment and clothing developments in order to improve athletes' performance;
  * assistance for officials' decisions;
  * wider accessibility for fans in the manner in which they receive sport entertainment.
* The modern Olympic Games:
  * began in the nineteenth century, to bring nations together and for athletes to take part in fair competition;
  * has become the world's biggest and most prestigious sport competition;
  * reflects many of society's problems, such as political turmoil and the commercialisation of sport;
  * tempts athletes to take unfair advantage of opponents to reap the rewards.
* It is hoped that the London 2012 Games will bring:
  * economic growth;
  * regeneration of poor areas;
  * increased participation in sport among the general population.

Review questions

1 Provide a definition of sponsorship.
2 In table form, state the advantages and disadvantages of sponsorship to sport and sporting performers.
3 How has the media helped to sustain discrimination in sport?
4 How can sporting situations encourage aggression?
5 What elements within a football match can lead to spectator violence?
6 What are anabolic steroids and how can they help sport performance?
7 What social issues can encourage a performer to take drugs?
8 What are the problems associated with a performer taking drugs?
9 What strategies can be implemented in order to prevent athletes from taking drugs?
10 What reasons did Coubertin have for reinventing the modern Olympic Games?
11 Describe four symbols of the Olympic Games.
12 What were the reasons for the political upheavals at the 1936, 1956, 1968, 1972 and 1980 Olympic Games?
13 What benefits do sponsors of the Olympic Games achieve?

Acquiring, developing and evaluating practical skills in physical education (G452)

This unit will help you acquire the knowledge and understanding necessary to achieve success. Through participation in the roles of a performer, coach/leader and/or official you will learn of the different pathways to success which include:

- outwitting opponents,
- accurate replication of skills,
- exploring and communicating ideas, concepts and emotions
- performing at maximal levels
- identifying and solving problems
- exercising safely and effectively.

This unit will also help you to acquire the knowledge and understanding of the short and long-term health and fitness benefits of participation in physical activity and the opportunities for participation and progression in a chosen activity both locally and nationally.

How to be successful in your coursework

Learning outcomes

By the end of this chapter you should be able to:

- understand the requirements of the coursework unit;
- understand the assessment criteria for each area of the coursework;
- develop a plan to improve your ability in the role of performer, coach or official;
- appreciate and evaluate the performance of others;
- develop an action plan to improve the performance of others.

CHAPTER INTRODUCTION

This chapter seeks to help you get to grips with the coursework section of your AS Physical Education course. One of the underlying themes of this AS course is for candidates to show their ability to apply skills, knowledge and understanding through physical activity. This specification enables you to achieve this by having the opportunity to participate in physical activity, either as a performer, an official or a coach.

The coursework unit contributes 40 per cent to your overall AS mark.

What are the coursework requirements?

You have the choice of several different pathways to successfully complete your coursework at AS. Which pathway you choose will depend on your individual strengths and the advice given to you by your teacher. There are two components to this unit, both of which need to be completed. The choice of route through this unit is illustrated in Table 13.1.

Table 13.1

Unit G452	Component 1	and	Component 2
Pathway 1	Assessment in two practical performances	and	Oral assessment in the evaluation, appreciation and improvement of performance
Or			
Pathway 2	Assessment in one practical performance + one coaching/leading an activity	and	Oral assessment in the evaluation, appreciation and improvement of performance
Or			
Pathway 3	Assessment in one practical performance + one officiating an activity	and	Oral assessment in the evaluation, appreciation and improvement of performance
Marks available	60 marks (30 for each activity)		(20 marks)

Note: You must choose two different activities in component 1. For example, you cannot choose to perform and coach rugby.

Your ability to apply skills and demonstrate your knowledge and understanding from Part 1 (Unit G451) will therefore be assessed through:

- participation in two practical activities, as a performer and/or a coach and/or official;
- an oral assessment based on the observation of another performer.

Figure 13.1 You can be assessed in the role of an official

There are 80 marks in total available for this unit: 30 marks for each of your participative roles and 20 marks for the oral assessment.

What activities can I be assessed in?

Activities are grouped into activity areas. You must choose two activities from different areas for your assessment. For example, you could choose swimming and netball, but you cannot choose rugby and football. This is true whether you wish to be assessed as performer, coach or official. Table 13.2 outlines the different activity areas and gives some examples of activities that fall into each group. If you cannot see a particular activity in the table that you wish to be assessed in, ask your teacher if it is possible or check the OCR website (www.ocr.org.uk).

How will I be assessed?

You will be assessed in the first instance by your teacher. They will keep an ongoing record of assessment in your role as performer, coach or official throughout the year and must submit your marks to the exam board by 31 March (15 May for summer activities). They will also keep a video log of your performance to justify the marks that have been awarded to you. This video will also help you identify your strengths and weaknesses and determine what you need to do to improve your performance.

Table 13.2 Examples of coursework activity areas

Activity area	Activity examples
Athletic activities	Track and field athletics, Olympic weightlifting, track cycling
Combat activities	Judo, boxing, fencing
Dance activities	Contemporary dance, Irish dance
Invasion games	Association football, basketball, field hockey, netball, rugby league, rugby union
Net/wall games	Badminton, squash, tennis, volleyball
Striking/fielding games	Cricket, rounders
Target games	Golf, archery
Gymnastic activities	Gymnastics, trampolining
Outdoor and adventurous activities	Mountain walking, sailing, skiing
Swimming activities	Competitive swimming
Safe and effective exercise activities	Circuit training

For activities that are not offered in your school or college, it may be possible to be assessed by an external coach under the guidance of your PE teacher. At some point in May, a number of candidates from each centre will be subject to external moderation, led by a practical moderator from the exam board. This process guarantees the standardisation of marks across the country, so that all teachers are marking to the same level.

What are the assessment criteria?

The assessment criteria will vary depending on whether you are being assessed as a performer, coach or official. Table 13.3 highlights the general themes of assessment for each of these roles. These general themes can then be applied to each activity. The activity-specific assessment criteria can be viewed on the OCR website (www.ocr.org.uk).

Table 13.3 General assessment criteria for the roles of performer, coach and official

Performer	Coach\Leader	Official
Candidates will be assessed on their:		
<ul><li>level of acquired and developed skills, and standard of accuracy, control and fluency under pressure;</li><li>selection and application of advanced techniques, and standard of accuracy, control and fluency under pressure;</li><li>use of appropriate strategies demonstrating understanding of perceptual requirements.</li></ul>	<ul><li>level of basic and advanced coaching/leadership skills;</li><li>use of appropriate strategies demonstrating understanding of perceptual aspects;</li><li>level of awareness of health and safety.</li></ul>	<ul><li>level of basic and advanced officiating skills;</li><li>use of appropriate strategies demonstrating understanding of perceptual aspects;</li><li>level of awareness of health and safety.</li></ul>
And will need to:		
<ul><li>demonstrate a range of basic and advanced skills;</li><li>demonstrate appropriate tactical awareness;</li><li>demonstrate an understanding and application of rules;</li><li>demonstrate knowledge and understanding of the fitness and health benefits of the activity.</li></ul>	<ul><li>coach/lead sessions;</li><li>demonstrate competence in organisational skills related to the planning and delivery of sessions;</li><li>demonstrate an understanding of health and safety procedures;</li><li>implement risk assessment procedures;</li><li>demonstrate an awareness of the health and fitness benefits of the activity;</li><li>demonstrate an awareness of child protection issues;</li><li>operate the principle of inclusion in their sessions;</li><li>Keep a detailed log of coaching/leading over a three-month period;</li></ul>	<ul><li>officiate sessions;</li><li>demonstrate competence in decision-making skills related to the application of the rules/regulations and conventions of the activity;</li><li>demonstrate an understanding of health and safety procedures;</li><li>implement risk assessment procedures;</li><li>demonstrate an awareness of the health and fitness benefits of the activity;</li><li>demonstrate an awareness of child protection issues;</li><li>keep a detailed log of officiating over a three-month period;</li></ul>

Continued

Table 13.3 *Continued*

Performer	Coach\Leader	Official
And will need to:		
	• evaluate sessions delivered and plan for improvement.	• evaluate sessions officiated and plan for improvement.
NB: The skills are required to be performed in conditioned competitive situations. These are situations where you must perform your skills and tactics under pressure. You need to select the most appropriate skills to use and perform them with accuracy, fluency and under control.	NB: The Sports Leaders UK CSLA or a governing body level 2 coaching qualification gives you some idea of the level required. It may be a good idea to gain either of these during your course. However, you must still fulfil all the assessment criteria.	NB: A governing body level 2 officiating award gives you some idea of the level required. It may be a good idea to gain this during the course. However, you must still fulfil all the assessment criteria.

Figure 13.2 The conditioned competitive situation for trampolining is the performance of a ten-contact sequence made up of a number of required elements; the sequence is assessed using the movement phases of shape, form, consistency and control

How can I improve my level of performance, coaching and officiating?

It is essential that you dedicate some time to improving your skills as a performer, coach and/or official. Joining clubs, whether in school or outside, will give you the opportunity to perfect your skills through performing, coaching or officiating.

As a performer you will need to work on:

- quality and range of skills;
- fitness;
- tactics and strategies;
- knowledge, understanding and application of rules.

It is a good idea to ask someone to video you while you are performing, so that you can identify your own strengths and weaknesses and see for yourself what you need to improve on.

As a coach you will need to work on:

- control and organisation of individuals and groups;
- choice and delivery of appropriate drills and progressive practices;
- choice of appropriate fitness sessions;
- awareness of health and safety and child protection issues.

Again, it is a good idea to ask someone to video you while you are coaching, so that you can identify your strengths and weaknesses and see for yourself what you need to improve on.

Figure 13.3 A coach must have good control of the group in order to communicate information and instructions effectively

As an official you will need to work on:

- the rules and regulations of the activity;
- decision making related to the rules and regulations of the activity;
- fitness;
- awareness of health and safety and child protection issues.

Once again, it is a good idea to ask someone to video you while you are officiating, so that you can identify your strengths and weaknesses and see for yourself what you need to improve on.

Activity 3

Make a video of yourself as a performer, coach and/or official. Analyse your performance with your teacher or coach and develop an action plan for improvement.

Activity 4

Contact the national governing body for the activities in which you will be assessed and request the latest rules and regulations handbook.

Activity 5

If you are to be assessed as a coach or official you will need to demonstrate an understanding and appreciation of health and safety and child protection issues relevant to your activity.

1 Conduct a risk assessment for either a coaching session or a competitive fixture.

2 Contact the national governing body for your activity and identify the issues surrounding child protection.

Evaluating and planning for improvement

In addition to assessments of you in the role of performer, coach or official, you are required to observe a live performance of a fellow candidate in one of your assessed activities and carry out an oral response based on what you have observed. Your oral response should evaluate the performance and provide ideas on how the performance can be improved. Your response should therefore focus on:

- identifying the strengths of the performance in relation to skills, tactics and fitness;
- identifying the weaknesses of the performance in relation to skills, tactics and fitness;
- prioritising elements of the performance requiring improvement;
- formulating a realistic action plan that can be implemented to improve the weaknesses identified – this should include coaching points and progressive practices, as well as giving some idea of timescale;
- suggesting the local and national opportunities for performers to participate in and improve their performance;
- detailing the health and fitness benefits of participation in the activity.

Figure 13.4 You will be required to observe and evaluate the performance of others

What questions can I expect in the evaluation and planning for improvement section?

The questions posed by your teacher and/or the moderator will be very open-ended questions which will allow you to demonstrate and apply your knowledge. You will be directed to the performer or aspect of performance you should focus on. For example: 'I would like you to observe the performance of _____. I would like you to comment on:

- the strengths of the performance observed in relation to skills, tactics and fitness;
- the weaknesses of the performance observed in relation to skills, tactics and fitness;
- the areas of the performance you would prioritise for improvement;
- creating a viable action plan to improve those areas of performance (this should include

detailed coaching points and progressive practices);
- the opportunities locally and nationally for performers to participate and improve in the activity;
- the health and fitness benefits of the activity observed.'

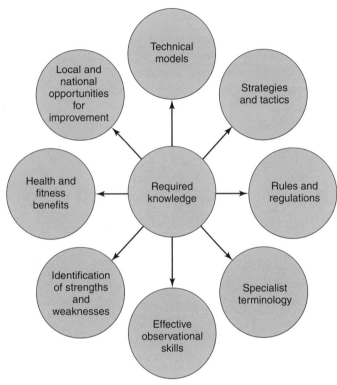

Figure 13.5 Required skills and knowledge for the successful completion of the oral response

How should I structure my oral response?

It is best to break down the response into a number of logical steps, otherwise you can end up confused, losing your train of thought and becoming tongue-tied. The points set out below provide a suggested route through your oral response.

Step 1: Observe the performance

Observing a performer is more difficult than it may appear at first. In order to gather all the required information, it may be necessary for you to observe from a number of different vantage points. For example, when observing individual skills, it may require you to view from the side, from the front and from behind. Observing tactical appreciation, on the other hand, may require you to get a much broader picture and observe from further away.

When observing the live performance it is a good idea to make a few notes to prompt you when outlining the performer's strengths and weaknesses. However, you will not be allowed to use pre-prepared notes in your assessment.

Step 2: Identify the movement or analytical phases of your activity

The phases help you to focus on particular aspects of performance, such as the arm action in swimming or the preparation phase when performing an overhead clear in badminton. Identifying the phases of movement should feature early in your response.

You might start by saying something like: 'The phases of movement for throwing the javelin are:

● initial stance, grip and preparation;
● travel and trunk position;
● throwing action;
● release;
● overall efficiency.

I will now comment on the strengths and weaknesses of the throw related to these phases.'

Activity 6

Find out from the OCR website (www.ocr.org.uk) the phases of movement related to your activity.

Step 3: Identify the strengths and weaknesses of the performance

You should focus on the strengths and weaknesses of the following three areas of the performance:

● skills when performed under pressure;
● tactics and strategies;
● fitness.

Skills when performed under pressure

You are required to be aware of the relevant technical models of the particular skills you are observing. These technical models refer to the performance of textbook skills, considered to be of very high standard. You can find technical model resources in coaching manuals, instructional videos, photographs and other live events. Knowing how a skill should be performed will help you justify your evaluations (strengths or weaknesses).

When performing under pressure, the competitor may perform some skills poorly (compared to the technical model) or inconsistently, make the wrong choice of shot, or even choose not to perform the skill at all. These would all constitute weakness in skill reproduction.

Try to refrain from saying that the arm action in swimming, for example, is simply good or bad, without offering any justification. You should phrase your response in a similar way to the following example:

> The pull phase of the arm action is strong. It pulls down the midline of the body, which ensures that the swimmer maximises her forward movement in the water. However, the straight arm recovery is a weakness as it slows down the arm pull. A bent arm recovery with a high elbow is favoured, as this is more efficient, wasting less energy and ensuring a quicker recovery phase of the stroke.

Activity 7

Using a variety of coaching media, such as coaching manuals, Internet sites (e.g. www.bbc.co.uk/sportacademy) and software (e.g. Dartfish or Quintec), begin compiling your own coaching handbook, based on the technical models for a range of skills for your activity. Your manual should include:

● images or photos of correct technique;
● video footage of correct technique;
● coaching points for each skill;
● a list of common faults for each skill.

Tactics and strategies

You will need to have a good level of understanding of the main tactics and strategies that are appropriate in the activity you are observing, and then comment on the performer's application of these. Tactics and strategies will vary greatly from activity to activity. Some activities, for example, may require you to comment on the effective use of team plays and strategies; other comments might refer to an individual's decision-making ability or their selection of the most appropriate skill. It really depends on the activity.

- coordination;
- balance;
- strength.

For example, you might comment that suppleness at the hip joint is fundamental to an effective split leap in dance and gymnastics, but the lack of flexibility about the hip of the observed performer has resulted in a poorly executed leap. However, the dancer has demonstrated some high levels of leg strength, confirmed by the height of the leap; this is to be expected of the dancer as it allows more time for movement into and out of the splits position.

Activity 8

Using a variety of coaching media, such as coaching manuals and Internet sites, research a number of tactics and strategies appropriate in your activity.

Fitness

You will need to determine the required components of fitness used in the observed activity, and compare the performer's demonstrated level with the required or expected level of these components. For the purpose of AS study, the following components could be used:

- stamina;
- suppleness;
- speed;
- power;

Activity 10

Using a variety of coaching media, such as coaching manuals and Internet sites (e.g. www.brianmac.co.uk) research a range of coaching sessions aimed at improving each of the following:

- stamina;
- suppleness;
- speed;
- strength.

Make sure you include information on the FITT principle:

- **Frequency** – How often you should train.
- **Intensity** – How hard you should train.
- **Time** – How long each session should last.
- **Type** – What method of training should be used.

Activity 9

Use the fitness wheel to identify the fitness requirements of the activity. Observe a friend or classmate in this same activity and compare their level of fitness to the required fitness.

Key: 10 = excellent; 1 = poor

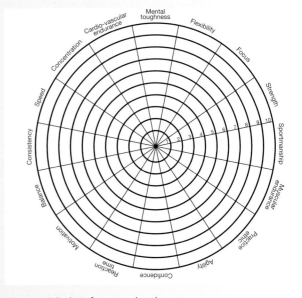

Figure 13.6 A fitness wheel

Step 4: Formulate an action plan to improve performance

Once you have observed and identified the strengths and weaknesses of the performance, you will need to arrive at an action plan which addresses the weaknesses recognised.

Your action plan should include the following information:

- Timescale – How often will training take place and how many weeks will your action plan take in total? If it is relevant, you might make a comment such as the following:

> The performer will follow a strength-training programme that requires them to attend the gym three times per week for one hour over a period of 12 weeks.

- Method of achieving your goals – What coaching points, drills, practices or fitness training methods will you use to improve performance? If it is relevant, you might make a comment such as the following:

> In order to promote the bent arm recovery in front crawl, I will demonstrate the correct action to the swimmer. I will have them place a pull buoy (float) between their legs, so that the swimmer is concentrating solely on the arm action, and ask them to perform the following exercises:
>
> - 4 x 50m catch-up, which encourages a high elbow recovery.
> - 4 x 50m drawing the thumb up the side of the body from waist to armpit, which encourages a high elbow recovery.
> - 4 x 50m arms only, concentrating on the relevant teaching points: high elbow, entry point in line with shoulder, and so on.

- Detailed teaching points – If it is relevant, you might make a comment such as the following (for the overhead clear in badminton):

> Preparation:
>
> - Shake hands grip
> - Get underneath or slightly behind the shuttle
> - Adopt a sideways receiving stance
> - Your racquet foot should have most weight on it
> - Your non-racquet shoulder should point towards the net
> - Keep both arms up: the racquet arm should be bent at the elbow so the racquet head is

about shoulder height (or 'scratch back' = position). The non-racquet arm should point to the shuttle to improve timing and balance

Execution

- Extend your arm while rotating to face the target
- Keep your wrist cocked
- Strike the shuttle at the highest point possible, slightly in front of your body, using a strong throwing action as if you are going to throw your racquet high and forward through the air
- Snap wrist forward on contact
- Keep the racquet face open on contact with the shuttle

Recovery/ follow-through

- Continue the swing through
- Transfer your weight fully from front to back
- Move back to the base position

Activity 11

Observe a number of different performers and address the following points:
1 What are the major weaknesses in the performance?
2 Outline a corrective practice or drill to improve the performance.

Step 5: Discuss the role of the activity in promoting a healthy lifestyle and the opportunities for increased participation

You should conclude your oral response by making some comment on:

- the health and fitness benefits of the activity;
- the range of opportunities, both locally and nationally, for progression in the activity.

The health and fitness benefits of the activity

For this section, you need to consider the long-term adaptive responses of the body to training and the impact this has on the health and fitness of the individual. You should try to critically evaluate and perhaps acknowledge any negative impact that exercise might have on health. For example:

The health and fitness benefits of participation in an athletic event such as the 1,500m are great. The performer may notice many physiological adaptations, such as an enlarged heart, known as cardiac hypertrophy, which may lead to an increased stroke volume and a reduced resting heart rate (bradycardia). This places less stress on the cardiovascular system and can keep blood pressure within a healthy range. By performing aerobic-type exercise, bone density may also increase and so prevent skeletal diseases such as osteoporosis. However, the performer must be careful not to overtrain, as s/he may become susceptible to overuse injuries such as stress fractures or even osteoarthritis.

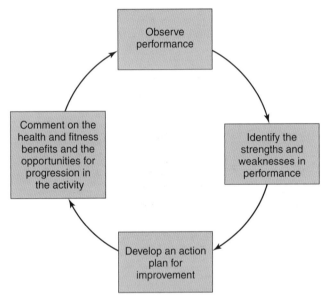

Figure 13.7 The evaluation and planning for improvement cycle

The range of opportunities, both locally and nationally, for progression in the activity

For this section, you need to consider factors that may have influenced the opportunity for development and improvement in the activity. Therefore it is important that you consider issues such as physical education experiences, provision of facilities, effectiveness of national and local organisations, government initiatives, funding and the influence of role models. For example:

In my local area there are a number of hockey clubs, but there are only two or three AstroTurf pitches. Demand for these pitches is high and they are always booked, particularly in the evenings and at weekends. I have to rely on my college in order to play hockey, but regionally it seems that fewer and fewer schools and colleges are putting out teams, so we mainly train and I only play a dozen or so matches in the season. I believe that England Hockey should provide more AstroTurf pitches and develop more grass-roots schemes to provide greater opportunities for participation.

Exam-style questions

1 The achievement of sporting excellence is influenced by many factors including funding and the media. How can both funding and the media help to develop sporting excellence in the UK?

(5 marks)

2 What are some of the possible causes of crowd violence at sporting events and what strategies can be implemented to prevent such occurrences?

(5 marks)

3 Discuss the advantages and disadvantages of technology within sport.

(10 marks)

What you need to know

* You are required to be assessed in two activities: one as a performer and one as performer, coach or official.

* The two activities must come from different activity groups.

* You will be assessed according to the relevant assessment criteria for your activity.

* Assessment criteria for performance consider your level of overall performance, level of physical and mental fitness, and level of understanding of the rules and regulations of the activity.

* Assessment criteria for coaching consider your overall level of coaching or leading, level of organisational skills, knowledge of rules and regulations, and awareness of child protection and health and safety issues.

* Assessment criteria for officiating consider your overall level of officiating, level of organisational skills, application of rules and regulations, and awareness of child protection and health and safety issues.

* You are also required to observe the live performance of another candidate, evaluate it and plan an appropriate strategy for improvement. This will take the form of an oral response.

* Assessment of your evaluation and plan for improvement will focus on: your description of strengths and weaknesses of the observed performance; your priority of performance improvement; your creation of a viable action plan; your appreciation of the health and fitness benefits of the activity; and your appreciation of the range of opportunities, both locally and nationally.

Index

Entries for illustrations are in *italics*, e.g. 8. Entries for essential information ('what you need to know') are in **bold**, e.g. 52